Furniture Design

DIS Scandinavian Furniture Design workshop. Drawing and sketching at full scale. *Photo: courtesy Erik Skoven, DIS.*

Furniture Design

Jim Postell

John Wiley & Sons, Inc.

Library of Congress Cataloging-in-Publication Data:

Postell, James Christopher, 1958–
Furniture design / James Postell.
  p. cm.
Includes bibliographical references and index.
ISBN 978-0-471-72796-5 (cloth)
1. Furniture design.   I. Title.
NK2260.P67 2007
749—dc22

            2007013717

Printed in the United States of America

10 9 8 7 6 5 4 3 2 1

Contents

chapter **7**
Materials   173

chapter **8**
Fabrication   213

chapter **9**
Professional Practice and Marketing   247

chapter 10
Historical Overview

265

Preface

ALVAR AALTO AND FRANK LLOYD WRIGHT were architects who integrated custom furnishings into their spaces and buildings. Interior designers such as Eva Maddox and John Saladino are renowned for their skill in blending textures and furnishings with interior space. Henry Dreyfuss and Bill Stumpf were industrial designers who considered ergonomics and industrial fabrication processes in their furniture designs. Woodworkers and artisans such as Sam Maloof and Pierluigi Ghianda create furniture with remarkable handcraft and finish. Consider for a moment the qualities and viewpoints brought to furniture design by these individuals and their unique disciplines. There are pronounced differences in the way architects and interior designers create a sense of place by designing and selecting furniture, in the way industrial designers seek to resolve industrial fabrication processes in design, and in the way artists are trained in their craft. Many individuals and disciplines contribute to the body of knowledge of furniture design.

Consider the influence that structural forces, material properties, the surrounding environment, and ergonomics have on furniture design. Reflect upon the historical, cultural, political, and societal conditions revealed by the way people sit, rest, work, and play, or the human factors research upon which furniture designers rely. Many factors should be considered when designing furniture. Most are situated within personal and professional frames of reference.

This book is written as a comprehensive survey, as a resource to give the reader a deeper understanding and provide knowledge and inspiration for designing and making furniture. It is organized into 10 chapters:

Experiments with bent and laminated wood—furniture components for the Paimio Sanatorium and the library in Viipuri, Finland. Designed by Alvar Aalto. *Photo courtesy Jim Postell.*

- Chapter 1, *Introduction to Furniture Design*, outlines basic relationships between furniture and design.
- Chapter 2, *Function and Social Use*, introduces fundamental notions of function (intended purpose) and categories of social use.
- Chapter 3, *Form, Spatial Organization, and Typological Orders*, addresses a range of physical and spatial characteristics in furniture design.
- Chapter 4, *Furniture Case Studies*, presents 21 furniture studies organized in chronological order.
- Chapter 5, *Furniture Design Theory*, delves into the nature of furniture design, focusing upon aspects of structural integrity and composition, how furniture works and feels, and notions of beauty and aesthetics.
- Chapter 6, *Design*, presents an overview of design principles and focuses upon the phases, processes, skills, and ethics of designing furniture.
- Chapter 7, *Materials*, outlines a broad palette of materials and discusses material properties relative to furniture design.
- Chapter 8, *Fabrication*, discusses ways of fabricating furniture, with an overview of hand tools, power tools, and digital tools.
- Chapter 9, *Professional Practice and Marketing*, covers professional aspects related to the practice, marketing, and business of designing furniture.
- Chapter 10, *Historical Overview*, highlights how societies have thought about, designed, fabricated, and used furniture up to the present.

Designing furniture relies upon judgment and technical information linked to several professional and academic disciplines. The breadth and depth of knowledge necessary to design, select, fabricate, and arrange furniture in space is extensive. This book draws upon this knowledge and, in doing so, reaches out to students, faculty, and professionals in several fields.

It is difficult for some individuals to acknowledge furniture design as a stand-alone profession or even as a vocation because it is intertwined with many established disciplines. It is a challenge to formulate a collective dialogue about furniture design because different disciplines approach design and fabrication from unique perspectives.

Look back to the time when *interior design* was an emerging field and consider its historical beginnings. One can determine that interior design developed from several fields, the work of key individuals, unique professional practices, and established academic programs. The fields of architecture, design, fine arts, and the decorative arts, in conjunction with the professional practices of James Adam (1732–94) and Robert Adam (1728–92), Elsie de Wolfe (1856–1950), and Florence Knoll (b. 1917) would likely receive recognition for influencing the emergence of interior design as a professional design discipline.

In the 1950s, *industrial design* began to emerge as a discipline. Consider the work of Norman Bel Geddes and Raymond Loewy, as well as the influence that industrial fabrication processes and mass production have had upon the field of furniture design.

It is important to acknowledge the collective influence architects, interior designers, industrial designers, and fine artists have had upon the professional and academic stature of *furniture design*, but one also needs to consider the important roles that fabricators, engineers, and human factor researchers have played as well.

It is the author's hope that this book will be useful as a survey textbook for students and faculty alike, and will serve as a resource for designers, fabricators, and individuals interested in furniture and design.

Acknowledgments

THERE ARE MANY INDIVIDUALS to acknowledge for their contribution and support in writing this book. I want first to thank Paul Drougas, acquisitions editor at John Wiley & Sons, with whom I have worked closely over a 2-year period. Paul and the team at Wiley have done a remarkable job of guiding this project from conception to publication.

My wife, Florine, has been encouraging and supportive throughout the entire process of writing and has edited several drafts. My parents, Brad and Carol, and my mother-in-law, Inge, have provided support as well.

I am fortunate to teach at the College of Design, Architecture, Art, and Planning at the University of Cincinnati. DAAP is composed of many design disciplines and has a long history of cooperative practice providing students with professional internships in firms across the country and around the world. DAAP provides a collaborative environment in which faculty and students have provided support while I was writing this book. I am grateful for the contributions of a number of faculty, including G. Thomas Bible, Ann Black, Gil Born, Brian Davies, Gülen Çevik, Ericka Hedgecock, Nnamdi Elleh, Bradley Hammond, Soo-Shin Choi, John Stork, and Craig M. Vogel.

Specifically, I want to convey my appreciation to the following DAAP colleagues: Patrick Snadon, Jeff Tilman, Elizabeth Riorden, Ray Laubenthal, and Jerry Larson, as well as Eva Frederiksen, Ole Gormsen, Erik Krogh, and Jens Overbye from Danmarks Designskole in Copenhagen, Denmark, for their contributions to Chapter 10.

Nothing travels far without theory, and I appreciate the insights of David Saile and Gordon Simmons. David and I have discussed theory for years; his thinking about built form and culture has inspired my experiential outlook toward design.

Designing and making furniture are core subjects of this book. I value the input from my colleague David Lee Smith in Chapter 6, as well as the contributions of Jeff Arnold, Steve Mickley, Jonathan Bruns, and DAAP Shop Superintendent Jim Berns to Chapters 7 and 8. Special acknowledgment is due to Michael Toombs, a colleague with whom I have taught and collaborated on many furniture design commissions and whose input has significantly improved the book in general and Chapters 7 and 8 in particular. I have learned a great deal about woodworking, craft, and fabricating high-end case goods and casework from Michael, and have grown as a designer from our collaborative experiences.

This book is written for students working in the fields of furniture design, architecture, interior design, industrial design, and fine art. Inspiration for writing it developed from years of teaching human factors and contemporary furniture design at DAAP. During the past 2 years, I have worked closely with many students to complete the manuscript, and I am particularly indebted to Nora Luehmann, who digitally modeled (using FormZ) the majority of the furniture studies in Chapter 4. Sylbester Yeo helped model furniture studies in this chapter as well, and I appreciate the precision and detail of their work. Matthew Althouse, Mehmet Ziya Cetik, Peter Chamberlain, Nicole Desender, Ryan Newman, Ian

Ramous, Carly L. Snyder, and Chris Sommers have also contributed to the book in a variety of ways. Greg Bleier, an alumnus of the School of Architecture and Interior Design, edited several manuscript drafts. I am grateful for everyone's contribution and help in producing this survey on furniture design.

Images are critical for any book on furniture design. I wish to thank Julia Bryan, Peter Chamberlain, Lauren Farquhar, Ben Meyer, Chris Sommers, John Stork, and Will Yokel for use of their images. I am especially appreciative of Scott Hisey of the Cincinnati Art Museum, Linda Baron of Herman Miller, David Bright of Knoll, Inc., Jeanine Holquist of Steelcase, Renee Hytry of the Formica Corp., Michelle Nirenberg and Tom Revelle of Humanscale, Malene la Coeur Radmussen of Rud. Radmussen, Erik Skoven, and Bjørli Lundin of DIS, and Tina Taul of GUBI for their permission to use many remarkable images.

Generally, textbooks do not have a foreword, but I am pleased that John Pile agreed to write one. His books on modern furniture and interior design are marked by a balance of technical information and thoughtful insight about design, which are supported by great images. John has had a remarkable career as a teacher, author, and practitioner—always with focus on *design*. He has contributed significantly to the study of furniture design and interior design and was influential in the development of this book.

Writing this book has sparked a desire to reread the works of David Pye, Ralph Caplan, Galen Cranz, Ernest Joyce, Ezio Manzini, and Edward Lucie-Smith. It has also been a time to discover new books such as *Materials and Design* by Mike Ashby and Kara Johnson. Writing is somewhat related to rewriting, that is, analyzing and synthesizing the thoughts of others and expressing them in a personal way. I would like this book to complement those already on the shelves and inspire students to better understand the comprehensive and extensive nature of designing and making furniture.

Foreword

THE FIELD OF FURNITURE DESIGN is strangely diverse. It does not have a well-established definition and is not regularly studied in colleges or universities.

It is also odd to remember that most of the world's population does not make use of furniture except, perhaps, for a few stools or benches. Western civilization, however, beginning thousands of years ago, has become addicted to the use of furniture of the most varied sort. In the modern world, we are in touch with furniture at almost every moment. We sit in chairs, work and eat at tables, sleep in beds, and are hardly ever out of sight of a number of furniture items, for better or for worse.

Furniture is now produced and distributed for homes, for offices, for schools, for hospitals, and for every other situation in which people are to be found. In spite of this near glut of furniture, the sources of the designs that are so ubiquitous are obscure. Most furniture now comes from factories, but the designs factories produce are generally anonymous, the work of staff that exists mostly to develop variations on earlier designs whose origins are lost.

There are, of course, some exceptions. Most historic furniture can be traced to cabinet-makers such as Chippendale and Sheraton or to architect-designers such as the Adam brothers, but these are rare exceptions mostly to be found only in museums and auction galleries. In the modern world, we know the names of the designers of those special creations we call *classic:* Eames, Breuer, Mies van der Rohe, Bertoia, Rietveld, and Le Corbusier. If we look into the backgrounds of these famous figures, we find that they were not trained to be furniture designers. They were architects, sculptors, or, in some instances, industrial or interior designers. When they turned to furniture, they had to rely on their background knowledge of structure, materials, human body mechanics, and the many other issues that relate to successful furniture design.

Design history is full of examples of many efforts by distinguished designers that have fallen by the wayside, while a few highly successful designs have come from unexpected sources—one thinks of the Rowland stacking chair, the Pollack office chair, or the Noguchi coffee table. Efforts to establish some form of training for designers who wish to work on furniture have not met with much success. A brief course in furniture design is offered in some interior and industrial design programs, but architectural training is too demanding to include even limited exposure to the field. Some schools with major programs in furniture design are oriented toward craft techniques and train master woodworkers who produce a single, one-of-a-kind effort demonstrating craftsmanship but offering little to the broader world of furniture. In the end, it must be admitted that furniture design is generally self-taught, whether the learner is also a craftsperson, architect, sculptor, or layman.

To turn at last to this book, we find an author determined to give aid to the would-be furniture designer, whatever professional background or lack of professionalism that person may have. In this one volume, we can confront issues of function, materials, structure, production techniques, and whatever philosophical and theoretical matters may have a bearing upon the realities of furniture.

Although many books deal with furniture (as this book's bibliography can attest), most are histories, picture books, or studies for collectors. Very few even touch on furniture *design* as a process, a skill, or a matter for serious study. Here we have a book determined to make up for the furniture design shortage. It is hard to imagine a more complete and comprehensive coverage of this neglected subject brought up-to-date with such tireless effort!

John Pile

1 Introduction to Furniture Design

DICTIONARY AND ENCYCLOPEDIC sources use words like *equipment* and *movable* to define furniture.[1] Words can describe furniture, but students and professionals know that *furniture design* extends far beyond dictionary or encyclopedic sources. It takes design skills, experience, intuition, and knowledge in many areas to develop a thorough understanding of how to design furniture. Designing furniture also requires inspiration, a concept or idea, and a commitment to give pleasure to those who use it.

Furniture design is deeply rooted in the human condition. It is a social science that belongs to the humanities, an applied art that draws upon many design fields, and a tangible reality that relies upon a working knowledge of materials and **fabrication** techniques. It is a holistic and all-embracing field of study.

Before delving into the nature of furniture design, it will be helpful to examine the terms *furniture* and *design* and reflect upon the fundamental relationships between these two words.

FURNITURE

> **furniture**
> • *noun* **1.** the movable articles that are used to make a room or building suitable for living or working in, such as tables, chairs, or desks. **2.** the small accessories or fittings that are required for a particular task or function: *door furniture.*[2]

By many accounts, furniture includes a broad range of human body support devices, surfaces for various activities, storage and display pieces, and partitions[3] designed to help

Figure 1.1 Chairs at the Trapholt Furniture Museum, Kolding, Denmark.

Figure 1.2 Outside café tables and chairs.

Figure 1.3 Case goods (cabinet and bookcase) designed by Mogens Koch, fabricated by Rud. Rasmussen since 1932.

people sit and rest, work and play, organize items, and partition space (Figures 1.1–1.4). This view suggests a utilitarian framework, which more often than not underscores the intended purposes of designers. Though utility and social use are important aspects of furniture, so too are **aesthetics,** environmental matters, and fabrication processes.

Utility can inspire design ideas and is often grounded by social use. In this book, categories of social use include healthcare, hospitality, institutional, office, recreational, religious, residential, retail, and storage furnishings and are introduced in Chapter 2.

The word *furniture* is derived from European verbs, nouns, and adjectives. The Latin adjective *mobile* means "movable," which is an important characteristic of furniture. The

Figure 1.4 Dupont Corian exhibit, designed by SOM, 2005.

French verb *fournir* means "to furnish." The French *meubles,* the Turkish *mobilya,* and the Danish *møbel* translate into the English word *furniture.* Freedom from the physical structure of a building provides designers with an opportunity to create spatial relationships between movable elements and interior space. Though most furnishings are freestanding, some are built in or mechanically attached to a floor, wall, or ceiling. In either scenario, space can be made complete through the location and orientation of tangible form and intangible use.

DESIGN

design
- *noun* **1.** a plan or drawing produced to show the look and function or workings of something before it is built or made. **2.** the art or action of producing such a plan or drawing. **3.** underlying purpose or planning: *the appearance of design in the universe.* **4.** a decorative pattern.
- *verb* **1.** conceive and produce a design for. **2.** plan or intend for a purpose.[4]

One can think of design as *structured play*[5] resulting from creative thinking, intuitive judgment, and hard work—guided by technical information, theory, and communication skills. Design is a process that utilizes both the right and left sides of the brain. As such, furniture designers consider structural, functional, **tactile,** aesthetic, spatial, economic, and cultural needs and desires all at the same time.

The word *design* is distinct from the word **project.** While design entails processes of inquiry and methods for exploring and synthesizing ideas (Figure 1.5), a project is the coherent resolution of purpose and presence (Figure 1.6). At some point in time, design efforts transform into projects. A project can be revealed in a drawing, model, working prototype, or fabricated work. It's not the medium that distinguishes a design from a project; rather, it is the presence of resolved and synthesized aspects—very often with the intent to make real.

The words *design* and *designate* are derived from the Latin verb *designare. Designare* translates "to mark out," taken from *de,* "of," and *signare,* "to mark," or the noun *signum,* "a mark or sign."[6]

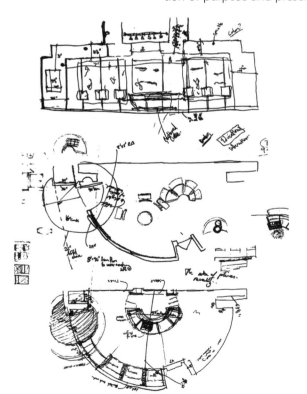

Figure 1.5 Design study exploring spatial relationships with furniture, Children's Chapel, Cincinnati Children's Medical Center.

Figure 1.6 Children's Chapel—furnishings fabricated and installed by Heartwood Furniture Company, 1995.

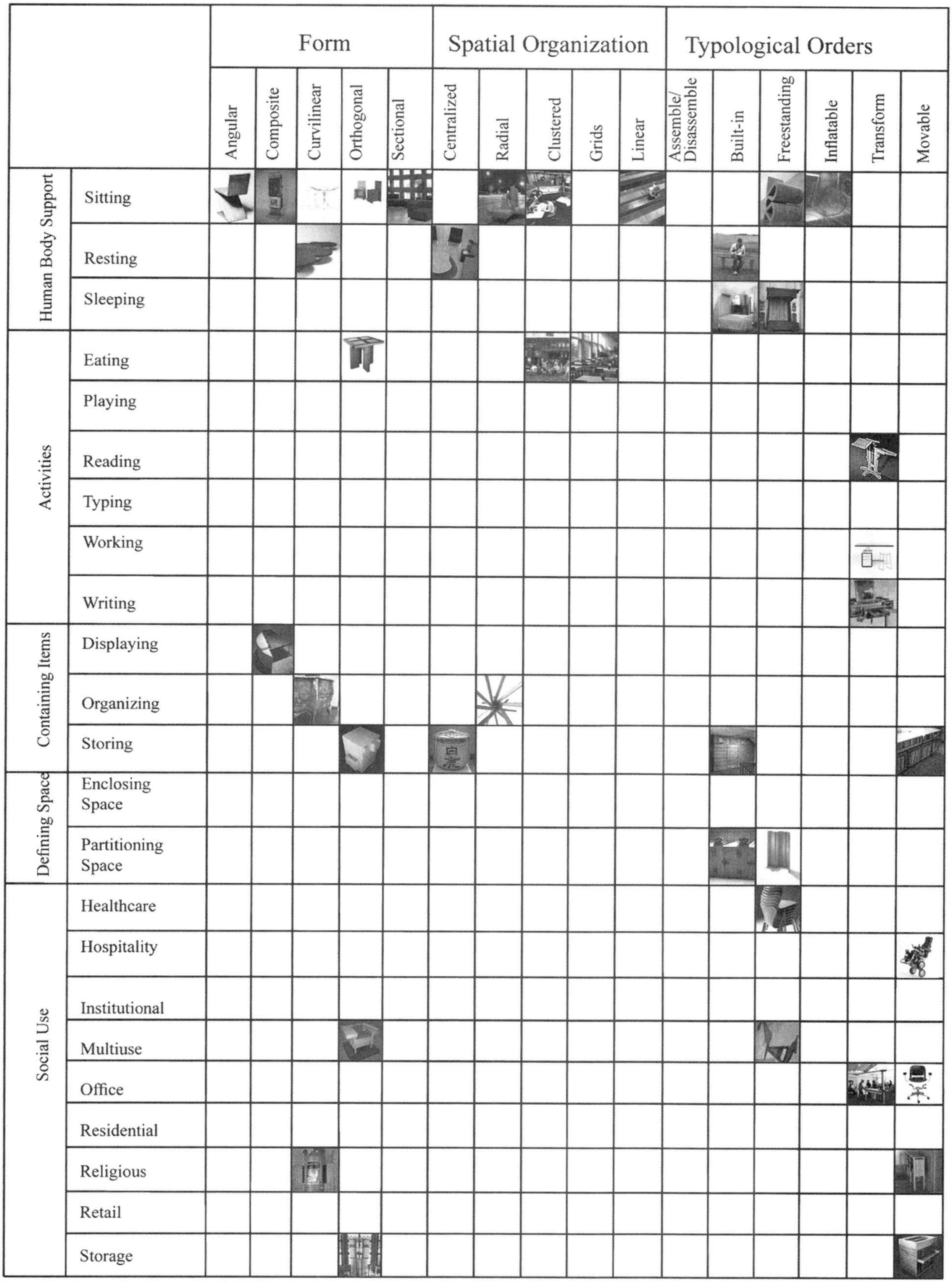

		Form					Spatial Organization					Typological Orders					
		Angular	Composite	Curvilinear	Orthogonal	Sectional	Centralized	Radial	Clustered	Grids	Linear	Assemble/Disassemble	Built-in	Freestanding	Inflatable	Transform	Movable
Human Body Support	Sitting	■	■	■	■	■		■	■		■			■	■		
	Resting			■			■						■				
	Sleeping												■	■			
Activities	Eating				■				■								
	Playing																
	Reading															■	
	Typing																
	Working															■	
	Writing															■	
Containing Items	Displaying		■														
	Organizing			■				■									
	Storing				■		■						■				■
Defining Space	Enclosing Space																
	Partitioning Space											■	■				
Social Use	Healthcare												■				
	Hospitality																■
	Institutional																
	Multiuse				■								■				
	Office														■		■
	Residential																
	Religious			■													■
	Retail																
	Storage					■											■

Figure 1.7 Furniture design lexicon.

The Italian word for project is *la progettazione*. *Il progetto* translates into "the plan." The word *design* is sometimes used to mean "the plan" and implies planning or intending for a purpose.

At the core of designing furniture is a body of knowledge and the skills necessary to compose the tangible and intangible aspects of furniture. Technical information includes a working knowledge of materials and fabrication processes, **ergonomic** theories, knowledge about the human body, marketing, and professional practice. Design skills include visual and spatial communication skills and the ability to conceive and develop ideas. Technical instruction can be taught. Design skills need to be exercised and generally improve with experience. Furniture designers learn how to design, sketch, draw, draft, make study models, and use computer programs while simultaneously developing a working knowledge about materials, fabrication techniques, and the human body. In regard to the skills and knowledge necessary to design furniture, experience is one of the best teachers a student can have.

The **lexicon** in Figure 1.7 delineates synthetic boundaries of use and form. The lexicon is an attempt to organize furniture design into related but discrete components, which are physical, spatial, and functional. The organization of the lexicon is less important than the process that led to its development. As an exercise, consider completing the lexicon or determine other organizational approaches to bring order to the many categories and typologies of furniture.

Furniture designers generally work within semantic boundaries, drawing upon professional and personal experiences in the process. The primary goal for many furniture designers is to create designs that improve upon existing products or to provide entirely new designs. In doing either, designers broaden the world through fresh and personal points of view.

As a tangible reality, furniture is composed of materials and finishes held together by joinery and experienced physically and spatially. However, furniture is also composed of intangible aspects that reveal ideas about engineering, ergonomics, cultural meaning, social status, use, spatial organization, and aesthetics. These intangible aspects serve as a basis for theory. Not all dimensions are measurable, and neither are all details limited to physical properties. It is imperative to consider tangible and intangible aspects concurrently when designing and making furniture.

chapter

2 Function and Social Use

THE BEST OF TODAY'S furniture provides for many needs and desires, revealing the latest conceptions of function and social use. In this book, *function* is interpreted broadly; it is concerned with matters of structural integrity, utility, and aesthetics. We shall begin with the following categories of utility: *Human Body Supports, Activities, Containing, and Defining Space.*

Figure 2.1 Human figure seated; sketch by Gil Born.

HUMAN BODY SUPPORTS

Sitting, Resting, and Sleeping

Furniture directly supports the human body in the course of sitting, resting, and sleeping. **Beds,** benches, car and plane seats, **chairs, couches,** futons, hammocks, inflated therapy balls, mattresses, rockers, **sofas,** and wheelchairs are some of the many furniture pieces designed to support the human body (Figure 2.1). At a minimum, human body supports should allow for body movement, support the weight of the body as evenly as possible, and minimize uncomfortable pressure points.

Conventionally, furniture serves to keep people and activities off the ground. Even sleeping bags and picnic blankets offer some degree of separation from the moisture and dirt of the ground. But when the grass is dry and the ground is clean, either can be a wonderful place

Figure 2.2 Sitting and lying on the grass.

to sit, rest, or sleep (Figure 2.2). Before we focus upon furnishings that support the body for various purposes above the ground, consider how people enjoy sitting, resting, working, and sleeping on the ground.

Man-made body supports include elevated platforms and raised surfaces used for sitting and resting. Backless benches made from logs, retaining walls, and steps can support a wide range of people and activities. These furnishings are often site-specific, incorporated into the surrounding landscape (Figure 2.3).

Figure 2.3 Sitting on a log bench.

Figure 2.4 Egyptian-grown and carved stool with splayed legs, ca. 1560 B.C.

Figure 2.5 Sauna stool designed by Antti Nurmesniemi (1952), fabricated by Vuokko. Laminated birch seat, teak legs.

Stools are considered the oldest portable human body support. The three- and four-legged stools that existed in ancient Egypt remain a popular furniture type today. Consider the similarities and differences in the form, materials, and fabrication of the hand-worked three-legged Egyptian stool in Figure 2.4 and the **laminated** sauna stool designed by Antti Nurmesniemi in Figure 2.5.

Chairs can be thought of as stools with backs. Backs give spatial orientation and provide lateral support for sitting. Backs can also denote social order. The Greek ***klismos*** chair has been referred to as "the chair with a back"[1] because up to 500 B.C., chairs with backs expressed significance in social status and were considered thrones. Throughout history, sitting has denoted social status. Chairs have been used to distinguish between being served and serving others. Individuals who stood generally served those who sat (Figure 2.6). The *klismos* chair gave dignity and poise to a broad spectrum of users, underscoring an emerging social and gender equity within the Greek democracy. The draw-

Figure 2.6 Egyptian stone relief: king makes offering to Throth, 1070–712 B.C.

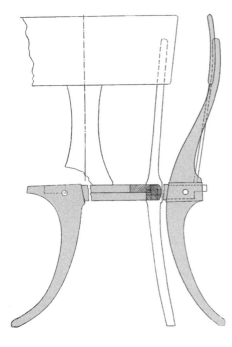

Figure 2.7 Greek klismos chair, 700–400 B.C.

ing overlay of the *klismos* chair in Figure 2.7 is based upon an interpolation of surviving pottery and sculptural relief.[2]

It is a challenge to integrate formal aspects of composition, material properties, fabrication techniques, and functional use in the conception of furniture, but the best designers do so. Consider the upholstered foam over a molded plastic shell in Eero Saarinen's *Womb* chair (Figure 2.8) or Grete Jalk's folded and laminated plywood *Easy* chair (Figure 2.9). These chairs resulted from material exploration and rigorous design iteration. Through the process, the designers were able to transform materials and processes of fabrication into furnishings that are structurally sound, comfortable, and beautiful.

Figure 2.8 Womb chair, designed by Eero Saarinen (1948), manufactured by Knoll International.

Figure 2.9 Easy chair, designed by Grete Jalk (1963), molded plywood and Oregon pine veneer, manufactured by Poul Jeppesen, Denmark.

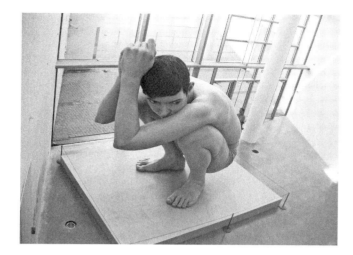

Figure 2.10 "Boy," by artist Ron Mueck, 2000. Aarhus Museum of Art, Denmark.

Squatting and Sitting

Squatting is considered by many to be the first and most natural means of sitting and is especially prevalent in nomadic and Eastern societies. Squatting works a variety of muscles and places the body close to the ground (Figure 2.10). Today, out of the tens of thousands of chairs available, stools and inflated therapy balls are among the few furnishings designed to accommodate a squatting posture. Squatting is physiologically healthy and doesn't rely upon the use of or need for chairs. But most people in Western societies have cultural and societal preferences for chairs. They desire the comfort and posture achieved by sitting.

Large pillows and beanbag chairs on the floor can accommodate a range of postures conforming to specific uses by adults or children. However, pillows and beanbag chairs limit body movement during use. Further, they are difficult for many to get into or out of. Most beanbag chairs offer little support for the body; consequently, the body tends to collapse inward in a captive, static posture, which over time becomes uncomfortable (Figure 2.11).

Figure 2.11 Il Sacco (three bean bag chairs), designed by Piero Gatti, Cesare Paolini, and Franco Teodoro (1969), manufactured by Zanotta Spa.

Figure 2.12 Mirra (designed by Studio 7.5), Aeron and Equa chairs (designed by Bill Stumpf and Don Chadwick). All chairs manufactured by Herman Miller.

In contrast to the static position created by the beanbag chair, many contemporary office chairs are designed for dynamic movement and multiple tasks such as typing, writing, and reading (Figure 2.12). The best are designed to accommodate a wide range of users, who perform multifunctional tasks for extended periods of time. Consumers seek comfort, appropriate support, and ergonomic resolution in today's office environments and are willing to spend several hundred dollars for an appropriate chair. Furniture companies have invested significant resources in the research and development of ergonomic chairs, which in turn require mass production and a high volume of sales for economic feasibility.

Can a chair that is designed specifically for reading a newspaper be used to type a report? Typing requires the maintenance of correct eye position relative to the top of the computer monitor. Arms and wrists need to fall at the level of the keyboard. The spine often leans forward when typing. Reading a newspaper assumes a different posture altogether. Conventional theories suggest that an ideal **seat rake** (the angle between the seat pan and the seat back) for reading depends upon a number of factors: what one is reading, how long one is reading, and one's preferences concerning how to read. Most researchers and designers would agree that the seat rake for reading should be greater than 90 degrees and less than 110 degrees. Though the angle of the seat rake is important to consider in designing a chair, this measure is directly related to other aspects such as the height of the **seat pan,** the surrounding furnishings, the intended purposes, and the physiology of the user. Even when one considers these aspects thoughtfully, body posture will change frequently. Allowing for different postures and body movement is as important as determining appropriate dimensions and angles.

The Dànish designer Niels Hvass designed and fabricated *Yesterday's Paper* (1994), a **chaise lounge** made entirely out of recycled newspaper. In one operation, an **ottoman** for the lounge was cut out of a block of laminated newspapers, resulting in a place to sit and a support to rest one's legs (Figure 2.13). Under the chair is a support with wheeled casters that keeps the lounge off the ground. *Yesterday's Paper* works well as a place to read the newspaper, but it would be a challenge to sit in it in a reclining position and type a report. Different functions require different postures, which often means different chairs.

Figure 2.13 Yesterday's Paper, designed and fabricated by Niels Hvass (1994), Copenhagen, Denmark.

A **bench** typically serves as a place to rest for a brief period of time. But not all benches serve the same purpose. A bench used for sitting in a cross-legged manner needs to have a deeper seat pan and a lower profile than a bench designed for people to sit in an upright manner. Benches that are subdivided or have contoured or predefined seating areas can be difficult to lie upon or incorporate personal items (Figure 2.14).

Benches seem to be everywhere. They are used at bus stops, in parks, and in lobby spaces. Benches are generally used for sitting and waiting, and perhaps for reading, talking, or writing as well, but people find uses that extend beyond conventional utility. The idea of standing on a bench in order to gain extra height to see into the distance may seem unusual,

Figure 2.14 A bench's center stile makes it difficult to lie down.

Figure 2.15 Unconventional use: *standing* on a bench to see into the distance.

but the additional 17 inches (42.2 cm) provided by the bench in Figure 2.15 enabled an exceptional view of the bay.

Beds provide places to sleep. Beds also express social and cultural meaning. Consider the Japanese futon and the *shikibuton,* the blanket in a teepee, the canopy beds designed and fabricated during the Rococo and Victorian periods, and the waterbeds of the 1970s. Beds can be built in, as were the once popular *Murphy beds* of the 1930s, or freestanding platform beds, which were popular in the 1960s. Because one conventionally enters a bed from the side, beds divide rooms spatially and socially. Thomas Jefferson (1743–1826) placed his bed in an alcove located between his study and the bedroom, making it visible and accessible to both spaces while simultaneously drawing together and separating the principal bedroom from the study at Monticello (Figure 2.16).

Figure 2.16 Thomas Jefferson's bedroom and study at Monticello, near Charlottesville, Virginia (1768–81).

ACTIVITIES: EATING, READING, TYPING, AND WRITING

People depend upon furniture for a variety of purposes and activities. Furniture influences how one experiences a meal, reads a book, types a report, works at a computer, or writes at a desk, though the relationships between design and experience need to be studied further. The ability to identify the measurable and material aspects of furniture that contribute to structural integrity, use, and pleasure is key to understanding basic relationships in design.

Eating, reading, typing, and writing are *performance-based* activities. Observing and analyzing correlations between furniture, the human body, and activities can help design-ers better understand how and why furniture performs well or poorly. **Bureaus,** desks, **lecterns, tables,** work-benches, and workstations are designed to accommodate many intended purposes and a broad range of users, which further complicates the parameters of design. Such furnishings are distinct from human body supports in that they primarily support activities rather than the human form.

Consider the activities involved in sharing a meal, and reflect upon how a table's form and shape, size, height, materials, structural stability, **edge profile,** weight, and spatial location can influence patterns of behavior and communication during a meal (Figure 2.17). An effective and sensitive design can assist the behaviors and contribute to the psychological and physical experience of dining.

Observe people reading and typing at a chair and table. Note how often posture changes during each activity. How often do people shift their posture in order to keep their blood moving and stay comfortable when sitting? Observe how chairs and tables support and compromise various activities. Consider sitting as a dynamic and ever-changing activity.

The height and depth of horizontal surfaces influence the utility of furniture. Designers may wish to consider sketching or modeling a human figure when exploring and delineating horizontal surfaces (Figure 2.18). One needs to consider furniture relative to standing, leaning, and sit-ting as well as the various ways of working, resting, speak-ing, reading, typing, and reaching. Most contemporary societies have developed dimensional standards for spe-cific activities. The following conventional standards apply to work surfaces and tables throughout many Western societies:[3]

- Accessible counters for wheelchair use are 30 inches (76.2 cm) high.
- Kitchen counters range in height between 30 and 38 inches (76.2 and 95.7 cm) and are typically 24 inches (61 cm) deep.

Figure 2.17 Solid-surface round dining table (Great American Kitchen exhibit).

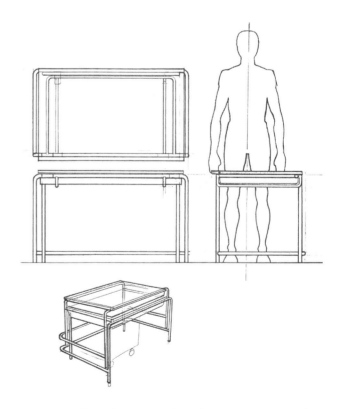

Figure 2.18 Orthographic drawings of a drafting table with a human figure included for scale.

- Standing bar-height surfaces are 42 inches (106.6 cm) high.
- Reading tables are between 25 inches (63.5 cm) and 33 inches (83.8 cm) high, depending upon clearance needs for youth, adults, and wheelchair users.
- Lecterns and reading podiums should be adjustable between 42 inches (106.6 cm) and 48 inches (122 cm) in height.

CONTAINING: STORING, DISPLAYING, AND ORGANIZING

Storing, displaying, and organizing items are also determinants of function. Storing and displaying are separate functions that can occur simultaneously, as in a jeweler's display case (Figure 2.19). Box-like furniture such as chests of drawers, **dressers,** bookcases, storage units, and buffets are **case goods.** Case goods are freestanding elements, generally made of wood. The early-17th-century **cabinet** shown in Figure 2.20 is a decorated case good used to store personal items. The detail in the cabinet contrasts with the conventional white painted pedestals used to display art in many gallery settings (Figure 2.21), which, in turn,

Figure 2.19 Jeweler's display cases.

Figure 2.20 A 17th-century Pakistan cabinet.

Figure 2.21 Custom pedestals designed and fabricated by artist William Christenberry (2001), Dorothy W. and C. Lawson Reed Jr. Gallery, College of Design, Architecture, Art, and Planning, University of Cincinnati.

Figure 2.22 Shaker casework ca. 1800s, Massachusetts.

reveals fundamental distinctions between storing possessions and displaying art. But both examples demonstrate the shared necessity to organize items.

Storage and display solutions can also be inexpensive, sustainable, and *ready made*. In the 1970s, wooden orange crates and plastic milk crates were popular as simple ways to store books, record albums, and clothes. They were portable, lightweight, sturdy, and stackable.

Many contemporary societies find it difficult to live with few possessions. Furnishings are needed to provide adequate storage and function to contain, display, and organize personal possessions acquired in this modern age. These furnishings include **armoires, buffets, chests,** coat racks, **coffee tables, commodes, credenzas, cupboards,** filing cabinets, flat files, gallery pedestals, **hutches,** shelving systems, storage bins, and **tambours.**

Built-in storage and display units, wall-mounted cabinets, and kitchen pantries are considered **casework.** Casework is typically custom-fabricated for the specific contents and environment in which it resides (Figures 2.22).

DEFINING SPACE: ENCLOSING, SHAPING, AND PARTITIONING

Partitioning space is another determinant of function. Space can be subdivided or unified through the use of built-in furnishings, privacy screens, and shelving systems. Consider how **built-in** and partitioned pews have influenced the perception of interior space in many older churches and cathedrals across Europe. At the other end of the spectrum, consider the many office environments, hotel lobbies, museum exhibits, libraries, and restaurant spaces in which freestanding furniture functions to partition and define zones of activity, independent of

Figure 2.23 Partitioned space using office furniture.

the interior or architectural frame. Office storage systems can provide flexible arrangements, dividing and subdividing large spaces into more manageable spaces, or more private spaces (Figure 2.23). Residential **fire screens** help control the heat from an open fire and in so doing provide a greater utility for those near a fireplace.

CLASSIFICATIONS BASED ON SOCIAL USE

Furnishings influence social use and facilitate the functional needs required in many different environments. Healthcare, hospitality, institutional and educational, office, recreation, religious, residential, retail, and storage are social-use headings. Retail stores, on-line web sites, catalogs, and production companies market furniture using social-use headings to reach targeted audiences who might be looking for specific categories of furniture.

Social-use classifications change over time. Retailers try to keep current with social-use trends and respond by offering new products to satisfy the changing demand. Consumers want safe furnishings for newborn babies, products that are nontoxic, and finishes that emit few volatile organic compounds (**VOCs**). Multimedia furnishings are designed much slimmer today, catering to a shift in the market toward thinner plasma and LCD TVs. Many outdoor residential furnishings are lightweight, comfortable, and designed to resist fading or damage caused by the sun. *Home goods* is a phrase used by many retailers to describe lifestyle (residential) design. Williams-Sonoma, Arhaus, Target, and IKEA are retail corporations that offer lifestyle furnishings and target middle- to upper-middle-class consumers.

Healthcare Furniture: For Those Who Need Assistance

Several large furniture companies produce furnishings and equipment specifically for the healthcare industry. Healthcare equipment includes **wheelchairs,** rollaway carts, lift chairs, and adjustable tables to help people with disabilities or those requiring hospitalization.

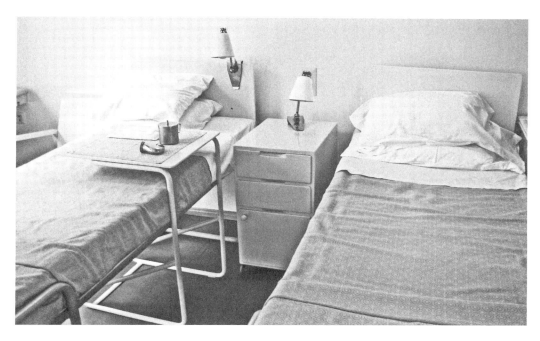

Figure 2.24 Patient room and furnishings, designed by Alvar Aalto, Tuberculosis Sanitorium, Paimio, Finland, 1933.

Generally, healthcare equipment and furnishings are mass-produced; however, architects, designers, and artisans have also focused upon designing limited-run, custom furnishings. When architect Alvar Aalto designed the Tuberculosis Sanatorium at Paimio, Finland, in 1933, he designed the furnishings and casework for each of the patient rooms (Figure 2.24).

Today, many medical beds designed for Intensive Care Units (ICUs) are air inflated, temperature controlled, movable, and adjustable in length, height, and width. Medical beds are designed as components of a complex system of devices that work together to ease body discomfort and save lives.

In the 1800s, wheelchairs were little more than rigid chairs on wheels that were pushed from behind (Figure 2.25). Early 20th century wheelchairs had spoke wheels and wire-wound rubber tires. They were made of chrome-plated steel tubing and stiff vinyl upholstery. They were heavy, averaging between 45 and 50 lb in weight. Today, lightweight titanium wheelchairs are available for athletic competition or negotiating challenging urban spaces.

Many of today's power wheelchairs utilize digital and computer technologies that help control special features such as automatic brakes and antitipping devices. Many of these wheelchairs take into account the need for back, neck, head, and leg support. Power wheelchairs can have electronic controllers to help users drive smoothly, brake easily, and allow independent movement with just the touch of a hand. Dean Kamen's *iBOT* mobility system (1999) transcends traditional

Figure 2.25 Wheelchair from the early 1800s.

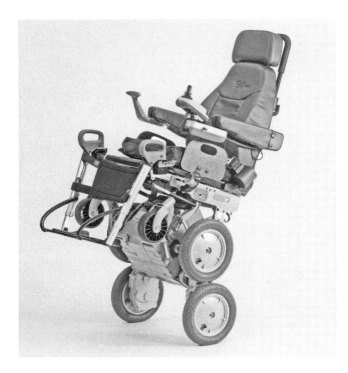

Figure 2.26 Dean Kamen's iBOT Mobility
System (1999), produced for Independence
Technology, L.L.C.

ideas about the wheelchair (Figure 2.26). Though it is designed to help those with a disability, it is not considered a wheelchair. It is a device that can climb stairs, balance on two
wheels, and, in four-wheel mode, can go on any terrain including sand, pebbles, and even
an uncut curb. The *iBOT* enables users to enjoy the same eye height and reach as nonwheel-
chair users.

Lift chairs, bath lifts, and toilet lifts assist those with a disability in getting into and out
of a seated position (Figure 2.27). They offer support for people who are unable to sit and
stand independently and allow caregivers to hold patients physically when tending to their

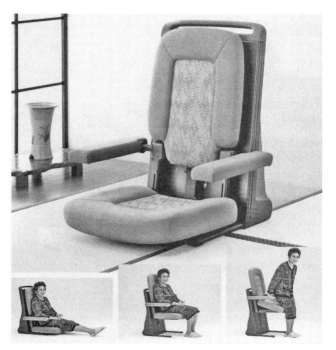

Figure 2.27 Adjustable lift-seat for use
on tatami.

needs. They address the difficulty many individuals have with limited lower back and hip movement. Healthcare furnishings in general and lift chairs or wheelchairs in particular raise issues of semantics that blur the boundary between furniture and equipment. This is happening in other markets as well, but it seems more pronounced in the healthcare industry due to the technical, mechanical, and material innovations that have occurred there.

Hospitality Furniture: Restaurants, Lobbies, and Reception Areas

Hospitality furniture is designed and fabricated for public and social interchange and includes lounge seating, restaurant chairs and tables, lobby seating, and reception desks. Hospitality furniture accommodates a broad range of users and uses. Consequently, accessibility, durability, and flexibility are important criteria to consider in design.

Restaurant Dining Tables and Chairs
Restaurant furnishings are components of hospitality furniture. Despite specific characteristics and features of the tables and chairs used in restaurants and lobbies, overall dimensions are often based upon industry standards:[4]

- The standard height of dining tables is 29 inches (73.6 cm).
- The standard table-width dimension per individual adult is 24 inches (62 cm).
- The standard seat pan height of mass-produced chairs for Western markets is 17 inches (42.2 cm).

Small dining tables occasionally may need to accommodate larger gatherings. With all tables at standard sizes, they can be rearranged as needed to form space for larger groups.

Lobby and Reception Furniture
Lobbies and reception areas are social-centered places that draw people together for relatively short periods of time (Figure 2.28). Verner Panton's *Living Tower* (1969) is composed

Figure 2.28 Social-centered space.

Figure 2.29 Living Tower, designed by Verner Panton (1969), produced by Vitra.

of interrelated components that make possible a variety of spatial configurations and body postures (Figure 2.29). The sectional seating design is ideally situated for lobby and reception areas. Related to Panton's *Living Tower* was *Vision II,* an exhibit space also designed by Panton, composed of many upholstered components. It was conceived as a three-dimensional body landscape using sinusoidal curved shapes, interlocking components, and bold use of color.

George Nelson's *Platform bench* (1946) is modest in form and flexible in use (Figure 2.30). It can be configured and arranged in a number of ways. Lobbies and reception areas need flex-

Figure 2.30 Platform bench, designed by George Nelson (1946), manufactured by Herman Miller.

Figure 2.31 Sectional lobby seating in the Seattle Public Library, designed by architect Rem Koolhaus, 2006.

ible and multifunctional furnishings in order to accommodate changing and temporary uses. The lobby furniture in Rem Koolhaus' Seattle Public Library (Figure 2.31) is filled with colorful, sectional upholstered seating elements designed to accommodate diverse users (i.e., young, old, individuals, groups, or even Seattle's homeless population) and multiple uses (i.e., talking, gathering, reading alone, and resting).

Institutional Furniture: Education

Institutional furnishings are used in classrooms, libraries, and training facilities. The term **contract furniture** is often used to describe institutional furniture. On occasion, institutional furnishings are custom designed for specific places, but generally, they are anonymous products. Stackable chairs such as Arne Jacobsen's *Series 7* (Figure 2.32) and David Rowland's

Figure 2.32 Ant and Series 7 molded plywood stacking chairs, designed by Arne Jacobsen (1955), manufactured by Fritz Hansen, Denmark.

Figure 2.33 The 40/4 stacking chairs, designed by David Rowland (1963), manufactured by GF Furniture Systems. The stamped-out sheet metal has a protective PVC coating applied.

40/4 stacking chair (Figure 2.33) were designed for conferencing, auditorium seating, and institutional use. The best designs are durable, comfortable, flexible, lightweight, and easy to store. Arne Jacobsen's *Ant* chairs are available in three- and four-leg versions, with or without arms, and in a variety of back profiles. The *40/4* stacking chair (1963) can be stacked 40 high within a space of 4 feet (1.2 m) because the design nests closely and the frame is made of ⁷⁄₁₆-inch (11-mm) diameter high-strength steel rod. Over 8 million *40/4* stacking chairs have been produced, and many are still in use around the world.

Design criteria for institutional seating include:

- Lumbar vertebrae support
- The ease with which and number of chairs that can be stacked (4 to 40)
- Lightweight design
- Comfort and freedom for body movement
- Gauge of the metal supports (16-gauge and ⅞-inch [2-cm] tubing are standard)
- Durability
- Stain and scratch resistance of the chair's finish
- Price

Fixed institutional seating includes educational lecture seating, auditorium seating, theater seating, stadium seating, and courtroom seating. The folding auditorium seating designed by Poul Kjærholm and in collaboration with cabinetmaker Ejnar Pedersen (1976) is attached to a stepped floor in the concert hall at the Louisiana Museum of Modern Art in Humlebaek, Denmark. The seating incorporated plaited maple seat pans and backs (woven slats) that were remarkable for both their craft and comfort (Figure 2.34). The maple com-

Figure 2.34 Concert hall seating at the Louisiana Museum of Modern Art, Humlebaek, Denmark. Designed by Poul Kjærholm, 1976.

plemented the dark wood flooring, but the plaited inserts caused a distracting noise from maple rubbing against maple. Wax and soap flakes were applied in an attempt to address the problem but without success. Eventually, the maple inserts were replaced with ash wood, which solved the noise problem.

Fixed seating often incorporates extendable writing tablets or cup holders. These elements should be accessible, easy and quiet to operate, and durable. Most writing tablets are designed to favor right-handed users because 90 percent of the population is right-handed, but the challenge remains to accommodate all users.

Shelving systems are significant institutional furnishings, particularly in libraries. They need to be flexible, adjustable, accessible, and durable. Wall-mounted or freestanding shelving systems often define and partition space in a significant manner (Figure 2.35).

Figure 2.35 Library shelving, the Seattle Public Library, 2006.

Multifunctional Furniture: Sit/Sleep and Store/Display

Furniture becomes multifunctional the moment we toss clothes on a chair or sit on a table. Tabletops function as places to set items and serve as places to eat, drink, and work. Tables can also accommodate the desire or need to sit and rest (Figure 2.36), just as chairs can incorporate drawers and open shelving for storing and organizing items (Figure 2.37).

Many furnishings are designed to serve more than one purpose, especially in small spaces where efficiency and economy are required. The *Valet* chair (Figure 2.38) designed by Hans

Figure 2.36 Sitting and reading *on* a table.

Figure 2.37 Heavy study chair, Lars Tingskov Mikkelsen, 1998.

Figure 2.38 Valet chair, designed by Hans J. Wegner (1953), fabricated by PP Møbler.

J. Wegner (1953) is a stool conceived to function as a clothes valet for students living in dormitories at Saint Catherine's College in Oxford, England. The seat pan is hinge-mounted near the front, which can be lifted to access a small recessed tray that is useful for storing personal items. The chair's back is profiled to support a shirt or jacket.

Futons

The **futon** is a traditional Japanese bedding system. It includes the *shikibuton* (floor mat) on which a person sleeps and the *kakebuton* (duvet/comforter) that covers the body. Its portability allows it to be stored when not in use. This is an important feature because traditional Japanese living spaces are compact. The futon is placed on *tatami* mats, which are traditionally 2-inch (5 cm) thick woven reed flooring mats that are 35.5 inches (90 cm) wide by 71 inches (180 cm) long and inset into the floor.[5] Futon mattresses are simple cotton mats that are flexible and foldable. Western societies utilize adjustable wooden frames to help place the futon in either a sitting or sleeping position to offer a night of rest.

Storage/Display Units

Retail environments rely upon shelving systems to store and display products as well as to organize space. The primary goal of retail display is to promote the sale of merchandise. Consider the baker's rack, which is typically used in the food preparation industry. A baker's rack is easy to assemble, offers a flexible arrangement, provides clear lines of sight, and can be configured in multiple shelf heights. It is a transferable shelving system for settings as diverse as warehouses, pharmacies, and personal garages. Verner Panton and Peter J. Lassen collaborated on a similar shelving system made with chromed metal rods called the *Wire Cube* in 1970 (Figure 2.39). The *Wire Cube* is produced for commercial use by Montana and recalls the pragmatic utility and visual language of the traditional baker's rack.

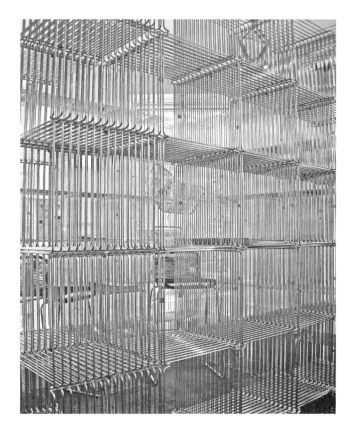

Figure 2.39 Wire Cube, designed by Verner Panton and Peter J. Lassen (1970), manufactured by Montana.

Office Furniture: Ergonomic Seating, Workstations, and Systems Furniture

Office furniture constitutes a large segment of the furniture industry. The U.S. office furniture industry has grown significantly over the past 20 years, reaching $12 billion in gross sales in 2006.[6] Ergonomic seating is a large portion of this market. Today, many well-designed ergonomic chairs are available. Some of these include Herman Miller's *Equa, Aeron,* and *Mirra* chairs, Humanscale's *Freedom* chair, and Steelcase's *Leap* chair (Figure 2.40).

Office furniture systems have undergone significant transformations because of social and economic change, new ergonomic theories, and technological innovation. The influx of computer and digital technology, new products, and cultural shifts in the way office work is organized and managed have changed the workplace from the heavy, dark environments that were typical 100 years ago (Figure 2.41).

In 1968 Herman Miller introduced *Action Office* (see Chapter 4), the first panel-based, open-plan office system in the world.[7] The designer, Robert Propst, developed a system of components that could be configured and reconfigured as needed over time. The ability of individuals to control their physical and ambient work environments responded to a growing trend. The *Action Office* system transformed the workplace, as well as Herman Miller and the entire furniture industry, into a systems-based approach in thinking about the role of design.[8] Since then, the concepts of *networking, teaming,* and *hoteling* have developed in the culture of the workplace, and these, in turn, have inspired new office systems and new product lines. Primary themes behind *Action Office* are open communication areas, flexibility for spatial and functional change, and incorporating a greater sense of user control throughout the workspace.

Nearly 35 years later, Ayse Birsel's *Resolve* office system (Figure 2.42) reestablished the success of Herman Miller's original office system by expressing new ideas about flexibility and

Figure 2.40 Leap office chair, designed by Steelcase and IDEO (1999), manufactured by Steelcase.

Figure 2.41 Heavy, dark office environment typical 100 years ago.

individual control over one's environment. *Resolve* utilizes geometries based upon 120-degree angles that create inviting, attractive, space-efficient, and open workstations. The system is composed of vertical poles of various heights and tiered support trusses that manage power and define space. It has a high recycle content and offers supporting products that include canopies, specialized work surfaces, and lighting fixtures.

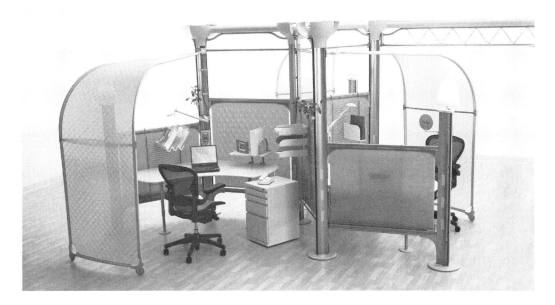

Figure 2.42 Resolve-propeller application, DOT on rolling screens, poles support arms and tool rails, metallic silver finish, designed by Ayse Birsel (1999), manufactured by Herman Miller.

Figure 2.43 Foosball table with telescoping rods manufactured by Bonzini.

Recreational Furniture: Play, Leisure, and Outdoor Furnishings

Poker tables, foosball tables, and Ping-Pong™ tables are equipment and gaming furniture designed for leisure and play. Concepts of health, safety, and welfare have transformed the landscape of recreational gaming. Today's furnishings are safer than before, minimizing the risk of injury and limiting exposure to liability. Many foosball tables have telescoping rods (Figure 2.43). Some swings and play equipment are now made from recycled plastic and rubber synthetics, and many game tables have materials and decorative finishes that emit fewer VOCs.

Outdoor Furnishings

A significant percentage of outdoor furniture is manufactured from exotic hardwoods such as teak or jarrah (from Australia) and maintained yearly with a UV protecting and penetrating oil or allowed to **patina** to a natural silver-gray color. Other woods that perform well outdoors include redwood, cypress, cedar, mahogany, and white oak. Aluminum is a popular metal for outdoor furniture because it is lightweight and weathers well. Water-resistant materials and fabrics often are used to improve comfort where the metal comes in contact with the body. The classic aluminum folding lawn chairs of the 1950s and the wooden director's chairs of the 1970s are precedents for many contemporary folding chairs used for camping and watching sports events. Roto-molded polyethylene (PE) furnishings are lightweight, comfortable, and weather well, but generally are bulky and rarely are designed to fold.

Religious Furniture: Altars, Arks, and Minbars

Religious environments and the practice of unique rituals require specific furnishings. Liturgical furniture is determined by collective ritual practices that help structure how a given set of

Figure 2.44 Altar at Saint Francis of the Providence of God, motherhouse chapel, Pittsburgh, Pennsylvania (1994).

people worship together. A summary can be drawn from the similarities and differences among three major religions as experienced in Catholic, Jewish, and Islamic places of worship.

Catholic Church Furnishings

The **altar, ambo, ambry, cantor stand, credence table, gift table, ossuary, presider's chair, processional cross,** and **tabernacle** are standard liturgical furnishings within a Catholic church.[9] These furnishings are typically conceived as a suite. Liturgical guidelines for the Catholic furnishings illustrated in this section were based upon the *Environment and Art in Catholic Worship,* published by the National Conference of Catholic Bishops (1978).

The **altar** is a focal point for the celebration of the mass. It is located in the midst of the people who gather to receive the Eucharist. The form and location of the altar shown in Figure 2.44 maintain its liturgical focus and accessible ideal position in space.

Originally, the **ambo** was conceived as a raised platform located in the nave of Greek Orthodox churches, marking the place to stand and read the Gospel or the Epistle.[10] Today, it is comparable to the altar in the liturgical setting since the first part of the liturgy centers on the word of God. In recent years, accessibility has become increasingly important in liturgical furnishings. The ambo shown in Figure 2.45 responds to the challenge of incorporating accessible and **universal design** directives in new liturgical furnishings.

Figure 2.45 Accessible ambo with retractable book shelf, shown in closed and opened positions (1999).

Figure 2.46 Tabernacle at Saint Charles Borromeo Catholic Church, Kettering, Ohio, 1993.

Figure 2.47 Ambry at Holy Family Catholic Church, Poland, Ohio, 2000.

The Eucharistic chapel is a unique space in a Catholic church. Its primary purpose is to serve as a place for the **tabernacle** and *sacramental candle.* The Eucharistic chapel can be defined by an **iconostasis screen,** partitioned in any manner or set apart from the assembly area in a variety of ways. The sacramental candle is located close to the tabernacle. The candle is always lit (usually a 7- or 8-day candle) and serves as a sign that Christ is present. The tabernacle contains a ciborium (a container for the bread used in the mass) and host. The tabernacle for Saint Charles Borromeo Catholic Church in Kettering, Ohio, displays the ciborium through its tempered glass and cherry wood frame (Figure 2.46). In addition to the celebration of the liturgy, people may be invited to vigil in the Eucharistic chapel for private silent prayer. For these occasions, **prie-dieux kneelers** are used.

Holy Oils are among the most highly revered sacramentals of the Catholic Church and are stored in an **ambry.** Recently, the Holy Oils have become more visibly prominent in the Catholic Church. The ambry shown in Figure 2.47 displays and secures the Holy Oils and is located close to the baptismal font.

Baptismal fonts are liturgical furnishings that are either portable or physically incorporated into the architecture. They are often located near the entry, in a gathering area, or placed on the sacramental platform along with the altar and ambo. They are used periodically and serve an important function in the church.

Synagogues

Reform and Orthodox Jewish synagogues are liturgically similar to one another, as are their furnishings. The **ark** is the most important liturgical furniture in a synagogue. It refers to the *Ark of the Covenant,* where the word of God was kept safe during the time of Moses. The ark is also called the *Crown of the Torah.*[11] Freestanding and built-in arks (Figure 2.48) contain Torah scrolls and are located close to the *ner tamid* (all-burning light). The interior of the ark is illuminated and often screened (by a veil or glass) so that the Torah scrolls are not visually prominent during the service.

The **Torah table** usually has a canted surface in order to read the Torah. The size of the Torah table is generally large enough to accommodate a Torah scroll and up to four people gathered around it. A reading table or **lectern** is used for reading a book, singing, or speaking. Liturgical pieces are located on the bima (a raised platform). The bima spatially defines the functions of worship and indirectly guides the layout of the assembly seating for regular services and High Holy Days (Figure 2.49).

Figure 2.48 Ark at the Plum Street Temple, Cincinnati, Ohio, 1866.

Figure 2.49 Chapel and bima at the Isaac M. Wise Center, Cincinnati, Ohio, 2006.

Figure 2.50 Minbar and mihrab, Rustem Pasa.

Figure 2.51 Mihrab, New Valide Mosque, Üsküdar, Turkey. Architect: Kayserili Mehmet, 1710.

Figure 2.52 Prayer rugs.

Mosques

Within a mosque, the **mihrab, minbar,** and **prayer rug** are liturgical elements designed for worship. The minbar is a high pulpit, an elevated structure from which the *khutba* (an Islamic sermon) is given during Friday communal prayers. It is located in front of the assembly. Metaphoric elements are typically incorporated in the minbar and include a *gate, ascending steps up to heaven, portal,* and *open door.*[12] The minbar (Figure 2.50) is located near the mihrab (Figure 2.51), a niche indicating the direction of Mecca.

A prayer rug (Figure 2.52) is a rug upon which an individual prays. It provides a clean, flat surface on which to submit oneself to Allah while praying on one's knees and hands. During the call to prayer, prayer rugs are oriented toward the mihrab. Chairs are not used in a mosque.

Residential Furniture: Social Gathering, Resting, Dining, and Organizing

A home can be considered an "organized closet," shaped by personal possessions and members of a family. Residential furniture provides the basic necessities of dwelling and includes freestanding and built-in furnishings that help meal preparation and dining, the organization of possessions, social gathering, work, rest, and play.

Architects Charles Mackintosh (1868–1928) and his wife, Margaret MacDonald (1864–1933), designed the interior spaces, furniture, **millwork,** and textiles when they designed *Hill House* in Helensburgh, Scotland (Figure 2.53). The location and orientation of the furnishings throughout the house are site-specific and complement the architecture and interior spaces.

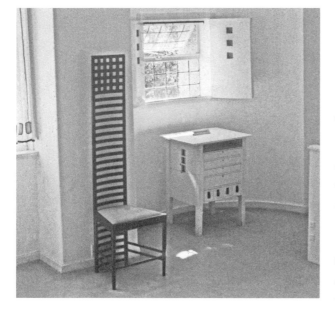

Figure 2.53 Bedroom furnishings at Hill House, designed by Charles R. Mackintosh and Margaret MacDonald (1904), Helensburgh, Scotland.

Figure 2.54 Canopy state bed, designed by Robert Adam for Osterley Park, Middlesex, England.

A place to sleep is an important component of a home. Beds can be built in or freestanding. They can stack vertically upon one another as **bunk beds** do or they can be designed as low beds on casters that can be rolled out from or into another, as a **trundle bed. Canopy beds** were popular in many large homes from feudal times to the early 1900s (Figure 2.54). Most canopy beds were fabricated out of wood and had draperies that could be closed for privacy and warmth. Canopy beds can be considered rooms within rooms that enclose space within a space. Defining space in a figural manner is distinct from creating and working with open space. Many of today's platform beds (such as the Maly bed shown in Figure 2.55) emphasize horizontal lines and are designed to complement open, contemporary spaces.

Figure 2.55 Maly platform bed (2006), manufactured by Ligne Roset.

Figure 2.56 Portable outdoor stretcher.

Cots and stretchers serve as portable and folding structures for rest and sleep when conventional beds are not available. The portable stretcher shown in Figure 2.56 is made of wood, canvas, and galvanized hardware. Cots are versatile furnishings used for camping, natural disaster relief, and temporary bunking.

Organizing

In Western societies, storage units and shelving systems have become necessities of contemporary life. Even in hotel rooms (homes away from home), storage units and shelving systems are desired amenities. Architect Arne Jacobsen incorporated built-in and freestanding furniture in the guest rooms he designed when he worked on the Radisson SAS Royal Hotel in Copenhagen, Denmark. Room 606 is preserved today exactly as it was originally designed in 1958 (Figure 2.57). The furnishings in the room include wall-mounted storage cabinets,

Figure 2.57 Built-in furnishings, room 606, Radisson SAS Royal Hotel, designed by Arne Jacobsen (1958), Copenhagen, Denmark.

built-in modular desks, sliding wall-mounted luminaries, open shelves, and freestanding chairs. The built-in desks organize personal items and are accessible by raising their tops.

Kitchen Furnishings

Kitchens are places where meals are prepared and shared, equipment and food are stored, and people gather. Cabinets, counter spaces, built-in storage units, pantries, tables, and chairs serve pragmatic purposes and express cultural values. Contemporary American kitchens are generally open spaces with built-in counters, cabinets, and equipment integrated into the perimeter of the space (Figure 2.58). Older kitchens are generally smaller spaces and in many cases are composed of freestanding equipment, cupboards, tables, and chairs (Figure 2.59).

Figure 2.58 Contemporary kitchen (2005) with perimeter built-in and wall-mounted casework.

Figure 2.59 A 1924 kitchen, a small space with freestanding fixtures and equipment.

Retail Furniture: Displaying, Storing, Transactions, and Sales

Retail furnishings should be flexible, durable, and require low maintenance, but above all else, they need to promote the sale of merchandise. In addition to the design of product storage and display furnishings, the location, size, material, and form of cash-wraps and reception areas should be considered carefully. **Cash-wraps** and reception areas are places of communication and transaction (Figure 2.60). They incorporate equipment, computers, credit swipes, cash registers, supplies, merchandise, and people in their design. They attract and welcome customers, yet keep valuables secure from theft. Cash-wraps and reception kiosks often function as *sociofugal* (outwardly oriented) spaces, and they need to maintain the visual lines of sight throughout a retail environment to function well for both staff and customers.

Wall systems can be used to display items for self-assistance or are often located behind counters to help promote the sale of merchandise. Typically designed as a system of components, wall units are often shallow in depth and serve as a background component to the surrounding retail space.

Figure 2.60 Retail cash-wrap and reception area for a card shop, Connecker, Pennsylvania.

Storage Containers: Organizing and Accessing

The significance of a container is often related to the significance of its contents. It is not surprising, then, that the quality and value of jewelry and other personal collections are expressed by the design and material of their containers. The design and fabrication of a flatfile can express the importance of drawing equipment and paper supplies (Figure 2.61) by its materials and quality of workmanship. **Hope chests** were made to store the dowries of young women, and often were personalized and crafted with care. They were one-of-a-kind pieces that projected a narrative or allegory through form, material, ornamentation, or decoration. Though not strictly considered furniture, Japanese sake casks are remarkable for their craft and workmanship. The workmanship of these wooden casks reinforces the importance placed upon the communal ritual of opening and consuming sake.

Storage and wardrobe furnishings (armoires) can be sizable. The congregation at Viikki Church in Helsinki, Finland, had a need for substantial coat storage, which easily could have overwhelmed the entry and gathering space of the

Figure 2.61 Flatfile on wheels—organizing writing utensils, equipment, and sheet paper (1988).

Figure 2.62 Open storage units, Viikki Church, Helsinki, Finland.

church, designed by JKMM Architects in 2005. Freestanding coat closets (Figure 2.62) were designed without fronts and backs to maintain lines of sight throughout the lobby area and keep the lobby/gathering area visually open when not in use.

Shelving Systems

One of the intended purposes of shelving is to maximize accessibility to stored material (in most settings). Adjustability, structural integrity, visibility, and aesthetics are further design considerations. Shelving systems can be wall-mounted or freestanding. Typically, these systems are modular and, due to their size, can have a significant influence upon the experience and spatial composition of a room (Figure 2.63).

Figure 2.63 Library shelving, Bartholomew County Public Library, Columbus, Indiana, designed by I. M. Pei, New York City.

chapter 3
Form, Spatial Organization, and Typological Orders

THIS CHAPTER FOCUSES upon the physical and spatial characteristics of furniture and is organized in three parts: *Form, Spatial Organization,* and *Typological Orders.*

FORM

Form constitutes the physical and spatial structure of an entity; however, *form* is not a synonym for *mass* or *volume*. Music and poetry have structure as well as form. A drawing or sketch of a chair can express form just as a model of a chair might. When shape is governed by structural or cognitive considerations, it becomes form. We perceive form in our minds as we perceive sitting in a chair. The *Circle* chair designed by Hans J. Wegner (1946) is considered form because its shape characteristics are determined by the structure of sitting in conjunction with the conditions of its geometry (Figure 3.1).

Figure 3.1 Circle chair, designed by Hans J. Wegner (1946), fabricated by PP Møbler.

Figure 3.2 Folded corrugated cardboard chair.

Figure 3.3 Sciangai Clothes Stand, designed by Jonathan de Pas, Donato d'Urbino, and Paolo Lomazzi (1974), manufactured by Zanotta.

Consider the forces that can influence form (i.e., moment, shear, compressive, tensile, and lateral forces) resulting from gravity, daily use, and live loads. Reflect upon the sturdiness and strength that can be achieved by folding corrugated cardboard, as shown in Figure 3.2, or in the mechanical hardware in the *Sciangai* clothes stand designed by Jonathan de Pas, Donato d'Urbino, and Paolo Lomazzi (Figure 3.3). Think about how details, materials, form, and fabrication techniques help to achieve structural integrity in design.

Forces applied to furniture during use place significant demands upon design. Structural forces are present in all of the physical systems and components of furniture, keeping them from falling apart.

Figure 3.4 Conoid cushion chair with a walnut seat and hickory spindles, crafted by George Nakashima.

A review of internal and external forces during design might help to develop a better understanding of how shear, moment, and lateral forces affect furniture. Quick study models and thoughtful, intuitive sketches can help designers confront basic forces in their designs. Eventually, **prototypes** may need to be fabricated in order to test the structural integrity of a design. Furniture designers need to be attentive to basic engineering principles throughout the design process and aware of concepts such as deflection, **creep,** and load failure as materials and dimensions are determined.

Materials and fabrication techniques influence form. In addition, form can inspire the appropriate use of materials and fabrication processes. The natural figure and grain in wood inspired George Nakashima's handcrafted furniture (Figure 3.4). The interlocking laminated and formed plywood components give order to Kristian Vedel's children's furniture, designed in 1957 (Figure 3.5). Verner Panton's stackable *Panton* chair

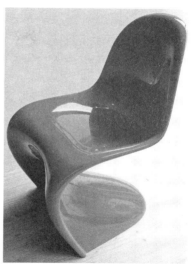

Figure 3.5 Children's furniture series, designed by Kristian Vedel (1957), fabricated and assembled with formed plywood.

Figure 3.6 Stackable Panton chair, designed by Verner Panton (1960), manufactured by Nienkämper.

(Figure 3.6) expresses the dynamic, fluid potential of rigid polyurethane injection-molded in one piece.

Form is influenced by the purposes it serves. In a chair or stool the fundamental purpose may seem clear, yet there are many ways that people sit. This is evident in the wide spectrum of sitting devices available, ranging from inflated therapy balls to the upholstered **settees** of the Victorian period.

Space and geometry are formal constructs in design. Consider the profile sketch of a **laminated** chair designed by Erik Krogh and the unfolding geometries that result from a study of the chair's formal and kinetic characteristics (Figures 3.7a, 3.7b). The laminated plywood is staggered in an incremental fashion, which along with its profile creates a synthesis between the chair's design, the desire for body movement, appropriate body support, and the desire for an upright posture.

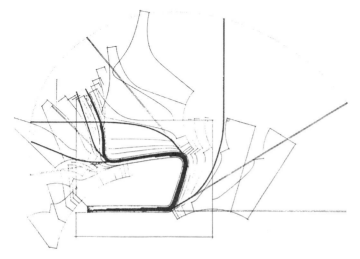

Figure 3.7a Drawing—reflective study of movement and space.

Figure 3.7b Laminated plywood chair, designed by Erik Krogh.

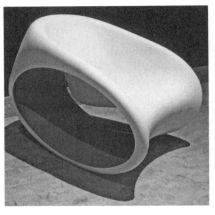

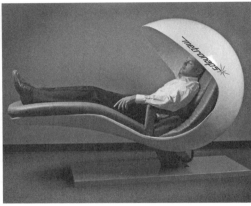

Figure 3.8 Mirra chair with Meridian lateral file and Action Office 2 system. The Mirra chair was designed by Studio 7.5 (Claudia Plikat, Burkhard Schmitz, Nicolai Neubert, Carola Zwick, and Roland Zwick), produced by Herman Miller in 2003.

Figure 3.9 Ron Arad's roto-molded rocking lounge seating.

Figure 3.10 MetroNaps pod—side view.

Sit in a *Mirra* chair (Figure 3.8) designed by Studio 7.5 for Herman Miller and experience the various body postures and body movements allowed by the chair's active and passive adjustments. Experience the rocking motion of one of Ron Arad's roto-molded lounge chairs (Figure 3.9). These designs integrate an anticipated experience, technical processes, ergonomic inquiry, social use, and aesthetics.

Furniture can express personal (private) and communal (public) space. Personal space is experienced in the *MetroNaps pod,* created in 2004 by MetroNaps. The reclining pod offers users a semiprivate space and expresses quiet and individual repose (Figure 3.10). The *MetroNaps pod* is a place to recharge the mind and body—ideally situated for use in stressful environments such as airport terminals. In a different manner altogether, the arrangement of desks and chairs organized in a circular pattern in a town hall expresses the political ideal of individuals working together to constitute a collective and unified public voice, creating, in turn, a communally shared space (Figure 3.11).

Figure 3.11 Tables and chairs arranged in a circular pattern, Town Hall at Århus, Denmark.

Form results from the many ways of thinking about structure, materials, function, social use, and technical considerations. Form also reveals physical and spatial subcomponents, one of which is shape. Shape is dependent upon descriptive geometry and in this section is organized into five categories: *angular, composite, curvilinear, orthogonal,* and *sectional/modular.*

Angular

All geometry is composed of angles, lines, and planes, but **canted,** nonorthogonal and noncurvilinear geometries are referred to as *angular.* Gerrit Rietveld's stackable *Zig-Zag* chair (1934) is visually dramatic due to the bold angular relationships between the chair's support, seat pan, and seat back (Figure 3.12). The diagonal cantilever incorporates dovetailed, glued, and screwed joinery.

Figure 3.12 Zig-Zag chair, designed and fabricated by Gerrit T. Rietveld, 1934.

Composite

Composite furnishings utilize two or more geometric systems such as *curvilinear* and *orthogonal* or two or more distinct materials such as stone and wood in one piece. The bent, welded, and chromed tubular steel frame is distinct from the black leather seat pan and backrest in Marcel Breuer's *Model B32* (Figure 3.13). *Nintendo Power* is a display and storage unit organizing the media and hardware for Nintendo's original 8-bit gaming system. The geometry is entirely orthogonal, but the design is a composite of various materials and iconic references (Figure 3.14). Isamu Noguchi's coffee table is a composite of biomorphic-shaped wood supports and a curvilinear glass top (Figure 3.15).

Figure 3.13 Model B32, designed by Marcel Breuer, 1928.

Figure 3.14 Nintendo Power, designed and fabricated by Jim Postell, 1990.

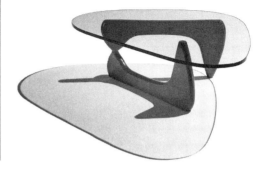

Figure 3.15 Coffee table, designed by Isamu Noguchi for Herman Miller, 1947.

Figure 3.16 Circular forms—inflated gym balls.

Figure 3.17 Drawing overlay of PK 9. Chair designed by Poul Kjærholm (1961), manufactured by Fritz Hansen.

Figure 3.18 Dondolo rocker, designed by Cesare Leonardi and Franca Stagi (1967), manufactured by Elco-Bellato.

Curvilinear

Inflated therapy balls (gym balls) are simple curvilinear forms (Figure 3.16). Gym balls have neither front nor side, unless these are implied by other characteristics such as material, seams, or branding logos. They offer a practical, inexpensive, and healthful means of sitting.

Compound curves are curvilinear shapes that bend in two or more directions. Poul Kjærholm's *PK 9* is composed of a compound curved fiberglass seat covered with leather, with curved steel supports, as seen in the overlay drawings in Figure 3.17. Cesare Leonardi and Franca Stagi designed the *Dondolo* rocker in 1967. It is made from molded fiberglass-reinforced polyester strengthened by incorporating ribbing, and has an unusual curvilinear shape, which relies upon the posture and weight of the user to function properly (Figure 3.18).

Orthogonal

Orthogonal furniture is composed of rectangular geometric forms created by lines, planes, and volumes positioned at 90 degrees to one another. Armoires, beds, buffets, shelving, and sofas are often orthogonal due to their size, cost of fabrication, and spatial proximity to a wall. Donald Judd's precisely crafted Baltic birch plywood box chairs (1991), shown in Figure 3.19, complement his lifelong artistic exploration of light, form, and order, which nearly always is expressed through orthogonal geometries.

Sectional/Modular

The terms *sectional* and *modular* are often used interchangeably, but distinctions should be made. Sectional furnishings are arrangements of components that can be composed in various ways. The components need not be similar or even proportional to one

Figure 3.19 Computer rendering of two (Baltic birch) plywood chairs designed and fabricated by artist Donald Judd, 1991.

Figure 3.20 Sectional seating arrangement—lobby area, Simmons Hall, Massachusetts Institute of Technology.

another. Modular furnishings rely upon proportional correlations between components, having repeatable or geometric correlations between parts, which may be arranged in a variety of ways. Sectional and modular furnishings are inherently flexible, designed as a system of components that can be assembled, disassembled, and very often reconfigured (Figure 3.20). Shelving systems, office workstations, lounge seating, and storage units are generally sectional or modular.

Music Machines is an ensemble of four furniture pieces designed to organize a variety of components and media (Figures 3.21a, 3.21b). Two custom-fabricated speakers, a storage unit for records and CDs, and another unit that organizes stereo components were designed as an ensemble, interconnected and interrelated with one

Figure 3.21a Music Machines, designed by Jim Postell, 2002.

Figure 3.21b Music Machines—furniture for organizing records and CDs.

another. The pieces were fabricated of laminated plywood, cherry, and neoprene 70, and the storage and display units incorporate wheeled casters. The design utilizes modular components, internally arranged and externally expressed as parts of a larger whole.

SPATIAL ORGANIZATION

Space is the medium that architects, designers, and artists use to compose form. Space and form are codependent. Without space, form would not exist, and without form, space could not exist. Thinking about the space between the fixed elements of a chair can clarify your thinking about the form of a chair. The next time you draw a chair, consider sketching the space between its parts. The exercise may help you to better see the spatial structure of the chair's composition. Try it!

Music can be denoted graphically and spatially, giving visual measure to the structure and rhythm of a musical composition. Similarly, the placement and orientation of furnishings give measure to the structure and rhythm of interior design. Spatial relationships exist between as well as within furnishings. Furniture designers should consider the following spatial relationships:

- Spatial relationships between people and furniture
- Spatial composition of furniture and interior space
- Spatial relationships between various components of furniture
- Spatial extensions based upon the geometries of furniture

Plan diagrams, as shown in the overlay of the before and after plans in Figure 3.22, can appear abstract, but the exercise of thinking in terms of plan and section, while simultaneously thinking in terms of perspective, is important to practice. Designers draw in plan, section, elevation, and perspective, and must be able to communicate design ideas in a didactic as well as a perceptual manner. Throughout the design process, designers often switch from abstract to perceptual representation. To follow this point, the spatial organizations discussed in this section develop both an analytic and a perceptual understanding of some of the characteristics and principles that render space. These include *centralized, clustered, grid, linear,* and *radial organizations.*

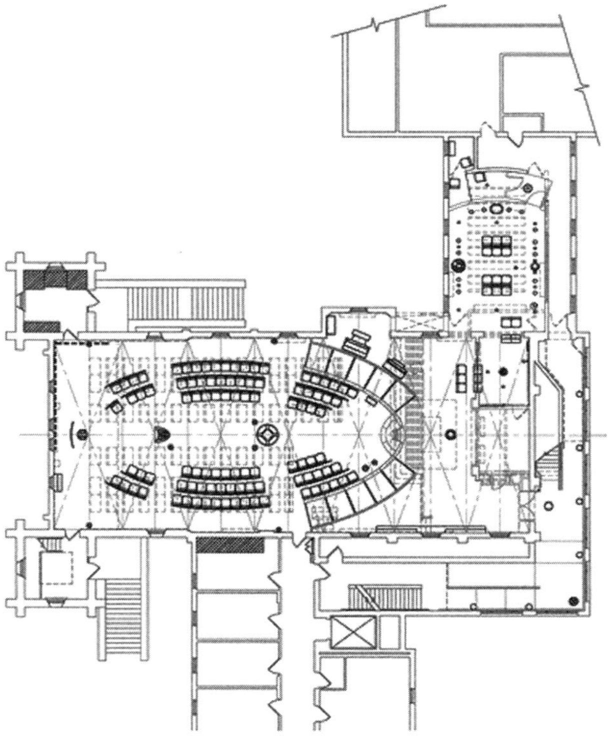

Centralized

Centralized spatial order draws focus toward the center of a space. The interior of Eero Saarinen's chapel at the Massachusetts Institute of Technology relies upon three elements to draw the visitor's focus toward the center of the space: a built-in marble altar, a circular light lantern located in the chapel's ceiling, and a metal sculpture by Harry Bertoia centered above the altar and suspended below the lantern (Figure 3.23). The size, location, orientation, and surface articulation of these three

Figure 3.22 Furniture overlay—existing and proposed interior plans. Chapel, Sisters of Saint Francis, Tiffin, Ohio.

Figure 3.23 Centralized space—altar, suspended sculpture, and lantern at Kresge Chapel, Massachusetts Institute of Technology, designed by Eero Saarinen (1955). Suspended light sculpture by Harry Bertoia.

components, in concert with the dynamic effect of daylight brought into the chapel from the lantern, influence the perception of a centralized **typology.**

A centralized space (or any spatial typology) is an experienced phenomenon that is influenced by many factors. Furniture, material, people, activity, acoustics, and lighting are variables that influence the perception of space. The existing centrality of the chapel shown in Figure 3.24 was made more pronounced in the renovation through the transformation of material, lighting, acoustics, and new furniture.

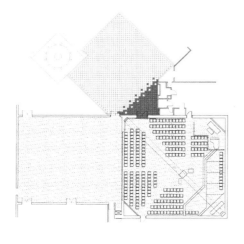

Figure 3.24 Reinforcing a centralized space—before and after plans, Isaac M. Wise Center, Cincinnati, Ohio, 2006.

existing plan   new plan

Figure 3.25 Action Office showing different work surfaces, designed by Robert Propst for Herman Miller, 1968.

Clustered

Clustered arrangements are apparent whenever a group of three or more elements (or axial orientations) share the same field (Figure 3.25). Many office systems are designed to enable a broad range of options regarding spatial layout. Office systems such as the *Action Office* series can result in clustered spatial arrangements when the layout of workstations and privacy screens is based upon functional relationships as well as communication needs within the corporate culture. A clustered spatial organization based upon public and private activities can appear random in plan, even though substantial thought has gone into the spatial arrangement.

Open loft spaces are spatially organized by the location and orientation of furniture. Clustered arrangements of furnishings can create zones of activities, with each zone defining a specific component of "home." There is the private sleeping area defined by the bed; the work area shaped by office furnishings and equipment; the social gathering area composed of seating, a coffee table, and an area rug; the dining and kitchen area for meal preparation and consumption; as well as the recreation area defined by chairs, television, computer, game table, or shelving for books. Space between clustered furnishings, when liberated from the confines of structural columns and wall partitions, can result in **interstitial space** (in-between space).

Andrea Zittel's *A-Z Comfort Unit,* shown in Figure 3.26, was conceived to accommodate and render a new social and formal typology of home furnishings for people who share space but desire privacy. The Comfort Unit challenges traditional notions of domestic space through a series of habitable and transformable pods designed for open, loft-type, and shared living environments.

Figure 3.26 A-Z Comfort Unit (1994), designed and fabricated by Andrea Zittel.

Grids

Furniture designers rely upon grids and underlying templates in their development of form and spatial organization. Grids are useful in transferring the order of an underlying spatial organization. The modular display system shown in Figure 3.27 is an arrangement of extruded cubes organized along x, y, and z grid coordinates. The spatial layout of the office

Figure 3.27 An orthogonally arranged system for display.

Figure 3.28 Orthogonal spatial arrangement of an office environment.

desks and lighting fixtures in Figure 3.28 is based upon a 5-foot (1.5-m) orthogonal grid. Distinctions between grids can vary by measure and/or geometric order.

Linear

Lines are made from two or more points and generally are conceived as being straight (Figure 3.29), but they also curve, warp, and transform, as illustrated in *Bookworm,* designed by Ron Arad (Figure 3.30). Every line has an underlying spatial structure. The eye follows lines

Figure 3.29 Linear organization of pews, The Chapel of the Holy Cross, designed by Pekka Pitkänen.

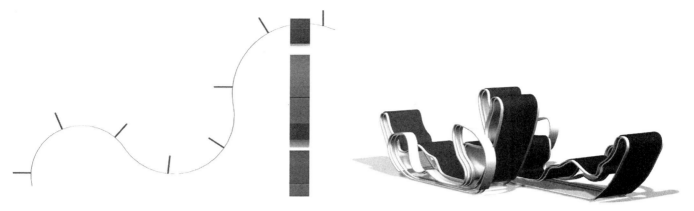

Figure 3.30 Sinusoidal lines—Bookworm, designed by Ron Arad (1994), manufactured by Kartell.

Figure 3.31 DU lounge seating, designed by Gülen Çevik and Jim Postell, 2004.

from beginning points to intersecting endpoints. Sinusoidal linear characteristics are often expressed through the edges, seams, and planes of furniture. *DU* (Figure 3.31) integrates upright and reclining postures and relies upon its sinusoidal edges and juxtaposing planar surfaces to visually express linear movement.

Radial

Sociofugal spaces are perceived as outward-oriented spaces. *Sociofugal*[1] is a term coined by Edward T. Hall to describe space that radiates outward from an implied or marked center. The *Tatlin II* settee is designed to orient users outward into space (Figure 3.32). Radial spaces are distinct from inwardly focused, centralized, *sociopetal* spaces.[2]

Figure 3.32 Tatlin II, designed by Semprini/Cananzi, 1989 (sociofugal seating).

TYPOLOGICAL ORDERS

Order results from the confluence of ideas present in the conception and development of design. Furniture is nearly always movable, but not all furnishings are designed to move easily. Furniture can be stationary, but not all furnishings are mechanically attached to the floor, wall, or ceiling. Furniture can be adjustable, but not all furnishings are specifically designed to transform from one form into a different form. Most furniture can be taken apart, but not all furnishings are designed and distributed as knock down or flat-pack. Generally, most furnishings are freestanding; however, not all pieces are specifically designed to be seen and experienced in 360 degrees. Freestanding pieces can take advantage of a sculptural and dynamic quality inherent in the nature of form.

The typological orders determined in this book are distinguished by whether or not furniture is:

- Flat-pack/knock-down
- Built-in (casework)
- Freestanding (case goods)
- Inflatable
- Transformable
- Movable

Assembled/Disassembled (Knock Down)

Ready-to-assemble (RTA) furniture is distributed and sold in an unassembled state and assembled by the consumer. RTA furniture is also known as flat-pack or knock-down furniture. The Artek company has produced a series of flat-pack furnishings designed by Alvar Aalto. Most of Artek's furniture is sold unassembled and shipped throughout the world (see Chapter 4).

The writing desk shown in Figure 3.33 was designed for easy disassembly and reassembly so that the relatively large writing desk could fit through a narrow doorway. The verti-

Figure 3.33 Knock-down writing desk, designed and fabricated by Jim Postell, 1989.

cal Baltic birch panels and horizontal shelves are mechanically fastened to the underside of the writing desk using pins and dowels. The horizontal shelves and the curvilinear shape of the top help stabilize the desk to balance the lateral forces generated by writing.

The Swedish furniture and accessory company IKEA sells unassembled, flat-pack furniture and controls expenses in getting products to market by having customers shop at large distribution outlet centers located throughout the world. The company's success is due in part to controlling the costs of distributing furniture and passing the savings on to its consumer.[3]

Built-in/Stationary

When built-in furniture is carefully integrated with its surrounding space, it can enhance the continuity of the architecture. Built-ins and casework require on-site installation and mechanical attachment to a floor, wall, or ceiling. In these situations, designers must consider ways in which relatively imperfect or irregular existing conditions will receive precisely fabricated elements. Reveals, shims, and scribed edges must be incorporated in the design of built-in furnishings. Plaster and wallboard partitions are rarely flat, floors and ceilings are seldom level, and what lies behind interior surfaces is often a mystery. In addition, the placement of built-in furniture is critical in regard to its impact upon the circulation of the surrounding space, as illustrated in the built-in study carousels of Exeter Library designed by the architect Louis Kahn (Figure 3.34).

Wall-mounted panels and cabinets attached to interior partitions are generally supported by **French cleats,** which are interlocking hardware devices—one applied to the panel, the

Figure 3.34 Built-in study carousels at Exeter Library, designed by architect Louis Kahn.

other secured to the wall. French cleats are conventional means of supporting heavy wall-mounted panels, cabinets, and display systems.

Freestanding

Most furnishings are freestanding, but a few are designed to be experienced in the round. Beds, couches, case goods, and rectangular tables are often placed against a wall or next to other furnishings. Coat racks and video shelving units are typically located in corners. However, lounge seating, dining, conference, and coffee tables are designed to be experienced from multiple directions.

Finn Julh's leather *Chieftain* chair (1949), Troels Grum-Schwensen's *Waterlily* seating (2003), and Poul Kjærholm's dining table *PK 54* (1963) are designed to be experienced in the round. Juhl's comfortable lounge is as attractive from the back as it is from the front or side. In his own modest home, the upholstered chair can be seen from all sides (Figure 3.35). Grum-Schwensen's *Waterlily* seating is a sectional module seating design that works well in a large lobby space or museum setting. Its modular nature and curvilinear form complement its versatility of use and flexibility in arrangement (Figure 3.36). The circular forms contribute to its sculptural presence, making it an ideal choice in large and open spaces. Kjærholm's *PK 54* is an expandable circular dining table that needs sufficient space for the extensions (Figure 3.37). The circular flint-rolled marble table with maple wood extensions complements the orthogonal steel frame of its base, resulting in a circular and freestanding form that relates well to orthogonal elements in a room.

Figure 3.35 Chieftain lounge chair, designed by Finn Juhl (1949), fabricated by Niels Roth Andersen. Photo taken at Juhl's residence, Copenhagen, Denmark, 2006.

Figure 3.36 Waterlily, designed by Troels Grum-Schwensen (2003), manufactured by Globe Furniture.

Figure 3.37 PK 54, designed by Poul Kjærholm (1963), manufactured by Fritz Hansen.

Inflatable

Waterbeds, inflatable air mattresses, therapy balls, and beanbag chairs are internally "filled" and externally "sheathed." The *Blow* chair (Figure 3.38), designed by Jonathan de Pas, Donato d'Urbino, Paolo Lomazzi, and Massimo Scolari (1967) for Zanotta, was one of the first commercially produced furniture products that relied upon a thin membrane of polyvinyl chloride (PVC), low-voltage weld-seams, and air. Inflated therapy balls have recently gained popularity due to their versatility and the body movement experienced through their use. Inflated furnishings are often designed for temporary uses and can be made compact for easy

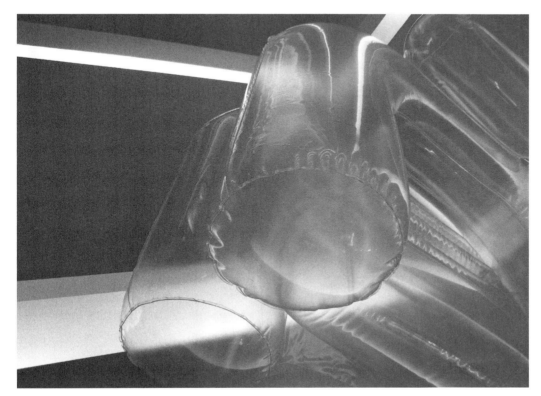

Figure 3.38 Blow chair, designed by Jonathan de Pas, Donato d'Urbino, Paolo Lomazzi, and Massimo Scolari (1967), manufactured by Zanotta.

storage or transport when required. Some inflated furnishings utilize heat-activated expanding gas or air-activated expanding foam, while others depend upon rapid inflating and deflating techniques, cellular substructures, and integrated components designed to improve the support and experience of the user.

Mechanical (Transformative Machines for Living)

Mechanical joinery can allow furniture to transform into different shapes, as shown in the American drop-leaf table (Figure 3.39). The classic **chair-table** was an armed chair resembling a throne with a pivotal back that could easily convert to a table. This idea inspired *Zabro,* designed by Alessandro Mendini in 1984, and manufactured by Zanotta (Figure 3.40). Folding chairs, **butterfly tables,** extending **draw tables,** and transformable cribs can be changed from one state to another. The classic aluminum folding chair, the wooden folding director's chair, and *Trefoldestolen* (Figure 3.41) are examples of remarkably simple fur-

Figure 3.39 American drop-leaf table, 1815–30.

Figure 3.40 Zabro chair-table, designed by Alessandro Mendini (1984) for Zanotta.

Figure 3.41 Trefoldestolen, designed by Mogens Koch (1932), fabricated by Rud. Rasmussen, Denmark.

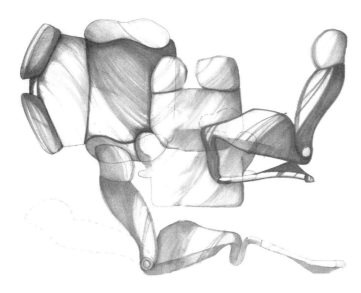

Figure 3.42 Marker studies of the Wink Lounge, designed by Toshiyuki Kita (1980), manufactured by Cassina.

nishings that physically transform for use, transport, and storage. The *Wink Lounge,* designed by Toshiyuki Kita in 1980 and produced by Cassina, utilizes an internal system to transform its profile, which enables one to recline close to the floor or sit upright in a conventional manner (Figure 3.42).

Movable

Movement can enhance function. Alvar Aalto's *Tea Trolley* serving cart (1936) was designed to roll about easily (Figure 3.43). The large wheels are painted wood and are banded with rubber to reduce the noise caused by movement. Frank Lloyd Wright's office chairs pro-

Figure 3.43 Wheeled Tea Trolley serving cart, designed by Alvar Aalto (1936), produced by Artek.

Figure 3.44a Office furniture designed by Frank Lloyd Wright for the S. C. Johnson Wax headquarters (1937); chairs with casters (originally manufactured by Steelcase).

Figure 3.44b The "great room" of the administration building, S. C. Johnson Wax factory (1936–39), designed by Frank Lloyd Wright.

duced for the S.C. Johnson Wax headquarters in Racine, Wisconsin (Figures 3.44a, 3.44b), utilize **casters** to promote functional movement. The chairs were specifically designed to freely roll about in space at a time when many chairs of the same typology did not.

SUMMARY

The first three chapters of this book have introduced aspects of function and social use, and have outlined characteristics of form, spatial organization, and typological orders related to furniture design.

Analyzing classifications of use and characteristics of form is a process of thinking about furniture in terms of synthetic and semantic components. This process is helpful to introduce important considerations that can influence the design and fabrication of furniture. What remains is the need to synthesize this introduction into a more holistic understanding of furniture.

The furniture studies that follow in Chapter 4 build upon the ideas presented thus far. The background, tectonics, and ideas in the selected pieces are presented in a more comprehensive and integrated manner and underscore the importance of time and place in design.

4 Furniture Case Studies

IN THIS CHAPTER, 21 furniture case studies are organized chronologically. Computer-rendered images, hand drawings, and photographs help present the context and background, tectonics, and aesthetics of the studies. The studies reveal ideas about sitting, working, storing, and partitioning space and present a spectrum of furniture types, production techniques, and social-use examples.

As you read through the studies, reflect upon the time and place from which each of the selected pieces were designed and fabricated.

OVERVIEW OF FURNITURE CASE STUDIES

700–400 B.C. Greek *Klismos* chair

1745–50 A.D. French Rococo commode, by Jean Baptiste/J. B. Hedouin, stamped JME.

1754 *Chippendale chair*, designed and fabricated by Thomas Chippendale

1855 *Model No. 14*, designed by Michael Thonet, manufactured by Gebrüder Thonet

1917–18 *Roadblauwe Stoel—Red and Blue Chair*, designed and fabricated by Gerrit T. Rietveld

1922 *Blocs Screen*, designed by Eileen Gray

1925 *Wassily club chair*, designed by Marcel Breuer, fabricated by Standard-Möbel/Lengyel/Knoll International

1928 *Siège à Dossier Basculant (B301)*, designed by Charlotte Perriand, Pierre Jeanneret, and Le Corbusier, manufactured by Gebrüder Thonet, H. Weber, and Cassina

1932–33 *Stools 60/65*, designed by Alvar Aalto, manufactured by Artek

1950 *Eames Storage Unit (ESU)*, designed by Charles and Ray Eames, produced by Herman Miller

1950 *Antony chair*, designed by Jean Prouvé, produced by Jean Prouvé

1951 *Wire Side chair*, designed by Harry Bertoia, produced by Knoll International

1968 *Action Office*, designed by Robert Propst, produced by Herman Miller

1987 *Ghost chair*, designed by Cini Boeri, produced by Fiam Italia

1992 *Cross Check armchair*, designed by Frank Gehry, produced by Knoll

1993 *Trinidad chair*, designed by Nanna Ditzel, produced by Fredericia Stolefabrik

1994 *Living Units*, designed and fabricated by Andrea Zittel

1994 *Aeron chair*, designed by Don Chadwick and Bill Stumpf, Herman Miller

2000 *Pathways*, produced by Steelcase

1999 *The Block*, designed and fabricated by Erik Skoven

2004 *Jimmy's Buffet*, designed and fabricated by Jim Postell, Janet Flory, Steve Wethington, and Matthew Cornell

Furniture:	*Klismos* **chair**
Design:	**Greek craftsmen**
Fabrication:	**Greek craftsmen**
Context:	**Social democracy, craftsmanship, and proportion**
Date:	**700–400 B.C.**

Figure 4.1 Gravestone of Hegeso—*klismos* chair, carved marble bas-relief, National Museum, Athens, Greece, 410 B.C.

NEITHER A THRONE NOR A STOOL, the *klismos* chair was unique in both form and social use and has been cited as the most characteristically Greek of all chairs.[1] The *klismos* chair is both graceful and functional, combining comfort, simplicity, and elegance in one typological form whose proportions evolved over several hundred years. It is assumed to have been a relatively light chair, with a curved back and outwardly curved legs. Gisela Richter referred to the *klismos* as "the chair with [a] back"[2] because seats with backs during this time were considered thrones. The *klismos* chair is a throne for everyday use. Based upon surviving representations on vases, paintings, and sculptural **relief** (Figure 4.1), the *klismos* chair is often associated with domestic life, depicting women who appear to be seated comfortably.

From carefully executed depictions on vase paintings and other sources, it is possible to obtain a fairly good idea about the design and fabrication of the *klismos* chair. The back and legs were generally plain, but their angle, proportion, and profile varied. The back ended in a curved horizontal board at about the height of the shoulders and was supported by two or three uprights. The **stiles** and rear legs were made, as a rule, in one piece. This helped to achieve the fine, continuous curve of its profile. The frame

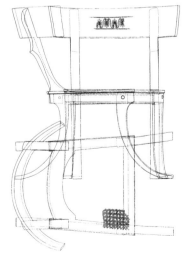

Figure 4.2 Drawing of a *klismos* chair designed by N. A. Abildgaard, c. 1800.

pieces of the seat were **mortised** into the legs. The **tenons** passed through the upright bars. Wood joints were held together with tenons, hide glue, and nails. The seat frame was never higher than the top of the legs. Generally, the front legs terminated in pointed projections extending slightly above the seat frame. Drapery, fabric, animal hides, and pillows were placed on the seats (Figure 4.2).

The dimensions of the computer-rendered images (Figures 4.3, 4.4) are estimated and based upon interpolated dimensions of the *klismos* chair: 36 inches high (85 cm), 30½ inches deep (77 cm), and 20 inches wide (51 cm).[3] Significantly, no two *klismos* chairs were exactly alike. Each chair was a unique handcrafted creation.

The *klismos* chair marks a correlation between furniture design and the political ideology of Greek democracy, expressing dignity and providing practical comfort to the individual user. The chair evolved over a period of 300 years into a remarkably well-proportioned design whose formal characteristics and elegant fabrication techniques have inspired many designers throughout history. It served as a precedent for Roman chairs and was resurrected as a source of inspiration for the *French Directoire* and *English Regency* styles during the 1800s. The painter and architect Nicolai Abildgaard fabricated a version of the *klismos* chair in 1800 as **Neoclassicism** emerged as the dominant style throughout Europe. By that time, the United States was politically secure and found individual and expressive freedom in the **Federal Style,** whose source of inspiration came from Greece. For a young emerging democracy, the Greek ideal was the preferred standard on which to cultivate a new society.

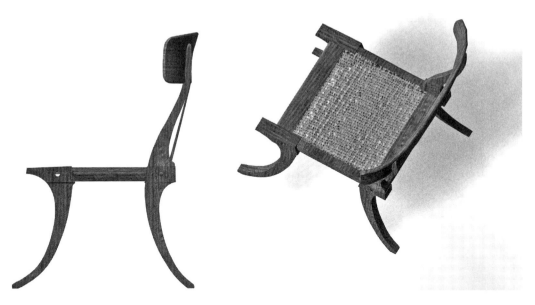

Figure 4.3 Computer rendering of a *klismos* chair—profile view.

Figure 4.4 Computer rendering of a *klismos* chair—aerial view.

Furniture:	French commode
Design:	Jean Baptiste/J. B. Hedouin
Company:	Craftsmen working in a variety of French guilds during the reign of Louis XV. Stamped JME
Context:	French Rococo (ornate workmanship, fabricated by special trades and guilds)
Date:	ca. 1745–50

COMMODES FIRST APPEARED at the beginning of the 1700s at the court of Louis XIV. The furniture type and form were quickly adopted by other countries and adapted to particular needs. The word **commode** comes from the French word *commodité* and the Latin word *commodus*—both of which mean "convenience."[4] The two-drawer commode illustrated in this study was typical, but later versions during the Regency period had three drawers.

The front of the commode was treated as a single element, and the visual distinction between the drawers and the frame was generally ignored. The compound curve that is apparent in cross section is known as **bombé,** while the curves apparent in plan view are described as *serpentine.* The commode has a cambered form with a curved **apron** and high-curved supports. Decorative cast metal mounts made of bronze protect the feet of the legs. The commode has a continuous ¾-inch (2-cm)-thick, highly variegated marble slab as the top, which was typical of the commodes produced between 1745 and 1750. The commode stands 38½ inches (96.5 cm) high (Figure 4.6).

During the **French Rococo,** there existed a strictly controlled **guild** system for fabricating a wide variety of furniture, as shown in Figure 4.5. **Ébénistes** were makers of veneered

Figure 4.5 An 18th-century Louis XV oak-paneled room.

Figure 4.6 French commode by Jean Baptiste/ J.B. Hedouin (1750), stamped JME (*jurande des menuisiers—ébénistes*)—front view.

furniture, **menuisiers** were makers of solid-wood furniture, **fondeurs** were makers of metal mounts, **ciseleurs** were makers of bronze chasing, *vernisseurs* were lacquerers, *marqueteurs* were makers of **marquetry,** and **doreurs** were gilders. The commodes produced during the French Rococo period engaged a majority of these trade guilds, and the quality of the workmanship of this furniture type was typically remarkable (Figures 4.7, 4.8).

Figure 4.7 French commode by Jean Baptiste/ J. B. Hedouin (1750), side corner. Note the compound curve and cambered form.

Figure 4.8 French commode by Jean Baptiste/ J. B. Hedouin (1750), corner detail.

Furniture:	*Chippendale* chair
Designer:	**Thomas Chippendale**
Company:	**Chippendale**
Context:	**Georgian period (an innovative design that allowed for a number of interchangeable carved parts)**
Date:	**1754–80**

BORN IN YORKSHIRE, ENGLAND, in 1718, Thomas Chippendale was the son of a joiner (a person trained in woodworking and carpentry). The **Chippendale** chair was a generic design that could be customized in a number of ways to suit different clients. The 18th-century armchair could have had any number of carved back *splats* and various leg profiles incorporated into the design. It was renowned for its exquisitely carved decoration, **cabriole legs,** and elaborate chair backs. The *Chippendale* chair is a transitional piece designed at a time when furniture was shifting from being designed and fabricated exclusively for the aristocracy to being marketed and produced for the upper middle class. Chippendale's booklet *The Gentleman and Cabinet-Maker's Director* (1754) illustrated various household furniture designs that could be ordered and reproduced around the world. His notes and illustrations in the *Director* were explicit, citing limitations in the height of the seat backs, allowable variations in design for the front legs of the chairs, and upholstery guidelines for the seat pans. His overall work in furniture, and particularly his *Chippendale* chair, became synonymous with the highest quality of late-18th-century furniture design (Figure 4.9).

All intersecting wood members were held together using **mortise-and-tenon** joinery. The chair's splats (decorative pattern on the back of the chair) and the **marlborough legs** are signature components of the chair's design. Thomas Chippendale was able to inventory a variety of splats and legs, which enabled quick delivery for the made-to-order chairs. French Rococo designs, as well as the interiors and furnishings of the Adam brothers, who had returned from Italy by 1760, added inspiration to the carved pieces (Figure 4.10).

Figure 4.9 Chippendale chair (1754)—drawing modified from Thomas Chippendale's Director.

During the mid-1700s, the trade of upholsterer equaled that of cabinet maker in importance. There were as many upholsterers as there were cabinet makers, and many firms advertised doing both. The *Chippendale* chair depended on the careful integration of both trades.

Made from hardwood mahogany discovered in Central and South America, the chair shown in Figures 4.11 and 4.12 is 39 inches (100 cm) high and 28 inches (71 cm) wide.

Chippendale had a significant reputation and influence on furniture design around the world. His reputation was chiefly founded on his book (*Director*), despite the fact that the designs in the book were largely derivative. Thomas Chippendale was a good craftsperson, but also one of the greatest entrepreneurs and businessmen in furniture up to the mid-18th century. His work was sold around the world, and quickly became a status symbol, satisfying an acquisitive society.

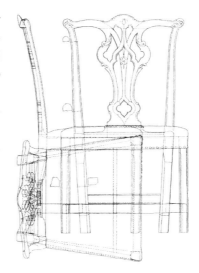

Figure 4.10 Study of a Chippendale-type chair.

Figure 4.11 Computer rendering, Chippendale chair—front oblique view.

Figure 4.12 Computer rendering, Chippendale chair—rear oblique view.

Furniture:	Side chair, *Model No. 14*
Designer:	Michael Thonet
Manufacturer:	Gebrüder Thonet (1853–1921)
Context:	Steam-bent beech wood fabrication, mass production, and flat-pack distribution
Date:	1855

MICHAEL THONET (1796–1871) created the Austrian furniture company Gebrüder Thonet in Vienna in 1853 with his five sons. The bentwood process of 1840, developed by Thonet, revolutionized the mass production of furniture. Almost immediately, the company experienced enormous success through the mass production of steam-bent and flat-pack beech wood chairs. Le Corbusier selected the side chair *Model No. 14* for inclusion in his influential l'Esprit Nouveau exhibit in 1925, which was the best-selling of all bentwood Thonet chairs. Between 1855 and 1930, Gebrüder Thonet sold an unprecedented 50 million units of Model No. 14, more than any other chair in the world up to that time[5] (Figures 4.13–4.15).

Originally designed for laminated wood chairs, the bentwood technique was utilized because sea travel and exposure to the elements during transportation caused delamination to occur. Steam bending required less work than laminating, and the chairs were more durable because of the limitations of the glues available at the time. Using steam-bending techniques, the leg supports and seat back were made from solid beech wood and the seat frame was made from laminated wood. The seat pan was made from solid wood or woven cane. *Model No. 14* was an ideal café chair for the coffeehouses and cafés emerging throughout Europe. It was called the *Vienna* chair after the Viennese coffeehouses where it first came into use. Coffeehouses were essential to Viennese social, intellectual, and artistic life, and the chair fit perfectly in this social and cultural context.

Figure 4.13 Side chair, rear oblique view.

Figure 4.14 Side chair, front view.

Figure 4.15 Side chair, Model No. 14 with the additional lower brace, front oblique view.

The beech wood was steamed until pliable and then bent into shape using clamps and forms. Craftsmen worked carefully together to manipulate the wood into the desired shape. The chair was assembled from six pieces of wood and held together with screws and nuts, eliminating complex joints. *Model No. 14* is 35½ inches (90 cm) high, 16¾ inches (43 cm) wide, and 20¾ inches (52 cm) deep.[6] It is elegant in its linear form and reductive in its shape. Lightweight and durable, its modest cost and flat-pack distribution made it an ideal choice for hospitality or residential use throughout the world (Figure 4.16). A crate measuring 1 cubic meter could hold 36 dismantled chairs.

It was one of the first pieces of furniture designed for all society rather than only for the wealthy. Conceived for mass production and flat-pack distribution, *Model No. 14* was far ahead of its time in form and in the direct use of materials. It embodied and foreshadowed the ideals and spirit of **modernism,** which emerged nearly 70 years later. Furthermore, *Model No. 14* is often cited as the flagship for the Thonet series of chairs. Due to the industrial production employed, Michael Thonet has been considered the world's first industrial designer.

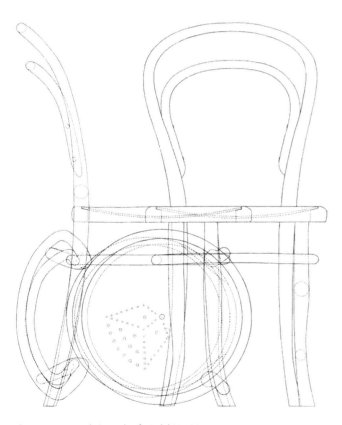

Figure 4.16 Analytic study of Model No. 14.

Furniture:	*Roodblauwe Stoel* (Red-and-Blue Chair)
Designer:	Gerrit T. Rietveld
Company:	G.A. van de Groenekan, De Bilt (reissued by Cassina, Italy, in 1971)
Context:	De Stijl movement (Utrecht, the Netherlands), furniture as a social art
Date:	1917–18

Gerrit T. Rietveld (1888–1965), along with Theo Van Doesburg (1883–1931) and Piet Mondrian (1872–1944), created the **de Stijl** movement and were dedicated to the creation of a universal aesthetic through the use of simple geometric forms and a color palette consisting of primary colors (red, yellow, and blue) as well as achromatic hues of black, white, and gray. Space was defined by line, plane, and color and was composed in an innovative fashion.

The *Red and Blue Chair* was based on standardized mass production. Rietveld considered its fabrication a social act, with the goal of mechanizing labor in order for the laborer to escape the boredom of hard, repetitive work (Figure 4.17). Six years later, Gerrit Rietveld designed the *Schroeder house* (in Utrecht, the Netherlands), in which the *Red and Blue Chair* appropriately fits.

The process by which Rietveld fabricated this piece is an allegorical representation of the ideals behind its creation. He took a board of wood and sawed the middle part in two for the seat and backrest. The assembly of the chair is based on a 4-inch (10-cm) module, which

Figure 4.17 Red and Blue Chair designed and fabricated by Gerrit T. Rietveld, 1917–18.

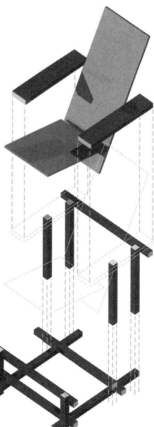

Figure 4.18 Exploded axonometric of the Red and Blue Chair.

is the thickness of three rails. The rails are doweled together. The seat and the back are mechanically attached to the frame with screws. Though the simple geometries and elements are clear, the mechanical systems are effectively hidden. The red 70-degree angled seat back and the blue 10-degree angled seat pan offer bodily support, and the black orthogonally positioned frame directs the loads to the ground through indirect transposition of forces. The frame is made of black-painted beech wood. The seat (blue) and back (red) are lacquered plywood. The chair is an abstraction of two systems—one composed of liberated, painted planes that support the body and the other a network of painted rails to support the painted planes. The *Red and Blue Chair* is approximately 33.7 inches (86.5 cm) high, 25¾ inches (66 cm) deep, and 34 inches (83 cm) wide (Figure 4.18).

The *Red and Blue Chair* is an expressive composition of form, space, and color. The black orthogonal components, combined with the intersecting, brightly colored planes, accurately represented the spirit of the age in the Netherlands (1918). The angle between the seat pan and seat back provides bodily comfort for rest, and even more significantly, the seat and back allow for body movement during use due to the flat painted planes. Within the social and formal context of the de Stijl movement, the design is effective and elegantly resolved (Figures 4.19, 4.20).

 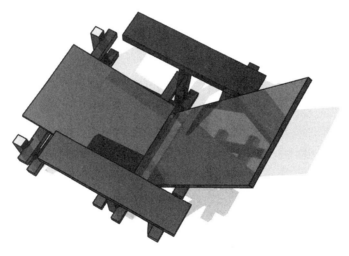

Figure 4.19 Detail—seat back, seat pan, and support members.

Figure 4.20 Computer rendering, Red and Blue Chair—aerial view.

Furniture:	*Blocs Screen*
Designer:	Eileen Gray
Company:	Jean Désert, Paris (reissued by Ecart International, Paris, from 1978 to the present by Alivar)
Context:	Partitioning space
Date:	1922

FABRICATED FIRST in white and then in high-gloss black polyester **lacquered** panels, Eileen Gray's *Blocs Screen* expresses a transitional moment in her design career. The screen marked a shift from her early decorative and hand-lacquered works to her later work that incorporated industrial materials and industrial processes of fabrication. The lacquered *Blocs Screen* was first designed as part of a larger interior commission for Madame Lévy's apartment in the rue de Lota in Paris. The design evolved into several variations, each of which employed small lacquer-painted blocks to create a freestanding articulated screen.

The *Blocs Screen* could be configured in a number of ways. The version presented in this study is four blocks wide and seven blocks high (other versions were five blocks wide and eight blocks high). The lacquered blocks in one screen could vary in size, proportion, and color from those in another screen. The lacquered modules illustrated in this study each have a square relief and are based upon the Golden Section, which was used throughout the career of the architect Le Corbusier, with whom Eileen Gray apprenticed. The individual blocks are 10 inches (25.4 cm) high, 16.182 inches (41.1 cm) wide, and ¾ inch (2 cm) deep. The frame is held together with **brass** pins that support and mechanically enable the visual transparency of the screen. Overall screen dimensions are 74½ inches (189 cm) high and 53½ inches (136 cm) wide (Figure 4.21).

The beauty and appeal of the *Blocs Screen* lay in its conception and formal composition. The flexible array of individual pivoting panels creates a simple, freestanding, and functioning screen that partitions space and extends the architectural quality of the surrounding walls. The screen was conceived as an interior accessory, as were many of Eileen Gray's chairs, tables, carpets, and lighting designs, which furthered the notion of an integrated interior space composed of discrete, carefully arranged elements. The screen is visually attractive; however, it is relatively narrow in width and awkward to move about in space. It is a visual element, not one to touch. Nonetheless, the screen is playful as a receptor of light and is effective in partitioning space.

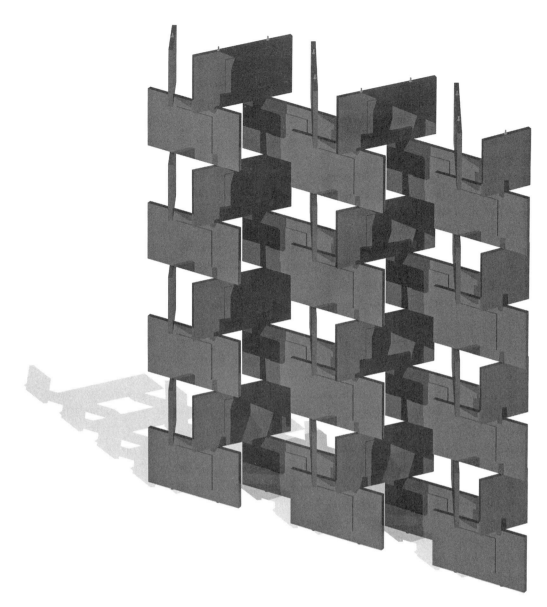

Figure 4.21 Blocs Screen, designed by Eileen Gray, 1922.

Furniture:	*Wassily* club chair, *Model No. B3*
Designer:	**Marcel Breuer**
Companies:	**Standard-Möbel Lengyel and Company, Berlin, and Gebrüder Thonet, Frankenberg, Germany (reissued by Knoll International, Inc., New York from 1968 to the present)**
Context:	**Dessau Bauhaus (modernism—use of industrial materials and fabrication techniques)**
Date:	**1925**

THE *WASSILY* CLUB CHAIR is an icon of the Modern Movement for its use of industrial materials and the clear expression of its fabrication (Figures 4.22, 4.23). Designed by Marcel Breuer in 1925, it is still in production. It was called the *Wassily* club chair because it was originally designed for the living room of Breuer's friend Wassily Kandinsky, a renowned abstract painter and faculty member of the **Bauhaus.** Expressing the ideas behind the *Wassily* chair, Breuer is quoted to have said:

> I already had the concept of spanning the seat with fabric in tension as a substitute for thick upholstery. I also wanted a frame that would be resilient and elastic. The combination of elasticity and of members in tension would give comfort without bulkiness. I also wanted to achieve transparency of forms to attain both visual and physical lightness. Mass production and standardization had already made me interested in polished metal, in shiny and impeccable lines in space as new components for our interiors. I considered such polished and curved lines not only symbolic of our modern technology, but actually technology itself.[7]

This leap toward modern technology was intended for manufacture by Standard-Möbel, but the materials and process proved to be too costly. Today, Knoll International, a division devoted to manufacturing classic 20th-century furniture, produces the chair.

The chair is 28¾ inches (73 cm) tall, 27½ inches (70 cm) deep, and 30¾ inches (78 cm) wide. One might assume that the Wassily chair is heavy; however, it is light. The idea of using tubular metal was inspired by Breuer's Adler bicycle, which he rode daily. The heavy cushioning of a comfortable chair has been replaced with tightly fitted, thick fabric (later be-

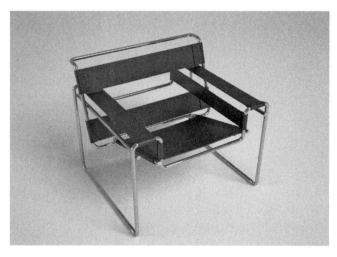

Figure 4.22 Wassily chair, designed by Marcel Breuer, 1925.

Figure 4.23 Exploded axonometric of the Wassily chair.

coming leather) held in tension around metal tubes. Breuer went to the Mannesmann steel works for the manufactured bent steel. The chair is fabricated from standardized parts and can be easily disassembled (Figure 4.24).

The *Wassily* chair is inventive in its use of new technology and aesthetically pleasing. Breuer himself wrote, "It is my most extreme work both in its outward appearance and in the use of materials; it is the least artistic, the most logical, the least cozy and the most mechanical."[8] The *Wassily* chair is a simple and graceful design. Due to the relatively flat leather planes and the generous space in which to sit, it allows users to move about freely (Figure 4.25).

The *Wassily* chair inspired many chair designers throughout the 20th century. "I thought that this out of all my work would earn me the most criticism," Breuer said, "but the opposite of what I expected came true."[9] It has been hailed by critics as one of the greatest chairs of the 20th century, but there are those who disagree. For some critics, it is problematic in its fixed posture, the backward angle of the seat back to the seat pan, and its tactile quality, all of which limit its utility. This raises the question, what qualities constitute a great chair in the 20th century?

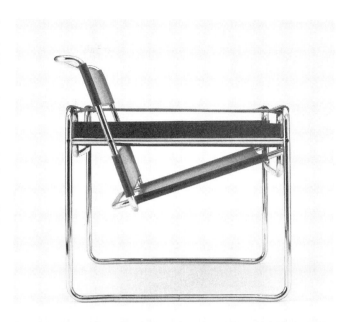

Figure 4.24 Side profile of the Wassily chair.

Figure 4.25 Detail—tubular chrome-plated steel and leather.

Furniture:	*Siège à Dossier Basculant (B301)*
Designers:	**Charlotte Perriand, Pierre Jeanneret, and Le Corbusier**
Companies:	**Gebrüder Thonet 1928, H. Weber 1959, Cassina from 1965**
Context:	**Ville d'Avray and Salon d'Automne Exhibition—1929 (Industrial materials—a machine for sitting)**
Date:	**1928**

LE CORBUSIER DESIGNED functional furniture that utilized new materials and industrial modes of production. Charlotte Perriand joined Le Corbusier's atelier in 1927 and contributed to the design, as did Pierre Jeanneret. Le Corbusier established the parameters for the furniture, but it was left up to Perriand and Jeanneret to resolve and detail the design. Conceived as a *machine for sitting,* the *Basculant* chair can accommodate numerous postures. It is Perriand who has been credited with the seat back's mobility and the use of tubular steel. The Basculant chair was created for "living room conversation" for a French villa in Ville d'Avray and, ultimately, for mass production.

The *Basculant* chair, inspired by the British army officer's Pel chair designed by F. M. Allen Roorkhee, was initially refused production by Peugeot's bicycle-making section. Le Corbusier then made an arrangement with Thonet to produce the chair in 1929. Despite the availability of the new technology of tubular metal, the chair was produced in wood and rush materials for a Brussels exhibit in 1935 (Figures 4.26, 4.27).

Figure 4.26 Model Basculant B301, designed by Charlotte Perriand, Le Corbusier, and Pierre Jeanneret, 1928.

Figure 4.27 Model Basculant B301, designed by Charlotte Perriand, Le Corbusier, and Pierre Jeanneret, 1928.

Figure 4.28 Detail—seat back, arm support, and chromed metal tubing.

The chair is 25¼ inches (64 cm) tall, 23½ inches (59.7 cm) wide, and 25½ inches (64.8 cm) deep. It weighs 29 lb. Today, it is available in several different upholstery and metal finishes. The *slingback* chair, as it is sometimes referred to, has a steel frame finished in either **chrome** or matte black. In 1929, it was fabricated of polished nickel-plated steel tubing to reduce the cost. Today, Cassina offers the chair in pony hide with black leather arms, Russian red saddle leather with matching arms, or black saddle leather (Figure 4.28).

The structure consists of an assemblage of metal sections, none of which forms a closed framework except for the chair's back. Both the front and rear elevations consist of an H design composed of two vertical supports and one horizontal support. The structure and stability of the chair rely entirely upon the welded connections of the joints, which differ from the bolted connections of other Bauhaus pieces. The seat pan consists of a stretched material over thin tubing with supporting springs underneath. The chair's back is similar to the seat pan, with the material held in tension by springs. The arms of the chair provide no structural support, and the leather straps freely rotate around the projecting ends of metal tubes.

The desire to create an affordable chair and to employ industrial materials and new technologies drove the design, yet the chair remains expensive to produce because of its details. Nonetheless, the chair is important as a model introducing the impact that female designers of the Bauhaus had in creating aesthetically pleasing, comfortable, and practical furniture designs.

Furniture:	Stools *60/65*
Designer:	Alvar Aalto (1898–1976)
Company:	Prototype by Korhonen, Eggers; manufactured by Artek
Context:	Designed for the Viipuri Town Library, Finland (and later mass produced by Artek).
Date:	1932–33

IN THE 1920S, Alvar Aalto began experimenting with bent and laminated wood. He was, in his own words, immersed in his "struggle against metal in furniture design." When he moved to Turku, Finland, in 1927 and teamed up with the factory owner Otto Korhonen, they perfected one of Aalto's most important discoveries in furniture design, the bent knee technique that is used in making the legs of *Stool 60* (Figures 4.29–4.31). The bent knee stacking stool with three legs was first introduced to the public at the 1933 London Exhibition and originally designed by Aalto for the Viipuri town library.

It has been said that as Aalto and Korhonen were throwing the working prototype around the factory floor in order to test its durability, Aalto exclaimed, "This stool is going to be made in the thousands!" Within 50 years, more than a million stacking stools were in existence. The stool became the most widely sold piece of Alvar Aalto's furniture and represents a turning point in Aalto's design work.

The legs of the stool are made of bent birch wood utilizing special cutting and joining technologies, while the seat is available in either black or red linoleum, white, yellow, red, or blue laminate with a thin birch band, or foam covered and upholstered to specification.

Figure 4.29 Stool 60 designed by Alvar Aalto, produced by Artek, 1933.

Figure 4.30 Formwork for the curved laminated birch leg—Stool 60.

Figure 4.31 Components of Stool 60 on display at the Alvar Aalto Museum, Jyväskylä, Finland.

Figure 4.32 Stool 60 designed by Alvar Aalto, produced by Artek, 1933.

Birch wood was readily available from local suppliers, but it was not good for bending and fractured easily. Aalto's idea was to take a solid piece of birch wood and saw it open on one end in the direction of the grain. Next, thin pieces of wood were glued into the grooves. This allowed the wood to be bent to the desired radius and angle, which in the case of *Stool 60* was slightly less than 90 degrees. As the wood dried, it straightened to a 90-degree angle and could be screwed directly into metal inserts placed in the bottom of the seat pan. The use of heat to bend the wood demanded fast-setting glue, and it was not until the 1960s that the legs could be bent mechanically. The stool is 17⅛ inches (43.5 cm) high and 13¾ inches (34.9 cm) in diameter. Various heights and finishes are available. The stool can be purchased as a three- or four-legged stool. *Stool 65* is a modified four-legged version with back (Figure 4.32).

Korhonen's factory fabricated most of Aalto's furniture until the 1940s. After World War II, Eggers, in Wisconsin, produced Aalto's furniture in the United States, with sales out of New York.

Today, the Finnish company Artek produces *Stool 60*. It is shipped flat-packed. *Stool 60* is both a designed and crafted object in which the mind and hand come together to create a simple, elegant, modern, and traditional stool—all at the same time (Figures 4.33–4.35).

Figure 4.33 Stool 65 with back—front view.

Figure 4.34 Stool 65 with back—side view.

Figure 4.35 Stool 65 with back—rear view.

Furniture:	*Eames Storage Unit (ESU)*
Designers:	**Charles and Ray Eames**
Company:	**Herman Miller**
Context:	**Design for Living Exhibit (kit of parts, industrial production—flat-pack distribution)**
Date:	**1950**

THE *EAMES STORAGE UNIT* (ESU) was a popular but short-lived storage system developed by Charles and Ray Eames in 1950. In 1940, Charles Eames and Eero Saarinen worked on a system of cabinets. The units could be used as benches, as shelves, or for storage. Four years later, Charles and Ray Eames developed the *Case Goods series,* which were displayed at the Museum of Modern Art (MOMA) in New York City in 1946. Inspired by the metal knockdown shelving units that people bought for use in their garages and basements, Charles and Ray Eames developed a new system for an exhibit entitled *Design for Living.*

Figure 4.36 ESU table, desk, and storage unit (400 Series) designed by Charles and Ray Eames (1950) for Herman Miller.

Figure 4.37 Room with various ESUs.

The idea of an inexpensive, lightweight, functional system was very important in the design. In 1950, Herman Miller marketed the *ESU.* Originally flat-packed, and requiring only a screwdriver and wrench to put together, the *ESU* did not sell well, so Herman Miller began making preassembled units. In this approach, dents and scratches proved to be problematic during distribution. As a result, the applied supports were set flush with the wood shelves. In 1955, Herman Miller stopped production of the *ESU* due to slow demand. Recently, with the renewed interest in the work of Charles and Ray Eames, Herman Miller has brought the *ESU* back into production (Figures 4.36, 4.37).

The *ESU* is a kit of standardized parts. The uprights, cross-bracing, and perforated metal backs are all zinc-coated steel. The legs have a nylon glide at their base. The cabinet doors are dimpled and laminated plywood. The shelves and drawer fronts are plywood. All of the plywood comes with a birch or walnut veneer on the exposed faces, while their side and bottom edges incorporate lacquered Masonite panels. The *ESU* is available in four sizes. The smallest is 24½ inches (62.2 cm) wide, 20½ inches (52.1 cm) high, and 16 inches (40.6 cm) deep. The second unit is 47½ inches (120.7 cm) wide, 20½ inches (52.1 cm) high, and 16 inches (40.6 cm) deep. All variations allow an arrangement of panels, cross-bracing, and shelves (Figure 4.38).

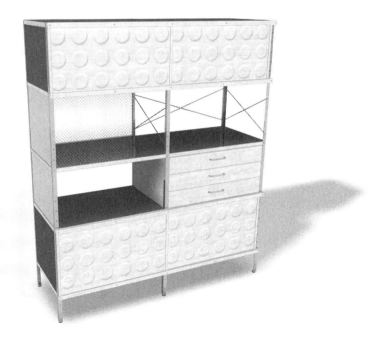

Figure 4.38 ESU (computer model).

The design expresses honesty in form and function. Fabrication and material selection are straightforward. The *ESU* foreshadowed the design of Charles and Ray Eames' home in Southern California, known as the Eames House. The *ESU* is significant in its economy, modularity, and ready-to-assemble fabrication. It has inspired many designers and architects since its conception in 1950 (Figure 4.39).

Figure 4.39 ESU—open.

Furniture:	*Antony* chair
Designer:	Jean Prouvé
Company:	Les Ateliers Jean Prouvé
Context:	Modernism (industrial materials with craft in fabrication)
Date:	1950

Figure 4.40 1:6 scale models produced by Vitra of the Antony and the Standard chair, both designed by Jean Prouvé.

JEAN PROUVÉ WORKED with industrial materials throughout his career as a furniture designer in the small town of Nancy, France. For him, the nature of laminated Baltic birch, painted steel, aluminum, and rubber was in line with the mechanization and industrialization of the early twentieth century. Prouvé's work captured the spirit of the times through his use of industrial materials and the hand-crafted approach in fabricating his working prototypes (Figures 4.40–4.42).

The *Antony* chair is characterized by its hand-welded and black-painted steel finish, expressive use of hardware, and mechanical connections juxtaposing the gracefully laminated birch compound seat. The bent and painted tubular metal and flat steel supports, along with the expression of the chair's hardware and overall form, have inspired many furniture designers. The

Figure 4.41 Computer model, Antony chair—side view.

Figure 4.42 Computer model, Antony chair—front oblique view.

primary feature of the *Antony* chair is the ⅜-inch-(1-cm)-thick molded plywood body support that serves as the seat pan and seat back. The molded plywood body support is a compound curve. In 1950 this was a remarkable accomplishment due to the complexity of the form and the tendency for veneers to split when simultaneously stressed in two or more directions (Figure 4.43).

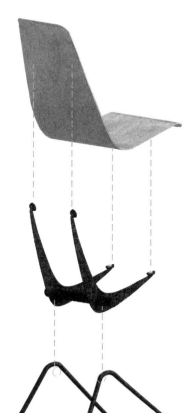

Figure 4.43 Exploded axonometric of the Antony chair.

Furniture:	*Wire Side* chair
Designer:	Harry Bertoia
Company:	Knoll International, New York
Context:	Synthesis of sculpture and function (mass production)
Date:	1951

HARRY BERTOIA ACHIEVED a synthesis of sculpture and function with his series of wire-framed chairs. These chairs were, in his words, "studies in space, form, and metal."[10] In terms of functionality, he thought that if a chair were used for an extended period of time, it should accommodate the movements of the human body in order to remain comfortable. That is what led him to use thin metal rods, thinking that they would adjust and respond to the body's movement (Figures 4.44, 4.45).

Figure 4.44 Wire Side chairs arranged around a table.

Figure 4.45 Detail—welded and chrome-plated steel rods.

Figure 4.46 Computer model of the Wire Side chair, designed by Harry Bertoia for Knoll Associates, 1950–52.

The *Wire Side* chair is a grid of steel wires, approximately ³⁄₁₆ inch (5 mm) in diameter, bent and welded to form a graceful, compound curved, and unified seat and back support. The seat and back form is composed atop a base of two steel rods, approximately ½ inch (1.25 cm) in diameter each, bent and welded. The entire chair is 29½ inches (74 cm) high, 21¼ inches (53.9 cm) wide, and 23¼ inches (58.7 cm) in depth.

The production process, although now quite common, was revolutionary at the time of the chair's initial production. A wooden mold was first created, in which all of the wires were bent in place by hand. It was easier to bend the rods by hand rather than by machine. Once all the wires were properly arranged, an electric current was applied to the steel, which welded every connection simultaneously. The final assembly was either given a chrome finish or coated with rilsan, an applied vinyl finish. Rilsan was applied by using a fluid-bed process in which the steel chair was heated and then passed through a chamber containing suspended vinyl particles. The heated steel caused the vinyl to melt and adhere to the steel in an even coating, which resulted in a durable finish. A seat cushion made of a padded fabric, vinyl or leather could be fastened to the seat (Figure 4.46).

The *Wire Side* chair is exceptionally comfortable. The steel rods bend just enough to mold to a range of human body shapes and a range of positions, yet remain stiff enough to provide appropriate support. The side chair works well in group settings, within courtyard and public gathering areas, alone or at a desk. Flaws in its stability are apparent in that it tends to tip forward when one stands up and can lean forward while one remains sitting.

Furniture:	*Action Office*
Designer:	**Robert Propst**
Company:	**Herman Miller, Zeeland, Michigan**
Context:	**Open-plan (systems furniture for an emerging office landscape)**
Date:	**1968**

AFTER 10 YEARS OF RESEARCH and development, Herman Miller introduced *Action Office* in 1968, the first panel-based, open-plan office system in the world.[11] The designer, Robert Propst, developed a system of panels and components that could be configured and reconfigured to respond to needs that would develop over time. Panels were available in a variety of heights, widths, and surface treatments. Components including work surfaces and storage units attach in 1-inch (2.5-cm) height increments, giving flexibility to the assembly and allowing users to work comfortably. As with most office systems, the ability of individuals to control their physical and ambient work environments was paramount.

Action Office marked a departure from the previous era's assumptions of what office furniture should be. The Action Office system transformed the workplace, as well as Herman Miller and the entire furniture industry, into a systems-approach business led by design (Figures 4.47, 4.48).

Action Office Series 2 reestablished the success of the original system by expressing the basic Action Office concept with new details and extended capabilities. The revised panels carried increased energy and cable loads to meet heavy technological demands. Work surfaces and storage components responded to changing aesthetic tastes. A number of new components offered options to suit each individual's work process. *Action Office Series 2* remained true to the fundamental principles of the original system: space-saving benefits, simple ordering and inventory, design options, and interchangeable components (Figure 4.49).

Figure 4.47 Action Office, C & S Bank, showing vertical storage on three-way panels amid offices, designed by Robert Propst for Herman Miller, 1968.

Figure 4.48 Action Office, C & S Bank, first big AO installation, on the seventh floor, uses hexagonal elements in a round building.

Figure 4.49 Action Office—a departmental cluster taken at the Batts Building shows panels at various heights, with mounted storage units and integrated lighting.

Action Office is easy and quick to install and reconfigure. It is a systems-based product, a kit of parts allowing the user to configure and compose various components as desired. It is a remarkable concept that transformed both an industry and the office workplace (Figure 4.50).

Figure 4.50 Action Office Series 2 with curved work surface and panels.

Furniture:	*Ghost* chair
Designer:	**Cini Boeri**
Company:	**Fiam Italia Spa**
Context:	**First all-glass, one-piece chair**
Date:	**1987**

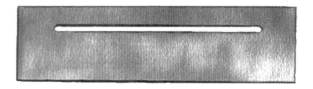

THE STATED PHILOSOPHY OF THE ITALIAN GLASS furniture company Fiam is to produce works that "free glass from its historical role of ornamental accessory and make glass a protagonist in furnishing, resulting in an unobtrusive and important presence in people's lives." Located in the heart of Brianza in northern Italy, Fiam is renowned for producing glass furniture. Fiam hires top designers such as Cini Boeri, Philippe Stark, and Danny Lane to realize their ideals. The *Ghost* chair is an important piece for Fiam and for furniture design in general. It is considered to be the first successful fabrication of an all-glass chair without adhesives or mechanical connections. It is constructed from a single sheet of crystal and is reported to be stackable (two high) (Figures 4.51, 4.52).

The ability to fabricate the *Ghost* chair resulted from a revolutionary type of glass called *float glass,* which was developed in the 1960s by Pilkington, an English furnishing producer. The term refers to the flat, perfectly smooth sheets of glass, which are produced by causing magma to oscillate on a bed of molten tin. But Fiam takes this process further in order to produce furniture designs in glass. The fabrication process begins by taking a piece of float glass and cutting out a single oval shape using the high-precision Paser system (high-pressure water spray mixed with an abrasive powder), with the remaining portion forming the seat, back, and armrests. Inside a curving chamber, the glass is heated

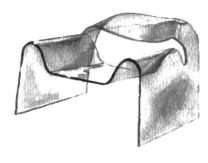

Figure 4.51 Plan and elevation watercolor study, Ghost chair, designed by Cini Boeri for Fiam.

Figure 4.52 CNC device cutting glass for the Ghost chair at Fiam.

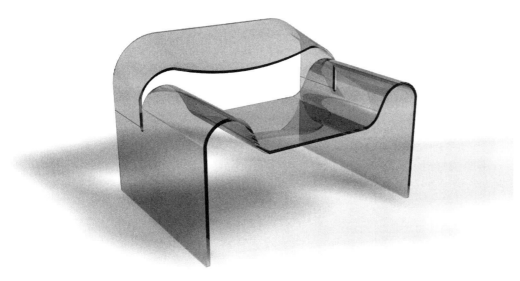

Figure 4.53 Computer model of the Ghost chair.

and reaches the maximum level of thermal stress. At approximately 700 degrees Celsius, the glass can be molded like wet clay—stretched over a chair mold by the force of gravity.[12] Patented technologies applied during the cooling stage and the absence of residual stress allow the glass to become exceptionally strong. The chair weighs 79 lb and can carry a load of 300 lb. The chair is 26¾ inches (67.8 cm) high, 37½ inches (95.3 cm) wide, and 29½ inches (74 cm) deep. It consists of a single sheet of ½-inch (1.25 cm) crystal glass that is folded and cut during the process on a computer numerical control device (CNC machine) and moved by an applied force of air (Figure 4.53).

The *Ghost* chair is intriguing because the designer uses and expresses the full potential of glass as a weight-bearing material and as an aesthetic medium. Although the use of glass in design often conjures up rigid, box-like interpretations, this chair has a relaxed air in the compound curves that form the arms and back rest. Although it is proportioned to be comfortable as a device for sitting, one can't quite imagine the user feeling fully relaxed in a glass chair for both thermal and psychological reasons. These reactions may be due to the limitations of human imagination rather than the limitations of the design itself; however, glass does feel cool to the touch. Nevertheless, in this context, comfort was not the primary reason for its production.

Furniture:	*Cross Check* armchair
Designer:	Frank Gehry
Company:	Knoll International
Context:	One material serving as the generator of form, structure, and function
Date:	1992

THE LAMINATED HARD WHITE MAPLE CHAIR series was initially inspired by bushel baskets. The *Cross Check* armchair is one of a series of comfortable bentwood chairs each given a name based on hockey terms: *Power Play* armchair, *Hat Trick* side chair, and *Face Off* table. The supports and the chair's seat are formed from the same lightweight, slender wood strips. The laminated plywood strips create a single coherent form. Frank Gehry explored the possibility of bentwood through many working prototypes and proved it to be pliable, with "spring" and lightweight effectiveness. The *Cross Check* chair is one of the last chair designs developed in Gehry's bentwood series.

The primary intent was to develop a diagonally woven chair. Gehry accomplished this by taking loose strips of bentwood and working the material into expressive form. The first prototype was achieved in 1990. The second prototype became the first diagonally woven chair that was structurally stable, and this opened the door for the development of the final *Cross Check* chair.

To improve the back support, the arms were brought forward and attached to the front of the chair. This brought the chair into balance while simultaneously softening the geometric angularity of earlier triangulated bases. The new arm design suggested providing another leg, which was further integrated into the final design of the chair in addition to the second over-arm. In keeping with the curvilinear theme, the back slats extend to loop over, which strengthen the final design. Knoll developed an environmentally sound water-based dip finishing system to seal and finish the chair.

Figure 4.54 Laminated maple chairs and tables inspired by the woven construction of apple crates. Designed by Frank Gehry (1992) for Knoll, Inc.

The chair is made from maple veneers harvested from sustainable forests and cut into 2-inch (5-cm) wide, 1/32-inch (0.7-mm) thick strips. It is laminated to six-, seven-, and eight-ply thickness using high-bond urea glue, with all wood grain running in the same direction for resilience. Thermoset glue provides structural rigidity, minimizing the need for metal connectors while allowing for ergonomic movement and flexibility. The backs of all chairs flex for added comfort. No glues are used in the seat assembly to allow flexibility in unison with spring-like movement. The total weight of the chair is 12 lb. The seat height is 18⅛ inches (46 cm), 28 inches (71.1 cm) wide, 33⅝ inches (84 cm) high (arm height), 28½ inches (72.4 cm) wide, and 24 inches (61 cm) deep (Figure 4.54).

The design process was a successful collaboration between Gehry's studio and Knoll International. The *Cross Check* chair is a high-quality chair that in production rekindles many notions of the Industrial Revolution and the craft trades of the nineteenth century. The design of the *Cross Check* chair provides an exciting sitting experience and infuses structural and technological innovation (Figures 4.55–4.57).

Figure 4.55 Cross Check chair, front oblique view.

Figure 4.56 Computer model—side view.

Figure 4.57 Computer model—top view.

Furniture:	*Trinidad* chair
Designer:	Nanna Ditzel
Company:	Fredericia Stolefabrik, Denmark
Context:	Hospitality seating
Date:	1993

NANNA DITZEL WAS BORN in Copenhagen in 1923. She began her work in furniture design through cabinet making before attending the Industrial Arts and Crafts College and the Royal Academy of Fine Arts in Copenhagen. Following World War II, she was one of the very few women working in furniture design. The *Trinidad* chair is a lightweight, comfortable, stackable café chair. Inspiration for the design came from a time in Nanna's life when she lived in the Caribbean islands and developed an interest in colonial-style wooden architecture. The chair's name comes from the country of Trinidad, whose traditional fretwork techniques inspired Ditzel (Figure 4.58).

The *Trinidad* chair is available in laminated maple, beech, cherry, teak, or lacquer-painted wood and can be purchased with or without arms. A high-density foam seat-cushioned model is also available. The chair's seat and back are supported by a metal tubular frame. The fabrication process involves laminating several sheets of wood, applying a veneer, and cutting the overall shape and flexible slits. The wooden back and seat pan are attached to the metal frame with metal fasteners located along the bottom and back of the chair. Synthetic rubber footings are placed on the ends of the four legs. The chair weighs 22 lb and

Figure 4.58 Trinidad chair—high stool version, designed by Nanna Ditzel (1993), manufactured by Fredericia Furniture A/S, Denmark.

Figure 4.59 Computer model of the Trinidad chair.

is 19¾ inches (50 cm) wide, 22½ inches (57 cm) deep, and 32¾ (83 cm) high, with a seat height of 17½ inches (44 cm) (Figure 4.59).

The design is elegant and the proportions are graceful. The design won the APEX Award first prize in 1997, and the following year it won the Danish Industrial Design Award (Figures 4.60–4.62).

Figure 4.60 Trinidad chair—front view.

Figure 4.61 Trinidad chair—side view.

Figure 4.62 Trinidad chair—rear view.

Furniture:	*Living Units*
Artist:	**Andrea Zittel**
Context:	**Transformative living—furniture as a social art**
Date:	**1994**

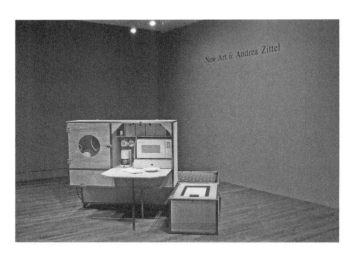

Figure 4.63 A-Z Living Units, 1994, designed by Andrea Zittel.

Figure 4.64 A-Z Living Units, © Andrea Zittel.

Figure 4.65 A-Z Living Units.

ANDREA ZITTEL IS AN ARTIST who uses her own day-to-day living as the impetus for her artwork. The *A-Z Living Units* were a series of fabrications (hybrids between furniture and shelter fabrications) designed to change one's sense of personal space. The various designs left no area of daily living, no matter how basic, untouched. The initial *Living Units* were conceived and fabricated in the early 1990s, when Zittel was living in New York.[13] The images of the *A-Z Living Units* were taken from an installation at the Cincinnati Museum of Art entitled "New Art 6" (1995). The materials were kept to a simple kit of parts, including angle iron, Baltic birch plywood, hardware, and upholstery. As the fabrications sold and began to be used, the designs began to be modified by their new owners. Nonetheless, the structural framework and transformative nature of the fabrications remained intact (Figures 4.63, 4.64).

In discussing her work, Zittel explains:

I lived in contained spaces that weren't mine. I wanted to create a highly personalized space. It was like owning a house that would fit inside a shell within a house other people owned. I would do all the modifications within the capsule of the Living Unit. That series ended when I bought a building in New York in 1994.[14] (Figure 4.65).

Several versions of the *pit bed* were made. The *pit bed* is an assembly referred to as the *Comfort Unit* in the

Living Units series. Some versions were exact copies and others were radical take-offs. But at the core of the various fabrications in the *Living Units* series such as the *pit bed* is an idea of a solution designed to satisfy the conflicting needs for security, stability, freedom, and autonomy. Owning a *Living Unit* created the security and permanence of a home, which would then be set up inside the homes that other people owned. It provided freedom because whenever the owners wanted to move, they could collapse the unit and move it to a new location. The *Living Units* were remarkably simple social constructions, transformable and functional spaces in which to live (Figures 4.66, 4.67).

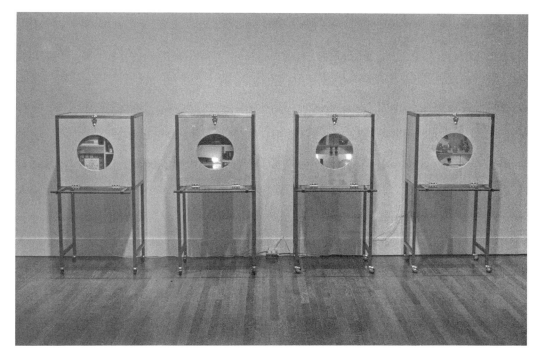

Figure 4.66 A-Z Living Units.

Figure 4.67 A-Z Living Units.

Furniture:	*Aeron* chair
Designer:	**Don Chadwick and Bill Stumpf**
Company:	**Herman Miller**
Context:	**Ergonomic office chair**
Date:	**1994–95**

DON CHADWICK AND BILL STUMPF designed the *Aeron* chair in 1994 for Herman Miller. The design is significant because the chair was made largely from recycled materials and was remarkably ergonomic. The transparency of the chair as a visual element was in keeping with the idea of transparent architecture and technology. Transparency is the effort to make technology less opaque, to communicate the inner workings of things, and to make objects less intrusive upon the environment (Figures 4.68, 4.69).

The design team conducted anthropometric studies, using a specifically developed instrument to calculate average dimensions ranging from popliteal height to forearm length. The team did pressure mapping and thermal testing to determine the weight distribution and heat- and moisture-dissipating qualities of the pellicle suspension mesh made of polyester and lycra on the chair's seat and back.[15] Field studies examined the relationship between the sizes of people and their preference for chair size (Dowell 1995). The unique form of the *Aeron* expresses its purpose and use, as well as the material composition of its parts and the way they connect. The slightly translucent and reflective nature of its surfaces gives it an airy quality. The *Aeron* chair becomes part of the person who uses it and the environment that surrounds it (Figure 4.70).

Figure 4.68 Aeron chair, designed by Don Chadwick and Bill Stumpf (1994) for Herman Miller—front view.

Figure 4.69 Aeron chair—side view.

Figure 4.70 Aeron chair—rear oblique.

The chair functions well in the workplace, where there are many different multifunctional tasks to perform over extended periods of time. The material feels cool but not cold, making the haptic experience inviting and comfortable. The woven pellicle material offers appropriate support. Depending upon the weight and size of the user, the *Aeron* chair can be purchased in one of three sizes, from A (small) to C (large) (Figure 4.71).

Figure 4.71 Aeron chair—available in sizes A, B, and C.

Furniture:	*Pathways*
Design:	**Steelcase Design Team**
Fabrication:	**Steelcase**
Context:	**Office system (furniture as a framework for creating flexible spatial arrangements)**
Date:	**2000**

PATHWAYS TOOK EIGHT YEARS and $150 million to develop.[16] Steelcase responded to the market forces that require companies to move and reconfigure themselves with inconceivable speed. Pathways includes every element of an office, from flooring to walls to lighting, all designed to work together seamlessly.

The need to constantly integrate new technologies into offices was a prime focus for Pathways' designers. Steelcase realized that many clients were renovating older buildings, such as loft warehouses or existing offices, and facing prohibitive rewiring costs in the process. Consultants from Xerox's research division had advised Steelcase that these issues would become more complex over time. *Pathways* is a design solution to avoid cable gridlock, which meant creating extensive cavities inside the furniture system for equipment cables (Figures 4.72–4.74).

Starting with its flooring systems, the designers define private areas with walls and doors, then customize the surfaces of exterior or immovable walls with the *Pathways Addition* components (i.e., selecting fabrics for acoustical privacy or whiteboards for meeting areas). Individual niches can be formed from the open spaces that remain, using 2-foot (61 cm) and 4-foot (122 cm) partitions (Figure 4.75).

To create teamwork areas, the *Pathways Conjunction* system forms post-and-beam structures that can be closed off with curtains and fitted with shelving, whiteboards, and digital screens. Feeding off wiring that runs through the floor, its hub posts and tables offer spots for free-floating workers to plug into the company's data flow. Its ambient lighting line illuminates the space with a soft glow.

Figure 4.72 Pathways, in context, designed and manufactured by Steelcase, 2000.

Figure 4.73 Pathways, enabling open and flexible space, designed and manufactured by Steelcase.

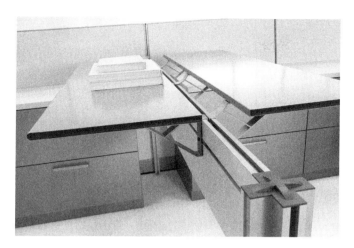

Figure 4.74 Pathways, shelving and accessory detail, designed and manufactured by Steelcase.

Figure 4.75 Pathways, in use and in context, designed and manufactured by Steelcase.

Furniture:	*The Block*
Designer:	Erik Skoven
Fabrication:	Werner Furniture
Context:	A contemplative place to sit—allegory by design and fabrication
Date:	1999

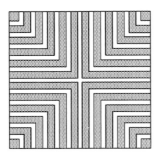

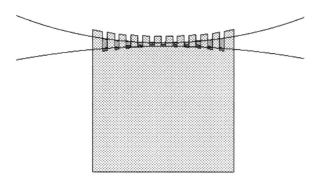

Figure 4.76 Plan and elevation drawing of The Block, designed by Erik Skoven, 1999.

THE BACKGROUND for this particular design is a sad one; however, it is important to understand in order to comprehend the significance of the work:

> A 26 year old Danish woman, pregnant with her second child, is found to have leukemia. A choice is to be made and the baby is taken by caesarian after which the mother receives full chemotherapy—and dies. The child, now two years old, lives with the father and thrives. The grief of the family members was deep and the thought of designing something for them to sit on at the grave came to the designer. Something simple and yet beautiful: a sitting block of wood that would last for a long time, and yet disintegrate years from now, when perhaps the memories of Therese begin to fade.[17] (Figures 4.76–4.78)

The outdoor wooden stool was conceived and fabricated in a meaningful way during a difficult time of grieving the loss of family (Figure 4.79). Erik Skoven describes an underlining theme for the wooden stool in a brief poem:

Figure 4.77 Two Blocks.

Figure 4.78 The Block in context.

With knots and cracks, like our love
No empty and hollow spaces
It will age, and one day—when I am no more—disappear
He transformed into mortal clay or ashes.[18]

The design is a solid wooden cube. The sitting surface is concave over grooves that are convex—the lower and upper parts of a sphere—thus symbolizing the convergence of life and death, heaven and earth. Since it is designed for outdoor use, rain runs off in the grooves. When fixed, the solid oak block sits on a foundation, raised 1 inch (2.54 cm) above the ground. An indoor version is also available. Both are 15 × 15 × 15 inches (38 × 38 × 38 cm). The direction of the oak's grain runs vertically; thus, one sits on the end grain of the block. To get oak of a sufficient diameter in Europe, the tree must be between 450 and 500 years of age.

In 2001, *the Block* was selected as one of five pieces for the annual SE cabinetmakers' exhibition at the Museum of Art and Design in Copenhagen. In 2004 *the Block* was acquired and exhibited at the Trapholt Art Museum in Kolding, Denmark.

Figure 4.79 The Block, outdoor stool, designed and fabricated by Erik Skoven, 1999.

JIMMY'S BUFFET IS A MOVABLE SIDEBOARD for a residential dining room setting in which guests can serve themselves. The design allows dining accessories to be stored and easily retrieved from five compartments. In addition, the top surface of the buffet allows ample space for serving and displaying food (Figure 4.80).

The buffet incorporates 10 full-extension drawers, each 16 inches (40.6 cm) deep, and offers a variety of widths, ranging from 6 inches (15.2 cm) to 24 inches (61 cm), and a variety of heights, ranging from 6 to 12 inches (15.2 to 30.4 cm). Six clear **acrylic** casters enable the piece to roll freely for cleaning and spatial rearrangement.

The buffet is fabricated using handcraft technology and industrial materials. The layout

Figure 4.80 Jimmy's Buffet, designed and fabricated by Jim Postell, Janet Flory, Matt Cornell, and Steve Wethington, 2004.

of the drawers was inspired by the video game *Tetris,* with various shapes stacking tightly over one another. Materials for the buffet include ⅛ inch (3 mm) bending birch plywood, cherry lumber and ¾ inch (2 cm) cherry plywood, neoprene 60, full-extension glides, acrylic casters, and stainless steel drawer pulls. The

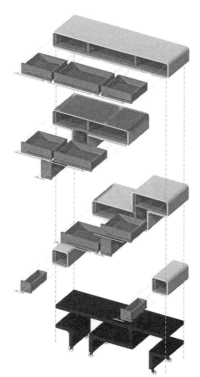

Figure 4.81 Exploded axonometric of Jimmy's Buffet.

form is composed of five individual storage components. Each component is "wrapped" with four ⅛ inch (3 mm) thick bending birch plywood laminations, mechanically assembled using ½ inch (1.25 cm) through-bolts, composed by using 2 inch (5 cm) thick blocking to isolate each component. The recessed reveals are faced with ³⁄₁₆ inch (5 mm) thick, black neoprene 60. Overall dimensions of the buffet are 36 inches (91.4 cm) high, 60 inches (152.4 cm) wide, and 21 inches (53.3 cm) deep (Figure 4.81).

The buffet expresses part-to-whole relationships in both form and function (Figures 4.82–4.84).

LESSONS FROM THE FURNITURE CASE STUDIES

What recurring themes or cumulative lessons are apparent from the furniture studies? Some furnishings were the first to use a specific material or a new fabrication technology. Some have remarkable workmanship. Some studies reveal a pronounced sense of social use or formulate cultural links to a particular place and time. Some are precedents for designs that have followed. Collectively, the studies highlight a range of cultural, technical, and functional ideas about furniture design, but every study is linked to a particular place and time. **Zeitgeist** is a fundamental notion that tempers how one might consider each of the furniture studies. Furniture is very often part of a larger systemic context, linked to societal norms and to both place and time.

The organization of the furniture studies illustrates an important consideration, which becomes evident upon hindsight. Following the introductory remarks about background and context, the studies emphasize three recurring themes:

1. A description of material, dimension, weight, and joinery (how the piece is made, how well it holds together, etc.)
2. A discussion on how the piece functions (how it feels and issues of utility, social use, comfort, and ergonomics)
3. Aspects of beauty, meaning, aesthetics, spatial organization, and proportion (how the piece looks)

These themes serve as a basis for a common thread of inquiry and develop a framework for considering and formulating theories of furniture design.

Figure 4.82 Detail—cherry, bending birch, and black neoprene 60.

Figure 4.83 Front elevation—Jimmy's Buffet.

Figure 4.84 Jimmy's Buffet in context—dining room, the furnished house, Cincinnati, OH, 2004.

chapter

5 Furniture Design Theory

theory
- A set of statements or principles devised to explain a group of facts or phenomena. A belief or principle that guides action or assists comprehension or judgment.[1]

Figure 5.1 Final reviews, Denmark's International Study program, summer furniture workshop, DKDS, Copenhagen.

INQUIRY

THEORIZING SHEDS LIGHT on the nature of something through individual and collective inquiry. Regarding our interest in the subject of furniture design, the questions asked are broad and encompassing. What is furniture design? What is its place in the world? Who are furniture designers? How is furniture design done, and for whom is it undertaken? What are the principles of furniture design, and why are they important to know?

The Latin word *theria* and the Greek word *theoroi* mean "to see," "seeing the sights," or "seeing within" and are the origins of the English word *theory*.[2] These origins point to the importance of looking within oneself as well as looking outward to the world. Furniture designers rely upon intuitive judgment (looking inward), utilize materials and processes (looking under), draw upon prior experience (looking backward), and observe how people do things (looking outward) when seeking inspiration for their own work (see Figure 5.1).

Inquiry directs the discussions of furniture design toward technical, functional, and aesthetic matters. In doing so, theory reveals knowledge to help determine good design. Knowledge and ethos in design change over time, and so does theory. When new evidence about an area or subject emerges, theory will adjust accordingly. Our understanding of aesthetics, comfort, and fabrication technologies is different today than it was 30 years ago and likely will continue to evolve.

Inquiry sustains a body of work—all types of work. What ideas contribute to good design? Can one design be considered better than another? Aside from aspects of comfort and workmanship, what makes a good chair good? We have a host of "best-sellers" in many different typologies, designed and marketed according to theories of ergonomics, human factors, and **anthropometrics.** Which designs are the best? Aside from considerations of price and comfort, what qualities make them the best? Expanding upon the relationships between furniture and space, how might the variables of placement and orientation draw furniture into an architectural thesis?

During the past 300 years, as technology has advanced and social concerns have evolved into more democratic ideals, furniture makers and furniture designers have begun to acknowledge these cultural shifts within vocational and professional arenas. In the past 50 years, industrial designers, interior designers, architects, and fine artists have contributed to social change through the design and fabrication of furniture. Designers have sought a better understanding of science, ergonomics, comfort, production, and the business of marketing, branding, and distribution. Today, theory engages aspects of industrialization and mass production, green design, health and welfare concerns, universal design, transgenerational design, and social use. The culture of design continues to reach out to a broader market and is fueled, in part, by designers working on designs that are more or less within economic reach.

Theory is the conglomeration of many voices. Thomas Chippendale, Gustav Stickley, Mies van der Rohe, Charles and Ray Eames, David Pye, Galen Cranz, Bill Stumpf, and Sam Maloof are a few of the many designers who have contributed ideas about composition, technique, ergonomics, and social utility through their efforts in writing, designing, and fabrication. The lessons and ideas drawn from others are important to assimilate because they can help inspire and formulate personal views about furniture and design.

Mies van der Rohe once said; "A chair is a very difficult object. A skyscraper is almost easier."[3] Consider the following explanations:

1. A chair is an extension of the user, and no two users are exactly alike. No two users sit, squat, or move about in the same manner.
2. A chair is used for many different purposes (e.g., to rest, write, type, read, talk, etc.). Each of these activities could result in a specific chair, yet often chairs are intended to be multifunctional.
3. Sitting is inherently a challenge to one's well-being. Research indicates that standing is healthier than sitting. The body needs to move about, frequently change positions, and adjust itself constantly.

Sitting is considered by many to be a static activity, but in fact, the human body needs to move and stretch continually. The challenge in designing a chair extends beyond physical parameters of static posture. Theories abound regarding the dynamics of body movement. Ideas about ergonomics have evolved significantly, and knowledge in the area of anthropometrics has developed as well. It is important to study ergonomic theories, and it is generally useful to produce working prototypes and take the opportunity to experience and evaluate design ideas.

Designing and fabricating furniture is one way of learning about furniture design. Remember to note the successes and failures that occur from conception through the life of a piece. Inquiry is an active part of the process of design, making observations and taking notes along the way. Successes and failures during the process are part of one's research. Theories develop from designing, fabricating, and experiencing furniture, as well as through reading, writing, observing, and studying furniture.

FIRMITAS, UTILITAS, AND VENUSTAS

Architectural theories are dependent upon three interrelated terms—*firmness, commodity,* and *delight.* The Latin terms of origin *firmitas, utilitas,* and *venustas* are attributed to Vitruvius' text, *The Ten Books of Architecture,* originally titled *de Architectura,* written in 79 A.D. Sir Henry Wotton translated the Latin terms in his 1624 treatise, *The Elements of Architecture,* as follows: "The end is to build well. Well building hath three conditions: firmness, commodity, and delight."[4]

From this phrase—"*firmitas, utilitas,* and *venustas*"— a theoretical framework emerges that is useful in guiding broad inquiry relative to furniture design. In this book, theories of furniture design are outlined accordingly:

> *Firmitas:* Structural integrity, tectonics, and composition (how furniture is made and held together)
>
> *Utilitas:* Use and experience
> (how furniture functions and feels)
>
> *Venustas:* Form, spatial organization, and aesthetics (how furniture looks, fits within space, and expresses meaning)

This model builds upon an interpretation of Vitruvius and Wotton, but it also acknowledges the writings and designs of many individuals who have contributed to a larger collective framework.

Keep in mind the links that theory has with time and place. Theory is connected to, and intertwined with, the spirit of the age in which it develops. Furniture design supports this fact and needs to be considered in context. Ideas and perspectives about furniture embrace a range of issues that change over time and are influenced by culture, politics, economics, and place. Theories of furniture design consider the composition of parts (i.e., tectonics and structural integrity), function (i.e., ergonomics, comfort, and social use), and meaning (i.e., aesthetics and semantics) of built form (Figures 5.2–5.4).

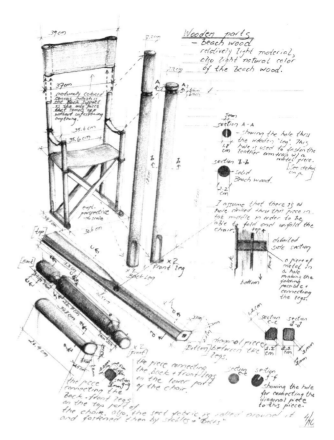

Figure 5.2 Analytic study by a DIS student of the Folding stool, designed by Mogens Koch.

Figure 5.3 A man sitting in four different leaning positions— depicting motion of sitting. DAA chair, designed by George Nelson, manufactured by Herman Miller, 1958.

Figure 5.4 Bound-Un-Bound, upholstered seating, designed by Komplot Design, 2002.

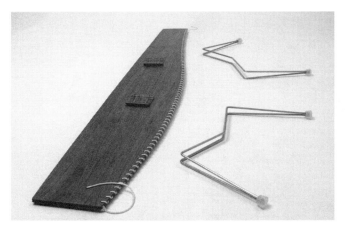

Figure 5.5a Unassembled Deck Chair, designed by Erling Christoffersen (2004), fabricated by Rønne & Askou.

Figure 5.5b Assembled Deck Chair.

Firmitas

Firmness (*firmitas*) refers to the structural integrity and tectonic composition of furniture. Firmness is dependent upon fabrication techniques, the quality of workmanship, and the spatial relationships among the parts and between the parts and the whole. Applied forces, such as lateral forces, challenge the physical integrity of furniture. Lateral forces, live loads, and gravity should be carefully considered when designing furniture. Lateral forces routinely cause joints and connections to fail. Braces, skirts, folds, and applied hardware serve to resist lateral forces and improve the structural integrity of furniture.

Consider the economy and structural integrity achieved in the *Deck Chair* (Figures 5.5a, 5.5b) designed by the Danish architect Erling Christoffersen and fabricated by Rønne & Askou. The individual elements of the lounge are relatively flexible when unassembled, but as the contoured wood planes are drawn tight, the lounge transforms and becomes rigid.

A solid walnut **trestle table** (Figure 5.6a) is detailed differently than a **veneered** table (Figure 5.6b). This is so because lumber expands and contracts due to changes in humidity, while veneer demands a stable substrate. A solid lumber table must allow for expansion and contraction perpendicular to the wood's grain or the design will fail.

Figure 5.6b Veneered table, designed by Jim Postell (2002), fabricated by Contract Fixtures, Inc.

Figure 5.6a Trestle table, fabricated by Jonathan Bruns of Sachi Woodworking, 2005.

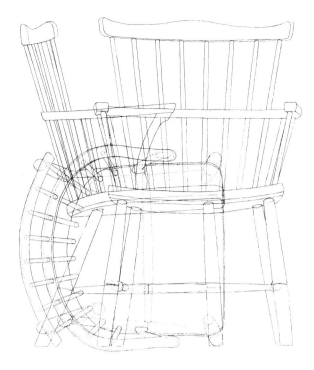

Figure 5.7 Windsor-type armchair by Børge Morgensen, 1944.

Børge Morgensen's *Windsor-type* armchair (1944) is remarkable in its structural integrity and the economy of its parts (Figure 5.7). As in most **Windsor chairs,** both legs and stretchers are turned with increased thickness where they receive smaller members. The back spindles are placed in compression, and the curved outer member is in tension as pressure is applied to the back. The open spindles are ideal solutions for outdoor settings, allowing breezes to pass through without blowing the chair over. The Windsor chair is a generic design. There are many variations, all of which are lightweight and durable.

Wood is not a uniform material. It has a range of physical characteristics and properties. Some **hardwoods** are relatively soft, such as basswood, and some **softwoods** are relatively hard if allowed to grow slowly (as was once the case for southern yellow pine). Some woods adhere well with carpenter's glue, such as Honduran mahogany, while others require polyurethane glue or epoxy glue to adhere freshly cut boards, such as ebony due to its density. Some woods are inherently stable (they don't easily cup, warp, or bend after using the **jointer** or planer), such as walnut, while other woods are dimensionally unstable, such as beech. Most hardwoods have an open cellular structure, such as red oak, but some hardwoods, such as white oak, have a closed cellular **grain.**

Wood has many properties, which demonstrate how important it is for both the designer and the fabricator to understand the unique characteristics of each species when using it in design. The cellular structure, the type of adhesive, the joinery, and the moisture content of lumber affect the structural integrity of the design. Wood is one of several materials used to make furniture. The physical properties of other materials such as fabrics, metals, and plastics are equally important and are discussed further in Chapter 7.

Ideas are expressed through details. Workmanship, structural integrity, and aesthetics are clarified through joinery. The word *detail* shares its origin with the word *tailor,* meaning a craftsperson who knows how to sew together individual pieces of fabric to make a complete set of clothes for the human body.[5] The tailor, furniture designer, and furniture maker face similar challenges in how to join materials properly and consider human form and function in doing so.

Utilitas

> Utility must precede beauty.
> Christopher Dresser, "General Principles of Ornament," *The Furniture Gazette,*
> London, 1877, pp. 173–174.

Commodity (*utilitas*) is determined from a range of observations and experiences based upon how well furniture functions and feels. In this book, commodity refers to comfort, ergonomics, social use, and the tactile experience of furniture. It introduces ideas that contribute to an area of knowledge known as **human factors,** which involves scientific research on the interface between the human body and the built form. Human factors data are objective and scientifically determined, but the data are always subject to political and social frames of reference. Human factors encompass many areas of research including accessible design, anthropometrics, ergonomics, posture, proxemics, and universal design.

Human factors specialists are advocates for the user. Relatively expensive, mass-produced office chairs such as the *Freedom chair* (Figure 5.8) rely significantly upon human factors research. Before the *Freedom chair* went into production, Humanscale invested in extensive anthropometric research and considered theories of ergonomics, body position, and body movement. Niels Diffrient designed the *Freedom chair* in 1999 for Humanscale. Diffrient brought his background in industrial design and his engineering know-how to complement the need for an ergonomic chair that emphasized the "human factors" in today's office designs.

Furniture physically and spatially embraces the body. One can sit and lie upon, work at, and touch furniture (Figures 5.9–5.11). Designers need to experience their designs physically before they can accurately evaluate their work. Considering tactile experiences (**haptic sensations**) in design is important.

Figure 5.8 Freedom chair, designed by Niels Diffrient (1999), manufactured by Humanscale, 2000.

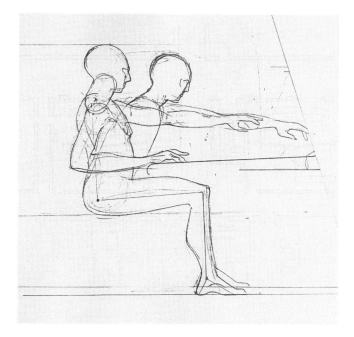

Figure 5.9 A study of the parameters of reaching while sitting upright.

Figure 5.10 Reclining recliners.

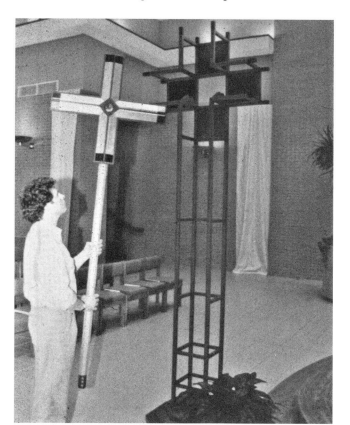

Figure 5.11 Carrying a 12.5 lb processional cross.

Ergonomics (i.e., fitting the task to work within the limits of the human body) presents challenges through which design is often measured. Commodity can be considered the interface between function and ergonomics. Design solutions seek to find a match between the measure and physiology of the body, the tactile experiences of use, and aspects of health, welfare, and pleasure.

Figure 5.12 Observing the inward compression of the lower vertebrae.

Observing, documenting, and analyzing how people sit reinforces compelling arguments for the need to maintain muscular strength, provide easy access, and allow for a range of postures and body movement while being seated (Figure 5.12). Personal observations and individual inquiry may challenge traditional theories of ergonomics, which in the past attempted to facilitate static seated postures for extended periods of use.

Changing body postures, body movement, supporting the body's weight, and maintaining lumbar lordosis are important aspects to consider when designing a chair. Today we understand more about the measurement and physiology of the body than ever before. However, designers should remain open to new ideas about comfort and use, because our knowledge of ergonomics and human factors is in a constant state of flux.

Anthropometrics

Anthropometrics is the science of determining anatomical measurements and understanding the physiology of the human body[6] (Figure 5.13). Researchers working in the area of anthropometrics generate statistics from different age groups, body sizes, and body proportions, different ethnicities, gender distinction, and different populations to understand the similarities and differences in the human form. Knowledge of the physiology and measurement of the human body is critical for designing furniture. However, the application of anthropometrics does not require the designer to assume that comfort is scientifically achievable by "fitting" the structure and movement of the body with furniture. Nonetheless, anthropometric data are an important resource for furniture designers and are helpful in determining the dimension, size, and material of their designs.

What is a reasonable height of a chair's seat pan for the average adult? What is the height of the seat pan relative to the length of the body's **popliteal dimension?** What is a

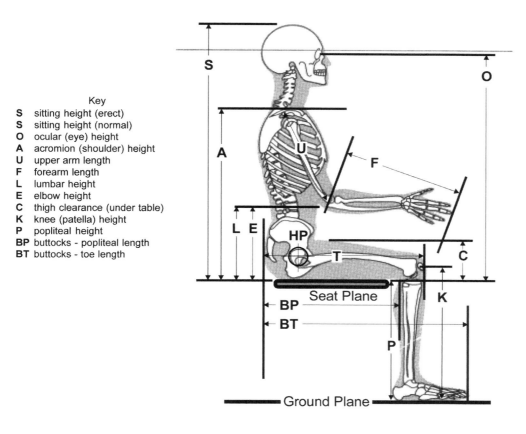

Anthropometry
Seated Adult Male
Variables

Key
S   sitting height (erect)
S   sitting height (normal)
O   ocular (eye) height
A   acromion (shoulder) height
U   upper arm length
F   forearm length
L   lumbar height
E   elbow height
C   thigh clearance (under table)
K   knee (patella) height
P   popliteal height
BP buttocks - popliteal length
BT buttocks - toe length

Seat Plane

Ground Plane

Figure 5.13 Anthropometric terms and measurable lengths for sitting.

reasonable angle of the seat rake for reading? How might the choice of materials contribute to the experience of sitting? What is a reasonable height of a table surface for dining for an average man, woman, child, or adult in a wheelchair? Where on the body is the vascular flow most susceptible to outside pressure? Body posture and appropriate support are some of the many dependent relationships that furniture designers need to consider (Figure 5.14), and one can analyze these in plan as well as section. To help determine dimensions, materials, and form, designers may inquire: What is the intended purpose of the chair or table? Who are the intended users? How will the furniture be used? The significance of these questions becomes evident when a chair or table is designed for the first time.

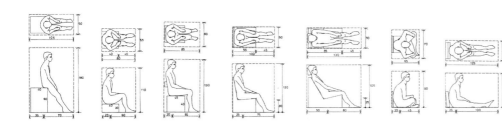

Figure 5.14 Human supports for a range of sitting postures.

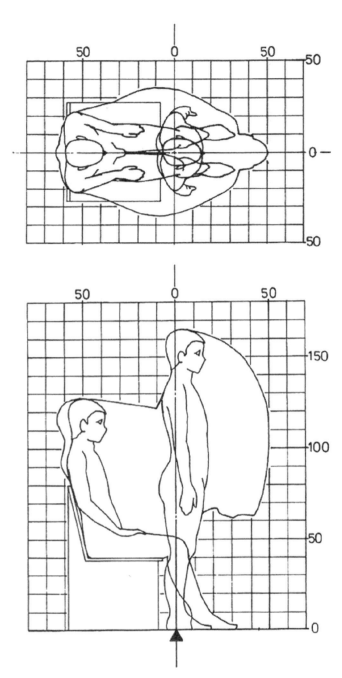

Figure 5.15 Technical body, motion, and space study of sitting (plan and elevation).

Anthropometrics is a term that industrial designers, interior designers, engineers, and architects share with researchers working in the area of human factors. The works of Henry Dreyfuss, *The Measure of Man* (1960), *Human Scale* (1974; reissued in 1981 with his protégé, Niels Diffrient), and *The Measure of Man and Woman* (revised edition, 2002) are important in the field of anthropometrics. *Human Scale* was a significant step forward in the process of documenting the physiology and measurement of the human body. Though Dreyfuss initially emphasized white males in gathering data on the physiology and measurement of the human body, his research expanded and eventually included the physiology and measurement of women in the revised edition of *The Measure of Man and Woman.* The revised work presented a statistical analysis of the human body in a range between the 5th and 95th percentiles of the American population. This extensive range (90 percent of the population) contributes to our understanding of the measurement and physiology of the human body and establishes a political and social context of the extent that design ought to accommodate.

This work, and the work of others, has challenged preliminary theories of ergonomics, advancing a collective understanding about design in general relative to the physiology and measurement of the human body. Researchers have also investigated the space that sitting in different postures occupies in both plan view and section (Figure 5.15). Furniture designers should seek to understand as much as possible regarding the physiology and measurement of the human body and its interface with built forms.

Ergonomics

Ergonomics focuses upon the study of work and how work is done. It seeks to establish a healthy fit between performing a task, the limits of the human body, and the designed product (Figure 5.16). This thesis is based upon the assumption that the body is healthier if it is not stressed beyond the normal limits of muscle, bone, posture, and so on. The term *ergonomics* entered the modern lexicon when Wojciech Jastrzebowski used it in an 1857 article on the subject.[7] Since then, *ergonomics* has often been used synonymously with the total application of human factors, including the phrases *universal design* and *accessible design,* but semantic distinctions between these terms are important to understand.

The term *ergonomics* comes from the Greek words *ergos,* meaning "work," and *nomoi,* meaning "natural laws." An ergonomic design solution adapts the task to fit the natural limits of the person rather than forcing the limits of the person to conform to the task or the space. The goal of ergonomics is to optimize how well design (or habits) can enable work

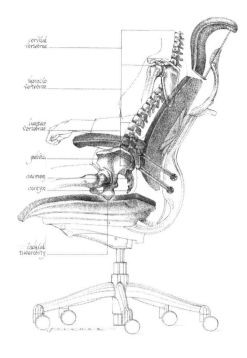

Figure 5.16 The relationship between the lower lumbar vertebrae and hip while seated.

to be accomplished, considering the physical and psychological limits of the human body. Body posture and the physical limits of reaching, pulling, lifting, and pushing are factors to consider in ergonomic design.

Many office chairs are labeled *ergonomic seating.* A chair is ergonomic only when the limits of the user correlate with the task at hand. A chair with a right-handed tray is not ergonomic for a left-handed user, and fixed auditorium seating is not ergonomic for interactive class discussions. The term *ergonomics* applies to experiences and tasks (which are temporal) and less directly to objects and furnishings.

Consider *ergonomics* by looking at its prefix, *erg,* a unit of measure of work or energy, and render the suffix, *nomics,* as having to do with efficiency. A body of knowledge regarding the efficiency of work grew out of funded research for the United States military in the 1940s and 1950s. This research was extended to include the study of blue-collar work considerations in the 1960s and eventually to white-collar office environments in the 1970s. In the 1980s, with the introduction of computers and other equipment into the workplace, ergonomic research concentrated upon repetitive strain injuries as well as neck and lower back disabilities caused by poor spatial arrangements, inflexible furniture and equipment, and poor work habits. Ergonomic research responded to the growing cost of injuries and disabilities that occurred in factories, laboratories, and office environments.

In recent years, there have been dramatic increases in *cumulative trauma disorders* (CTDs), repetitive motion disorders, and other work-related injuries and illnesses due to ergonomic hazards. These injuries, which affect the musculoskeletal and nervous systems, may be caused or aggravated by repetitive motions, forceful exertions, vibration, mechanical compression, hard surfaces, and sustained or awkward postures held for extended periods of time. CTDs affect nearly all tissues. Nerves, tendons, tendon sheaths, ligaments, and muscles are frequently injured by poor design and poor use. CTDs are recognized as a significant health hazard in the workplace and account for the largest share of occupational illnesses known as *repeated trauma disorders,* according to the Bureau of Labor Statistics.[8]

Today, the need to make work efficient incorporates concern for making work and the tools used to work with more healthful, safe, and environmentally green.

Furniture designed from an ergonomic perspective focuses upon task-specific operations. Ergonomic research also considers multiuse and multiusers. Ergonomic furniture is marketed to businesses where liability and public welfare are of concern and functions such as typing, lifting, and pulling may cause medical problems. Smart seating, adjustable work surfaces, wrist relaxers, posture guidelines for working at a computer keyboard and monitor, policy concepts regarding the need to take breaks, the importance of vascular circulation, and body movement have been introduced and integrated into ergonomic research topics. The *Ergonomics Data Sheet* compiled by the U.S. Department of Labor in 1989 states that "ergonomists, industrial engineers, occupational safety and health experts, and other trained individuals believe that at least one-half of all workplace safety and health problems could be reduced by changes in ergonomic conditions."[9] Nearly all of the ergonomic changes proposed by the Department of Labor impact the design and use of furniture.

The size, material, and form of chairs should provide ergonomic support and utilitarian function. Dimensions of the user and operative tasks are important considerations in chair design. In addition, four utilitarian factors ought to be considered when designing human body supports:

1. Supporting the weight of the user
2. Eliminating pressure points
3. Enabling body movement
4. Maintaining lumbar lordosis

Supporting the Weight of the User The first consideration is how to support the weight of the user for the task at hand. Traditional views suggest that ergonomic seating should distribute the weight of the user evenly. However, supporting the body is often limited to selective areas: the lower back, ischial tuberosities, and arms. The **seat rake** is the angle of the seat back to the seat pan. Designers and ergonomic researchers study the correlation between seat rake and posture. Studies of different seating profiles, including Clara A. Ridder's body-neutral posture research (resulting in the *Ridder Curve*[10]), are important to consider in chair design. Further, an inclined seat back may help distribute the weight of the body.

Eliminating Pressure Points A second consideration is the need to eliminate or minimize pressure points. Pressure points can constrict the flow of blood through the body and can affect the nerves that transfer sensation to the brain. This can cause discomfort, lead to the sensation of pins and needles, **parasthesia,**[11] and eventually lead to numbness. The area behind the knee is particularly sensitive to pressure and applied force. In ergonomic seating, a waterfall seat front, a seat height that is no higher than the popliteal dimension, an upholstered seat, or a contoured seat pan are strategies to minimize uncomfortable pressure points while being seated (Figure 5.17).

There are two triangular seat bones inside the buttocks called **ischial tuberosities.** Research indicates that approximately 65 percent of the body's weight is transferred through these bones to the seat of the chair when sitting.[12] The shape, angle, and curvature of the seat pan affect the amount of pressure applied to these two bones when sitting. The height of the seat pan ought to be slightly less than the length behind the user's knee to the floor. The vertical dimension from the underside of the thigh at the knee to the bottom of the foot on the floor is the **popliteal dimension.** After adjusting for heels, clothing, and other

Figure 5.17 A stool's contoured seat pan.

issues, the popliteal dimension is useful in determining the height of the chair seat. The height of the seat pan in mass-produced chairs is generally 17 inches (43.2 cm)—falling in the middle of the American National Standards Institute (ANSI) recommendation for the range of seat height adjustment: 15 to 20½ inches (38.1 to 52 cm).[13] It is critical that the seat pan be no higher than the popliteal dimension of the user. Traditional theories suggest that the feet ought to rest firmly on the floor. This will minimize pressure points, increase the stability of sitting, and help distribute the weight of the body more evenly. In theory, consider a 135-degree angle between the spine and the thighs as a place to start, bringing the knees significantly below the seat pan. This angle places the pelvis and spine in a body-neutral position; however, very few chairs accommodate this angle. A different but related angle to consider is the seat-to-back angle, which generally ranges from 95 to 105 degrees. ANSI recommends that this angle be between 90 and 105 degrees.

Enabling Body Movement A third ergonomic consideration is to enable body movement while being seated. Though posture is dependent upon time and societal norms, it is not a static condition. The human body is always moving, seeking comfort and different positions when sitting or resting. Consider chair designs that allow people to distribute their weight, adjust their posture, and use their muscles when sitting. Designers should allow enough space and appropriate body support in their designs.

Maintaining Lumbar Lordosis The fourth aspect to consider in supporting the human body is the curvature of the lower lumbar vertebrae and the angle of the hip when seated. Contemporary theory seeks to maintain **lumbar lordosis** while seated, which is the natural curvature of the spine when standing. When the lower lumbar vertebrae are compressed forward (which occurs when sitting on a flat surface), they become pinched. This can be painful and harmful to the vertebrae over time. Inward compression of the lower lumbar vertebrae is called **kyphosis.** Designers should avoid this condition through design whenever

Figure 5.18 Sitting on cases of beer.

possible and consider ways of maintaining lumbar lordosis for the seated user. Rotating the pelvis forward helps maintain the natural curvature of the spine.[14]

Moving from a standing position (lumbar lordosis) to an upright sitting position bends the hip joint and rotates the pelvis, flattens the lumbar curve (kyphosis) of the back, and strains the muscles in this region. One should attempt to maintain lumbar lordosis while in a seated position.

Posture Furniture affects posture, which in turn influences how people sit, work, rest, and socially gather. Conversely, observing how people naturally sit, work, and rest can inspire design ideas (Figure 5.18). Posture expresses cultural, societal, and gender-based considerations. Posture also reveals formal and informal patterns of behavior, spatial communication, and social interaction. An ideal posture does not exist because human beings cannot hold any single posture for long periods of time. Posture is always changing, driven in part, by the need to redirect the flow of blood and relieve pressure applied to the body over time. How people communicate in and through space and how people sit directly affect how well furniture functions and feels.

Posture is a concept that reveals continuous body movement when sitting, standing, or walking. The position of the body is always shifting to seek comfort. Posture expresses social-spatial communications between people, driven by cultural norms, and physiological factors.

Poor posture has been a factor in litigation cases involving worker's compensation claims and loss of income due to medical disabilities resulting from improper design and use. Poor work habits and bad posture contribute to physical problems with the back, neck, and wrists, which motivates further research on ergonomics and posture.

During the 20th century, chairs and desks in schools were designed to keep the body and eyes forward and to place the hips, knees, and ankles mostly at right angles in an upright-seated position. Often, desks and chairs were integrated with one another (Figure 5.19). Today, this is

Figure 5.19 Integrated chair and desk (school furniture).

Figure 5.20 Body profile studies

not considered a healthful design. The integration of chair and desk offers little flexibility of use. Further, it is difficult to maintain a static or fixed position for a substantial period of time.

Research studies during the past 20 years have pointed out that when sitting in this manner, the hip joints actually bend only 60 degrees. An additional 30 degrees of bending occurs in the lumbar region of the lower back.[15] This bending flattens the lumbar vertebrae, straining muscles in this critical region. Figure 5.20 shows how the angles of the hip, knee, and back correlate with one another in different postures ranging from standing to lying down (with and without body support).

Contemporary thinking suggests that a sitting posture in a natural resting position is healthful (Figure 5.21). This allows the spine to carry the body's weight in a more comfortable way. This concept has been called *balanced seating,* a term coined by A.C. Mandel, chief surgeon of the Finsen Institute in Copenhagen, Denmark.[16]

Figure 5.21 Sitting in a relaxed position.

Correlations between a chair's formal characteristics and body posture, use, and comfort are important to investigate. The paired images in Figures 5.22a,b and 5.23a,b reveal interesting correlations between chair designs and body postures. The chairs were designed and fabricated by students enrolled in Denmark's International Study Program's (DIS) summer furniture workshop taught at the Danmarks DesignSkole in Copenhagen. Each summer since the year 2000, Professors Erling Christoffersen, Flemming Jensen, and Bjørli Lundin have taught a summer workshop in which design students from different American programs design and fabricate a chair (human body support). The choice of what to design and fabricate is left to the students, but the designs had to utilize one primary material: a limited amount of veneer, lumber, or metal rod. The images of the chairs paired with the images of students sitting on their chair designs reveal interesting correlations between furniture, posture, and personal intention.

Figure 5.22a Denmark's International Study Program: Summer Furniture Design Workshop—chair designed and fabricated by Jessop Kozink.

Figure 5.22b Denmark's International Study Program: Summer Furniture Design Workshop—chair with design student Jessop Kozink.

Figure 5.23a Denmark's International Study Program: Summer Furniture Design Workshop—chair designed and fabricated by Emily Lauren Green.

Figure 5.23b Denmark's International Study Program: Summer Furniture Design Workshop—chair with design student Emily Lauren Green.

Figure 5.24 Observing—body posture and spatial communication.

Figure 5.25 Observing—social gathering around Når Enden er God; designed by Søren Petersen, fabricated by Davinde Savvaerk, 2006.

Proxemics is the study of how people communicate in and through space. It links the study of human behavior with social, cultural, spatial, and geographic contexts. It is an area of study that considers eye contact, body language, posture, and social customs, as well as intimate, personal, social, and public spatial zones of interaction and communication (Figures 5.24, 5.25). Notions of privacy, intimacy, crowding, defensible space, and territoriality are aspects to consider when arranging furniture in space.

Benches designed by Gunnar Asplund for one of the grieving chapels at Skogskyrkogården (The Woodland Cemetery in Stockholm, Sweden), have a 15-degree angle incorporated in plan, dividing and joining the benches into two nonsymmetrical parts. This angle promotes eye and body contact better than a conventional bench would and symbolically draws together two parts into a whole (Figure 5.26).

The term *proxemics* is attributed to the research and writing of anthropologist Edward T. Hall.[17] In 1963 Hall described the measurable distances between people as they interacted. Hall's work in the areas of sociology and anthropology was reinforced and developed further by the research and writing of psychologist Robert Sommer, Donald Preziosi, and the video documentaries of William Whyte.

Cultural and societal notions of how people interact with one another and their patterns of behavior are important to understand. The size, location, and orientation of furniture directly influence patterns of behavior. Seating and table arrangements can influence the perception of space and contribute to the social and psychological experience of space.

For example, crowding is known to increase irritation and stress, leading to friction, arguments, and even crime.[18]

Figure 5.26 15-degree bench detail, designed by Gunnar Asplund, Skogskyrkogården (Woodland Cemetery), Stockholm, Sweden.

But curiously enough, crowding is not entirely dependent upon density; rather, it has to do with one's personal ability to maintain a sense of control in a given spatial context for a period of time. Crowding is a mental construct of how people react to a given situation as much as it is a quantitative measure of the density of people per square foot. Configuring furniture in a classroom or restaurant into clustered arrangements can help reduce the perception of crowding. Furniture designers need to understand the social grouping dynamics and behavior patterns of those who will use their designs as much as they need to understand code regulations and occupancy standards when organizing and composing furniture in space.

In *The Hidden Dimension,* Hall pointed out that social distance between people could be measured and described in four categories:

- Intimate distance for embracing, touching, or whispering (6–18 inches or 15.2–45.7 cm)
- Personal distance for interactions among good friends (1.5–4 feet or 0.45–1.21 m)
- Social distance for interactions among acquaintances (4–12 feet or 1.21–3.65 m)
- Public distance used for public speaking (12 feet or over 3.65 m)

The idea of navigating through one's environment and the environments of others, including the cultural nuances in how people interact with one another, contributes to the study of proxemics.

Hall recognized that different cultures maintain different standards of personal space.[19] Proxemics concentrates upon places and spaces where people congregate or pass through, such as airports, lobbies, and plazas, as well as private spaces, personal residences, and office environments. Design can influence how people communicate in and through space, depending upon the public or private setting, the people in the study, the characteristics of the furnishings, and the placement and orientation of the furnishings.

Reflect upon the traditional elongated, rectangular dining table. The table's form suggests a social hierarchy revealed through the correlation of its dominant axis and the place where the "head" of the household traditionally sits. Compare a rectangular dining table to a circular table, where there is no dominant axis (Figure 5.27). One might infer that primary and secondary orders, relative to spatial layout, suggest primary and secondary orders relative to social status. One can conclude that a circular table expresses an equitable group sharing without bias the collective activity of working, talking, or eating. Following this line of thought, one might begin to see political, social, cultural, and gender-biased intentions in the conception and development of other pieces of furniture.

Figure 5.27 Sectional and circular Petal table, designed by Richard Schultz (1960) for Knoll.

Venustas

What distinctions can be made between aesthetics, beauty, and delight? Delight is a personal reaction to physical or visual stimuli and is subjective. Pleasure is revealed by sensation through the tactile nature of materials, finishes, and comfort as well as the visual nature of color, shape, and form. For centuries, delight has been associated with concepts of pleasure; however, delight elicits a range of emotional reactions (positive and negative) closely linked to the notion of arousal.

Arousal theory has been influenced by the work of Daniel Berlyne, Joachim F. Wohlwill, Albert Mehrabian, and James Russell during the 1960s and 1970s. Laboratory work in experimental aesthetics and studies in the physical environment conclude that pleasure is related to the observer's level of arousal, and arousal is influenced by the uncertainty created by the environmental stimulus.[20] The pleasure-arousal hypothesis is based upon Berlyne's finding that pleasure and stimulus uncertainty are related. Berlyne theorized that pleasure resulting from exposure to a visual stimulus increases with stimulus uncertainty until the observer's arousal level becomes uncomfortably high, at which point pleasure decreases.

If pleasure results from exposure to a stimulus, then we might consider unpleasant as well as pleasant stimuli as inherent within the nature of beauty. The bombing of a Basque town during the Spanish Civil War inspired Pablo Picasso's painting *Guernica*. The painting intends to make the viewer feel the horrors of the war, but the experience results in the sensation of pleasure.

Traditional ideas of beauty suggest that geometry, proportion, and form inspire and please both the mind and the soul. In architecture, design, and art, ideas about beauty, geometry, proportion, and form fuel the sensation of delight. In furniture design, placement and orientation in space along with the visual and tactile experiences generate delight.

Beauty

> When I'm working on a problem, I never think about beauty. I think only how to solve the problem. But when I have finished, if the solution is not beautiful, I know that it is wrong.[21]
>
> —Buckminster Fuller

Leon Battista Alberti (1404–72) established theoretical principles that defined *beauty* as "the harmony and concord of all the parts achieved in such a manner that nothing could be added or taken away or altered except for the worse."[22] Alberti's statement emphasizes wholeness—an important concept to consider in design. Alberti describes the joining of lines and angles as an important and difficult task. Furniture designers must contend with the complete integration of structure, utility, spatial context, material, and aesthetics, in which any one factor can disrupt the harmony of design. Achieving harmony in furniture design is an ever-present challenge.

One way to understand the idea of beauty in furniture is to consider the notion that design is the organization of parts into a coherent whole. Consider the *Eames lounge* chair and ottoman by Charles and Ray Eames for Herman Miller (Figure 5.28). The lounge and ottoman share intertwined relationships of material, form, and use. The totality achieves a whole out of carefully integrated parts. The chair reveals a disciplined order that demonstrates the capabilities of the designers and offers inspiration for other designers to build upon.

Figure 5.28 Leather lounge and ottoman in rosewood, designed by Charles and Ray Eames (1956), manufactured by Herman Miller.

Beauty is not limited to aesthetics. A significant aspect of beauty lies in the experience of furniture, and in this regard, beauty is something that is entirely tangible. The essence of beauty is intertwined with use, experience, and aesthetics. Beauty is a complex phenomenon that is dependent upon several tangible and intangible components working together.

Aesthetics comes from the Greek word *aisthetikos,* meaning "perceptive, especially by feeling."[23] Aesthetics is the branch of philosophy dealing with the beautiful. Aesthetic theories intertwine with design principles. They serve as lenses through which judgment is made about formal qualities in furniture design. In the design phase, aesthetics are studied and modified by using drawings and models. These efforts require a thorough understanding of geometry and the communication skills necessary to explore and refine design ideas.

Geometry

Euclid's *Thirteen Books of the Elements* was written around 300 B.C. and was translated by Sir Thomas L. Heath in the 19th century. It presents the rules and principles of geometry, with a focus upon lines, angles, planes, circles, ratios, proportions, polygons, and cylinders. It is an important source that covers the mechanics of geometry. Geometry is the foundation of composition. In order to conceive, design, and draw furniture, one must have a technical or intuitive knowledge of the rules and principles of geometry.

Proportion

Proportion is derived from relationships within the human body (digit, cubit, head, arm, proportion of elegance) and from relationships between door size, windowsill height, room dimension, and so on. In many ways, furniture responds proportionally to the human body and to the interior space in which it is placed.

Ad Quadratum and ad Triangulatum

Ad quadratum ("by the square") and **ad triangulatum** ("by the triangle") are geometric systems that designers have used to create unity in their work. Ad quadratum is based on the ratio of the side of any square to its diagonal (1:$\sqrt{2}$). Spatial and formal relationships in the chair shown in Figure 5.29 were derived using ad quadratum geometry.

Figure 5.29 Ad quadratum geometry used to compose a chair made of Baltic birch plywood, cherry, and neoprene 80.

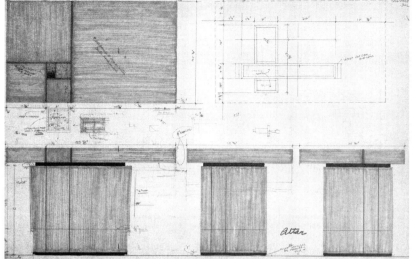

Figure 5.30a Fabrication drawing for an altar; the Golden Section can be seen in plan, elevation, and section.

Figure 5.30b Altar, designed by Jim Postell (1994), fabricated by Heartwood Furniture Company.

The Golden Section

The Golden Section is a ratio that results when a line is divided so that the short segment has the same relationship to the long segment that the long segment has to the sum of the two parts. It works out to be a unique mathematical proportion 1:1.6182 . . . as well as .6182:1.[24] The Golden Section was the principal proportional system used to resolve the plan, elevation, and section of the altar shown in Figures 5.30a and 5.30b.

Analysis of the geometric basis for many design elements that employ the Golden Section illustrates an almost exact mathematical progression known as the *Fibonacci series* of numbers 0, 1, 1, 2, 3, 5, 8, 13 . . . in which each number is the sum of the two numbers preceding it.

The Golden Section and the Fibonacci series are related. Regarding the Fibonacci series, continuing to divide the larger number by the one that directly precedes it will, as the numbers increase, approach the Golden Section (1.6182 . . .)

The Golden Section and the Fibonacci series are proportional systems that have influenced aesthetic theories for centuries. From the Renaissance to modernism, systems of geometry have been inherently, intuitively, and deliberately incorporated in the design of furniture. Beginning with the shift to functionalism, however, the importance of geometric systems began to give way to more humanistic considerations of commodity, social use, and ergonomic theories. In today's culture of digital design, there has been a reconsideration of Euclidean geometry and the Golden Section for more complex and organic formal possibilities through the use of digital hardware, digital software, and digital production machines.

Modernism

Modernism is more than a style. It is a philosophical way of thinking about architecture and design. It came into being in an emerging industrial world that rapidly embraced

Figure 5.31 Chaise Longue, designed by Charlotte Perriand, Pierre Jeanneret, and Le Corbusier (1929), manufactured by Cassina.

mechanization. When modernism emerged in the Western world in the 1930s, design had difficulty building upon or acknowledging history. It was an ideology encapsulated by the statement "form follows function," often attributed to Louis Sullivan but initially used by the 19th-century sculptor Horatio Greenough (1805–52).[25] The modernist idea is that function and utility can and should create form. The question is, what is function?

Modernist theory in furniture seeks to integrate social function and structural integrity, incorporate industrial materials and industrial fabrication processes, and determine how well furniture performs its job. Modernism considers *function* as a broad term with meaning at many levels. The following list outlines a few concerns that affect the notion of function within the view of modernism:[26]

- What is the intended purpose of the furniture?
- Are there secondary or tertiary purposes (social uses) to consider?
- Who will use the furniture, in what context, and how often?
- What tools, resources, energy, and processes are needed for fabrication?
- What are the waste by-products of fabrication and the resources needed for distribution?
- What societal or economic impacts result from either the fabrication or consumption of the furniture?
- At the end of its life span, how will disposal, recycling, or biodegrading occur?

The modern understanding of function relates back to *utilitas* but has a broader definition. The *Chaise Longue* (Figure 5.31) by Le Corbusier, his brother Pierre Jeanneret, and Charlotte Perriand epitomizes the modernist ideal through the use of industrial materials, deliberate expression of joinery, connectors, reveals, and expressive form that is dependent upon a broad view of function and fabrication. In the context of its conception, function is aligned with logical thinking, tectonic assembly, and industrial processes more than with a desire for comfort or ergonomics.

Systems Theory

The human body is a network of interrelated systems (nervous, skeletal, muscular, vascular, etc.). Similarly, furniture can be conceived of as a series of interrelated systems. In the 1960s and 1970s, it was popular to think about design as the management of systems. One did not design a chair or a table; one designed systems with which human and building systems interacted. Office furniture was known as *systems furniture* because of its integration of physical, structural, spatial, and electrical systems. Seating devices were referred to as *human body support systems*.

Systems theory grew out of *human factors engineering* and deconstructed the modernist use of the word *function* into an array of systematic relationships.

In systems theory, the primary objective of design was to optimize the fit between humans and machines. Systems theory promoted an engineering and scientific approach to the world. It was a powerful notion and contributed to a paradigm shift in the way people thought about design in general and furniture design in particular.

When design is considered as a series of interrelated systems, it reshapes one's thinking about style and aesthetics. Mapping and modeling the human body while standing, leaning, squatting, or sitting down is a good exercise to help designers understand body posture and body space (Figures 5.32, 5.33). Human factors specialists rely upon scientific methods and an enormous amount of research to better understand aspects of measure, posture, and physiology. However, the paradigm shift toward this line of research never took root within the design community, and systems theory lost its momentum by the mid-1980s to more cultural, humanistic, and phenomenological considerations. The awkward terminology contributed to its demise, but the rigorous and scientifically based research influenced the modern office workplace.

Figure 5.32 Mapping the human body at 1:1.

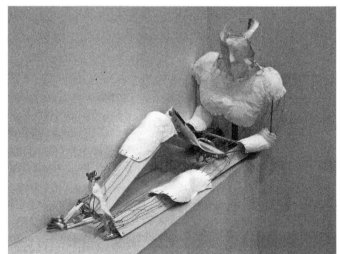

Figure 5.33 First-year design studio construction exercise at the University of Cincinnati—human figure reclining, design by Elizabeth Rajala, 2003.

Built Form and Culture

People from different cultural backgrounds view the built environment in different ways. Correlations between furniture, culture, and use develop into complex associations between built form and culture. Culture is a frame of reference through which furniture is given social meaning, but culture is not the only referent. The 1960s was a time of social change for many people. It was time to question authority, and in design it was a time when designers began to focus upon humanist perspectives including program briefs and *postoccupancy evaluations* (POEs). POEs are research studies that focus upon a building after it has been occupied and used for a period of time. Scholars, architects, and designers sought stronger relationships between design theory and humanist theory. The late 1960s marked a renewed interest in *programming,* which focused attention upon the processes and methods used to better design complex buildings. It was also the time when vernacular design began to reemerge as something deeper than a minor interest in cultural geography. John A. Kouwenhoven coined the term **vernacular** to refer to designs carried out in everyday or routine ways without much conscious or formal planning.[27]

Sociologists, cultural anthropologists, engineers, and psychologists have developed a body of knowledge that has advanced the importance of cultural and social theories in design and architecture. The groundbreaking work of Irwin Altman, Leanne Rivlin, Amos Rapaport, and Edward T. Hall led to second- and third-generation scholars such as Michael Brill, Clare Cooper Marcus, David Saile, David Seaman, and Setha Low, who have contributed to the study of environment and social behavior. The fields of sociology, cultural anthropology, and cultural geography, in conjunction with the study of transgenerational design and advanced studies of ergonomic relationships, have all contributed to a body of knowledge useful to furniture designers. Contemporary furniture designs express societal and cultural meaning, despite how subtle the references may appear to be.

Our evolving understanding of societies and cultures relative to built forms has influenced the collective view of theory, making humanism a primary consideration in design research. Theory began to shift its perspective from aspects of form and function (modernism) to more humanistic, societal, and cultural orientations during the late 1960s. Furniture designers began to break traditional and conventional rules of design, which in turn opened the door for new ideas and paradigms about furniture and design. The period from the late 1960s to the mid-1970s was one of formal and social experimentation in furniture design. Studies about the experience of furniture began to emerge in humanistic and *user-centered* research. Placing people first generated an interest in indigenous societies, vernacular design, and cultural geographies, and this in turn fueled an emergence of knowledge that evolved into *built-form and cultural research* and formation of the Environmental Design Research Association (EDRA).

Furniture addresses the needs of larger societal and behavior patterns that belong to specific institutions, regions, or global communities. Regarding societal patterns of behavior, furniture can be fully integrated within the daily life of people, as seen in the outdoor chairs and tables in many European cafés. For millennia, places of worship have embodied evolving and collective patterns of liturgical use. A pulpit rising well above freestanding chairs or pews hardly seems out of place, as do vernacular Turkish furnishings, Shaker furnishings hung on pegs on a wall when not in use, or office workstations arranged in a grid. In every case, when a clear sense of cultural identity aligns itself with any given standard in regard to established patterns of behavior, links between furniture and specific societal groups appear seamless, revealing correlations between the behaviors and values of these groups and design.

Consider **Shaker furniture** and reflect upon the image that comes to mind (Figure 5.34). Most likely, the image is of a naturally finished, handcrafted wooden stool, table, or box. But this is, in actuality, out of step with what is Shaker. Shaker culture can be diagrammed as one that grew in the early 1800s, reached its zenith in the mid-1800s, and then began its descent by the end of the 19th century. At the beginning and ending points of this culture, Shaker furniture was well crafted, naturally finished, and expressively detailed. No one piece was exactly like another, and the workmanship and wood grain were valued by both the maker and the user. At the height of the Shaker culture, furniture and millwork were painted with a milk-based paint (Figure 5.35), which gave a uniform appearance to the furniture and casework. All woodwork was made to appear similar. Different woods could be used and the paint hid the faults, details, wood grain, and craft distinctions, generating a formal and social sameness of the furniture. This way of thinking about furniture reflects upon the correlations between culture and built form. Though the Shaker way of life has long disappeared, its furniture remains popular today, but it

Figure 5.34 Shaker stool, Pleasant Hill, Kentucky.

is the natural, uniquely crafted pieces that are popular rather than the painted works, calling into question whether Shaker furniture is deeply appreciated as a cultural phenomenon or as a handcrafted work of beauty.

Figure 5.35 Shaker furniture, finished using a milk-based paint.

People around the world interact with the built environment in different ways. Distinctions in the way people interact with one another and with built forms can be seen as cultural folds, which in turn help define the seams between local, regional, and global communities. The terms *local* and *regional* have geographic and vernacular boundaries. People who live in a particular place and time tend to generate a collective identity through a shared view of how things are done.

Despite the economic influence that global corporations have upon design worldwide, the intent and extent of the origin of design contributes to the nature of its regional versus global status. Global design is similar to universal design by definition, immune from local or regional boundaries. A left- or right-handed computer mouse and the *Segway* transportation device are examples of products designed for a global community, without the influence of regional nuances or local ways of doing something.

Consider the communal nature of a sauna experience and the influence of the built-in wood seating upon the enjoyment of a sauna with others. Finnish, Norwegian, Swedish, and Danish people understand the rituals, conditions, and communal experiences that determine this specifically Scandinavian practice, which indeed is culturally distinct from how a sauna might be understood and experienced elsewhere in the world. Consider the outdoor gathering place located in Hammarby Sjöstad, Sweden (Figures 5.36, 5.37), and try to formulate connections between its design and intended use and the deep cultural heritage its designers drew upon to express a sense of place and regional identity.

Similar transformations occur whenever a regional norm is well established. However, disconnections between form and meaning begin to emerge when spaces and objects rooted in one culture are placed in a completely new cultural or geographic context. This has occurred many times in history: oriental rugs or kilims brought to Europe; the furnishings of Britain exported to India, the Chinese sea captain's chair copied for a dining suite in South Africa. This even occurs between generations when antiques and furnishings are transferred to grandchildren who live in societies that are significantly different from those of their grandparents or great-grandparents. Furniture, because of its mobile and temporal nature, often introduces a mix of cultural heritages and patterns of behavior to its setting and to its users.

Figure 5.36 Outdoor seating pod at Hammarby Sjöstad, Sweden.

Figure 5.37 Interior of an outdoor seating pod at Hammarby Sjöstad.

NEW FORMALISM: THEORIES OF DIGITAL FORM

Digital software programs and digital machines have begun to affect our thinking about design. Greg Lynn is an architect and professor at both UCLA and Yale University who uses advanced computer technologies to design complex forms. Making full use of the digital characteristics and properties of the software *Maya,* Lynn conceived of a chair that resulted from the digital interpolation of several of Michael Thonet's earlier bentwood chair designs. The idea is more significant than a study in digital representation. It marks a precedent for furniture design in which the capabilities of digital technology have extended beyond the human ability to generate (or comprehend) such complex forms.

Digital technology may well become more than a tool in the design process. It may become the vehicle and the means of generating form. The opportunity to reconsider traditional processes of design and fabrication is open to all designers now. And these opportunities may help designers in their inquiry to determine what makes good furniture good. Or, more to the point, digital technology may shape the very frame of reference used to determine how designers think about technical, functional, and aesthetic matters.

chapter

6 Design

Design-Fab-Func is the new term for furniture design because it expresses the simultaneity of systems.[1]

Coop Himmelblau (Wolf D. Prix, Frank Stepper, Helmut Swiczinsky)

DESIGN IS A PROCESS. The process can be simple or complex. It can take a few minutes or several years to accomplish. It can involve one person or a group of people. There are intuitive processes and there are systematic processes (Figures 6.1a–6.1c). This chapter focuses on the processes of designing furniture. It introduces principles of furniture design and covers the phases, processes, and skills involved.

Figure 6.1a Poul Kjærholm (1929–1980), furniture architect, working at his desk.

Figure 6.1b Design sketches for a two-piece aluminum chair by Poul Kjærholm, 1953.

Figure 6.1c Working prototype of a two-piece aluminum chair by Poul Kjærholm, 1953.

Figure 6.2a Exploded components of the Equa 2 work chair, manufactured by Herman Miller.

Figure 6.2b Equa 2 work chair, designed by Don Chadwick and Bill Stumpf (1984), manufactured by Herman Miller.

The ultimate goal of design is to synthesize tangible and intangible aspects and to create a unified whole out of an array of parts. Achieving part-to-whole relationships between components and interrelated systems is an important goal of design. In this sense, designing is a means of attaining order, arranging physical and spatial components along with intangible aspects to form a unified whole. Order governs the composition of any entity, such as the human body, furniture, a building, or a natural landscape.

Gestalt psychology, formulated in 1930 by Max Wertheimer (1880–1943), Kurt Koffka (1886–1941), and Wolfgang Köhler (1887–1967), stated that human experience should be considered in a broad, comprehensive way, suggesting that *the whole is greater than the sum of its parts.*[2] Building upon this perspective, furniture design can be understood as an effort to infuse any number of intended purposes with physical parts, interrelated systems, structural forces, and utilitarian needs in greater wholes, with attention placed upon the simultaneity of systems (Figures 6.2a, 6.2b).

Designing furniture is parallel to but different from designing a building or creating art. Furniture takes less time to create than a building and is one of many elements in interior space. Unlike art, furniture has pragmatic responsibility to function and often serves several intended purposes.

Furniture design is disciplined work that combines technical information with prior experience, observation, and intuitive judgment, but systematic design will not guarantee good results. There are many paths one can take in designing furniture. In every case, the design process influences the final product. If you change the way you design, then you will change the way you think about design and, consequently, what you design. **Paradigms** about the design process (methods, required skills, anticipated outcomes, etc.) vary significantly based upon professional, academic, and programmatic boundaries.

Disciplinary boundaries are acknowledged in this chapter because many designers approach furniture design from unique perspectives that often rely upon discipline-specific means. Nonetheless, design principles are a common thread in all disciplines, so we begin with a brief review of design principles.

DESIGN PRINCIPLES

Design principles provide criteria that describe formal intentions. The intended purpose of a chair or table can begin with a range of needs or desires and develop through any number of processes. Along the way, furniture designers are confronted by design principles, which require the eye and the hand to work together in a complex system of thought and action. The principles of design covered in this chapter are:

- Balance: Structural and Visual, Symmetry and Asymmetry
- Continuity, Unity, and Variety
- Dynamism and Stasis
- Hierarchy and Emphasis
- Juxtaposition
- Rhythm and Pattern
- Scale and Proportion

Balance: Structural and Visual, Symmetry and Asymmetry

Visual balance is the spatial weighing of a composition around an axis. Structural balance involves the physical equilibrium of freestanding elements such as chairs and tables. Furniture must be able to withstand lateral, shear, live, and moment forces. Visual balance and structural balance are related but distinct concepts.

Structural Balance

Structural balance considers the forces in furniture to be in equilibrium. When forces are not in equilibrium, cantilevers can fail, shelves can sag, and furniture can tip over. Furniture must be able to withstand **lateral forces** (forces applied from the side), shear forces (internal forces working in parallel but opposite directions), and moment forces (rotational forces applied to joints).

Structural forces inspire design ideas and are an important consideration in the conception of form. Frank Gehry's bentwood chairs resulted from a structural and material investigation using ³⁄₃₂-inch (2.4-mm)-thick maple veneers assembled and composed in various ways (Figure 6.3).

Figure 6.3 Computer rendering—bentwood Hat Trick chairs, designed by Frank Gehry for Knoll.

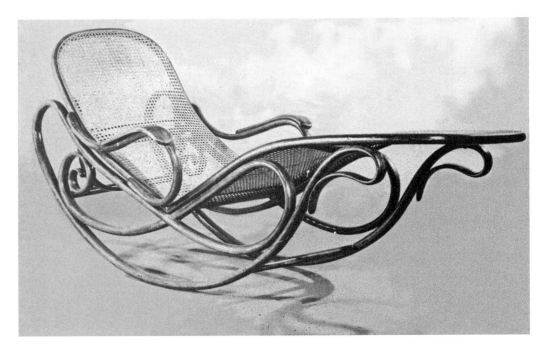

Figure 6.4 Rocking chair c. 1880, steam-bent beechwood, produced by Gebrüder Thonet.

Figure 6.5 Bilateral symmetry—Art Nouveau selette.

Rocking chairs move back and forth and rely upon the weight and motion of the user, the form of the chair, and the center of gravity of both the user and the chair to function properly. Rocking back and forth creates significant dynamic forces, stressing both the form and joinery of the rocker. The goal of the classic bentwood rocker by Michael Thonet (Figure 6.4) is to obtain a fluid and balanced rocking motion through a symbiotic relationship between the rocker and the user.

In cases where furniture is precariously tall and narrow or where the center of gravity lies beyond the tipping point, it may become necessary to attach furniture to a floor, wall, or ceiling in order to maintain structural stability.

There are dimensional limits to the horizontal span of shelving before deflection occurs and imbalance appears. Shelving systems, bed frames, music stands, grandfather clocks, cabinet doors, and speaking podiums all depend upon basic engineering principles to maintain structural balance and function safely.

Visual Balance

The spatial weighing of visual balance expresses either symmetrical or asymmetrical composition. **Symmetry** is a form of balance where a component (or several components) is mirrored along an axis. The Art Nouveau *selette* shown in Figure 6.5 is **bilaterally** symmetrical, which places emphasis upon its vertical axis and, consequently, upon the object displayed on top of the selette. Symmetry can be expressed *bilaterally* (around a common axis) or *radially* (around a common point).

Visual balance does not rely entirely upon symmetry. Much of the abstract cubist furniture from the 1930s and the *de Stijl*–style furnishings by Gerrit Rietveld and Theo Van Doesburg express balance but are not symmetrical. **Asymmetrical** balance is dynamic and appears in equilibrium along an axis through its form, though it cannot be mirrored. Gerrit Rietveld's *Berlin* chair (1923) and Charles and Ray Eames' fiberglass-reinforced plastic *Eames Chaise* (1948) are visually balanced, asymmetrical compositions (Figure 6.6).

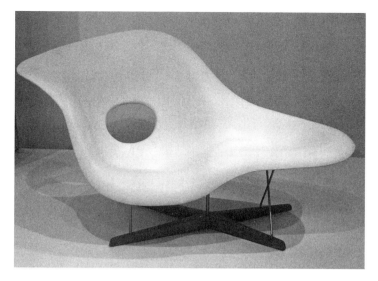

Figure 6.6 Asymmetry—Eames chaise (1948), manufactured by Vitra.

Figure 6.7 Continuity—wall seating at Woodland Cemetery, Stockholm, Sweden.

Continuity, Unity, and Variety

The wall-mounted wood paneling that transforms into a sinusoidal bench in Gunnar Asplund's chapel at the Woodland Cemetery in Stockholm, Sweden, expresses continuity, unity, and variety. The panels are evenly modulated and create a datum (unifying reference) from which the sinusoidal bench gives variety to the otherwise rectangular elements and planar surfaces. The uninterrupted plane of the laminated plywood gives continuity, and the integration of wall and furniture in material and form gives unity to the design (Figure 6.7). Unity and continuity underscore fundamental principles of design that draw together part-to-whole relationships.

Variation is expressed through differences and distinctions perceived within the bounds of constancy and regularity. The regularity of the vertical supports in Charles and Ray Eames' *Eames Storage Unit* (ESU) expresses continuity (see Chapter 4). The supports establish a repeatable pattern, while the lacquered Masonite panels give variation to the design through their placement and color. Unity is achieved in the dynamic interplay between the unit's components and its geometric order.

Figure 6.8 Visual and visceral movement—Maloof rocker, designed and fabricated by Sam Maloof.

Dynamism and Stasis

The handcrafted wood rockers designed and crafted by Sam Maloof express movement in both a visual and visceral manner (Figure 6.8). The visual and tactile characteristics contribute to their dynamism. Furniture that appears static, such as Erik Skoven's *Block* stool (see Chapter 4), expresses stasis (the characteristic of being at rest). Dynamism and stasis are contrasting attributes in built form.

Figure 6.9a Florence Knoll conference table (1961) with flat bar and Brno chairs expressing a formal and social hierarchy.

Figure 6.9b Profile distinction between presider's and deacon's chairs indicating a liturgical hierarchy.

Hierarchy and Emphasis

Hierarchy and *emphasis* point to priority and relative value in design. Hierarchy and emphasis are achieved through the manipulation of location, color, size, texture, and shape. Form, color, and material can emphasize primary, secondary, and tertiary levels of importance and meaning. Formal hierarchy can reinforce social status, such as the person sitting at the short end of a long rectangular conference table (Figure 6.9a) or the profile distinctions suggesting a social hierarchy between a **deacon's chair** and a **presider's chair** in the Catholic Church (Figure 6.9b). In this sense, social, cultural, and political meaning parallel formal characteristics of hierarchy.

Emphasis is drawn from dominant and subordinate relationships. For example, one can emphasize the vertical elements of a shelving system by using distinct materials and details to draw the eye. Shape differences and contrast levels can help designers distinguish dominant and subordinate relationships in their work.

Figure 6.10 Rivertime in the making, designed and fabricated by Michael and Rob Toombs (1986).

Juxtaposition

Juxtaposition is the simultaneous experience of the relationships between contrasting elements or characteristics. Examples include a curvilinear form juxtaposed with an orthogonal shape and a light, reflective surface juxtaposed with a dark matte finish. In Michael and Rob Toomb's *Rivertime* (1986), the light, figured, curvilinear maple top is juxtaposed with the dark, segmented lower portion of the cabinet (Figure 6.10).

Rhythm and Pattern

The word *rhythm* derives from the Greek term *rhuthmos,* meaning "to flow."[3] Rhythm is the foundation of music, dance, poetry, and design. Rhythm is the structure and order of elements in space or time. The fabrication drawing of an ark in Figure 6.11 expresses an array of horizontal and vertical elements, which create subsets of interrelated rhythm and variation. Rhythm is also the order of temporal daily experiences such as waking and sleeping, including monthly and seasonal patterns, and life-cycle events such as birth and death.

Pattern is the arrangement of elements that determine a whole and are made from points, lines, and shapes. Rhythm and pattern are codependent and inherent aspects in design. They reveal the underlying structure of form through physical, spatial, or temporal compositional order.

Scale and Proportion

Scale and *proportion* are dependent upon physical and spatial relationships, although important distinctions need to be made between these terms. **Scale** is based upon the size of one thing relative to another, such as the size of a sectional sofa in relation to the size of a room. The floor lamp in Figure 6.12a is based upon a series of reference points taken from the vertical axis of a human body (Figure 6.12b). The individual parts of the lamp reference various heights of the body, which were determined from the figure. The sketch explores proportional relationships between the floor lamp and the human form at a scale of 1 to 1.

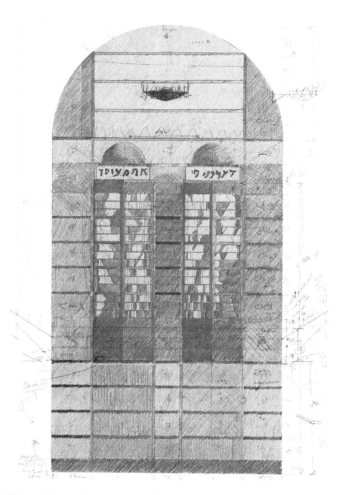

Figure 6.11 Rhythm—an array of horizontal and vertical elements in the drawing of an ark, 1994.

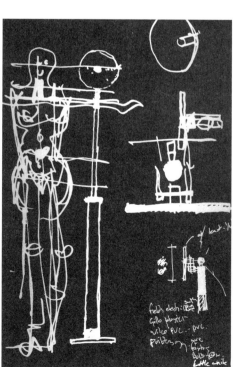

Figure 6.12a Sketch of a floor lamp (1985) scaled to the human body.

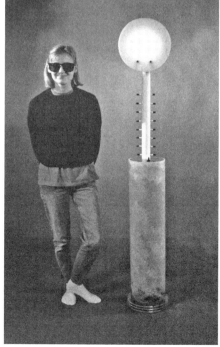

Figure 6.12b Correlations between the human body and a floor lamp.

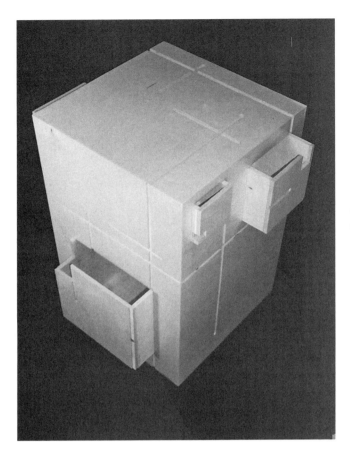

Figure 6.13 Proportional study using the Golden Section, by Janet Flory, 2000.

Proportion is the geometric correlations between parts and between parts and the whole. The design of the storage unit shown in Figure 6.13 is concerned primarily with proportional composition (formal geometric order) and secondarily with size or scale.

Scale

Furniture very often appears larger or smaller in its intended spatial context than it did in the shop where it was fabricated. The perception of **scale** depends upon the size of the furniture and the spatial context in which it is placed. When the surrounding spatial environment changes, the relative perception of size will change as well, though the proportions of the furniture have not changed. Furniture draws relationships between objects and space, thereby giving scale to a room, but it also draws relationships to the human body, thereby indirectly giving scale to the room based upon the body.

Parallel to the idea of *relative size* but different in focus is the scale in which designers sketch, draw, draft, or think about furniture. Initial conceptual ideas may be delineated at any scale. A plan of a space showing the furniture layout might be sketched, drafted, or plotted at ¼" = 1'-0" or at ⅛" = 1'-0". Interior elevations or sections showing furniture in elevation may be sketched, drawn, or plotted at ½" = 1'-0" scale (Figure 6.14). Detailed hard-line drawings or plotted *working drawings* at a scale of 3" = 1'-0" (25 percent of full size) is the conventional scale used to document the overall dimensions of individual pieces of furniture (Figure 6.15). It is helpful to show the edge profile, joinery, and mechanical features (as detailed section drawings) at full scale.

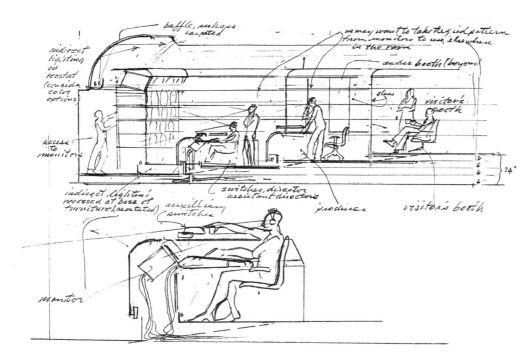

Figure 6.14 A ½″ = 1′-0″ scale plan, schematic furniture layout for NBC studio, sketch by Gil Born.

Placement and orientation are important aspects of furniture design. Because architects and interior designers incorporate furniture into the plans and sections of their drawings, designers should think about the context of furniture in the conception of design and be able to sketch, model, and develop furniture designs in a range of scales from ⅛″ = 1′-0″ to full scale.

Proportion

Proportion is not about size, nor is it about the perception of scale. It is the mathematical relationships of a part, or parts of a design, to other parts within a given field or frame of

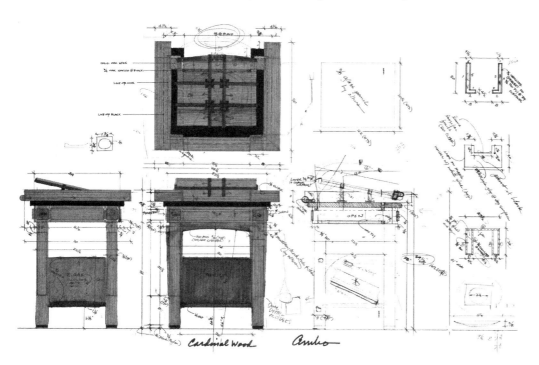

Figure 6.15 3″ = 1′-0″ scale—working drawings.

reference. We recognize furniture by its proportions, identifying the relationships between seat pan to seat back and leg dimensions to table height dimensions. Proportion is the relationship between width and length and, concurrently, between height and depth. Furniture can appear visually heavy or light, compressed or extended. How we characterize the physical and spatial relationships of furniture reveals proportional relationships of the design.

Proportion is based upon a variety of tangible references. The human body is the most common reference used in the design of furniture. Other proportional systems include mathematical or geometric systems such as the *Golden Mean,* the *Fibonacci series of numbers,* the *root system, fractal geometry,* and *logarithmic* or *parabolic geometry. The Power of Limits,* written by Gyorgy Doczy, is a good resource for further reading on proportion.

DESIGN THINKING

Design draws upon working methods and processes guided by specific ways of thinking:

- **Empirical knowledge** gained by doing, synthesized from prior experience (e.g., painting, driving, cooking, etc.)
- Intuition and judgment guided by subjective and objective assessment
- Deductive and inductive reasoning based upon rational, logical, and linear working methods to formulate connections between ideas and concrete realities
- Abductive modes of operating, creative associations—improvisational methods of working

Furniture design results from all four ways of working. However, deductive and inductive reasoning are the most teachable methods of design and therefore are described in this section.

Inductive reasoning involves an understanding of ideas and concepts that stem from specific knowledge and concrete realities. Designing a chair around the limitations of a particular material or specific joinery techniques entails the use of the inductive process in a search for form. Mistakes encountered along the way are considered research for both the designer and the maker. Mistakes can help improve ideas and processes that over time develop into intuitive working processes.

Deductive reasoning is a process of generating concrete realities from conceptual or form-inspired beginnings. It involves working and thinking that begin with conceptual ideas and develop into grounded specifics. Based upon a *conjecture-analysis* model, designers put forward ideas through sketching, drawing, or modeling and then proceed to analyze and critique the effort, seeking to refine and transform the idea into a specific resolution. The process is repeated (many times) until the designer is able to synthesize all areas into a workable, resolved design.

Deductive and inductive reasoning are linear processes involving conjecture and analysis, but design is not always linear or logical. Furniture designers are creative individuals with a capacity to think laterally, intuitively, tangentially, or thematically. However, lateral thinking knows no conclusive endpoint in the design process, and at some point, designers need to stop designing and test what they have accomplished.

Abductive modes of operating are processes that formulate associative links—often guided by metaphor or allegory. Abductive operations are not rationally directed; however, these often guide the process that most designers use to design. Designing furniture is a mix of rational-linear working processes and intuitive-subjective decisions made throughout the conception, development, and resolution phases of the design process.

Construing and Constructing

Designing furniture is a creative activity shaped by the dialogue between thinking and making. Thinking and making bond the processes of design with the limits of fabrication. With hands firmly grounded in the world of materials and tools and the mind engaged in the ever-expanding realm of ideas, furniture designers work to connect and infuse ideas with physical realities.

How furniture looks and feels is often dependent upon how well it was made. Furniture designers attempt to design well-engineered, sturdy furniture, but the academic and professional division between design and fabrication can make the process of investigating and resolving engineered solutions difficult. Hand drawings and computer renderings respond neither to applied forces nor to the properties of material. Scaled models can respond to gravity and lateral forces but cannot reveal the integrity of materials and the strength of joinery in the reduced scale of a study model. Full-sized **mock-ups** communicate a sense of scale and function to the designer but may have little correlation to the actual material or the tactile experience of furniture (Figure 6.16). The full process of design must include making a prototype, an exact or nearly exact version of the finished or manufactured piece, capable of experiential use and testing. There are many variables to consider in designing furniture. Full-sized model studies can help investigate and determine many variables in the process of design (Figure 6.17).

Reflecting upon "the making" often results in better-engineered and better-fabricated furniture. In this regard, the design process should include a three-dimensional sketch, one or more studies of structural promise, scale model(s), full-scale mock-ups, mechanically tested models, and working prototypes.

Figure 6.16 Mock-up of a reclining design, Denmark's International Study Program's summer workshop.

Figure 6.17 Full-sized 1:1 study model for a garden chair, molded steel wire, by Poul Kjærholm, 1953.

Bold Studies

Bold Furniture's CEO turned to design students in the College of Design, Architecture, Art, and Planning at the University of Cincinnati to design a new line of Bold workstations with tables, storage units, and more. For two academic quarters in 2005, students researched, sketched, modeled, and fabricated a series of full-sized mock-ups exploring ideas for the frame, the need for storage space, various solutions for security, and pragmatic aspects such as where to put the laptop, drawings, books, and so on. Students worked collaboratively and developed several design ideas using hand and computer drawings and a series of working prototypes (Figures 6.18a–6.18c). Full-sized mock-ups gave students the opportunity to analyze technical aspects, test how the designs functioned, and judge the aesthetics of their work. Mock-ups indicated that further depth was needed for storing equipment and helped to determine the height of the shelves and work surfaces. Using plywood and welded steel,

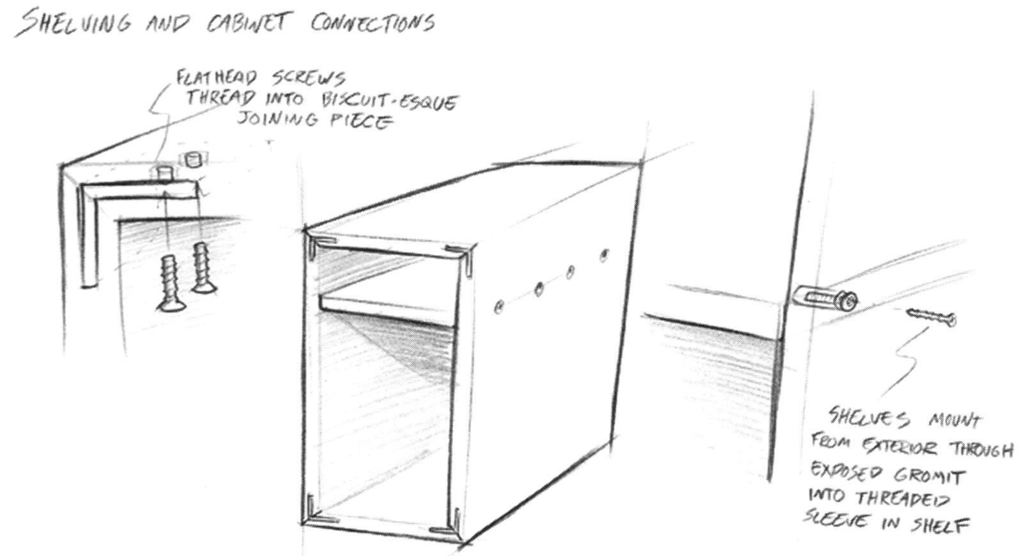

Figure 6.18a Bold studies—initial idea generation, pencil studies.

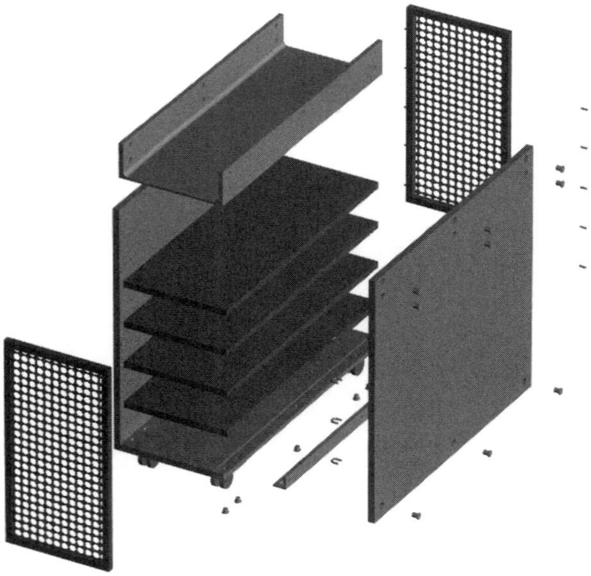

Figure 6.18b Bold studies—computer-rendered exploded axonometric view of the storage unit on casters.

Figure 6.18c Bold studies—computer-rendered perspective of a workstation, 2005.

Figure 6.19a Bold studies—working prototype of one of the workstations.

Figure 6.19b Bold studies—working prototype in use.

Figure 6.19c Bold studies—working prototype in use.

students verified their design ideas within the spatial context of the design studio and took the opportunity to test and resolve many details (Figures 6.19a–6.19c). The design explorations generated new ideas being considered by Bold Furniture.

Making Prototypes

Detail studies can be modeled or drawn at full scale and are useful in resolving difficult or complicated aspects of design. When the opportunity arises, making a working prototype at full scale can help test and analyze aspects of the design. A working prototype allows one to refine design ideas before committing to production. Charles and Ray Eames were renowned for making working prototypes of their designs. Figure 6.20 shows a rough but effective full-sized mock-up fabricated in 1945 to help resolve the dimensions and angles

Figure 6.20 Mock-up for the Eames Lounge (1945), fabricated by Charles and Ray Eames.

Figure 6.21 Museum board model, Saint Paul United Methodist Church, Dayton, Ohio, at ⅛″ = 1'-0" scale.

of the classic *Eames Lounge.* These efforts were absolutely necessary. Through their continued efforts in fabricating prototypes and making models, the Eameses were able to design and produce many classic furniture pieces. In this regard, modeling efforts in the process of design can be seen as a collection of explorations and tests. These explorations not only improve the current project, but also carry over to the next series of projects.

Scaled Models

Scaled models of furniture placed in interior models show relationships between furnishings and interior space and reveal notions of scale, layout, and proportion. Models of buildings and interior spaces can be fabricated precisely and relatively quickly out of white museum board, *foamcore,* or basswood (Figure 6.21). These models serve as excellent means to study furniture in its intended spatial context. Interior models can be fabricated at a small scale (e.g., ⅛″ = 1'-0" or ¼″ = 1'-0") to resolve general spatial relationships so that decisions about material selection, color, and texture can be explored in rendered drawings or in larger, more detailed models (e.g., 3″ = 1'-0") once the overall spatial context is resolved.

Materials can inspire design ideas. Working with materials in the development of design increases the effectiveness of the design process. In this regard, *material boards* and material sample arrangements are effective means of helping designers consider physical and visual materials for interior space, furniture, or a building. Composing material boards is an art. Consequently, the presentation can either inform and inspire or misinform and mislead. The time and effort required to compose material boards are significant investments. Designing with immediate access to materials is the key point.

The tooling and molds that produce cast or molded elements are essential to preproduction testing of mass-produced furniture. A rough scaled model of a two-piece mold

(Figure 6.22) was necessary in order to understand how to produce *Non Rubber,* a chair designed by Boris Berlin of Komplot Design (Figure 6.23). The mold would eventually be made out of aluminum, but the quick study model gave the designers and fabricators confidence in how to proceed with the design. This knowledge was used to refine important details of the single-formed iron and polyurethane rubber (PUR) chair so that it could be produced and easily released from an aluminum mold.

Tools, materials, and digital fabrication technologies have significantly evolved over the past 20 years. With the advent of plaster printers and five-axis computational numerical control (CNC) devices, working prototypes are easier and more economically feasible to produce than in the past.

In the digital age, will furniture designers maintain an understanding of when to use a hand block plane or the distinction between shellac and tung-oil finishes on wood furniture? What might happen when designers are able to go directly from digital design to digital production entirely by digital means using only digital tools? The challenge to keep current and maintain comprehensive breadth and extensive depth regarding hand, machine, and digital technologies affects every designer today and requires constant effort.

Figure 6.22 Scaled 1:5 model of a two-part form for Non Rubber.

It often takes an enormous number of sketches, explorations, and iterative model studies to end up with a design that is well composed, technically resolved, comfortable, functional, aesthetically pleasing, and economically feasible. Designing furniture has *iceberg-like* connotations in the sense that 90 percent of the time spent on design is typically used to

Figure 6.23 Non Rubber chairs, designed by Komplot Design (2000), for Källemo AB, Sweden.

explore alternative variations and subtle iterations, many of which are abandoned in the process of design. Processes of exploring and refining design ideas are critical, even if the efforts do not seem apparent in the final result.

DESIGN ETHOS

Accessible Design

Accessibility is concerned with issues of access and egress, while **universal design** is a concept of designing for transgenerational use, left- or right-handed users, pan-cultural uses, individuals without vision, and so on. Furniture designed with accessibility in mind would exclude beanbag chairs, hammocks, and chairs with narrow seat pans and tall arms because of the difficulty some persons have in accessing these designs. In these examples, getting in can be difficult and getting out often more so. Tables too high or too low and chairs in which the seat pan is too high or too narrow can be challenging to access.

Accessible furniture includes lift chairs, adjustable tables, and adjustable seating. Chairs and tables that are lightweight, have movable casters, and are stackable so that the floors can be cleaned or the space rearranged respond to issues of accessibility. Arms on a chair can help the elderly sit down and stand up, but care must be taken so that they don't prevent larger people from gaining access.

Accessible work surfaces include tables, desks, and countertop heights that can be used by people in wheelchairs. To be considered accessible, table heights should be 28 to 34 inches (71 to 76.5 cm) above the floor, with at least 27 inches (68.5 cm) clear for knee space.[4]

Codes, Guidelines, and Standards (Health, Safety, and Welfare)

Codes and technical standards exist for the health, safety, and welfare of individual users. Many have been developed for specific types of furniture, especially chairs. Dental chairs are specified by the *International Organization for Standardization* (ISO) standard 6875. Beanbag chairs are specified by the *American National Standards Institute* (ANSI) standard ASTM F1912-98. ASTM is the *American Society for Testing and Materials*. The *National Fire Protection Association* (NFPA) establishes standards for flame spread and smoke development ratings for furniture finishes and fabrics. Ergonomic requirements for office work with visual display terminals (VDTs) have been specified by ISO 9241-5:1988. ISO 7174 specifies stability of rocking and tilting chairs. ASTM F1858-98 specifies lawn chairs.

In public and common use areas, seating space must be provided for wheelchairs. Restaurants must provide wheelchair access to tables. Fixed-seat assemblies must allow for wheelchair placement at various seating locations. These regulations are enforced by the *Americans with Disabilities Act Accessibility Guidelines* (ADAAG).

The *Business and Institutional Furniture Manufacturer's Association* (BIFMA) establishes guidelines for testing commercial-grade chairs. Performance specifications include:

- Chair back strength of 150 lb
- Chair stability if weight is transferred completely to the front or back legs
- Leg strength of 75 lb applied 1 inch (2.54 cm) from the bottom of the leg
- Seat strength of 225 lb dropped from 6 inches (15.2 cm) above the seat

Figure 6.24 Testing the Equa chair's split shell made of glass-fiber-reinforced polyester, which permits the seat to operate independently of the side elements. Manufactured by Herman Miller.

■ Seat cycle strength of 100,000 repetitions of 125 lb dropped from 2 inches (5 cm) above the seat

Technical specifications define "proof" loads for chairs, which determine that under higher loads a chair may be damaged, but it must not fail. Institutions will often reference these standards or add their own specifications when purchasing furniture. Companies depend upon standards for quality assurance (Figure 6.24).

Green Design

> Concern for sustainability is more than a matter of compliance with industrial regulation or environmental impact analysis. It embraces a commitment to conceive of the work of design as a part of a wider context in time and place.
>
> The Hannover Principles, William McDonough Architects, 1992

For years, the mantra for *sustainable design* was "renew, reuse, and recycle." Today, furniture designers invoke **green design** in more complex and subtle ways. Green design considers distribution and packaging, biodegradability, the life cycle of materials and products, **off-gassing,** toxicity in fabrication or use, and a number of other important factors including human rights and labor standards.

Sustainable design solutions minimize negative and maximize positive impacts including social, economic, ethical, and environmental considerations. Leading-edge environmental thinkers and policy makers believe that sustainable development will require a "factor 4" improvement in the environmental performance of goods and services. This means reduc-

Figure 6.25 IKEA—furnishings in the showroom (distribution center) are sold flat-pack.

ing by at least 300 percent over the next 20–30 years the amount of resources needed and the pollution generated to deliver goods and services to consumers (Dr. Ernst Ulrich von Weizsäcker et al. 1997).

Flat-pack furniture can reduce the cost of distribution. IKEA has marketed and sold furniture to the public using this method and is recognized as the industry leader for producing inexpensive, practical, and well-designed products (Figure 6.25). The conservation of endangered materials such as Brazilian rosewood is sustained because many companies no longer offer the material for public consumption. Herman Miller stopped manufacturing the *Eames Lounge and Ottoman* in Brazilian rosewood.

Today, many major lumber retail chains buy wood from sustainable forests and offer certified harvested wood to their customers. There are two international forest certification programs, both of which monitor and certify the harvesting and transportation of lumber. The Forest Stewardship Council (FSC) offers a control certification that monitors the transportation and purchase of lumber, giving consumers assurance that the wood was harvested in sustainable forests and certified from stump to retail.[5] The Sustainable Forestry Initiative (SFI) is another international program, which monitors the harvesting and transportation of sustainable lumber. Retailers pay a fee to receive certified woods and advertise to consumers that they have done so.[6]

Since 2003, Brazil no longer exports mahogany wood species, as mandated by its government. Up to that time, Brazil exported 30 percent of the world's supply of South American mahogany woods, which along with Cuban mahogany is considered to be the highest-quality mahogany in the world. In response, many retailers and production factories have secured woods with grain and color characteristics similar to those of Brazilian mahogany, such as sapele.

Figure 6.26a Z BENCH—wood support, fabrication, Juan Zouain, design by Emiliano Godoy, 2005.

Figure 6.26b Z BENCH—detail of *Zacate* and wood.

Figure 6.26c Z BENCH—in use.

Many ready-made cabinets are fabricated with a thin wood veneer, covering a substrate of wood shavings pressed together with a lot of glue, which can emit formaldehyde gases for years. Consider cabinets made from solid wood, such as a hard pine cut from sustainable forests, or materials that are not endangered or in limited supply. Regenerative bamboo grows quickly, yet is comparable in strength to red oak wood. Choose stains and finishes that contain no volatile organic compounds.

Furniture designer Emiliano Godoy has been researching biodegradable materials for use in design for several years and came upon *zacate*, a rush used in Mexico and other countries of Latin America to scrub dishes or as a bathing sponge. Inspired by the rush, he designed the *Z-Bench* to highlight the contrast between zacate and wood, treating the materials in completely different ways. Conventional cabinet-making techniques were used for the wooden structure, while the uncovered and basically raw zacate generates visual tension and surprise (Figures 6.26a–c).

According to Godoy, "Biological materials are renewable, carbon neutral, and they can share disposal mechanisms. However, we have yet not enough options to substitute technological materials with biological ones. It is clear to me that we need more materials to work with, which participate as active components in Nature's biomes, and which can be designed to have no environmental impact, or even contribute to the regeneration of what industrial activity has destroyed."[7]

The Z-Bench was designed for the show "Diseño Muerto" in Mexico City, organized by Edgar Orlaineta in 2005 for the Galería de Arte Mexicano (GAM).

A series of chair and table designs were conceived and fabricated by Bär + Knell Design between 1993 and 1997. The furniture was produced by heat-forming 100 percent recycled plastic waste. Their furniture designs achieve aesthetic and ecological targets, raise the ethical bar of green design, and increase environmental awareness. The chair and table shown in Figure 6.27

Figure 6.27 Chair and table made from recycled plastic waste— Bär + Knell Design (1996).

are two of the many furniture pieces (chairs, tables, and screens) designed by Bär + Knell Design.

A study of the material life cycle of furniture has determined that most products are made of nonrenewable materials and, at the end of their useful life, will be discarded and become landfill. The dilemma today is that the sum of the undesired by-products from furniture and other commercial products exceeds the capacity of the environment to absorb them. Traditional cradle-to-grave concepts are beginning to be reconsidered out of concern for the planet's environment and ecosystem. William McDonough and Michael Braungart, from McDonough Braungart Design Chemistry, in conjunction with many other individuals and firms, have reconceived the paradigm of green design to embrace the concept of *cradle-to-cradle* thinking and have developed a collective body of knowledge in biological and technical areas of design. Green design reflects a new way of thinking about design. It is an important frame of reference and is in the foreground of many creative designers.

GUBI II is stackable, lightweight, comfortable, durable, and green. Boris Berlin and Poul Christiansen of Komplot Design designed the chair for the furniture company GUBI. The chair is available in a plain color or two-colored (front different than back) felt made from polyester fibers, a major part of which has been extracted from used plastic water bottles and transformed into a felt material (Figure 6.28). In one single process, two mats made from this felt are molded around a steel tube frame. In this way the industrial process is minimized considerably, since no subsequent upholstery or mounting process is required. There is no inner wooden or plastic shell to support the construction. The supporting qualities are incorporated in the felt. The combination of a straightforward look, great strength, light weight, and easy maintenance makes *GUBI II* ideal for cafeterias, meeting areas, restaurants, and auditoriums.

Rohner Textile AG is a textile company based in Switzerland that produces textiles for Design Tex and Herman Miller, among other companies. This relatively small company

Figure 6.28 GUBI II, designed by Komplot Design (2006), manufactured by GUBI A/S.

Figure 6.29 CH 24—the Y Chair (or Wishbone Chair), designed by Hans J. Wegner (1949), fabricated by Carl Hansen & Son, Denmark.

produces *Climatex Lifecycle™*, which is made of 65 percent wool and 35 percent ramie. It is considered a Jacquard textile, and is biodegradable and environmentally sound, with climate control aspects (making it a good choice for a variety of climate-sensitive situations). It took 18 months to research and manufacture Climatex. When the finished product was introduced to the market at the Solomon Guggenheim Museum in New York City, William McDonough commented in his speech to the attending designers and architects, "This is the first product of the Next Industrial Revolution. What we are now saying is that environmental quality can be an integral part of the design of every product. It is no longer a wishful option."[8]

Many furniture designers, including Kaare Klint and Hans J. Wegner, incorporated twisted paper and cane woven in the seat pans of their chair designs during the 1950s and 1960s because alternative means of upholstery were too costly (Figure 6.29). **Twisted paper** is biodegradable, readily available, local, inexpensive, and comfortable. As one considers green solutions, it becomes easier to recognize environmentally friendly materials, many of which were used before the terms *green* and *sustainable design* became part of today's design lexicon.

Universal Design

Universal design attempts to meet the needs of people of all ages, abilities, and cognitive skills. Set forth as a concept by Ron Mace of the Center for Universal Design at North

Figure 6.30 Universal design—left- or right-handed *Whale* mouse, manufactured by Humanscale.

Carolina State University in 1990, universal design focuses on the "range of abilities" rather than the "limit of disabilities" (Figure 6.30). Universal design strives to accommodate the greatest range of users (8–80 years of age) and abilities (wheelchair users, arthritic users, blind and deaf users, etc.), regardless of the user's height, weight, or health. *Universal design* is an inclusive notion that seeks to eliminate barriers relative to use and social function.[9]

Adjustability and size transformation are strategies used to address the challenge of designing for all people. However, design that responds to a wide range of users without transformation or adjustment reveals inherent qualities of universal design.

Examples of universal design of furniture include:

- Desks that are designed for left- *and* right-handed users
- Desks and tables that have adjustable height work surfaces
- Mobile desks and pedestals to rearrange the work space for personal needs
- Writing tablets for both left- *and* right-handed users
- Tables that accommodate all users, if only for limited tasks
- Chairs that consider access and egress as well as ergonomic qualities
- Shelving that accommodates wheelchair users
- Case goods that can be opened and accessed by blind individuals
- Cabinets that can be utilized by individuals with arthritis

FURNITURE DESIGN PROCESS

Designing entails the transformation of ideas into physical form.[10]

Designing furniture relies upon a continual process of making informed, objective, and subjective judgments. The process involves formulating conjectures about form and function, analyzing the efforts, and synthesizing design ideas into a product. It is known as the *conjecture/analysis/synthesis* method. The process is cyclical, one that the designer revisits time and time again with every project. As previously discussed, designers generally begin the process of design with a sketch or simple model and proceed to explore ideas and conjectures by sketching, drawing, using computer software, and making study models. Sometimes designers begin the process of design in the shop and work directly with tools and materials to generate or explore ideas that can result in new forms or induce new ways of considering design ideas. During this phase, assumptions may need to be suspended in order to synthesize fresh ideas, consider new materials, and integrate aspects of utility into a coherent whole.

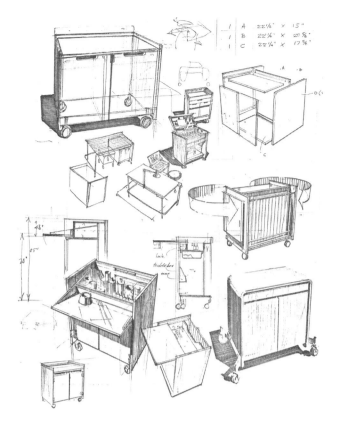

Figure 6.31 Initial furniture design studies.

Sketching, Drawing, Computer Rendering, and Model Making

Sketching is an important design skill that helps designers think visually on paper. Design generally evolves by sketching—typically in a freehand manner, freely annotated, allowing the designer to explore ideas as they occur (Figure 6.31). Sketching is an informal, image-based investigation. It is a way of graphically communicating ideas.

Model studies can serve the same function as sketching and are an equally valid method for beginning the design process. At a later stage, design ideas are drawn, technically drafted by hand, or plotted and can be rendered by the computer (Figure 6.32). Today, modeling

Figure 6.32 FormZ computer model used to visualize the design of an ark and bima, Isaac M. Wise Center, Cincinnati, Ohio.

Figure 6.33 Drawing and designing at full scale.

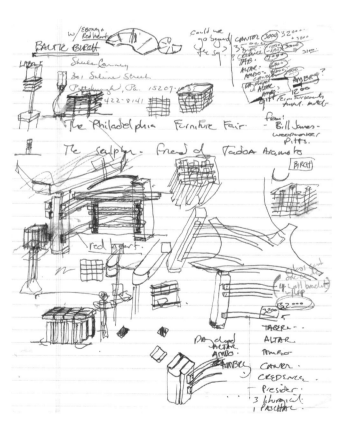

Figure 6.34 Initial design sketches for an altar.

software is becoming more intuitive, enabling the development and rapid visualization of initial design ideas. Computer software is beginning to emerge as a design tool in the initial phases of design as more and more designers are learning how to use software programs such as *Sketch-it, FormZ, AutoCad, 3-D Studio Max, Alias,* and *Maya.* Consider computer software as more than just a tool for visualization. Digital programs and digital tools to generate design are available to everyone.

Sketching and drawing help designers study composition. Ideally, drawing should be done at full scale (Figure 6.33). This helps designers consider aspects of form, proportion, and detail at 1:1 and consider accurate measurements and materials in the development of a design. It reduces the void between designing how something might look and how it might be fabricated. Drawing is more than a means to an end. It is a technique designers use to explore, see, analyze, and refine their work.

Full-scale drawing correlates with full-scale thinking, but there are times when it is best to begin the process by freely exploring ideas at a reduced scale such as 1:10 in metric or 1" = 1' (Figure 6.34). It is often easier to consider

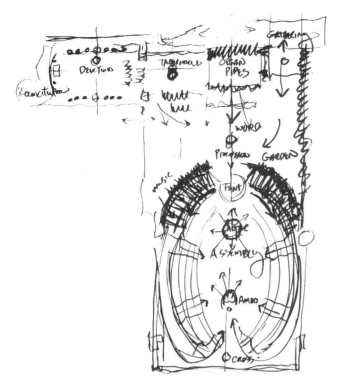

Figure 6.35 Esquisse sketch, showing initial ideas about layout and use of space.

and compare initial ideas and explore variations of design in this manner. Designers utilize this method often, usually in the initial phases, trying to get the fullest capacity out of their sketchbooks or anything available to draw upon.

An **esquisse** sketch (Figure 6.35) is an expression of the basic or essential idea/concept of a design. This drawing type stems from a methodology taught at L'ecole des Beaux Arts in Paris at the turn of the 19th century. An esquisse sketch can guide the design process through fabrication by serving as a reference for the designer in order to help clarify design intentions. Though the line quality, line weight, and medium used to communicate a design intention are often rough and unclear in technical detail, the basic composition and idea can be expressed in effective ways. Drafted drawings, computer renderings, and model studies typically cannot express such general ideas as effectively as an esquisse sketch.

A **parti** sketch (Figure 6.36) communicates the basic physical and spatial components of a design. It is an analytical diagram, useful in developing an understanding of compositional aspects in design. A parti sketch can take the form of a section, elevation, plan, or axonometric. Its primary use is to show the basic elements and components of a design in a simple and direct manner. A parti sketch is helpful in clarifying how a design is formally conceived, which can be useful in determining the materials and details in design.

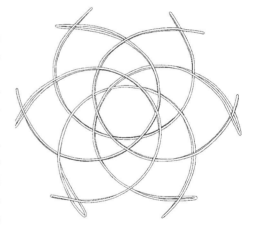

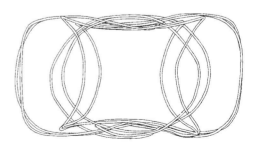

Figure 6.36 Parti sketch, showing the physical and spatial composition of elements.

Figure 6.37 Iterative sketches, overlay studies drawn at 1:2 scale.

Iterative sketches (Figure 6.37) help designers evolve and refine design ideas. Such sketches (and drawings) explore variations of selected aspects of design while other aspects remain constant. Iterative sketches could include a series of overlays used to investigate a detail of furniture while the overall composition remains constant. Table profiles, seat back angles, material joinery, and specific proportional investigations of an arm of a chair or a leg of a table are examples of specific areas that can be explored using iterative sketches. Furniture designers may complete hundreds of iterative sketches for a single piece of furniture. Iterative sketches can involve any drawing type (i.e. perspective study, elevation, or section study) and any scale of drawing, be it full-scale, reduced scale, or in some cases no particular scale but care for the relative proportions of the design. The overlay method of placing tracing paper over an existing drawing is a conventional means of producing iterations. However, the process can include a number of other methods ranging from filling a journal or notebook to executing a number of study models in the investigation or exploration of a detail, or any aspect of the design, be it material, color, or composition. Iterative sketches and study models are useful methods to refine and develop particular aspects or nuances of a design while keeping some aspects constant, which distinguishes them from explorative drawings.

The 1″ = 1′-0″ scale drawings and model studies of tables or chairs can help designers resolve compositional relationships early in the design process (Figures 6.38a, 6.38b). The 1″ = 1′-0″ scale is ideal for an initial study. It is similar to the European metric standard 1:10, which is frequently used to present the schematic resolution of furniture on a single sheet of A4 paper. The scale is large enough to resolve basic aspects of form, but larger-scale drawings are necessary to resolve technical aspects and details of a piece.

Working drawings for furniture are referred to as *fabrication drawings* (buildings are constructed, furnishings are fabricated). Fabrication drawings include the technical information necessary to fabricate the design, indicating dimensions, materials, and specifications for finish. Drafting precise hard-lined drawings is an important skill to acquire, despite the ability to use computer software to precisely render and plot furniture drawings. Fabrication relies upon exact dimensions, accurate details, use of appropriate materials, and resolved engineering. The process of drafting working drawings by hand can help designers understand each line and joint (Figure 6.39). Working drawings must represent design intentions

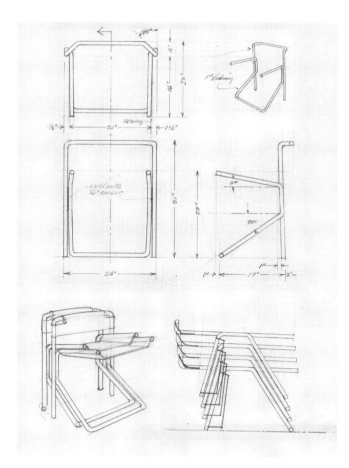

Figure 6.38a Fabrication drawing of a chair drafted at 3″ = 1′-0″ scale, by Gil Born.

Figure 6.38b Model studies at 1″ = 1′-0″ scale, by Gil Born.

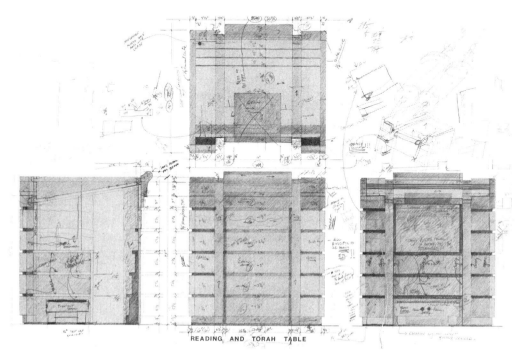

READING AND TORAH TABLE

Figure 6.39 Fabrication drawing, 3″ = 1′-0″ scale, torah table—Valley Temple, Cincinnati, Ohio, 1994.

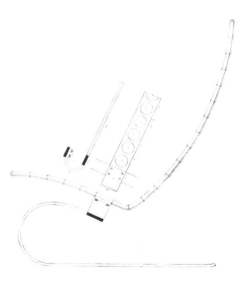

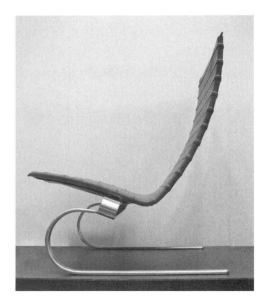

Figure 6.40a 1:1 scale working drawing—PK 20, by Poul Kjaerholm.

Figure 6.40b PK 20, designed by Poul Kjærholm (1967), manufactured by Fritz Hansen.

Figure 6.41 Wooden model, 3″ = 1′-0″ study of a lectern.

in a clear format. Fabrication drawings are typically drafted or plotted at no smaller than a 3″ = 1′-0″ scale (25 percent of full size). This is a conventional scale for submitting plans, elevations, and sections of furniture to a fabricator and is useful in resolving most aspects of furniture design. Drafting by hand or plotting computer-aided drawings (CAD) offers the degree of precision necessary to realize and communicate the dimensional relationships in furniture design (Figures 6.40a, 6.40b). Furniture drawings are usually dimensioned in inches or centimeters, not in feet and inches, which is the norm for interior and architectural construction drawings.

Model and detail studies at partial or full scale are useful means of testing and analyzing a detail, the center of balance, or any complex situation (Figure 6.41). The ability to work in three dimensions is critical to the process of developing furniture design. Models require a significant investment in time and material. Models made smaller than full size can help both designer and client see the relationships between furnishings and space, as well as notions of scale, layout, and proportion prior to fabrication. Models allow design ideas to be viewed and studied from multiple angles. Preliminary study models can be made of wood, clay, foamcore, or polymer foam to communicate the form and shape of the design. Detailed models can also be fabricated using a rapid prototyping machine. In these cases, CAD files made with various software programs can be converted directly into a polymer, wax, or plaster model using a CNC device or digital printer (Figure 6.42).

Museum board and foamcore are ideal materials to use in building models at a small scale ($\frac{1}{8}'' = 1''$-$0''$ or $\frac{1}{4}'' = 1'$-$0''$) because the off-white color of museum board enables form and space to be perceived clearly. Though museum board models lack material and color, they are quick to make, easy to modify, and photograph well in different types of light (Figure 6.43). These models can serve as explorative studies and as final presentation models. Small-scale studies are also useful in analyzing the spatial layout and compositional aspects of furniture and interior space. Models can be useful in exploring various lighting options and in studying the spatial relationships between furniture and interior space.

As the design of a chair develops, consider the effectiveness of making a mock-up of the seat pan and seat back. The mock-up might indicate whether or not further depth is needed for the seat pan and allow one to experience the design. Mock-ups are generally made at full size and communicate only partial aspects of design. Full-scale mock-ups include the entire form but are often fabricated from any available materials. A full-sized mock-up for a table can help verify the formal presence and relative scale of the table within the context of the space for which it is designed. Placing full-sized furniture mock-ups within their intended context is a good way to determine the sense of scale and spatial relationships between the human body, the furniture, and the surrounding space.

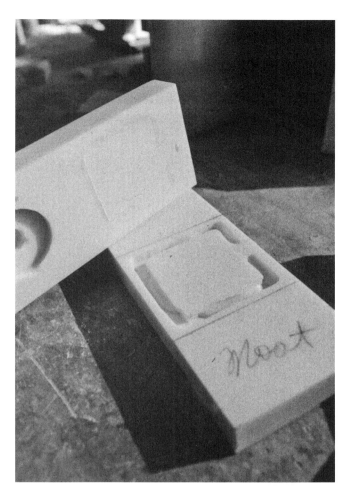

Figure 6.42 CNC—milling out solid surfacing material.

Figure 6.43 Museum board model, Chapel, Sisters of Mercy, Belmont, North Carolina. $\frac{1}{8}'' = 1'$-$0''$ scale, 2000.

In some cases, especially in the design of mass-produced furniture, working prototypes need to be fabricated. Working prototypes are the best means available to determine the size, detail, and technical nuances of a design. They can indicate aspects of design that might need to be further resolved. They serve as an effective means of evaluating the design and determining its fabrication. Full-sized working prototypes can help evaluate technical, functional, and aesthetic aspects.

FURNITURE DESIGN PHASES

Furniture design can be organized into phases. Designers can determine where they are in the process of designing furniture by understanding the expectations for each phase of work. Designers rarely skip a phase, though the process can move backward as well as forward. Designers can spend more time on one phase than another. There are few rules in design that cannot be broken.

It is ineffective to micro-manage the sequence of the design phases. However, a degree of flexibility should always be factored into the process of design. An enormous amount of time may be used to research and program ideas of "sitting" when designing a chair for the first time. The design development phase for a room divider might take a long time due to the complexity of the technical details. Nonetheless, designers are expected to understand where they are in the process of design. Organizing the phases of designing furniture into a linear structure is useful to determine where one is in the design process—if not for oneself, then for the client, who is likely to ask, "How far along in the design process are we?"

Regardless of the means and methods of design, there will always be phases to the process of design. An outline of design phases follows:

- Predesign, Research, and Programming
- Schematic Design
- Design Development
- Fabrication Drawings
- Pricing and Contract Negotiation
- Shop Drawings, Templates, and Working Prototypes
- Fabrication
- Delivery and Installation

Predesign, Research, and Programming

A well defined problem is 50% of the solution.[11]
Albert Einstein

The *predesign, research,* and *programming* phases involve necessary work that designers generally accomplish before designing a piece of furniture. Even before the research and programming phases, designers must prepare themselves by organizing their personal time and committing to the project. The design of a suite of Catholic Church furnishings may require a substantial investment of time to understand the purpose and environment in which the furniture will be placed. A significant effort may be required to understand the Catholic liturgy and the purpose of each liturgical furnishing. Designing furniture for a salon or spa may require a visit to various salons or spas to observe how hair is cut and how customers and staff interact with one another. When designing furniture for a particular space, existing architectural conditions may need to be recorded in order to accurately represent important aspects and dimensions of the space. Observation, documentation, and analysis provide an important foundation in the process of design and are considered predesign work.

Predesign, research, and programming may also entail research of technical standards driven by code, economic, or fabrication limitations. Generally, this phase of design takes a significant amount of time to complete—time that the client is not usually eager to pay for.

Programming can be as brief as a few written notes or as complex as a booklet. A program articulates in written form the goals and objectives of the design process. It is a tool to guide the design process and shape the parameters for how the design will be evaluated. It is an effort to organize and define the scope of work, the purpose of the work, the resources and conditions in which the work will be placed, and the schedule for all aspects of the work. Though they bring no guarantee of success, programming and research efforts may increase the likelihood for a successful project.

Regardless of the method one uses to determine the program and establish the intended purposes for the furniture that will be designed, basic questions can and should be considered by the designer. These questions are based upon six terms: who, what, why, when, where, and how.

WHO
- Who is in the market for this product?
- Who will use this product?
- Who will sell or distribute the product?
- Who will maintain the product?

WHAT
- What is its intended purpose?
- What are other things that it might do?
- What is the competition?
- What functions should be included?
- What is the life expectancy?
- What is the expected cost for the furniture?

WHY
- Why is the furniture design needed?
- Why would someone buy this product?
- Why is a new design needed?
- Why will the furniture be used?
- Why use hand, machine, or digital technology in its fabrication?

WHEN
- When will the furniture be used?
- When will the product require maintenance?
- When will it not have enough capacity?
- When will it be stored or moved?

WHERE
- Where will the furniture be located?
- Where should it not be located?
- Where will it be sold?

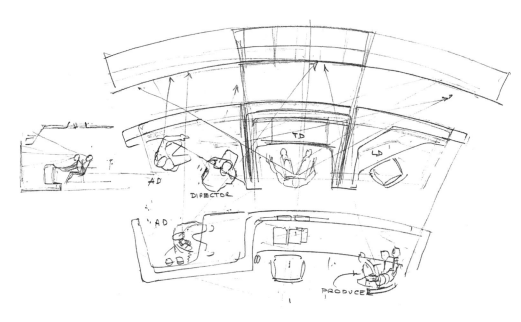

Figure 6.44 Schematic design NBC studies, drawing by Gil Born.

■ Where will its materials come from?
■ Where will it be fabricated?

HOW

■ How does it work?
■ How is it used?
■ How many functions will be served?
■ How well does it relate to all people?

Figure 6.45 Design development sketches by Gil Born.

Schematic Design

Schematic design is generally considered the first phase in the process of designing furniture. Generally, designers spend between 10 and 15 percent of their total design time on this phase of work.[12] During this phase, general decisions regarding size and form are explored. Sketches and rough study models are made to communicate ideas and study compositional aspects (Figure 6.44). There may be some degree of resolution regarding material selection or detail, but generally these aspects are unresolved.

Design Development

As a rule, designers spend between 15 and 20 percent of their total design time on *design development*.[13] In this phase, designers refine ideas, formulate general dimensions and materials, and resolve the direction of the work. At the end of this phase, decisions regarding size, proportion, material, color selection, and visual quality will have been explored and generally made. While further resolution of detail and joinery may be needed, the basic formal qualities of the design should be determined at this point (Figure 6.45).

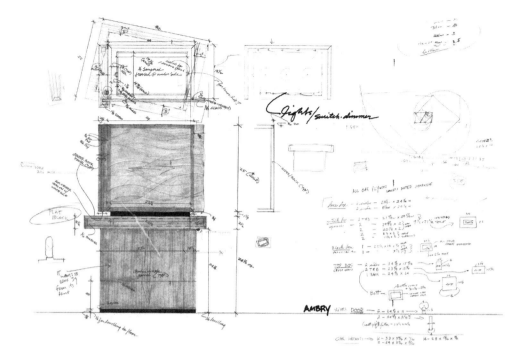

Fabrication Drawings

Fabrication drawings, also referred to as *construction drawings, working drawings,* or *contract documents,* are given by designers to fabricators for pricing and fabrication. All critical views of the design need to be shown and clearly delineated on paper or in the computer before fabrication can begin. Generally, designers spend between 30 and 40 percent of their time on this phase of work.[14]

In preparing fabrication drawings, designers explicitly resolve and delineate remaining design decisions before fabrication. During this phase, dimensions are specified within a sixteenth of an inch. Material selection, grain direction of the wood, specifications for quality, finish selection, fabrication details, and technical specifications must be complete. For mass-produced furniture fabricated out of metals and plastics, the tolerances are even finer, requiring dimensional resolution to within a thousandth of an inch. Depending upon the fabricator and the nature of the furniture, this phase of the work marks the point in time when the designer has satisfied his or her responsibility to the client for resolving the design prior to fabrication. Though more work lies ahead for the furniture designer, completed fabrication drawings are a major hurdle in the transformation from ideas into built form (Figure 6.46).

Technical sources are available to help designers determine how to specify and detail contract documents and how to avoid undesirable surprises in fabrication. The *Architectural Woodwork Institute* (AWI) produces an excellent reference that outlines standards and specifications for designing and fabricating wood furniture.

Pricing and Contract Negotiation

One can approximate the probable cost of fabrication during design development, but it is impossible to accurately determine the cost of fabricating furniture until the construction

Figure 6.47 Michael Toombs and Jim Postell discussing the scope of work and expectations for fabrication—bid negotiation phase.

drawings and specifications are complete. Mies van der Rohe said, "God is in the details";[15] he was right, but he neglected to add that "the Devil is in there, too." Details can significantly affect the cost of fabrication, which raises the question of why designers give fabricators their drawings after the contract documents are complete. It makes sense to work with fabricators as early as possible in the design process. Once the contract drawings are complete, a fabricator reviews and accurately determines how much it will cost and how long it will take to fabricate and install the proposed work. During this phase, the designer answers questions raised by the fabricator and organizes the process for submitting and receiving bids. If there are problems in fabricating the design, the fabricator discusses them ahead of time with the designer, who then works to resolve them, often in collaboration with the fabricator.

When the designer is not the fabricator, the most important thing the designer can do to promote the eventual success of the proposed work is to take an active role in determining the right fabricator for the job. A good fabricator can foresee problems in the design before fabrication occurs and work with the designer to resolve them and improve the design. A good fabricator will review the functional and technical aspects with the designer and work collaboratively to modify and improve the work whenever appropriate. Contract negotiation involves these considerations as well as determining the costs of fabrication. This phase requires communications and meetings with fabricators, artisans, and craftspeople. Managing the phase of pricing and contract negotiation consumes approximately 5 percent of the total time that designers spend on a project.[16] The result determines the scope of work and the cost, establishes the responsibilities of various individuals, and outlines a schedule for completing and installing the proposed work (Figure 6.47).

Figure 6.48a Emiliano Godoy preparing a two-part wood form.

Figure 6.48b Pressing *Maplex* (cellulose fiber material) in a two-part press.

Figure 6.48c A working prototype of the Weidmann chair.

Shop Drawings, Templates, and Working Prototypes

Once a fabricator is selected and a contract between client and fabricator is made, the fabricator prepares shop drawings and templates and, in some cases, produces a working prototype to test aspects of the design. Shop drawings and working prototypes represent the most detailed and explicit type of information about the design. They are made during the transitional phase between design and fabrication. Shop drawings might lead to a mock-up of a detail or indicate the need to review and modify the contract drawings. Shop drawings should always be reviewed and approved by the designer. These are the documents that remain well after production is over and are referred to if disputes or problems arise.

Working prototypes are useful in testing and resolving aspects of form and structure. They mark the last phase prior to producing the final work. This phase in the process of design is critical—taking carefully rendered drawings of design ideas into the most challenging phase. Some furniture designers, such as Emiliano Godoy, work comfortably in making formwork and working prototypes to test and help improve design ideas. A working prototype was made for the *Weidmann* chair (Figures 6.48a–6.48c), which was helpful in studying and testing aspects of the design prior to production (Figure 6.49).

Templates and forms are often made in order to fabricate a working prototype. In some cases, templates and formwork represent a significant part of the cost of fabricating a piece of furniture. Designing and making formwork is an art unto itself, and needs to be carefully conceived and resolved. This important task is typically left to the fabricator, as are the means and methods of fabricating furniture. However, due to the inherent integration of structure, form, and aesthetics in many designs, the boundaries between design and fabrication often are not apparent.

Figure 6.49 The Weidmann chair (2005), designed by Emiliano Godoy and Erika Hanson.

Figure 6.50 Furniture—in the making at Heartwood Furniture Company, 1993.

Fabrication

At this point in the design process, the significance of a good working relationship between designer and fabricator will become apparent. Designers can observe the fabrication process but generally do not *supervise* it, unless the designer is offering a *design/build* service to the client. Nonetheless, observation of the fabrication phase is an important responsibility of the furniture designer. Generally, designers spend between 30 and 35 percent of their total time on this phase of work.[17] When the scope of work is modified, the fabricator will invoice the client for the additional time and material.

The designer's role during this phase is to observe and monitor the process, describe the process to the client, and assist in problem resolution as issues arise. It is important to underscore that *observing* the fabrication is not *supervising* the work. Supervision would imply responsibility for the work and create liability for the designer should problems occur. Designers are responsible for the design, fabricators are responsible for the means and methods of fabrication, and clients are responsible for approvals and payment (Figure 6.50).

Delivery and Installation

Coordination with the client and fabricator for the delivery, installation, and final approval of the completed work marks the activities in this phase of work. This phase includes careful preparation to transport the work, repair damaged pieces that result from transport, install built-in elements, carefully place furniture throughout a space, and provide a schedule for the client for proper care and maintenance of the completed work. A suite of furnishings that includes case goods and casework can take several days to transport, deliver, and

Figure 6.51 Installation of liturgical furnishings for a chapel in Belmont, North Carolina.

install. Delivery and installation is an important phase of work that needs to be carefully planned and included in the overall cost of fabricating the work (Figure 6.51).

PROFESSIONAL AND DISCIPLINARY BOUNDARIES

> Where do architects and designers get their ideas?
> The answer, of course, is mainly from other architects and designers.[18]

Paradigms indicate and underpin general perceptions and assumptions about a subject held by a specific group of people. Architects, interior designers, industrial designers, and fine artists approach furniture design from different perspectives. Traditionally, architects and interior designers work to emphasize a "sense of place." Emphasis is placed upon the selection and location of custom furniture for a specific site. The architect works to create spatial, material, and ornamental correlations between a building and its furnishings. Furniture includes an enormous range of site-specific, mass-produced, built-in, and freestanding pieces. Furniture designed by architects and interior designers often complements the materials, details, and fabrication technologies of a building and its interior spaces. The furnishings generally are produced in limited runs, fabricated for spaces within and throughout a building.

An industrial designer is trained to focus on human factors and industrial processes throughout the development of design. Industrial designers are professionally invested in designing mass-produced work. Though architects incorporate mass-produced elements in their designs, architecture itself does not embrace the notion of being mass-produceable because of the unique characteristics of a place. The notion of *place* distinguishes the two fields in significant ways. Architects such as Frank Lloyd Wright, Charles Rennie Mackintosh,

Mies van der Rohe, and Alvar Aalto conceived, developed, and fabricated furniture for specific interior spaces and building environments. The mass production of their furniture designs for public consumption came later and is another story altogether.

Furniture designed for mass production is independent of specific architectural environments in both form and material. This establishes an independence of furniture from its surrounding environment and advances the notion of furniture's *detachment* from an architectural frame of reference. The differences between the professions are significant and directly impact the approach to furniture design, the design process, fabrication, and the delivery of products to the market.

Frank Lloyd Wright is renowned not only for his architecture but also for his furniture, which he designed for nearly every one of his 300 building projects. Some of these furnishings have been mass-produced by various companies for the open market. The furnishings and built-ins that Frank Lloyd Wright designed throughout his career extend the details, material properties, and geometric motifs of the spaces for which they were designed. Where his buildings have been preserved, such as *Fallingwater* in rural Bear Run, Pennsylvania, the furnishings have also been carefully restored or replicated whenever possible (Figure 6.52).

On the other hand, a majority of contemporary furniture designs, developed by industrial designers including Achille Castiglioni, Karim Rashid, and Bill Stumpf, were conceived and fabricated as solutions to lifestyle issues, were technical inventions, or resulted from explorations of form and material. Their work was not conceived for, nor was it dependent upon, a particular interior or architectural environment. Furnishings such as these find their way to a variety of spaces and are sold directly to the public through retail, Internet, and catalog venues or through showrooms and furniture representatives directly to architects and interior designers who specify furniture as contract furnishings.

Figure 6.52 Interior of Fallingwater (Edgar J. Kaufmann House), Bear Run, Pennsylvania, designed by Frank Lloyd Wright, 1936.

Figure 6.53 Rotory-molded Kite chairs, designed by Karim Rashid (2004), manufactured by Label.

The *Kite* chairs (Figure 6.53) designed by Karim Rashid and the *Iuta* chair (Figure 6.54) designed by Antonio Citterio and produced by B & B Italia are examples of industrial products that have broad appeal for a wide range of interior spaces, conceived and manufactured within the framework of an industrial design typology.

An interior designer is trained to think about furniture design similarly to an architect but differently than an industrial designer. Interior designers are primarily concerned with selecting furniture for their interiors. They generally focus upon interior aesthetics, contextual appropriateness, utility, comfort, form, finish, and product availability. Though purpose, comfort, and aesthetics are primary considerations for selecting furniture, the act of designing custom furniture for specific interiors has roots extending back to the 18th century. The

Figure 6.54 Iuta armchairs, designed by Antonio Citterio (2000), manufactured by B & B Italia.

work of Thomas Chippendale and George Hepplewhite, along with that of designers such as Robert Adam and Elsie de Wolfe, were precursors of what today is called *interior design*. Contemporary interior designers practice furniture design by offering a distinct "look" that doesn't yet appear in the catalogs. Their designs can influence change in the market when their lines successfully fill a niche overlooked by other designers. Florence Knoll (Knoll International) did just that.

Though architects and interior designers design furniture, most are not trained to design within the tolerances required for mass production. Furthermore, few architects and interior designers are trained to think about industrial processes as industrial designers are.

Engineers are trained to focus on mechanical function and address the efficiency and material quality of performance-based function. Filing cabinets and adjustable office seating are examples of engineered objects that demand a high degree of technological resolution due to the tight tolerances between design and form as well as between fabrication and function. It is not surprising to see engineers focus upon mechanical aspects and less upon the spatial and contextual relationships between furniture and interior environments.

Sociologists generally have a different perspective on furniture design than architects, designers, or craftspeople. Though sociologists don't usually design furniture, they are taught to observe interpersonal and behavioral patterns among individuals, analyzing how people gather and interact socially within public areas, reception spaces, office settings, and so on. Edward T. Hall's *The Hidden Dimension* and psychologist Robert Sommer's *Personal Space* explore the concept of proxemics in depth. Their writings and ideas have influenced a generation of designers.

Craftspeople and woodworkers focus upon the human skill of making and the visual and tactile quality of the overall finish of furniture. Craftspeople typically focus upon the properties of materials and fabrication methods, emphasizing *workmanship* and the making of furniture. It is in the making that they seek to master the craft of joining or to perfect a technique for finishing. David Pye, Ernest Joyce, George Nakashima, Sam Maloof, and Chris Simpson have written about furniture design from this perspective, and through their built work and writing, each has contributed to a body of knowledge concerning material, fabrication methods, and craft.

Architects, industrial designers, interior designers, furniture designers, artists, engineers, fabricators, craftspeople, theorists, sociologists, cultural anthropologists, historians, and business entrepreneurs actively contribute to furniture design in unique ways and hold distinct views about it. The sociologist and the cultural anthropologist represent one point of view and the interior designer and architect another. The industrial designer and product engineer provide yet another, and the craftsperson and artist represent a fourth perspective in thinking about furniture design.

7 Materials

MATTER IS THE MATERIAL OF DESIGN. Consider the self-expanding polyurethane foam *Anti-object* armchair, fabricated using pails of resin by Gunnar Aagaard Andersen in 1964 (Figure 7.1), or the hand-woven cane seat pan in *The Chair* designed by Hans J. Wegner (Figure 7.2). It would be a challenge not to acknowledge the influence that materials had in the design and fabrication of these furnishings.

Figure 7.1 Expanded urethane foam—Anti-object, designed and made by Gunnar Aagaard Andersen, 1964.

Figure 7.2 Cane seat pan—The Chair, designed by Hans J. Wegner, 1947.

In *The Material of Invention,* Ezio Manzini takes a philosophical approach to the science of material. Professor Manzini is specific about the physical properties of material and thoughtful regarding how materials can influence design thinking. He presents the argument that material and technology drive design by examining the relationships between matter and material (i.e., how material and its physical properties are an integral part of the process of transforming ideas into furniture). What was once considered impossible to make (let alone design) has become increasingly more possible to realize through evolving technology.

It is assumed that during prehistoric times, "furniture" was constructed from readily available natural materials and worked by hand into useful objects. As time progressed, materials were categorized, selected, and, in some regards, harvested. Metals were combined to form alloys. Recently, materials have been designed at the molecular level (i.e., polymers), and from those efforts, nanotechnologies have emerged as a means to create biomaterials, many of which are biodegradable. Today, the technology is available to design and make almost anything. Scientific investigations have led to molecule-sized machines, extraordinarily sensitive sensors, and revolutionary manufacturing methods.

Furniture designers do not need to understand the particulars of molecular science and nanotechnologies, or know the biomaterials currently available, but they do need to appreciate the distinction between matter and material. More importantly, designers need to understand why one material is better or more appropriate than another for a given situation. They should be informed about the newest materials and have a working knowledge of material properties. Doing so may help conceive and develop better furniture designs.

Materials contribute significantly to the structural integrity, comfort, and aesthetics of furniture. Considering the properties and characteristics of materials in the conception of design focuses the designer's thinking upon the limits and constraints of materials, which, ironically, opens the door to creative design ideas.

Today, material research focuses upon environmental issues, physical properties, health-related concerns, and performance-related characteristics. Digital technology and new materials have an enormous potential to influence the field of furniture design.

MATERIAL MATTERS

From the vacuum-molded studies produced by students using laminated veneers (Figure 7.3) to the translucent polymer tables industrially produced by Kartell (Figure 7.4), materials

Figure 7.3 Vacuum-molded studies, student furniture projects displayed at the International Furniture Fair in Copenhagen, 2006.

Figure 7.4 Plastic T-tables, designed by Patricia Urquiola, manufactured by Kartell.

matter. Some designers utilize new materials in traditional ways, and some designers seek unique ways of utilizing conventional materials. In either case, material is a significant determinant of form and function. At the fringe of material research are the working prototypes made from new polymers, new alloys, aerogels, new wood products, and biodegradable green materials. Before we seek to understand the appropriate uses and applications of materials encountered in contemporary furniture, we should look at the discoveries and inventions made during the past 6000 years. Consider how the methods of fabrication and the physical characteristics of furniture have evolved in tandem with the chronology of the discovery and use of materials.

4000 B.C.	**Copper** was used for implements and edges of tools.
3000 B.C.	The Egyptians used **bronze,** an alloy of copper and tin, in the ratio of nine parts copper to one part tin.
2600 B.C.	The Egyptians invented glass.
2300 B.C.	Bronze Age began in Britain.
1550 B.C.	The Hittites developed a crude form of iron extracted from iron ore.
1300 B.C.	Iron Age began in the Near East.
550 B.C.	Surviving Etruscan bronze furniture included thrones, chests, tables, couches, and circular barrel chairs.
500 B.C.	**Brass,** an alloy of zinc and copper, was widely used by the Romans.
50 B.C.	The Phoenicians developed glassblowing techniques.
105	The Chinese court official Ts'ai Lun invented papermaking from textile waste using rags. Later, Chinese papermakers developed sized, coated, and dyed paper.
700	The Chinese invented porcelain.
1284	Horners Company established an early plastics trade association.
1455	The Gutenberg Bible was printed, marking the first use of movable metal type.
1530	Peter of Anghiera (from Spain) provided the first printed mention of rubber (gummi optima).
1650	The use of bronze returned to furniture making in the cast supports and furniture mounts for tables. These were often gilded and in France were known as *bronze doré.*
1764	James Hargreaves invented the spinning jenny for cotton products (cotton is a natural fiber derived from the cotton plant).
1785	The power loom was invented by Edmund Cartwright to speed cloth production.
1791	Samuel Peal patented the waterproofing of fabrics with a rubber solution.
1805	Luigi Brugnatelli invented modern electroplating.
1829	Michael Faraday established a formula for natural rubber known as C5H8.
1834	Justus von Liebig developed melamine.
1843	Charles Goodyear and Thomas Hancock individually applied for rubber vulcanization patents.
1851	A process for thermosetting ebonite material was patented by Goodyear for pens, etc.
1856	Henry Bessemer developed the Bessemer converter to produce steel.
1873	Glass fibers that could be woven into cloth were made by Jules de Brunfaut.
1884	Hilaire de Chardonnet synthesized the first artificial textile.

1900	Invention of plywood, a sheet material made from built-up layers of wood veneer.
1907	Bakelite, the first totally synthetic thermosetting plastic, was derived from the reaction of phenol-formaldehyde that sets solid when heated.
1909	Dr. Leo Hendrik Baekeland received a "heat and pressure" patent for phenolic resins.
1912	Russian scientist Ivan Ostromislensky patented the use of plasticizers and developed polyvinyl chloride (PVC).
1913	Stainless steel was invented by Harry Brearley in Sheffield, England.
1920	Quick-drying, solvent-based lacquers that contain nitrocellulous were developed in the early 1920s by scientists at Dupont.
1922	Hermann Staudinger synthesized rubber.
1928	First commercial applications of urea-formaldehyde and PVC.
1930	Neoprene and polystyrene were invented.
1937	Wallace Carothers invented nylon, which is strong, resists water and mildew, and is a malleable plastic.
1939	First patent issued for epoxy.
1940	Invention of polyurethane, an important synthetic plastic used in furniture, which can be flexible, rigid, structural, or supplied as a textile coating.
1948	George de Mestral invented Velcro.
1954	Guilio Natta invented polypropylene, a plastic commonly used in injection-molded furniture.
1956	The Scotchgard fabric and material protector was developed by Patsy Sherman.
1958	Invention of polycarbonate.
1959	The float glass process was patented by Pilkington Brothers.
1960	**Medium density fiberboard** (MDF) was developed in the United States. This man-made wood-based sheet material consists of fine fibers of timber mixed with urea-formaldehyde resin and additives to form a felted material. The material is then subjected to heat and pressure to create rigid boards and panels.
1964	Leslie Phillips developed carbon fibers by heat treating acrylonitrile fibers.
1971	Invention of Kevlar, a fiber five times stronger than steel.
1975	Invention and patent for continuously **anodizing** aluminum by Howard Fromson.
1981	K. Eric Drexler promoted the idea of molecular manufacturing systems.
1986	Materials scientists developed synthetic skin.
1990	Two new biodegradable plastics, Novon and Biopol, were developed.
1993	The first international conference on "Green Goods" was held at the Hague, the Netherlands, from September 30 to October 1. Since 1993, five "Green Goods" conferences have taken place.
2000	New materials made with corn proteins became available.
2006	The technology for making thin film nanotubes by evaporation was invented.

The chronology of material parallels the evolution of concepts and design inquiry in the history of furniture design.[1] Generally, new materials are used to overcome the limitations of existing materials. It often takes years to generate fresh ideas about form and function based upon the physical properties of new materials. Cast iron lampposts were initially manufac-

Figure 7.5 GUBI Cinal shelving, designed by Chris Ferebec (2002), wood veneer on an aluminum core. Manufactured by GUBI, Denmark.

tured to look like carved stone. Plastic laminate tables were initially fabricated to look like finished wood tables. It is difficult to go beyond conventional thinking about materials, but innovative design can result by doing so (Figure 7.5).

Besides having economic value, materials have social and cultural value. Thus, when case goods are made from wood, typically expensive case goods are made from select woods such as Honduran mahogany (Figure 7.6), or materials that simulate select woods. Woods such as rosewood, walnut, cherry, and Swiss pear are valued for their associative meanings more than their material properties.

During World War II, Danish designers such as Kaare Klint began to use locally grown white oak in many of their furniture designs because imported rosewood and mahoganies (which

Figure 7.6 Round coffee table in mahogany, designed by Kaare Klint, fabricated by Rud. Rasmussen, Denmark.

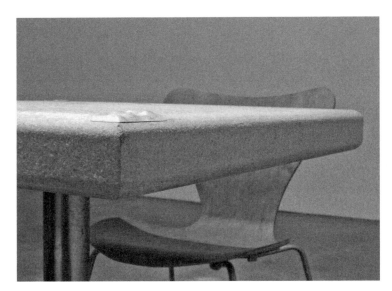

Figure 7.7 Release of VOCs through material, binder, and finish.

Figure 7.8 Computer drawing of the CO6 chair, designed by Pol Quandens (1996).

were preferred and widely used at the time) were unavailable. Light oak in furniture was used out of necessity, and it contributed to a new Scandinavian aesthetic that emerged in the 1950s.

The study of materials sheds light on important health-related issues. Fibrous asbestos in ACT tile, wiring insulation, and thermal insulation were concerns in the 1980s. Formaldehyde in MDF and composite woods, the carcinogenic fumes that result from metal plating processes, the arsenic in pressure-treated lumber, and VOCs released from PVC polymers, glues, and finishes also are of concern (Figure 7.7). Thoughtful selection and use of materials can contribute to the health, welfare, and safety of the public.

Many designers consider and utilize materials with specific physical characteristics and structural properties. Reflecting upon material as a structural element requires a willingness to suspend preconceptions and traditions about aesthetics in order to explore new correlations between form and function and materials technology. The *CO6* chair, designed by Pol Quandens (Figure 7.8), made from resin and polycarbon fiber, illustrates such thinking in getting the most out of the least material. In short, consider the basic properties and characteristics of material and allow that information to guide your thinking about design.

MATERIAL PROPERTIES

What are the material properties that furniture designers need to consider? What environmental conditions or structural characteristics influence the decision to use a specific wood or plastic in design? How might leather's ability to absorb odor, moisture, and oils affect the decision on whether or not to use it? How much do materials expand or contract when exposed to changes in moisture or temperature? How well do materials age?

Materials respond to changes in the environment in different ways. Wood expands and contracts with changes in relative humidity and tends to darken over time when exposed to UV radiation. Metals expand and contract when temperature changes, and most metals develop a protective patina when exposed to air and moisture. Leather is affected by temperature and moisture changes. Plastic is affected by UV radiation (full-spectrum light) as well as temperature. Concrete never completely cures, glass is always slumping, and organic materials decompose.

Material properties are important to consider when selecting material for furniture. Characteristics such as the *absorptive quality, cellular structure (open cell or closed cell), compressive and tensile strength, density, dimensional change, ductility, elasticity, expandability, stability, surface quality, VOC content, and workability* influence the performance of furniture, and these properties contribute directly and indirectly to the form and utility of furniture.

Absorptive Quality

A material's *absorptive quality* is its ability to absorb moisture, oils, and odors. Fabric and unfinished wood will absorb all three. Ring porous/semi-ring porous, open-grained woods, such as mahogany, can take a stain better than diffuse porous, closed-grained wood, such as hard maple; however, both woods can receive a deep-looking finish, but the processes may be different. Some woods are relatively high in oil content, such as teak, and are best finished in a shellac. Others are remarkably dense, such as ebony, and have difficulty absorbing oil finishes. Cork is soft to the touch and will stain, but it is not absorptive. Jasper Morrison used cork as the primary material in his series of table stools produced by Vitra (Figure 7.9). These stools appear unfinished.

Figure 7.9 Cork tables, designed by Jasper Morrison (2004), for Vitra, Switzerland.

Granite is igneous rock and will not absorb moisture or odors. It is remarkably dense, though sealing is suggested because bacteria can grow in the tiny pores of granite's surface. Marble and limestone are both calcium carbonates, will absorb moisture and oils, and are particularly susceptible to acids and to staining by olive oil. Metals are generally nonabsorptive. They can be affected by oils and acids, and some stainless steel metals will stain. Metals can be lacquered to preserve their appearance, but lacquer finishes on metal generally do not last; eventually, metal surfaces will oxidize. Powder coating is an effective alternative to consider as a finish for metals.

Cellular Structure (Open-Cell or Closed-Cell)

Wood is composed of open (straw-like) and closed (rod-like) cells that run with the grain. Hardwoods are generally open-cell materials, and softwoods are generally nonporous (rod-like). The cellular structure of wood affects grain quality and determines the characteristics of its stability and workability. Wood is strong in the direction of its grain and significantly weaker in tension perpendicular to its grain (Figure 7.10).

Compressive and Tensile Strength

The compressive and tensile strength of materials are related but distinct in their performance capabilities. *Compressive strength* is the ability of material to resist compressive forces (pushing), while *tensile strength* is the material's ability to resist tensile forces (pulling). Wood performs well in both compression and tension parallel to the grain, but when pulled at a right angle to the grain, it will split. Wood does not strongly resist shear forces applied along its grain, making it relatively easy to split with an axe or a chisel. Concrete performs well in compression but poorly in tension. Steel has excellent tensile and compressive strength, making it an ideal choice for the structural frame in Anders Hermansen's *Wire Sketch Chair* designed in 1985 (Figure 7.11) and Poul Kjærholm's folded spring steel frame in *PK 25,* designed in 1951 (Figure 7.12).

Figure 7.10 Turned and steam-bent wood—cut with the grain.

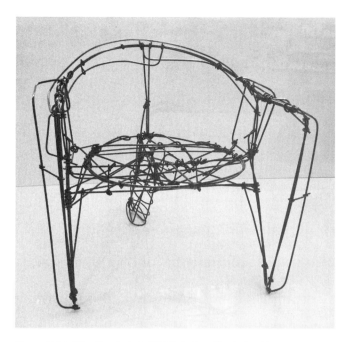

Figure 7.11 Wire Sketch chair, (1985) designed by Anders Hermansen.

Figure 7.12 Continuous folded spring steel frame for PK 25 (1951), designed by Poul Kjærholm.

Density

Density is the measure of the cellular structure of a material relative to its volume or mass. Brazilian cherry wood is a dense tropical hardwood that has a beautiful grain figure. Paper is a lightweight material and is relatively warm to the touch. It is the sole material in Toku-jin Yoshioka's *Honey-Pop Armchair,* designed in 2000. Another paper-based furniture design made from laminated corrugated cardboard is Frank Gehry's *Little Beaver* lounge chair (Figure 7.13). The tubular steel frame chairs by the early modernists Mart Stam, Marcel Breuer,

Figure 7.13 Little Beaver, cardboard lounge chair with ottoman (1987), designed by Frank Gehry.

Figure 7.14 MR lounge chair. Designed by Mies van der Rohe (1927), manufactured by Knoll, Inc.

and Mies van der Rohe were cool to the touch, with carefully placed leather, fabric, or caning whenever the chair came into contact with the body (Figure 7.14). Dense materials such as metals tend to conduct heat away from the body, resulting in the sensation of coolness to the touch.

The sensation of cool or warm materials is one consideration in furniture design that influences the haptic sensation (tactile experience) of furniture. Consider the apparent temperature of an aluminum chair in the same room as a wood chair. Metals, glass, and ceramics are heat-conductive materials. They feel relatively cooler than non-heat-conductive materials under the same environmental conditions. Thermal conductivity is a measure of the rate at which heat is transferred through a material and is generally related to density. Denser materials like concrete conduct heat away 15 times faster than wood; steel conducts heat away 300 times faster than wood.[2]

Dimensional Change

All wood species shrink upon drying and expand when the cells hydrate. Wood does not begin to shrink until all "free water" is removed and "bound-water" loss begins. Hardwood lumber must have a moisture content of 6–12 percent to meet the standard of the *National Hardwood Lumber Association* (NHLA) grades. Some woods shrink and expand more than others. However, there is a noticeable variation within any species between its tangential and radial shrinkage. Imagine a small slice of a log. The internal and inconsistent stresses in lumber are dependent upon how the tree was cut at the mill. **Quarter-sawn** lumber will expand and contract similarly to **plain-sawn** lumber, but quarter-sawn lumber is less prone to cupping. As plain-sawn lumber dries, it shrinks much more tangentially, causing it to split more often than quarter-sawn lumber.

It is important that furniture designers and fabricators understand the degree of compatibility between materials that connect to one another and know what precautions must be taken to allow for the relative differential in movement by different materials. In Figure 7.15, an **end grain** butt joint in the structural supports fabricated with two different woods (maple and cherry) necessitated core drilling twice through the entire length of the composite leg assembly. The different woods were then secured in compression using threaded rods and locking nuts. PVA or epoxy glue with dowels would not have secured the connection

Figure 7.15 Vertical supports joined using threaded dowels, secured in compression—Ambo.

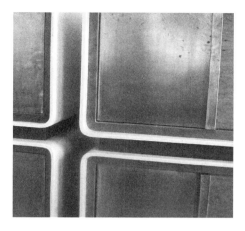

Figure 7.16 Folded copper drawer fronts with integrated copper handles.

Figure 7.17 Outdoor aluminum bench.

well enough, and over time, due to the differential in the dimensional changes of the two species, the joint would fail.

Wood is not a homogeneous solid material; consequently, movement that results from changes in relative humidity is not equal in all directions. Shrinkage takes place in every dimension of wood except along the length of the grain. As a general rule, one should avoid gluing wide and long pieces of wood cross-grain to one another (as in a skirt or apron for a table). When it is unavoidable, consider using a mortise and tenon or a slotted mechanical connection to allow for expansive and contractive movement.

Ductility

A material's *ductility* is its ability to be molded or shaped without breaking. Copper is a ductile metal. It folds, bends, and can be hammered or formed, as shown in Figure 7.16. Aluminum is far less ductile and is best when forged, cast, extruded, or rolled into shape (Figure 7.17). Polypropylene is a ductile polymer and can take a significant impact without breaking, especially when an elastomeric is added. Cork is ductile and is the primary material used in *KorQ,* a lounge chair designed by Kevin Walz in 1996 (Figure 7.18).

Figure 7.18 KorQ—design by Kevin Walz (1996), made with 100 percent cork. Drawing by Amy Ballman, University of Cincinnati.

Figure 7.19 Elastomeric—poly vinyl chloride tubing. Giandomenico Belloti's Spaghetti chair, 1983.

Elasticity

A material's modulus of elasticity is evident when deformations produced by low stress are completely recoverable after the load is removed. Giandomenico Bellotti's *Spaghetti* chair (1983), produced by Alias, utilizes elastic PVC tubing for its seat pan and seat back (Figure 7.19). The tubing gently supports the user and returns to its original shape when the load is removed from the chair. The ability of a material to return to its original shape can offer significant potential for wide-reaching products, which include the wooden skis made of birch in the 1940s as well as the memory foam pillows available today.

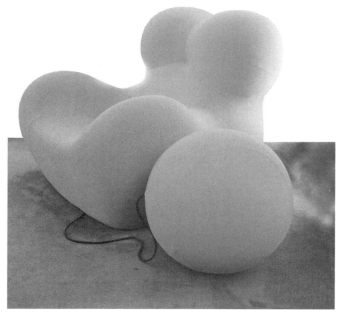

Figure 7.20 UP 5, expanded polyurethane foam upholstered in stretch nylon, designed by Gaetano Pesce for C & B Italia, 1969.

Expandability

Expandable polyurethane is a material that expands when exposed to air for the first time. Gaetano Pesce used this material in his *UP* series chairs (Figure 7.20). The chairs were shipped by the manufacturer, compressed in a thermo-sealed vacuum container at 90 percent of their actual size. When they were unsealed, the foam expanded back to its original size and gained full form approximately 1 hour after the seal was broken.

Most materials (except for thermosetting plastics) expand with either heat or moisture. Metal expands when heated. Wood and leather expand when moisture is increased. Plastic (polymers) expand when heat is applied. Fabric and rubber deform when tensile forces are applied.

Stability

Stable materials remain inert, with little or no dimensional change, when changes occur in moisture, temperature, or applied force. MDF is one of the most dimensionally stable wood composite materials and is used as a substrate for veneers. Marine-grade plywood is excellent for outside or wet conditions. It is able to withstand submergence in boiling water for an hour without delaminating at the core. (Cassina uses marine plywood to manufacture Gerrit Rietveld's *Red and Blue* chair.[3]) Ceramics, granite, stone, and thermosetting plastics are stable materials unaffected by moisture and temperature. The epoxy resin, *523 Broadway* chairs designed by Gaetano Pesce are made from a thermosetting plastic and are not affected by heat or daylight, as would a chair made from a thermoplastic (Figure 7.21). All materials **creep**—that is, deform over time when subjected to a constant load. This is evident when long, thin wood shelves gradually sag. Particleboard is a composite wood product that is particularly susceptible to structural deformation due to moisture. For this reason, particleboard should not be used in furniture unless it is adequately supported.

Surface Qualities

Surface quality is a general term that describes the visual and tactile characteristics of a material's surface. Descriptive characteristics of unfinished wood include figure, grain, and texture. Descriptive characteristics of finished wood include depth and luster. Metal can be polished or given a patina, and genuine leather has a "soft hand."

Visual Aspects of Finished Wood Surfaces

Depth
Depth is a visual quality that depends upon the process and type of finish used as much as it does upon the wood species itself. Wood surfaces with an open cellular structure can be enhanced with an oil finish. Open-celled wood when finished with oil or a **lacquer,** can be enhanced by the natural cellular structure and the depth of penetration by the finish. In

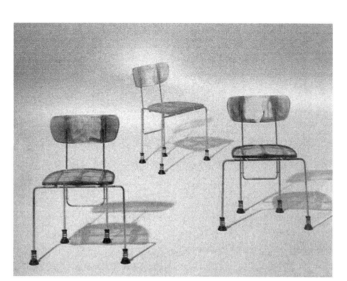

Figure 7.21 *523 Broadway* chairs, designed by Gaetano Pesce (1993), manufactured by Bernini Spa using epoxy resin.

Figure 7.22 Table finished using a nitrocellulose lacquer.

the past, the first finish coat applied to wood furniture, casework, or flooring was often thinned using mineral spirits to allow for deeper penetration. This, in turn, created a greater sense of depth in the finish.

Luster

The ability of finished wood to reflect and refract light gives **luster** to its surface. Luster is a visual quality that becomes apparent only when wood is finished. Compact and smooth woods such as curly or hard maple and special qualities in grain such as ribbon curl, when finished, can reveal a remarkable luster (Figure 7.22). Luster and color in finished wood are responsive and dependent upon one's viewing angle, the characteristics of the grain, and the source of the light. Walk around a finished table and study the visual transformation that occurs as the viewing angle and orientation change. It is remarkable how much variation can be perceived in the luster and color of finished wood.

Visual Aspects of Wood Surfaces

Figure

Figure is a term that describes grain anomilies. The natural characteristics of wood (i.e., medullary rays, growth rings, color variation, texture, knots, and abnormalities) all contribute to the characteristics of wood's **figure.** Imperfections such as stresses during growth and disease also contribute to wood's figure. Storing, drying, and seasoning lumber can affect a wood's grain. The formation of small checks, splits, or flaws on the surface of lumber can result from uneven seasoning. This is known as checking. Various types of figuring in wood include: ribbon stripe, flake, wormholes, block mottles, **bird's eye, fiddle-back,** quilted, **curly grain,** tiger, crotch, and **burl.**

Grain

Grain is the direction of the fibers relative to the long axis of the tree. Cut boards have three categories of **grain** based on location—face grain, **edge grain,** and **end grain.** In lumber where growth has been even and the cell structure is in line with the main axis of the tree, the wood will be straight-grained and relatively easy to work. Quarter-sawn straight grain results in uniform and stable lumber. Depending on how the tree is milled, wavy grain can give a rippled effect on tangential surfaces, while unusual growth malformations in the cambium layer of maple cause the cells to grow into a series of small, tight cellular structures called *bird's eye.*

The term *grain* is also used to describe the way wood is worked. Sawing, planing, and sanding are typically done with the grain. Cuts made at 90 degrees to the grain are known as *cross cuts* and often require finer blades for quality cuts.

Texture

The texture or feel of a wood's surface is the result of the cellular structure of the material. Lumber that has wide vessels or open cells, like red oak, is considered coarse-textured, whereas lumber with closed, porous cells and densely spaced cells is considered to be fine-textured (like the mahoganies). Softwoods are not open-celled. Their cells have a small diameter. As a general rule, think of softwoods as a bundle of tiny solid rods and hardwoods as a bundle of tiny open straws. The texture of softwoods results from the difference between early and latewood zones. When these zones are strongly marked, as in Douglas fir, the texture is considered uneven, and when there is little contrast between the zones, as in sugar pine, the wood is considered evenly textured.

Workability

Workability is the quality of a material's response to being cut, drilled, sanded, planed, folded, or shaped. For wood, the classifications applied to the resistance in cutting and the blunting effects on tools are based on kiln-dried wood of 12 percent moisture content. Mahogany is easy to cut and carve and is an ideal choice for many wood furniture designs. Woods that have changes in their grain direction are difficult to joint and plane. Cherry, despite its beautiful grain figure, often has directional changes in its grain, making it somewhat difficult to work. Tempered glass cannot be cut or drilled after tempering. Limestone, marble, and granite are easy to cut, using either a water jet cutter or a CNC device; they can also be drilled, sanded, **honed,** and carved. However, marble is especially fragile along its veins and can easily break when shear forces are applied. Stainless steel and copper can be welded, but it is difficult to weld copper because the heat required can also melt the copper. In welding copper, low-temperature/high-voltage welds are required.

Other Aspects

The visual, tactile, and structural characteristics of materials can be affected by changes in temperature, moisture, and time. Some woods, especially cherry, will darken when exposed to full-spectrum sunlight (UV radiation) and air (oxidation). With a proper finish, when allowed to age naturally, cherry has enormous visual depth and a rainbow of colors. On the other hand, American black walnut will initially darken, then slowly lighten over a period of time. Most metals, including aluminum, copper, and bronze, will develop a protective patina on exposed surfaces that results from the natural processes of oxidation. Leather and wood expand when exposed to moisture. Paints, stains, dyes, and applied finishes can dry out, fade, and crack over time. ABS plastics significantly fade and become brittle when exposed to full-spectrum sunlight. The surface quality of most materials is always changing, and this makes repairing or refinishing furniture such as antiques especially difficult.

Haptic Sensations

Haptic sensations are the physical and phenomenological experiences of touching and interacting with furniture (Figure 7.23). Aluminum feels cool to the touch, even in temperate and controlled conditions. Glass is also cold to the touch, and oils from the hand and fingers can leave marks if the glass is not treated. Vinyl does not pass moisture and can cause condensation to form when direct contact is made to exposed skin. Plastic laminates can be abrasive over time to clothes and skin. In response to these characteristics, designers and companies have sought to work with new materials and have utilized existing materials in ingenious ways. In the 1990s, Steelcase came out with *Silique,* a material designed for work surfaces, which was not as abrasive as traditional high-pressure (HP) plastic laminate. Herman Miller uses an open mesh, elastomeric fabric called *Pellicile* for their popular *Aeron* chairs. Many designers from the Bauhaus in Dessau, Germany, including Mart Stam, Marcel Breuer, and Mies van der Rohe, utilized leather and cane whenever their chairs came into direct contact with the human body.

Metals can be plated in a number of standard finishes and colors. Plating is done over a brass or nickel base in a broad variety of metals and in a range of surface qualities. Metal surfaces can be executed in polished or satin finishes. Concrete can be finished in either a hand trowel or broom finish, or can be etched, stamped, glazed, stained, waxed, or polished. Stone can be polished, hammered, flamed, or honed. Glass can be annealed, cast, distressed, floated, blown, or tempered. For every material used in furniture, there are many options to consider regarding the finish and characteristics of surface quality, and generally, different surface finishes will create different tactile experiences.

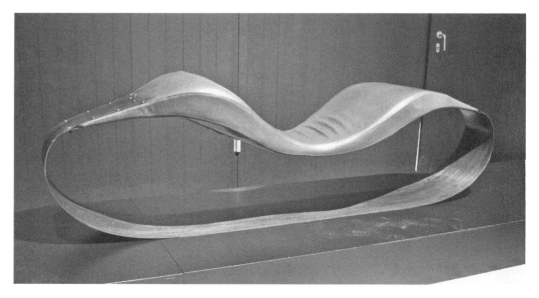

Figure 7.23 Ron Arad—dynamic seating exhibited at the Trapholt Furniture Museum, Kolding, Denmark.

Volatile Organic Compounds

Volatile organic compounds (VOCs) are emitted by many adhesives, paint thinners, and finishes. Low or no VOC emissions are desirable. VOCs can cause significant health problems, environmental damage, and annoying delays in getting products to market. Many large office furniture companies have had to warehouse their completed furniture products for several weeks to allow the vapor to dissipate before shipping them to the client. This step requires off-site storage, which adds time and cost to the furniture.

MATERIALS FROM A TO Z

Material classifications traditionally begin with wood and continue through metal, stone, glass, and composite boards. Some think of wood as a natural material, metal as somewhat less natural, and plastic as even further removed from nature; yet, all materials are natural. Even polymers, alloys, and synthetic materials are dependent upon a base of natural compounds.

The following materials are organized alphabetically to serve as a resource for furniture designers and fabricators interested in material properties. Though adhesives are technically not considered a material, we begin with them because of their importance in making furniture and the wide spectrum of their properties.

Adhesives and Glues

Adhesives and glues are designed to adhere materials together. Technically, glues are considered natural and adhesives are considered synthetic. There is no universal glue that will adhere anything to everything under all conditions. There are several general-purpose and special-purpose glues and adhesives. The first questions to ask when deciding upon which glue to use are:

- What materials are you bonding?
- Under what conditions do you need them to maintain their bond (waterproof, freeze/thaw)?
- How quickly must the bond reach full strength?
- How strong must the bond be?
- What properties (clear, sandable, etc.) must the glue have when it is dry or cured?

Animal Glues

Hide glue is made by boiling animal bones, hoofs, and skins, which results in a hard cake that is then soaked in water and heated. This produces a gelatinous mass. When reheated, this mass becomes liquid, giving it an instant "grab" when applied warm. Hide glue was once used for cabinet-making purposes and hand veneering processes. Its set time, however, takes up to 24 hours, and it is odorous. Warming the glue with applied moisture will reverse the adhesive process. Hide glue is a good adhesive for repairing antiques and has good workability. Its bonding strength, however, is not as great as that of PVA glues, and even the heat of an attic space can cause the glue to fail.

Nearly 5000 years ago, the Egyptians used hide glue to make furniture.[4] During the 17th century, the best glues were pure hide or fish glues. In the early 20th century, **animal glues** were still used for secondary or assembly gluing without the application of heat for a speedy turnaround time. Hide glue was generally used to glue wood joints and to lay down veneers, but it is only occasionally used today. Today, synthetic glues have replaced animal glues.

Vegetable Glues

Vegetable glues are made from a range of starch granules found in tapioca, rye flour, natural rubber, and soybean dissolved in a solution of caustic alkali. Starch glues were used primarily for plywood lamination and veneer work. Special rubber-latex vegetable glues have been formulated and used for contact adhesives to bond plastic laminates, upholstery, and foam work.

Synthetic Glues

Synthetic (also known as *white, yellow,* or *carpenter*) glues are a category of special-purpose glues developed during the second half of the 20th century. These glues respond to heat and special accelerants and therefore can have vastly accelerated setting times.

Polyvinyl acetate (PVA) is a white or yellow synthetic polymer that was first discovered in Germany by Dr. Fritz Klatte in 1912. It is a thermoplastic, water-based glue that sets as water diffuses into the materials being glued. It is prepared by the polymerization of vinyl acetate. Partial or complete *hydrolysis* of the polymer is used to prepare polyvinyl alcohol. PVA is sold as an emulsion in water and used as an adhesive for porous materials, particularly wood. It is the most commonly used wood glue.

> *Contact Adhesives:* Ideal for paper-backed veneers and laminating sheet materials together. **Contact adhesive** is not recommended for wood-on-wood conditions but is fine for phenolic-backed wood veneering. These adhesives are typically thinner-based and caustic, but newer water-based contact adhesives are available and are far less caustic.
>
> *Epoxy:* Extremely tough and durable synthetic resins consist of two parts that, when mixed together, bond a wide variety of dissimilar materials under relatively harsh conditions. Used for securing metal or stone to wood. Both the resin and the hardener are irritants, and their vapors are toxic.
>
> *Instant Glue:* An extremely fast-bonding adhesive. The chemical name is ethyl cyanoacrylate. Cyanoacrylate is the generic name for substances such as methyl-2-cyanoacrylate, which is typically sold under the brand names *Super Glue* and *Instant Krazy Glue®*. 2-Octyl cyanoacrylate is used in medical glues such as *Dermabond* and *TraumaSeal*. Cyanoacrylate adhesives are sometimes known as *instant adhesives*. They work best on smaller surfaces. Accelerators are available to speed their curing and bonding times. The bond is instant, colorless, transparent, and strong (except in shear). It was originally used for nonporous surfaces. Gel versions are now available for more porous surfaces.
>
> *Plastic Cement:* Used to join polystyrene plastic. It works by dissolving the areas that will be joined together, and in the dissolved areas, molecules from the two parts fuse together. It is very volatile and high in VOCs.
>
> *Polyurethane Glues:* These glues bond all wood, especially dense woods or those with high levels of oil such as teak. They expand as they cure and are messy to work with, but they hold materials together very well. Mortise-and-tenon joinery is excellent for polyurethane glues because they fill the voids and fully bond the joint.

Gorilla Glue is a brand name of polyurethane glue, but many companies make polyurethane glues.

Pressure Sensitive: Adhesives that bond on initial contact to most surfaces. Paper-backed veneers need the application of significant pressure (typically in refinishing cabinetry using pressure-sensitive veneers). The advantage of pressure-sensitive adhesives is that there is no drying or curing time. The strength of the bond varies with the formulation. Examples include no-lick stamps and envelopes, various tapes, and pressure-sensitive veneers.

Rubber Cement: Polymers mixed in a solvent such as acetone or benzene to keep them fluid enough during application make this glue one of the class of *drying adhesives.* As the solvent evaporates, a strong yet flexible bond remains. An advantage is the ease of rubbing to remove excess cement. It is used for bonding two- or three-ply paper-backed veneers and laminated components or components with a plywood backing. The fumes are toxic, and protective measures are needed when using rubber cement.

Silicon: One hundred percent silicon is a good adhesive for bonding glass or metal to wood. The process of curing can take up to 48 hours. Silicon is a relatively clean, transparent adhesive that works well when PVA and epoxy glues cannot be used.

UV Glue: UV glue uses UV light for curing. The result is a permanent and clear bond. One or both of the materials have to be clear, as the process needs UV rays from sunlight or artificial light sources. UV glues are especially useful for bonding glass furniture, as the process does not leave an unwanted "fog."

White Glue: Nontoxic, odorless, nonflammable, and dries clear in less than an hour. Used for bonding paper, wood, cloth, and pottery.

Yellow Glue: Used for bonding wood furniture. It is a higher-quality derivative of white glue that dries stronger and is more resistant to moisture.

Composite Boards

Composite boards are built-up boards used for specific applications. They often have a core with thinner plies of wood or other materials applied to each side of a core. They also include a range of **fiberboards,** such as oriented strand board (OSB), MDF, Medite II (which is one of many MDF products made without formaldehyde), and particleboard.

Plywood is a sheet good that consists of an odd number of plies that have been laminated at right angles in grain direction to each other. The alternating core laminations in American plywood are ⅛-inch (3 mm) thick and can be made from several species of woods including poplar, fir, and pine. Finished plywood is often sold in 4-foot by 8-foot (122 cm by 244 cm) sheets. Baltic birch plywood is made with ¹⁄₁₆-inch (1.5 mm) core laminations made from solid birch and is sold in 5-foot by 5-foot (150 cm by 150 cm) sheets. Bending plywood is typically ⅜-inch (0.95 cm) thick and is typically sold in 4-foot by 8-foot (122 cm by 244 cm) sheets to either barrel roll or column roll, depending upon the desired direction for the bend. In addition, ⅛-inch (3 mm)-thick bending plywood is available in 4-foot by 8-foot (122 cm by 244 cm) sheets and can be made to curve with a radius as tight as 2½-inches (6.3 cm). It is typically manufactured using Philippine mahogany (Luann) and birch, with the veneers laminated perpendicular to one another.

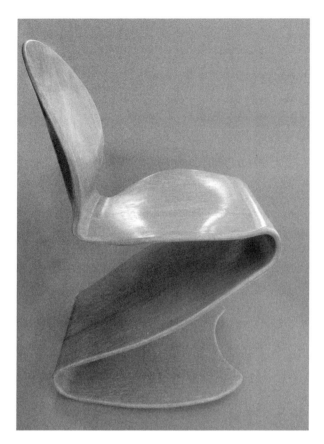

Figure 7.24 Mira Spectrum chair, designed by Verner Panton (1969), produced by Gebrüder Thonet.

American plywood can be purchased with a variety of wood veneer species and in a spectrum of surface and core qualities ranging from an A grade (high) to a D grade (low) on its face side and the number 1 (high) to 4 (low) describing the quality on its back side. The core of plywood is also rated using a letter system; K is a good-quality core, and lower grades are labeled with the letter L or M. Baltic birch has better structural qualities and a more attractive edge grain than American plywood, but is generally available only in a B grade surface and only in 5-foot by 5-foot (150 cm by 150 cm) sheets. Despite the limitations of its size, Baltic birch plywood is an excellent choice for cabinet and drawer fabrications but typically is not used as finish plywood.

The world's first cantilevered molded plywood chair, the *Panton S* chair, by Verner Panton was produced in 1966 by A. Sommer for Thonet. It is remarkably light and was a precedent for Panton's later laminated wood and injected molded and stackable *Panton* chairs. The laminated-wood Mira Spectrum chair (ca. 1969) is shown in Figure 7.24. It was produced in different colors and came with either a U-shaped or round-shaped backrest.

Fabrics and Leather

Fabrics and **leather** are materials commonly used where furniture comes into direct contact with the human body. *Fabric* is a generic name given to natural and synthetic textiles. *Leather* is a generic name given to animal hides prepared by a currier.

Figure 7.25 Velour upholstered pillow, designed and fabricated by a DAAP student, University of Cincinnati.

Historically, fabrics and leather have been used on seat pans, upholstery covers, cushions, wall hangings, the arms of chairs, writing desks, writing surfaces, reinforce joints and for selective uses as hinges. In the Middle Ages, some tables were covered with tapestries. Today's sofas and chairs are typically upholstered in wool, cotton, leather, synthetic leather, nylon, rayon, spandex, and micro fiber. The upholstered cushion in Figure 7.25 is covered with velour and functions as a hybrid between a beanbag and a portable pillow.

Some low-cost leather furniture uses genuine leather for cushions and back rests, while synthetic leather is used in high-friction areas such as armrests and at the base where shoe scuffs do the most damage. This increases the life of the furniture and minimizes the need for maintenance and repair.

Leather contracts as it becomes dry and expands with increases in humidity. Care should be taken to prevent excessive sunlight from fading and drying leather.

Genuine leather is available in various processed forms and has what is called *a soft hand.* Naturally dyed leather tends to show imperfections, grain, wrinkles, and veins more than synthetic leather. Naturally dyed leather ages well because there is no topcoat to crack with age. While this can make it more susceptible to natural oil stains, scrapes, and scuffs, these contribute to the deep, rich patina which leather gains with age. Lighter colors tend to show natural wear faster than deeper colors.

Leather is first dyed, and then a protective layer is absorbed into the surface to prevent staining, scuffing, and scarring, resulting in a *semisoft hand.* This provides excellent durability and is ideal for environments with children and pets. A manufacturer's recommended treatment can be used to prolong the life of leather and prevent unsightly cracking caused by long exposure to hard use and UV rays.

In 1938, Jorge Ferrari-Hardoy, Juan Kurchan, and Antonia Bonet designed the *butterfly* chair. It was composed of two iron frames covered in a leather sling. The *Sling/Butterfly* Chair shown in Figure 7.26a has full-grain leather sling upholstery with strengthening repair to the underside. Produced by Knoll, the chair is 34.5 inches (87.6 cm) high, 32 inches (82 cm) deep, and 30 inches (76.2 cm) wide.

The *Cab* chair is a full-grain leather chair designed in 1977 by Mario Bellini for Cassina. The first *Cab* was designed without arms, utilizing a steel frame and a plastic internal diaphragm incorporated directly under the seat pan to offer support and reinforce the leather seat. The full-grain leather slips over the metal frame and zips up along the inner seam of each leg. All seams are sewn together using polyurethane threading, and the end grain of the exposed leather seams is dyed black. In 1979, a second *Cab* chair was designed and produced with arms (Figure 7.26b).

Synthetic leather is durable. It won't stain easily, and does not feel as soft as natural leather. It is generally colder to the touch than genuine leather and will heat up in direct sunlight. It is generally nonporous; therefore, it does not breathe well. It is this quality, however, that enables synthetic leather to resist liquid and oil stains. It does not require treatment, but can crack with age if an inexpensive synthetic material is chosen. Enormous strides have been made in creating synthetic leather products that wear and feel like genuine leather.

Gilt leather, often called *Spanish leather,* was made from calves' skins faced with tin foil. Gilt leather is embossed or punched with patterns, which are then painted. Tooled leathers are produced in a similar manner. Gilt leather was extensively used for upholstery coverings and wall hangings.

Finishes

Historically, societies have placed a high value upon the finish of furniture. Wood, stone, and fabrics are porous materials that need sealers to protect them and enhance their visual ap-

Figure 7.26a Sling/Butterfly chair, designed by Antonio Bonet, Juan Kurchan, and Jorge Ferrari-Hardoy (1938), manufactured by Knoll International.

Figure 7.26b Cab chairs, (with and without arms) designed by Mario Bellini, (1977–1979), manufactured by Cassina.

Figure 7.27 Lacquer sample.

peal. Wood is finished primarily to protect and enhance its surface. Glass can be finished to minimize the oily finger marks left by touching. Metal can be finished to minimize the effects of oxidation (though the protection is temporary).

Natural lacquer is extracted from insects that secrete a resinous substance called *scale*. Scale was used in lacquer and in some varnishes, and has been known for a thousand years as the best finish for furniture. Once dried, the natural lacquer protects the furniture from humidity, water, heat, and chemicals. The process takes a long time to cure and requires repeated applications, so it is not suitable for mass-produced furniture. Modern lacquer was developed to mimic natural lacquer and is the industry standard for mass-produced furniture (Figure 7.27).

Wood furniture is commonly finished using a nitrocellulose *lacquer* in a matte, satin, or gloss sheen. Lacquer finishes protect wood surfaces and, when applied properly, greatly increase the perceived value of wood furnishings. When combined with aniline and pigmented dye stains, a fine lacquer finish can enhance the color, texture, and grain of wood. Boiled linseed and Danish oil finishes applied with a cloth or brush are beautiful but offer less protection from use.

Polyurethane finishes are less attractive and slower to dry than lacquer finishes. When polyurethane is applied, cold joints result between each application, because the applied coat does not dissolve the previous coats. For this reason, each coat must be applied to a properly prepared surface. Polyurethane-finished wood has the look and feel of plastic and turns increasingly amber in color with age. When moisture is an issue, a polyurethane or spar urethane wood finish is typically used, because lacquer finishes are subject to moisture damage.

Water-borne polyacrylic finishes have many advantages. They apply easily and dry quickly. They are environmentally better than petroleum-based finishes. Of all available finishes, gloss polyacrylic finishes are *water white* and retain the natural appearance of wood without causing it to amber or darken. The problem with polyacrylic finishes is that they appear to generate less depth and luster than oil-based or lacquer finishes. Polyacrylic finishes generally look better on light woods, such as maple, as opposed to dark woods, such as walnut.

In Denmark, a common method of finishing wooden furniture is to apply a mixture of soap flakes and water on unfinished wood. The number of coats varies from 1 to 10, depending on the desired sheen and depth of the finish. Soap flakes are mixed with water, applied in coats, and then rubbed to a finish. They offer an excellent satin sheen finish, retain the true color of the wood without causing it to turn amber, are environmentally safe, and can be easily cleaned and reapplied as necessary or desired.

Rubbing carnauba wax with a fine grade of steel wool over light scratches is an easy way to repair lacquer or polyurethane finishes. Using wax as a lubricant between the steel wool and the wood, one can rub the finish to the desired sheen. Once the wax has dried, it can be polished using a cloth diaper or cheesecloth. Wax, however, is not a good finish for furniture, because is offers little or no protection for the wood.

Purposes of finishing wood furniture include:

- To protect the wood from dirt, moisture, oils, odors, or minor scratches.
- To minimize the expansion and contraction of furniture due to changes in moisture content. It is important to finish all sides, not just the exposed surfaces.
- To provide a smooth, nonporous surface that is easy to clean.
- To improve the appearance of the wood by enhancing the color and quality of the grain.

Glass

Discovered by the Egyptians and perfected by the Romans, glass is one of the oldest man-made materials. Modern glass is approximately 75 percent silica with lime, sodium, lead, boron, or iron added to achieve different properties. Adding metals and oxides to silica generates a range of colors in glass. Chromium creates a green color. Manganese can remove the green-blue tint lent by iron. Cobalt yields blue. Tin and arsenic oxides make glass white. Copper oxide produces a turquoise color. Gold produces a ruby red color. Nickel produces a purple color. Uranium produces a green or fluorescent yellow color.

Glass is available in many different qualities and types. Annealed glass is formed by pouring molten glass onto an iron plate covered with sand, which is then made smooth with a roller before the annealing process. After annealing, the glass is ground and polished, but its faces are rarely parallel.

Float glass is produced by pouring molten glass on a molten tin surface. When the glass cools, it forms a surface that is smooth and uniform. It combines the distortion-free qualities of ground and polished plate glass with less expensive production methods.

Glass can be blown, cast, rolled, pressed, slumped, and tempered. Glass is joined by glaze (melt) bonding, clamping, or by using silicones, adhesives, and epoxies (Figure 7.28).

Stained glass is used in case goods and casework for its color, texture, and ambient quality. Came is used to secure ⅛-inch (3 mm)-thick colored glass in place. Came is made in lead, zinc, or brass extrusions and is available in C- and H-shaped profiles.

Enamel is finely powdered silica (technically considered a glass), colored with metallic oxide and suspended in an oil medium for ease of application with a brush. It was used as an inlay material in French Rococo furniture.

Tempered glass is float glass that is heated above 600°C and then rapidly cooled with forced drafts of air. This process cools the glass surface below its *annealing point,* causing it to harden and contract, while the inner portion of the glass remains free to flow for a short time. The final contraction of the inner layer induces compressive stresses in the surface of the glass balanced by tensile stresses in the body of the glass. Observing the glass with polarized light can reveal the pattern of cooling. The tempering process places tension in the

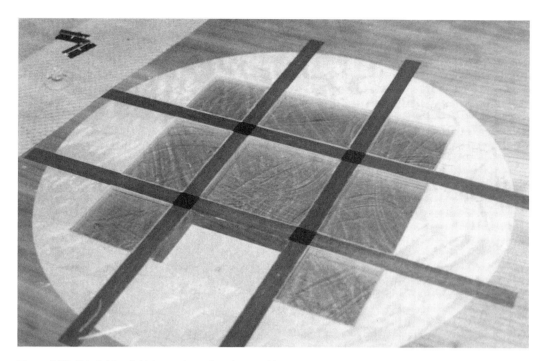

Figure 7.28 ⅛-inch (.3 cm) thick cast glass—inset into a table top.

glass, making it six times as strong as annealed glass. Tempered glass is sometimes incorrectly referred to as *safety glass,* which is glass laminated with plastic, as in automobile windshields.

The tensile strength of tempered glass comes with a penalty. Due to the balanced stresses in the glass, any damage or force applied to the glass edges will cause the glass to shatter into hundreds of tiny pieces. Thus, tempered glass must be cut to size and drilled before tempering, and it cannot be reworked once tempered. Ironically, while tempered glass can carry heavier loads, its surface is not as hard as that of annealed glass and it is more susceptible to scratching.

A recently developed technique to strengthen glass uses a heat-bonded transparent plastic film between two identical plates of glass. This chemical tempering process produces glass that is three times stronger than that produced by traditional tempering.

Glass can be cut using the Paser system, which involves a high-pressure pump that drives a mixture of water and abrasive powder through a cutting nozzle. The process is controlled by a computer. Preshaped and prebeveled glass is bent by placing it over heat-resistant steel and heating it in electric kilns that reach 630°C. The *Ghost* chair designed by Cini Boeri (see Chapter 4), produced by the Fiam company in Brianza, Italy, is an all-glass chair that results from both of these techniques. Glass can be welded using an adhesive that will cure only when exposed to full-spectrum UV light. The *Elica* table designed by Isoa Hosoe, produced by Tonelli (1988), and the *Atlas* table designed by Danny Lane, produced by Fiam (1988), result from the ability to weld glass in this manner.

Starphire glass is a glass with low iron content that is completely clear and without the pale green edge typical of most glass. *Laminated* or *safety glass* is annealed glass fused with plastic sheets that hold the glass in place when broken. **Cast glass** is difficult to control dimensionally but has a beautiful surface quality similar to that of ice.

Pyrex first became available in 1915. Corning research physicist Jesse Littleton cut the bottom from a glass battery jar produced by Corning, took it home, and asked his wife to bake a cake in it. The glass withstood the heat during the baking process and led to the development of borosilicate glasses for kitchenware and later to a wide range of glass products marketed as Pyrex.

In 1936, the Rohm and Haas Company of Philadelphia pressed polymethyl acrylate between two pieces of glass, thereby making a clear plastic sheet. It was the forerunner of what in the United States was called *Plexiglas*® (polyvinyl methacrylate). Far tougher than glass, Plexiglas is used as a substitute for glass in automobiles, airplanes, furniture, signs, and homes.

Metal

Metal is used in both the form and structure of furniture as well as for hardware and mechanical fasteners. It is, however, a material considered uncomfortably cool to the touch and therefore is conventionally used for surface and support elements in furniture. It is a remarkable material that can be curved, bent, and rolled. Metals are consistent in quality, stability, and hardness. Metal is a homogeneous material (without grain) and is given texture through a variety of techniques. It can be worked to precise dimensions far greater than those of wood, glass, or stone. Metal can be joined by being screwed, bolted, or welded. When joining different metals, keep in mind that **galvanic action** will occur when dissimilar metals touch and are exposed to moisture. Galvanic action is a chemical reaction that occurs in the presence of humidity or moisture and will corrode one or the other metal when two metals are in contact.

Aluminum is a relatively soft, lightweight metal that can be cast in sand, rolled, extruded, forged, and drawn. However, it is very difficult to weld. It is an exceptional material for outdoor use because its outermost layer converts to aluminum oxide when exposed to air, giving aluminum a nearly transparent layer that resists further corrosion. In the mid-1800s, aluminum was more expensive than silver. Thanks to an abundance of aluminum-bearing ores (bauxite) and development of modern means of extracting the mineral, aluminum today is widely available and inexpensive.

Brass is an **alloy** of copper and zinc that produces a soft yellow metal. Typically, brass is two-thirds copper and one-third zinc. It can be filed, sawn, drilled, bent, and braised. Brass is used as a base metal for plating other metals and finishes, making it an excellent choice for architectural or cabinet furniture hardware. Secondary uses include screws and decorative work.

Bronze was the first metal used in furniture. It is an alloy of copper and tin and is an excellent material for locks, hinges, and decorative elements because it is resistant to corrosion.

Copper saws, files, and solders easily. Though it polishes easily, copper will patina to a brown and then to a green color (copper carbonate) in clean air and to a black color (copper sulfide) in dirty air. Copper and its alloys are easy to cast, to roll to sheet, to draw to wire, and to shape in other ways. Copper and its alloys are particularly desirable for recycling.

Carbon steel is an alloy of iron and has up to 1.7 percent carbon. Early-20th-century furniture used tubular steel bent into various shapes. Mart Stam and Marcel Breuer of the Bauhaus were among the first designers who used precision steel tubing in their furniture (Figure 7.29). Many furniture designers, beginning as early as the second half of the 19th

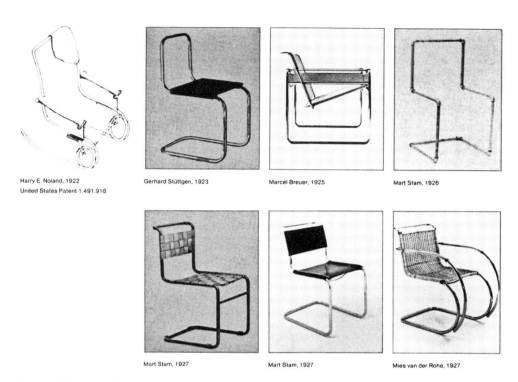

Harry E. Noland, 1922
United States Patent 1.491.918

Gerhard Stüttgen, 1923

Marcel Breuer, 1925

Mart Stam, 1926

Mart Stam, 1927

Mart Stam, 1927

Mies van der Rohe, 1927

Figure 7.29 Design offspring—tubular metal chairs.

century, used wire and steel rod. In the 20th century, Harry Bertoia designed a series of wire frame chairs that are still in production (see Chapter 4). Carbon steels are easy to recycle, and little energy is needed to recycle them.

Steel is often **galvanized** with a thin coat of zinc to minimize oxidation, but it is difficult to work. The process of galvanizing steel with zinc makes it problematic to weld or cut safely in a shop because cutting or welding galvanized steel produces a toxic off-gas. Zinc, in its pure form, was used to clad bar counters throughout France because of zinc's properties. It does not react to acids (wine) or cleaning fluids and is easy to shape.

Although created earlier in the 20th century by a Frenchman and a German, stainless steel was rediscovered in Sheffield, England, in 1913. Harry Brearley has been credited with popularizing the material. Made of iron with about 13 percent chromium and a small portion of carbon, stainless steel will not rust and welds easily. It is an excellent material for use in food service. There are many alloys of stainless steel, which include USD316, USD321, USD306, and USD630. USD304 is the typical grade, composed of 74 percent iron, 18 percent chromium, and 8 percent nickel.

Plastics

Plastics include a vast assortment of polymers used to mass-produce an enormous number of furnishings. Plastics are unique in the number of ways they can be shaped, formed, textured, and colored. They are often associated with modern life. In the early 1900s, plastic was used for small objects, eyeglasses, and containers. The late 1950s witnessed the use of plastic in furniture with the work of Charles Eames, Eero Saarinen, and Verner Panton. In the 1980s, companies such as Kartell and Artemide used plastic as the primary material in

Figure 7.30 Trådskitsestol, a one-piece stamped plastic lounge designed by Anders Hermansens, ca. 1985.

Figure 7.31 Tête-à-Tête lounge seating (1983)—designed by Stanley Tigerman, made with Formica's *Colorcore* material, a plastic laminate that has homogenous color.

almost all of their furniture production. Plastics have been made possible by their unique forming characteristics and offer excellent electrical, thermal, tensile, and insulation properties. Material scientists have developed many polymer materials for a wide number of applications. Particularly attractive to the furniture designer is the fact that plastic furniture can be made in one piece without joints or mechanical connections (Figure 7.30).

Plastics are made from polymers, which are chemical compounds composed of long molecules made up of chains of small, repeated units (monomers). Polymers are rarely used alone. Additives are often used to enhance the appearance, improve the strength, and change the characteristics of various plastics. Glass fibers can be used to strengthen plastic. Glass, carbon, paper, cotton, zinc, aluminum, magnesium, wood, talc, chalk, calcium, vegetable oil, and clay are some of the materials that can be incorporated into polymers to create different effects and properties. Polymeric products can be molded into any shape, are considered aesthetically pleasing, and have low density and a low coefficient of friction. Some plastics have excellent corrosion and impact resistance.

Plastics can be divided into two main categories. The first category has relatively short chains of molecules that are produced in the polymerization process. These polymers are called *thermosetting plastics*. In the second category of polymers, polymerization results in relatively long molecular structures called *thermoplastics*.

Thermosetting Plastics

A chemical change occurs in thermosetting plastics during the curing process. This irreversible condition is usually induced by mixing a resin with an activator, which coincides with the molding or forming of the component into its final shape. Thermosets cannot be re-formed after they have cured. Any subsequent shaping is carried out using traditional wood- or metalworking tools.

Phenol-Formaldehyde (PF) Resins: Used widely for laminate materials for tables and countertops (Figure 7.31). PF resins are also used in wood glues, reinforced laminates, and moldings such as car distributor caps and electrical plugs. Common trade names are *Bakelite* and *Melamine.*

Urea-Formaldehyde (UF): Used in wood glues, buttons, colored toilet seats, and domestic electrical fittings.

Epoxides: There are specific epoxy glues for metal, glass, and other materials. They are used for encapsulation of electrical components, glass reinforcement, powder coat-

Figure 7.32 Knotted Chair—epoxy coated knotted rope. Designed by Marcel Wanders (1996), produced by Dry Tech.

ings, adhesives, marine protection coatings, molds, and dies for thermoplastics (Figure 7.32).

Polyester: Used in finishes, **fiberglass**-reinforced boat hulls, car bodies, vehicle cabs, weather enclosures, and many applications where, in the face of weather conditions, aesthetics and durability are important. Polyester is also used in lacquers for wood finishing.

Thermoplastics

Thermoplastics soften when heated and regain their rigidity when cooled. Various *thermoforming* processes have been developed for changing the shape of thermoplastic sheets by exploiting this property, including *line bending, vacuum forming, dip coating, dome blowing,* **blow molding,** *rotational molding, injection molding,* and *extrusion* (*push and pull methods*). Unlike thermosetting plastics, no chemical change occurs when this type of plastic is heated and cooled. When a thermoformed object is reheated, it will soften again and can be re-formed or left to return to its original shape.

Between the 1920s and the 1940s, new synthetic fibers and resins such as nylon, acrylic, and polyester were introduced. These materials were used to make clothing, industrial equipment, and Plexiglas®. Nylon is strong and lightweight. Bases of office chairs are manufactured using nylon. These components are usually injection molded and filled with fillers such as glass or minerals to achieve higher durability. Because nylon absorbs humidity from the air, it is not recommended for humid areas.

Following the development of these materials, new compounds derived from the by-products of the oil-refining process entered the market. Four materials synthesized from such hydrocarbon by-products are:

■ *Polystyrene,* a brittle plastic known also as *Styrofoam™.* Polystyrene foam is used in packaging. It is processed by expanded foam molding.

- *Polyvinyl chloride,* used in plumbing fixtures and weather-resistant home siding.
- *Polyethylene,* which is flexible, inexpensive, and widely used in packaging and ski bottoms. Polyethylene foam is lightweight.
- *Polyurethane* is the most widely used of the elastomer foams. It is a self-skinning material.

ABS (acrylonitrile-butadiene-styrene) is a synthetic polymer plastic available since 1948. Mostly vacuum-formed and injection molded, it was used for making chairs in the mid-1960s. A fiberglass-reinforced plastic was used to produce Vico Magistretti's *Selene* (Figure 7.33), manufactured by Artemide in 1969, as well as Anna Castelli Ferrieri's *Stooble* (combining the words *table* and *stool*), produced by Kartell in 1987. ABS is used to make injection-molded chairs, storage systems, tables, and accessories.

Polyvinyl chloride (PVC) is a rigid or plasticized thermoplastic material first commercially developed in 1928–30. It is one of the cheapest, most versatile, and most widely used polymers. PVC is banned from use in some countries, as it produces carbon dioxide when it is burned—usually after the end of its useful life. It is also a known carcinogen. In its pure form as a thermoplastic, it is rigid. Joe Colombo's *Tube* chair (1969) is made of rigid PVC, plastic, foam, and fabric. The Tube chair was manufactured by Flexform. When incorporated with plasticizers, PVC can be made flexible as is the *webbing* for Giandomenico Bellotti's *Spaghetti* chair, produced by Alias.

Polyethylene (PE) is a lightweight thermoplastic material developed in 1933. As a high-density, rigid plastic, it is used in injection or blow molding for a range of plastic furniture. It has a waxy feel and is available in a wide range of colors. PE is characterized by easy processing and chemical resistance, and strikes a balance between strength and rigidity. PE is

Figure 7.33 Stackable Selene chairs, designed by Vico Magistretti (1969), manufactured by Artemide, injection-molded plastic.

a low-cost, recyclable material. The stacking PE child's chair designed by Richard Sapper and Marco Zanuso (1983), produced by Kartell, is an example of PE used for seating.

In 1953, Karl Zeigler developed a method for creating a high-density PE molecule with a very high melting point that could be manufactured at low temperatures and low pressures. It has been made into dishes, squeezable bottles, and soft plastic materials.

Polypropylene (PP) was discovered in 1954 but was not used in furniture design until 1963, when the first self-supporting injection-molded *Hille* stacking chair was produced. Many of the polymer components (seat pan) of the *4822-44 stools,* designed by Anna Castelli Ferrieri in 1979 for Kartell, were made of PP, which is recyclable.

Polystyrene (PS) is a rigid plastic used in molded products. It is the most familiar and cheapest of all polymer foams. The flammability of PS foam was, at one time, a cause for concern. New flame retardants allow PS foams to meet current fire safety standards. There are environmental concerns about using PS because it is not biodegradable.

Polyurethane (PU) is one of the most important synthetic plastics used in furniture. It can be made flexible, rigid, or structural, and is used for coating textiles and as a wood finish. It is used as an upholstery foam when flexible and as a chair frame shell when rigid. *Non Rubber,* designed by Boris Berlin and Poul Christiansen of Komplot Design, utilizes PU mixed with an elastomer as the primary material, which is then injected into a two-part aluminum form around a continuously welded steel frame (see Material Chapter). The result is a reductive, iconic, and functional stackable chair.

Polycarbonate (PC) offers one of the highest impact resistances among the polymers. It is many times stronger than glass. PC is available in several grades including UV stable, highflow, flame resistant, water resistant, high optical clarity, and wear resistant.

Lexan PC is one of the most widely known plastics. Available in sheets with a unique combination of high-impact strength and thermoformability, lexan is ideally suited for security applications. No other plastic can match lexan's combination of light transmittance (clarity) and the ability to withstand extreme impact. It is easy to machine and weathers well.

Less impact-resistant than lexan is acrylic. Kartell produces the *LCP Chaise* (Low Chair Plastic) designed by Maarten Van Severen, which is made from an engineered acrylic called *methacrylate.* The LCP Chaise is formed by a sculptural loop of clear or colored methacrylate, joined with rubber buffers to allow gentle movement by the user (Figure 7.34).

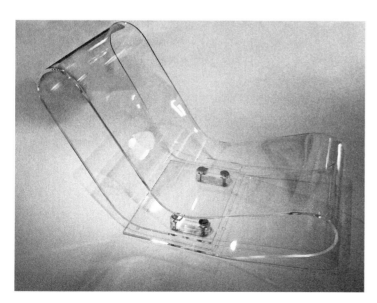

Figure 7.34 LCP Chaise (Low Chair Plastic), designed by Maarten Van Severen, manufactured by Kartell.

Figure 7.35 Bad-Tempered chair, designed by Ron Arad (2002), manufactured by Kartell.

Carbon and Poly Fiber Carbon

In 1964, British engineer Leslie Phillips made carbon fibers by stretching synthetic fibers and then heating them. The resulting fibers were twice as strong as the same weight of steel. Ron Arad's *Well-Tempered Chair* (1985) was originally fabricated out of sheet steel. In 2002, it was reintroduced at the Milan Furniture Fair entitled *Bad-Tempered Chair,* made of a specially developed plastic using glass, carbon, and Kelvar fiber laminated in resin. Both designs are produced by Vitra Edition (Figure 7.35).

The first chair to use molded carbon fiber in an epoxy-resin matrix and polyurethane foam is the *Light Light* chair, designed by Alberto Meda in 1987 for the Italian company Alias. It is remarkably light and durable. In response to the desire for improved comfort and increased sales, Alberto Meda designed *Soft Light* in 1989, a composite of an aluminum honeycomb core with a skin of carbon fiber and an elastomeric seat pan and seat back held in tension by the chair's side and back support.

Rubber and Elastomers

Wallace Carothers and a team at DuPont, building on work begun in Germany earlier in the 20th century, developed synthetic rubber in 1930, though natural rubber was known to the natives of Peru many centuries earlier. Synthetic rubber is called *neoprene,* a substance more resistant to oil, gasoline, and ozone than natural rubber. It is also used as an adhesive and as a sealant in industrial uses. Neoprene can be purchased as a soft foam (neoprene 10–20) as well as a hard synthetic rubber (neoprene 60–70).

Figure 7.36 Rubber Tire-Tube chair, exhibited at the International Contemporary Furniture Fair, in New York (designer unknown).

Rubber in furniture is generally reserved for wheels, bumpers, and mats. Natural rubber is an excellent, inexpensive, general-purpose elastomer. Some furnishings employ elastomers and rubber as an integrative and substantial material (Figure 7.36).

Stone

Marble is a beautiful stone; however, it is susceptible to breakage along its natural veins and faults. Though excellent in compression, it is fragile in both shear and moment capacity. It also needs to be sealed because it is easily stained and damaged by acids. Marble consists of calcium carbonate that is crystallized by metamorphism and ranges from granular to compact in texture. Typically, it is purchased in two slab thicknesses: ¾ inch (2 cm) and 1¼ inches (3 cm). Slabs available for purchase are typically 5 feet by 10 feet (152 cm by 304 cm).

Limestone is also *calcium carbonate* formed by seashells left behind millions of years ago. The shells formed sedimentary layers at the bottom of seas. Through a process called *metamorphosis,* they formed into limestone. Limestone, when further heat and pressure are applied, becomes marble.

Limestone and marble can be sanded, sawed, honed, and put on a **lathe** and turned. These stones are porous and will absorb moisture and oils. They need to be sealed and regularly maintained.

Granite is an *igneous* stone that results from volcanic activity. It is the hardest and most durable of the natural stones but still needs to be well supported. It is resistant to heat, moisture, acids, alkalis, and most chemicals. Granite receives its color by being combined with other minerals. Cobalt makes blue, iron makes red and black, and copper makes green granite.

Though granite is durable, it is a porous material and prone to developing bacteria within its surface. Therefore, it is not ideal for commercial food service applications. Popular synthetic stones, acrylic surfacing materials, and stainless steels are common substitutes for granite counters in food service or kitchen environments.

Stones can be cut and sculpted using a CNC machine. With the influx of digital software and digital modeling programs, stones can be worked in any imaginable manner using three-, four-, and five-axis milling machines.

Woods and Grasses

Wood

Wood has been the standard material used to make furniture since recorded time. Today, the process of working with solid lumber (by hand) to mass-produce furniture is generally considered economically unfeasible. This reality has caused furniture designers and companies to consider veneers and composite panels, computer-controlled cutting tools, and automated processes of painting and finishing wooden furniture. Laminated veneers and formed plywood designs became popular in the late 1940s, attributed to the initial studies by Charles and Ray Eames (Figure 7.37a). Since that time, many companies have developed furniture production and finishing technologies that utilize sophisticated machinery and processes of working with laminated and composite wood.

GUBI, a furniture company in Copenhagen, has produced a line of chairs made by pressing presliced veneer sheets under pressure into graceful compound curves (Figure 7.37b). The veneer sheets are fine-sliced before gluing and then formed into shape by a mold without cracking or buckling the veneers. The thin slices in the veneer fill with glue to set the veneer and are then sanded to look continuous. The chairs are well proportioned, comfortable, lightweight, and relatively inexpensive.

Despite the economic success that many designers and companies have had in making furniture that utilizes industrial processes, craftsmen and furniture designers continue to design and fabricate unique and limited-run studio furniture with lumber as the primary material. Therefore, knowledge of lumber and woodworking remains critically important for many designers and fabricators.

Furniture designers and furniture makers working with wood generally limit their selection to a few species from the several thousand available species throughout the world. According to Ernest Joyce, author of *The Encyclopedia of Furniture Making,* there are over 43,000 different species of wood-forming plants, of which 30,000 are regarded as timber producers and about 10,000 species are commercially available.[5]

As mentioned earlier, humidity and moisture changes in the environment will cause wood to move (mostly perpendicular to the direction of its grain). Different woods respond to changes in moisture at different rates. Generally, hardwoods are more susceptible to dimensional change than softwoods, with beech, maple, chestnut, and white oak enor-

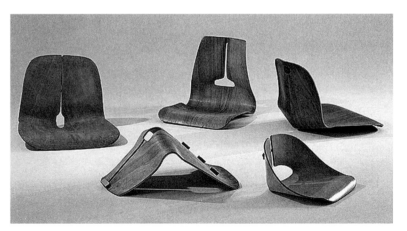

Figure 7.37a Laminated plywood chair studies, Charles and Ray Eames.

Figure 7.37b GUBI II, designed by Komplot Design (2006) for GUBI A/S Denmark.

mously susceptible to dimensional change. Walnut, poplar, and mahogany are some of the most stable.

The two main classifications of wood are *softwoods* and *hardwoods*. Softwoods are coniferous (cone-bearing), and though they will lose some needles, they usually remain green throughout the year. Hardwoods are deciduous trees that lose their leaves during the winter season. Generally, softwoods are physically soft, such as redwood, but some softwoods, such as spruce and yellow pine, can be very hard indeed. Hardwoods such as maple, birch, and ash are hard. Basswood, poplar, and balsa are "soft" hardwoods. Regardless of the general classification, what really matters are the specific material properties of each species.

Different species reveal unique properties that include ray patterns, cellular structure, dimensional stability, color stability, workability, grain configuration, oil and silica content, modulus of elasticity, and coefficient of deflection. A cross section of a tree trunk (Figure 7.38) reveals various layers from the bark to the center of its **heartwood.** The cambium layer is the layer just inside the bark and is made of a narrow ring of growth cells. The next layer inward is the **sapwood,** which distributes water and nutrients from the roots and is generally lighter in color than heartwood. Heartwood is the most generally desirable part of trees (darkened by extractives deposited over time) except for the maples, birch, and ash most desired for their lighter sapwood. The **pith** is the center of the tree and is impossible to use for furniture-making purposes because it is much too small. The outer protective layer of a tree is the bark. In birch and Spanish Oak trees, bark is a useful material. Cork is the subcutaneous bark of the cork oak, *Quarks sober,* which grows in the Mediterranean region. Cork is light, porous, easily compressed, and elastic. It is a natural, closed-cell wood product and is waterproof. Compressing granulated cork under heat makes corkboard.

While some lumber is **air dried,** most is sent to a kiln. Most lumber mills use kilns to dry wood at a temperature between 110 and 180°F. The desirable moisture content of dried

Figure 7.38 Cross section of a tree trunk.

lumber for interior use usually ranges from 6 to 12 percent, depending upon its use and intended location. **Kiln-drying** methods also usually kill most diseases or insects that might be present in the wood. Furniture used in controlled environments will have a moisture content close to 6 percent. It is ideal to work with wood and make all the joinery while the moisture content is compatible with its surroundings. Generally, wood will accept finishes better the drier it is.

The direction of the grain in lumber depends upon the tree's growth over time as well as the manner in which it was cut at the lumber mill. Plain sawn, quarter sawn, and **rift sawn** are three ways to cut lumber from the trunk of a tree.

The most economical way of securing lumber from a tree is to plain saw the tree by repeatedly cutting the log in a straight line from top to bottom (Figure 7.39). This process will produce a majority of plain-sawn lumber, but some of the lumber will be rift and quarter sawn as well. A "cathedral" grain pattern results from cutting straight down through the "stack" of the trees growth rings. **Plain-sawn** cutting produces boards that may cup or warp over time because of the inherent stresses in the lumber. Quarter sawing results in the straightest face grain possible and is also much more stable. This process also yields less lumber and is therefore more expensive.

Quarter-sawn logs are cut into four equal parts along the length of the log. Each quarter is then positioned on the saw and ripped at 90 degrees. When the resultant cut lumber is between 30 and 45 degrees to the tangent of the growth rings, the lumber is called *rift cut*. Rift and quarter-sawn lumber are equally strong. Quarter-sawn lumber is more stable than plain-sawn lumber and is also more uniform in its face grain appearance.

Lumber expands or contracts perpendicularly to the axis of the grain; consequently, the designer must consider movement due to moisture variations. Joints such as the mortise

Figure 7.39 A boule log, plain sawn mahogany lumber reassembled with spacer strips.

and tenon, lap, finger, and **dovetail** have evolved over time to join pieces of wood together. Maximizing the surface of the joint in order to maximize the surface within the joint is important to its strength and long-term durability. Dowel pins, screws, and adhesives are options to consider in mechanically attaching wood together. Care must be taken with simple metal screw-to-wood connections, because over time screws will loosen from the wood. It is always best to use metal-to-metal connections such as screws and threaded metal inserts.

Precompressed Wood

Precompressed wood is a method of forming wood three-dimensionally. The process uses regular lumber that is steamed until the wood is plasticized. Then it is placed in a compressor, which is a solid chamber. Enormous pressure is applied along the longitudinal direction of the wood, causing the fibers of the wood to fold. This process destroys the integrity of the cellular structure of the wood and enables it to be remarkably flexible while the wood retains its moisture (Figure 7.40). When fixed in a form, the wood can be dried, either in the air, in an oven, or by exposing it to high-frequency electromagnetic radiation. The steamed wood can then be used for several hours, or it can be wrapped in plastic to retain the moisture and stored for several weeks—still retaining its flexibility. Care must be taken not to store the wood too long because the high moisture will eventually cause it to rot. Though precompressed wood can easily be formed in a large number of compound curves, it is relatively unstable when dried and therefore is limited in use.[6] However, for making working prototypes of furniture designs with compound curves, no material is as easy to work with as precompressed wood. The compressors capable of creating compressed wood are expensive and limited in availability.

Figure 7.40 Soren Pedersen of PP Møbler explaining precompressed lumber to students.

Figure 7.41 Flitches of wood veneers.

Figure 7.42 Vacuum molding and veneer-laminated seating, Jose Alberto Casas Pena (2006), Denmark's International Study Program, 2006 summer.

Veneer

Wood **veneers** date to Egyptian times but became commonplace in the 18th century with the ebonite guilds. Veneering is the process of cutting thin layers of wood from a log using a veneer saw. A lathe will produce rotary cut veneers and a vertical knife will produce plain-sliced veneers. Veneers that are kept in sequence in batches are called **flitches.** Rotary-cut veneer is a continuous sheet of thin wood cut from a log that is turned on a very large lathe. Plain-sliced, rift, and quartered veneers are cut along the length of the log. Pine was used by English and American furniture makers as the carcass material and then covered with walnut or mahogany veneers. Once the thin layers of wood are cut (Figure 7.41), they can be applied to the surface of a substrate material such as MDF with glue or laminated together to create a curvilinear form (Figure 7.42). In some cases, it is very important to veneer both sides of a panel with the same or similar species of wood veneer. This will help maintain its dimensional stability and minimize warping.

Figure 7.43 Bamboo recliner—on display at Artek's showroom in Helsinki, Finland.

Grasses

A warp of stiff rods, usually made of willow, produces wicker. Other grasses include cane, reed, and straw. During the Roman Empire, wicker was a popular medium for furniture, as is evident in a number of stone reliefs. By the 17th century, wicker chairs were common throughout Europe. Several modernist designers have used wicker in their furniture designs. Mies van der Rohe's bent metal chair *MR* and the British officer's *Pel chairs* incorporated wicker in conjunction with tubular steel.

Bamboo is a grass. It has high sustainability. It can grow up to 3 feet (91 cm) in 1 month and can be harvested after a year. Generally, bamboo is prepared by laminating thin pieces of bamboo with an adhesive. Commonly utilized as a flooring material because of its resilient quality and as scaffolding for its strength, bamboo is an excellent material for furniture because it is relatively stable, hard, strong, and light, making it ideal for tables and shelving units (Figure 7.43).

Figure 7.44 PK 24 chaise lounge, designed by Poul Kjærholm (1965), manufactured using steel, braided cane, and black ox-hide by Fritz Hansen.

Other grasses utilized in furniture and upholstery include jute, hemp, reed, and straw. Braided cane seats have been used in many furniture designs, including Hans J. Wegner's *Cow Horn* chair (1961) and Poul Kjærholm's *PK 24* chaise lounge (1965) (Figure 7.44). Today, wheat and rye grasses have been formed into composite sheet goods and have opened up a world of new design possibilities.

chapter 8

Fabrication

We should make things as simple as possible but not simpler.[1]
Albert Einstein

Processes and Methods of Fabrication

In this book, *workmanship* refers to the quality apparent in the fabrication of furniture. Distinctions have been drawn between the workmanship of risk (handcraft) and the workmanship of certainty (machine and digital fabrication), but in every case, making furniture involves skills and a working knowledge of materials, tools, and processes (Figure 8.1).

Figure 8.1 Bottega di Pierluigi Ghianda—custom woodworking shop, Meda, Italy.

Furniture with a high level of workmanship usually takes more time to make than one might anticipate, so it pays to plan and be organized. Before beginning the process of making furniture, it is wise to make a list of the materials, tools, hardware, and supplies needed and to prepare a schedule to guide the fabrication process. Not only should one consider the quantity of materials necessary to make the furniture, but also the quality, availability, and cost of the materials specified.

For example, lumber is generally purchased at lumberyards or bought from timber merchants. Depending upon its grade, lumber can have excellent figure or have natural surface qualities that may be undesirable, such as sapwood, knots, wormholes, or fruit marks. It is becoming difficult to find woods such as cherry in widths greater than 6 inches (15.2 cm) due to the demand for these species. Plywood is graded by its surface and core and can vary widely in quality from one side to the other side of a single sheet. The quality of its surface veneers and its core are graded using letter and numerical ratings. Stone, especially granite and marble, can vary significantly in pattern and color within a single slab. The quality of plastics, metals, and glass, however, is generally consistent because of the uniformity of these materials and the manufacturing processes involved. The point is to keep in mind that some materials need to be hand selected by the designer. They can't be ordered over the phone or through the Internet due to their inherent variation.

Orders for hard-to-find materials such as specialty fabrics, veneers, and woods can take several weeks. Sources for newer green materials such as wheat board, Medite II, and the newest copper and aluminum foams can take time to locate and secure. Today, searches are made easier with the assistance of the Internet. (Several Web sites have been listed in the bibliography.)

Most hand tools for working materials are available at local retail stores, as are common shop supplies such as glues, screws, dowels, bits, sandpaper, and finishing materials. But special hardware, larger tools, and additional equipment may be needed and may require extensive lead times to secure. In addition to searching for and securing the necessary materials and tools, make schedules for fabricating the work and maintain them.

Preparing Shop Drawings and a Materials Takeoff List

Shop drawings are essential documents that delineate the parameters and expectations for the final product (Figure 8.2). They can be drafted by hand or executed on the computer and

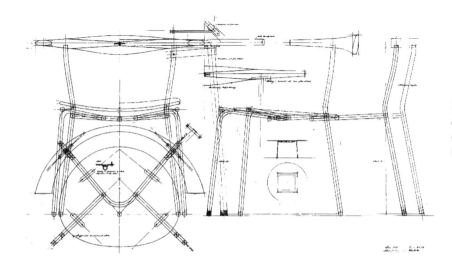

Figure 8.2 Shop drawing of The Chair, designed by Hans J. Wegner.

serve as a transitional phase between design and fabrication. Usually plotted or drafted at full scale, shop drawings delineate exactly how something will be made and the precise dimensions, material, and finish of the components.

A material *takeoff* list determines the quantity of material needed to fabricate the design. To do this accurately, it is helpful to sketch the required cut dimensions on scaled drawings of the available stock material. As a rule, depending on the species of wood, purchase 30 percent more wood than is considered necessary to complete the work. For materials with consistent properties such as glass, plastic, and metal, the overage can be as low as 10 percent.

Securing Materials, Equipment, Supplies, and Hardware

Consider the quality, grade, and availability of all materials needed to fabricate furniture as well as the width, length, thickness, and finished surface qualities of the materials as they are distributed. This process determines the necessary cuts and the yields of the materials needed. For example, ¾-inch (1.9-cm)-thick MDF is slightly thicker than ¾-inch (1.9-cm)-thick plywood. Though plywood is available in 48-inch by 96-inch (122-cm by 244-cm) sheets, MDF is purchased in 49-inch by 97-inch (124.5-cm by 246.5-cm) sheets. Baltic birch plywood is generally available in 60-inch by 60-inch (150 cm by 150 cm) sheets. If there are any doubts regarding the true dimensions and characteristics of the materials you desire to use, be certain to ask the supplier, distributor, or fabricator.

Lumber purchased S4S (surfaced four sides) is dimensioned lumber and is sold in linear feet using fixed, **nominal dimensions.** Rough lumber boards are planed and jointed (surfaced) on two edges. They are also available in prejointed boards for a noticeable savings in cost. Thus, a 1 by 2 is ¾ × 1½ inches (1.9 × 3.8 cm) and a 2 by 4 is 1½ × 3½ inches (3.8 × 8.9 cm). Their fixed dimensions can also influence design.

Rough lumber, which ultimately gives the fabricator the most flexibility, is sold by the **board foot,** and is available in thicknesses measured in quarters of an inch and referred to as ⁴⁄₄, ⁵⁄₄, ⁶⁄₄, ⁸⁄₄, ¹⁰⁄₄, and ¹²⁄₄ boards. One board foot is equal to the volume of lumber equivalent to 12 inches by 12 inches by 1 inch (30.5 cm by 30.5 cm by 2.54 cm) thick (144 cubic inches). Structural steel is purchased by the linear foot, thickness, and weight. Common stock profiles include flat bar stock, round tubing, bar tubing, square tubing, and angle. Plastic and glass sheet goods are purchased by the square foot, and pricing is based upon type, thickness, and edge treatment. Granite and marble are sold in ¾-inch (2-cm) and 1¼-inch (3-cm) thicknesses. A polished finish is standard on one side of stone slabs when distributed, but honed, thermal, hammered, and flamed finishes are also available. Leather is sold in full- and half-hide sizes and in full-thickness, split, and suede finishes. Sheet metal is sold in sheets and in various gauges and alloys. Sheet metals generally require professional fabrication and tooling. Keep in mind that most retailers that sell lumber, metal, stone, and plastic will charge to make cuts.

It is unrealistic to be dogmatic about what tools are needed to build furniture. The choice depends upon a number of factors, including the experience and personal preference of the fabricator, the furniture being made, available shop space, and financial resources available (Figure 8.3).

Figure 8.3 Hand tools—a craftman's wall cabinet in the Rud. Rasmussen woodshop, Copenhagen.

Many types of hand, power, and digital tools are used to make furniture. While good tools are often expensive, it is advisable to purchase and use quality tools because they are essential for producing quality results safely. As a rule, buy hand tools of superior quality and consider them all an investment.

A list of hand tools for making furniture might include:

- Adjustable block plane and jack plane
- Awl, calipers, and a marking gauge
- Metal **cabinet scraper** and a burnishing rod
- Bevel-edge chisels: ⅛ inch (3 mm), ¼ inch (6 mm), ⅜ inch (9 mm), ½ inch (12 mm), ¾ inch (18 mm), and 1 inch (24 mm)
- Mortising chisels: ¼ inch (6 mm), ⅜ inch (10 mm)
- Firm-edge chisels
- Wooden mallet
- Japanese saws (these "backsaws" cut on the pull) (Figure 8.4)
- **Coping saw**
- A set of **countersink** and high-speed steel drill bits
- A true square
- A combination square
- Sliding bevel
- Steel straight edge (30 inches [76.2 cm] with units visible) and a flexible steel ruler
- Marking knife
- Bench vise (wood)
- **C-clamps** (6-inch [15.2 cm] and 10-inch [25.4-cm] length)

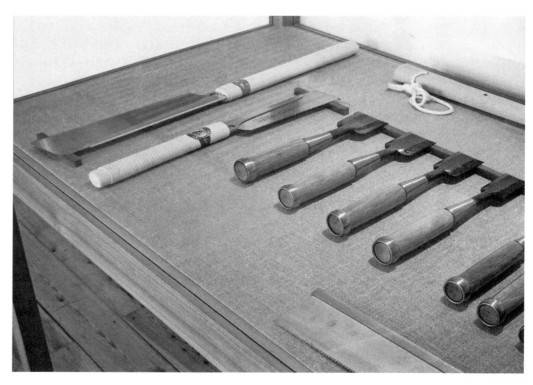

Figure 8.4 Hand chisels and Japanese saws.

- Sash or bar clamps (30-inch [76.2-cm] length)
- Framing corner clamps (minimum of four)
- Stones for sharpening cabinet scraper and chisels
- Level (24 inches [61 cm])
- An assortment of hand screwdrivers (flat-head, Phillips, and square-head), pliers, sockets, and wrenches
- An assortment of fasteners
- A tape measure

A list of power tools for making furniture might include:

- **Belt sanders** (24 inches [61 cm] long × 3 inches [7.6 cm] wide)
- **Disk sander** (13 inches [33 cm])
- Oscillating spindle sander (Figure 8.5)
- Orbital sander
- Routers (and a small hand-held trim router)
- Table saw
- Shaper
- Drill press
- Powered hand drills
- Air compressor
- Cut-off saw
- Panel saw
- Jointer (6-inch [15.2-cm] minimum)
- **Planer** (13-inch [33-cm]-width minimum)

Figure 8.5 Power spindle sander.

- Wood lathe (36 inches [91 cm] long)
- Metal lathe (36 inches [91 cm] long)
- Axis mill machine

Shop supplies might include carpenter's yellow glue, contact adhesive, polyacrylic, tung oil, Danish oil, or lacquer spray finishes, as well as sandpaper, screws, brads, finish nails, pencils, soap, beeswax, and dust masks.

- Yellow carpenter's glue generally works better than white PVA wood glue, but care must be taken in its application. To avoid making a mess in the application, an abundance of damp rags is suggested. Proper clamping pressure is also very important.
- Pencils need to be hard enough to give precise fine lines but soft enough to be seen and not leave an impression upon the wood. 2B pencils and 7-mm drafting pencils with 2H leads work well.
- Marking knifes are more accurate than pencils and provide a precise cut in the wood to guide work with chisels.
- Dust masks, ear protection, and protective eyewear are important safety measures. Working with wood and other materials generates fine dust and chemical fumes. The noise from power tools and compressor generators is damaging to the ears. Eyes are susceptible to fine particulates floating in the air, as well as to flying pieces of wood or metal from cut-off saws, sanding belts, and many other sources.

In addition to the necessary supplies, power tools, and hand tools needed to make furniture, a good horizontal work surface is essential in any furniture shop. Purchase or build one with a flat, sturdy top and a well-engineered base. Working at waist level is the conventional standard to use in determining the height of a workbench. Generally, 34 to 36 inches (86.3 to 91.4 cm) is a good workbench height.

Purchase additional quality tools as needed. It takes time to secure a set of tools and develop a sense of comfort, safety, and productivity with them (Figure 8.6).

Figure 8.6 Table saw with guard and splitter (riving knife).

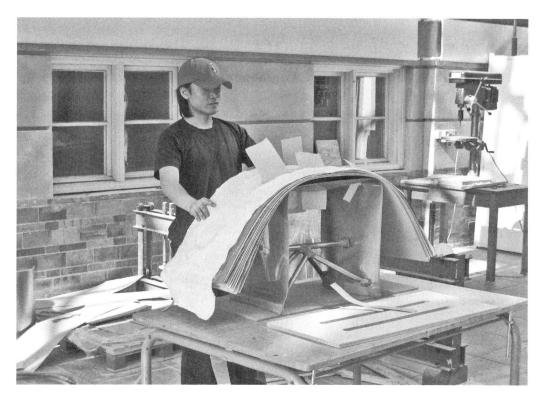

Figure 8.7 DIS student gluing wood veneers around a metal form prior to vacuum molding.

Bending

Bending plies of wood is an effective way to make natural forms with less waste. Beech or birch veneers are commonly used for this process. Thin veneers of these woods are layered with glue and pressed together around a metal form or compressed using a mold with heat and/or ultrasonic vibration (Figure 8.7). When taken out of the mold, the shaped form is sent to a trimmer. The result is high manufacturability, cost-effective fabrication (the initial tooling cost is relatively high, however), light weight, and a sturdy design, as shown in the laminated and molded plywood chairs by Charles and Ray Eames (Figure 8.8).

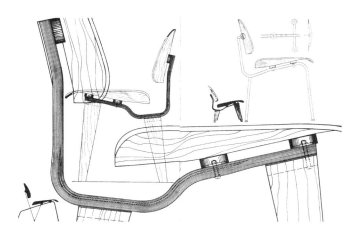

Figure 8.8 Collage of drawings, side views of Eames' laminated plywood chairs.

Figure 8.9 Handcarved detail in walnut.

Carving

Carving is an ancient art and a contemporary science, depending on whether it was done by hand or by machine. When it is done by hand, it is a craft in the true sense of the word. Woodworkers use chisels and gouges to carve and work wood (Figure 8.9).

Many designers and industries have begun to use CNC devices to carve into various materials for making furniture. Stone, polymers, and wood products can be transformed by CNC devices using digital programs and computer hardware. The most intricate patterns are possible, and the cost of the work is a fraction of the cost of doing the work by hand (Figure 8.10)

Figure 8.10 CNC-carved work in marble.

Cutting, Drilling, Milling, and Planing

There are rules of thumb worth considering when working with hand and power tools in a shop environment. The first and foremost priority is to learn how to use power saws properly and safely. Learn how to hold, cut, and shape wood, metal, or plastic in a safe and proper manner. Listen to the sound of the machine's motor. It will let you know when it is out of adjustment or being pushed beyond its limit. The motor driving a table saw can range from a small 2-horsepower motor to a large 10-horsepower motor, which directly affects the saw's cutting power. Observe the condition and sharpness of the saw blades and sanding belts frequently. Verify the jointer, planer, and table saws for accurate alignment. Regularly check the condition of the blades and the sanding belts. Confirm that the measurements on guide rails and the fences are accurate and square to the cutting blade (Figure 8.11). Working in a shop is a dynamic experience in which attention is required at all times, especially when you work alone.

Apply steady, consistent pressure when cutting wood. Let the blade do most of the work; do not force the wood through the blade. Working with metals also requires firm, constantly applied pressure while cutting, drilling, sawing, or sanding. Consider the high temperatures generated in the metal and the blade when cutting or sanding, and remember to wear gloves and a sturdy face shield. Cutting wood requires the use of proper blades that depend upon the type of cut desired. A *rip cut* (cutting along the length of a board) can be made using a 10-inch (25.4 cm) 24- (61 cm) to 48-(122 cm) tooth carbide-tipped blade. These blades have ample space between their cutting teeth, which prevents the blade and wood from overheating. *Cross cutting* wood perpendicular to the grain requires a finer-

Figure 8.11 Using a table saw.

Figure 8.12 Miter saw (also known as a chop saw) is used for making cross-grain cuts.

toothed cross-cut blade to minimize grain tearout (Figure 8.12). A cross-cut blade will not last long if it is used to rip lumber, and a rip-cut blade will produce poor results if used to cross-cut lumber. Combination blades are general, multipurpose blades used for ripping and cross-cutting wood. Dado blades are used for cutting channels of various widths and depths into lumber.

Many different hand and power tools are used to cut and shape wood. These include table saws, miter saws, panel saws, reciprocal saws (jigsaws), and scroll saws. The table saw is the most useful machine tool. It utilizes a variety of blades, a flat table, an adjustable fence, and a protective guard. Table saws are used to rip lumber, and cut dados and **quirk joints.** When one is using adjustable fence slides set in grooves, they can be used for cross-cutting. The safety of table saws has recently been improved with electronic sensors that can prevent serious injuries. Miter saws are adjustable in both angle and depth for precision cutting of angles and square ends. Reciprocal saws, also known as *jigsaws,* are used to cut freehand straight or curved profiles and can be used with a template or guide for precision cuts.

Assembling and Gluing

In the production of furniture, significant shop space is required for assembling and gluing pieces together. Clean, flat, work surfaces are needed to glue and clamp material together. Assembling furniture is a complex process that needs to be planned carefully. In addition to needing a lot of space, this phase requires a significant amount of time, primarily the set time required for the carpenter's glue to set and fully dry. Most PVA glues allow 30 minutes as an open time to work with and require approximately 1 to 1½ hours to set before one can remove the clamps (Figure 8.13). (Timers can make the process of assembly more efficient.)

Figure 8.13 Shop clamps, are essential for gluing assembly work.

Many types of adhesives are used in making furniture. Polyvinyl acetate (PVA) is the woodworker's glue of choice and comes as white glue, yellow glue, or an exterior-grade waterproof yellow glue. As a rule, let the glue do its job. Put no more glue than is needed on each surface to create a uniform bond. When gluing wood together, both sides should receive a continuous application, and should sit for a few minutes before one proceeds with assembling and clamping. This allows the glue to soak into the wood and will increase the strength of the joint. Remember not to overtighten a glued assembly because it will squeeze out the adhesive and reduce the strength of the bond. Further, remember to vent all blind holes that will be glued; otherwise, problems will result during finishing when you try to wipe glue off unfinished wood.

Applying glue to the end grain of wood will always produce an ineffective joint and should be avoided. The strength of any glue joint is proportional to the perimeter length of the joint, since the perimeter is the most highly stressed area.

Epoxy resins are useful for joining different materials together and are ideal for exterior work because they are waterproof.

Contact adhesives are available solvent and water based. These adhesives are applied to both surfaces, left until tacky, and then bonded together under the continuous pressure of a hand or machine roller. When laminating a substrate, it is important to laminate the back side so that the finished panel does not warp or twist.

Cyanoacrylates are instant glues that typically cure in 5 to 10 seconds.

Silicone is an adhesive caulk that can be used to bond materials that expand or contract very differently from one another, such as wood and glass or wood and metal, because silicone remains flexible when fully cured. Silicone is little affected by temperature or moisture and works well for interior and exterior uses. It requires 24 to 48 hours to fully cure.

Joinery, Mechanical Connections, and Fasteners

The way materials and parts of furniture come together is key to creating furniture design. The expressed joint is the beginning of ornament (Figure 8.14). At a utilitarian level, the joint must be strong enough to resist the forces placed upon it. This is especially important because the joint is often the weakest point of a fabrication. Yet, the joint can be more than a means of joining material together. There is an opportunity to communicate meaning through **joinery.** It is also important to consider the aesthetics of the expressed joint resulting from structural necessity and ending in patterns of visual delight.

Consider the techniques of detailing or joining together two or more elements. Broad categories of joining materials include:

- Adhesives
- Mechanical connections
    Sewing
    Nails, rivets, and staples
    Threaded fasteners
    Snap fits
    Applied hardware

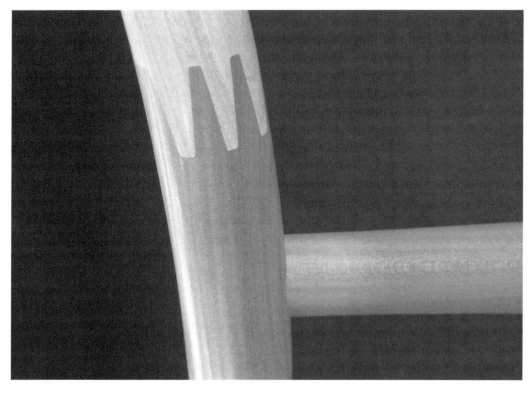

Figure 8.14 Wood joinery.

- Combining adhesive and mechanical connections
  - Dado
  - Dovetail
  - Finger joint
  - Miter joint
  - Mortise and tenon
  - Rabbet
- Welding
  - Spot and arc welding
  - Brazing
  - Metal inert gas (MIG) welding
  - Tungsten inert gas (TIG) welding
  - Diffusion and glaze bonding

Adhesive joints are virtually seamless unless the edge profile of the connection is made visible. Laminating high-density plastic laminate upon a ¾-inch (2-cm) MDF substrate or a simple butt joint of two similar woods are examples of adhesive joints. Wooden tabletops built up from strips of lumber do not need to be pinned or mechanically held in place with biscuits. Today's wood glues are sufficiently strong to do the job alone; they are able to hold the top of a table together for the life of the table.

Mechanical connections rely upon a variety of joining materials and methods. Sewing is the earliest method for joining material. Consider the ancient leg connections made by wrapping wet leather around joints and allowing it to dry. Consider the hammock, caned seating, and the art of sewing leather and fabrics along seams. Consider the hemp strapping used in Alvar Aalto's chairs, the woven cane seat pans of the Thonet chairs, or the twisted paper seat pans in Gio Ponti's café chair *Superleggera* (1951). Sewing and weaving can be significant means of joining and can be remarkable in their strength, comfort, and aesthetic qualities (Figure 8.15).

Figure 8.15 Cane seat pan from the Folding Chair, designed by Hans J. Wegner (1949), fabricated by PP Møbler, Denmark.

Figure 8.16 Section cut showing wood dowel connections in a chair.

Mechanical fasteners include a variety of wood and metal connectors. The wooden dowel or **dowel pin** is one way to hold a joint (Figures 8.16, 8.18). The language of the handcrafted wooden pin and through mortise-and-tenon connections drove the aesthetics and language of the **Arts and Crafts** movement. Finger joints and miter joints are sometimes held in place by a pin connection. Pin connections can also take the form of compressive joints where two materials are joined and held together through compressive means. Threaded fasteners are common means used to hold wood together. Threaded metal insets in wood allow metal-to-metal connections to hold wood pieces together and are better than metal-to-wood connections.

Knock-down furnishings rely on a host of mechanical hardware devices to hold together and easily disassemble individual components. The cam lock, tight joint, and dog bone are devices used to draw wood surfaces together to form one continuous surface. The tight joint and dog bone rely upon two recessed cylindrical holes in the wood connected by a recessed channel. The hardware device is then placed in the recessed holes and drawn tight using a threaded bolt and nut, bringing the edge surfaces of the wood pieces together.

Wood Dovetail Joints

There are three basic types of wood **dovetail joints** (Figure 8.17). The *through-dovetail* consists of tails and pins and is the negative counterpart on the joining board. The angle of the tail cuts should be 11 to 12 degrees. The *half blind dovetail* exposes only one side of the dovetail pattern. Tails should be twice the size of the pins. The dovetail joint is used widely in drawer construction. The *blind miter dovetail* is completely concealed within the joint. The

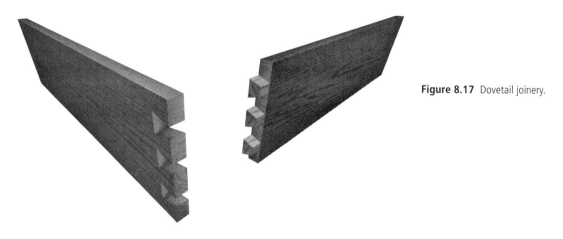

Figure 8.17 Dovetail joinery.

interlocking action of the connection makes the dovetail an especially strong joint, particularly in tension.

Edge Joints

There are five basic ways to join wood together along its edge. Board and batten joints add a piece of wood (shoulder or scab) behind a standard butt joint for increased strength. *A butt joint* consists simply of fastening two members edge to edge, usually with an adhesive. For a good joint, the pieces must be firmly clamped along the entire glue edge and must be of the same species of wood. A *scarf joint* extends the length of a wood member, in which two similarly sized members are joined at an acute angle of approximately 15 degrees for optimum strength. *Finger joints* require two pieces of wood cut with opposite matching notches and then fastened together. A *spline joint* uses a flat wood spline inserted into dadoes cut into the edges of the pieces being assembled.

Lap Joints

A *shiplap joint* receives a notch along the entire edge being joined, which increases the stability and surface area for the adhesive. *Tongue-and-groove joints* are commonly used in

Figure 8.18 Corner detail—wood dowel connections.

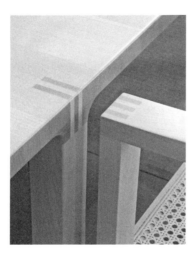

Figure 8.19 Finger joints.

cabinetry. One member receives a groove along its entire edge and the other member a matching and interlocking tongue. *Cross lap joints* allow two pieces of material to cross in the same plane. The same amount of wood is removed from each joining member. *End lap joints* can be used to extend the length of wood or to change direction. The *middle lap joint* occurs at the end of one member and between the ends of the other. The two pieces should fit snugly but should not be forced. In a *miter half lap,* the lap is cut at an angle so that the wood members can turn a corner with an angular expression. This joint is often used in making *frames* (Figures 8.19, 8.20).

Miter Joints

A **miter joint** is a type of butt joint where the two members are each cut with equal angles less than 90 degrees and joined. A *quirk miter* emphasizes the corner of the joint with a reveal cut into each member along the joint. A *spline* is a thin strip of wood inserted into a dado along the miter. In spline construction, the wood members must be thick enough so as not to be weakened by the groove (Figures 8.21, 8.22).

Figure 8.20 The strength of the glue joint is dependent upon the perimeter of the wood joint.

Figure 8.21 Rabbet and dado for stiles and rails—case good designed by Mogens Koch, fabricated by Rud. Rasmussen.

Figure 8.22 Insets used to strengthen a butt joint in the seat back of PP 52, designed by Hans J. Wegner (1975), fabricated by PP Møbler, Denmark.

Mortise-and-Tenon Joints

In a full mortise-and-tenon joint, the tenon is expressed on the outside face of the mortise member. This type of joinery is one of the oldest and strongest in woodworking. A *blind mortise-and-tenon joint* conceals the tenon within the mortise member (Figure 8.23). The tenon and remaining wood on either side of the mortise should be of equal strength. A *haunch* can be added to the tenon to aid in resisting lateral or racking forces. The *through mortise-and-tenon joint* places the joint at the ends of the wood members so that the end grain can be seen (Figure 8.24). A tapered wedge can be used to secure the tenon through the mortise. This type of connection, although it is very sturdy, can easily be taken apart and reassembled.

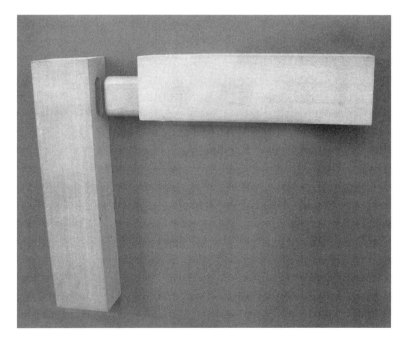

Figure 8.23 Blind mortise-and-tenon joinery.

Figure 8.24 Through mortise-and-tenon joinery.

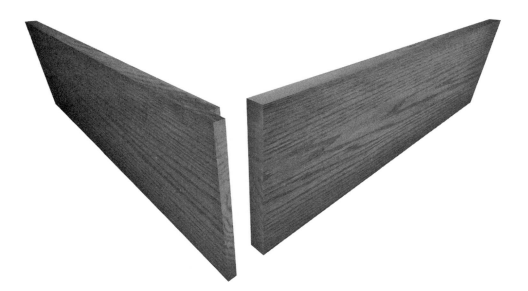

Figure 8.25 Rabbet joinery.

Rabbet and Dado Joints

A **rabbet joint** is fabricated where one or both of the members are recessed on an edge in order to turn a corner (Figure 8.25). A **dado** is a cut made in the wood to provide a shoulder on either side of the joining member. This joint is often used to fabricate cabinets and shelving. In a *dado and rabbet joint,* one member receives a dado cut and the other a rabbet on its edge. A *stopped dado* does not run to the edge of the wood member, so it looks like a butt joint.

Hardware includes square and Phillips tip drivers and stainless steel, brass, or wallboard screws (Figure 8.26). Hardware also includes bolts, nuts, washers, pulls, full extension glides, casters, special cabinet hinges, or plated continuous hinges. *Modez clips* are useful in mounting panels and heavy objects to a vertical surface. Similar to the **French cleat,** which relies upon gravity and two angled elements to secure the attachment, the modez clip is a two-part metal device that enables one element to fit into the other; then the two elements lock together via a keyhole with a simple sliding action.

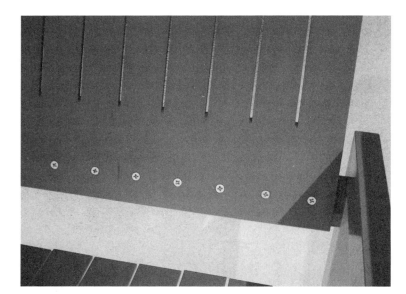

Figure 8.26 Mechanical connection—Phillips head screws.

- Drywall screws work well for most mechanical attachments. The length of the screw's shank is the main determinant of holding strength in a wood connection, not the thickness of the shank.
- Square drive screws and drivers are preferred by many craftspeople because they drive well, the heads won't strip out, and the screws have small, relatively attractive heads; the last is important, when considering them as an "expressed joint" detail.
- Hardware, glides, latches, and casters need to perform well. The best possible quality ought to drive the selection.

Upholstery

Upholstered furniture has been around since ancient Egypt, with seat pans made from various grasses. During the Renaissance, leather and velvet were applied to furniture. In 1620, the English Upholsterer's Company was granted a charter. It is one of the oldest of the London guilds and liveries companies. Traditional notions of upholstered furniture include pieces made with filling materials and covered with a surface material, but upholstery also includes furniture that uses jute, hemp, exposed web, or seat pans made of reed or other caning materials.

Upholstering in the 17th century developed from several trades, including that of the **cofferer,** who was responsible for using leather as a covering for trunks and later for chair seats; the *saddler,* who made saddles; and the *tapissier,* who supplied canopies, wall tapestries, table carpets, and *tent makers*. Tent making was a job for upholsterers, and it is not surprising that the coat of arms for the upholsterer's guild had three tents emblazoned on a shield.

In Europe during the 18th century, new concepts of upholstered furnishings and comfort emerged during the French Rococo. As a result of the Industrial Revolution, fully integrated and upholstered furnishings became common throughout the world. Upholstered furniture reached its zenith in the late Victorian and early Edwardian eras.

The *journeyman upholsterer* is considered a furniture-making specialist. Upholsters built upon a frame of wood or metal furniture padded with stuffing. This required measuring, cutting, and fixing soft material to the frame of furniture, and for the most part was a handcraft vocation. The industry grew so competitive that in the 1930s upholstery sweat shops were common. These shops often produced the cheapest and poorest-quality upholstered furniture.

Many chairs designed and fabricated between the 1930s and 1960s were handcrafted and used hemp webbing, halyard, cane, or braided paper to support the seat pan or human body while sitting. The craft of the woven seat pan in Hans J. Wegner's classic *The Chair* (Figure 8.27) is remarkable, as is Jorgen Havelskov's *Harp* chair (1968) made of ash and halyard.

By the 1950s, advances in polymer technologies had generated new ideas about color, shape, and form in upholstered furnishings. This technology advanced an

Figure 8.27 The Chair—cane woven seat pan and back rest, designed by Hans J. Wegner (1949), fabricated by Johannes Hansen.

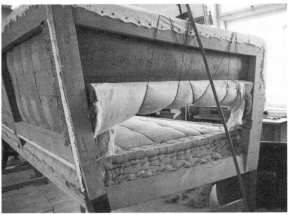

Figure 8.28 Upholstery in the making—Rud. Rasmussen, Copenhagen, Denmark.

Figure 8.29 Upholstery in the making—showing various types of materials: lumber, nails, staples, and wire.

ongoing investigation into ergonomics and sculpted form. Upholstered furniture often hid the structural elements of its frame. Formal ideas of **biomorphic** form began to drive design. Upholstered furniture examples include a wide range of furniture types, but the basic pieces were *sofas, chairs, sectionals, ottomans,* and *sofa beds.*

Conventional upholstered furnishings utilized woven springs and integrated bedding assembled by hand (Figures 8.28, 8.29). Today, machine production and integrated foam-injected molds have revolutionized the production of upholstered furniture and, for the most part, have improved its structural integrity. B & B Italia produces integrated upholstered chairs and sofas that utilize the latest fabrication technologies, in which the structural elements are completely integrated in both the design and fabrication of the expanded foam components. *Happy Hour* Sofa, designed by Andreas Storiko (1994), is a transformable upholstered sofa that adjusts for different postures (Figure 8.30).

Reclining chairs are a subcategory of upholstered chairs, including upholstered rockers and swivel chairs. Recliners can have adjustable backs and built-in footrests that allow a person to recline in a number of different positions. The original recliner was the **Morris chair,** named after the designer William Morris. The Morris recliners of the mid-1800s were bulky and required a significant amount of space to function properly. Advances in the reclining mechanism have greatly reduced the size of these chairs.

Sanding

In the process of making, shaping, and finishing furniture, it is important to have a working knowledge of abrasives, especially when working with complex and compound form (Figure 8.31). Abrasives are used to cut, etch, grind, sand, and texture material. Abrasives affect the finish quality of a material's surface and its visual appeal. In working with wood, the function of abrasives and sanding papers is to cut away the wood fibers by the rasping action of various tools and materials. Below is an outline of techniques to consider when using abrasives and sanding papers.

- When sanding wood for a lacquer finish, always sand (or scrape) in the direction of the wood grain. Never sand across the grain.

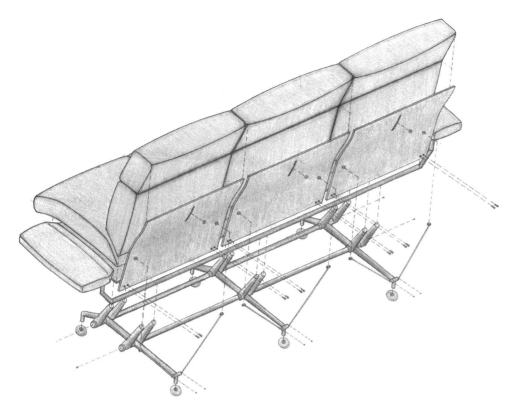

Figure 8.30 Happy Hour Sofa, designed by Andseas Storiko (1994), manufactured by B and B Italia.

Figure 8.31 Valet chair in the making at PP Møbler, Copenhagen, Denmark.

- In general, start with 80-grit, follow with 120-grit, and sand for finish with 150-grit, depending upon how well the lumber was milled. Do not skip between the 80-grit and 150-grit papers.
- Consider incorporating a **V-groove** or a quirk joint where two different woods meet. A V-groove is a shallow cut into the face of the grain with an angled or **chamfered** profile resembling the letter **V**. This will minimize the possibility of the darker wood discoloring the lighter wood in the sanding and finishing process.
- Apply even pressure when sanding by hand with a sanding block or with power tools. When necessary, use a rubber-backed hand-sanding block. *Paper scratches* caused by the sides of folded sandpaper are important to avoid.
- In order to determine where you have already sanded, consider drawing random pencil marks over the area to be sanded. When the pencil marks have been removed in the sanding process, the area has been uniformly sanded.
- Avoid using steel wool between coats of finishes; it can discolor the wood and agitate the surface. Rather, consider using 320-grit sandpaper or *Scotch-Brite*™ scuffing pads between coats.
- In some applications, try scraping the wood in the direction of its grain rather than sanding it. Scrapers, when used properly, can more quickly prepare wood for its final sanding for the finish. The effect is significant. Cabinet scrapers and hook scrapers require careful, regular sharpening using an oilstone.
- Do not oversand with the finer-grit papers. Oversanding polishes the surface of the wood, preventing the finish from penetrating into the wood or bonding mechanically to it.
- To dull or make satin a glossy lacquer, polyurethane, or polyacrylic finish, use a *Scotch-Brite* or similar pad over the finish when it is completely cured.
- Sandpapers can be used to sand wood finishes, metals, glass, and stone. Open coat garnet paper is available as a reddish-brown paper and is a good general-quality abrasive for sanding wood by hand. Open coat aluminum oxide paper is harder than garnet paper and is widely used as the abrasive sheet for power sanders when sanding wood. Closed coat silicon-carbide paper is generally used for finishing metals. It can be lubricated with water or thinner and is called *wet-or-dry paper.*

Finishing, Painting, Sealing, Staining, and Surfacing

Finishing a piece of furniture is the most important phase of the fabrication process and takes a significant amount of time to complete. It requires judgment, craft, and human skill to determine how much color and/or finish to apply and to decide when the finishing process is complete. Final finishes needs to be carefully considered at the outset of any project because they can significantly affect cost and can influence the choice and quality of materials selected to fabricate the furniture.

Wood Finishing

All finishes will darken wood by one to two shades. Polyacrylic finishes will retain the truest natural colors of light color woods such as maple or birch sapwood. They are easy to apply with a brush but should be applied in the direction of the grain. They are water-borne finishes that, when dry, are water resistant and referred to as *water white clear.*

Polyurethane finishes will darken the natural color of wood and cause it to turn amber. The first coat should be thinned for deeper penetration into the wood. Polyurethane finishes offer excellent protection against moisture. There will always be a cold joint between applications because polyurethane does not dissolve previously applied coats. Polyurethane is relatively easy to apply, and drying time is moderate.

Tung-oil and Danish oil are considered "drying oils." They can produce beautiful hand-finished furniture, but they are labor intensive and require periodic maintenance.

Waterlox is a blend of resin, mineral spirits, and other ingredients "cooked" with tung oil to produce a durable and beautiful finish. It finishes well with a cloth application (diapers work best) and is easy to apply; drying time is moderate.

Shellac finishes are ideal for teak because shellac will bond well to the wood despite teak's high oil content.

Steel wool and a good grade of furniture wax with carnauba will also produce a beautiful furniture finish, but it requires significant maintenance.

Precatalyzed and catalyzed lacquer finishes are the industry standard for wood furniture. Precatalyzed finishes produce a harder, more durable finish than regular nitrocellulose lacquers. Both are applied using a spray gun, and both can be touched up with a brush or spray (Figure 8.32). Applications of these finishes will dissolve the previous coats to produce a uniform finish. The thickness of these finishes is though limited to 0.005-inch or the cured surface may crack. Vertical surfaces generally receive two spray applications and horizontal surfaces no more than four applications. After 28 days, precatalyzed lacquers are nearly as resistant to moisture and chemicals as a polyurethane finish. These finishes only slightly amber the color of natural wood.

Plastic can be painted, sawn, drilled, sanded, or frosted. Plastic can also be buffed to remove tiny scratches.

Figure 8.32 Spray finishing using nitrocellulose lacquer.

Metals can be polished, brushed, and plated. Metals oxidize, but metal lacquer sprays can slow the oxidation process. Using a mild abrasive and special applicators, oxidized metals can be polished to rejuvenate their original finish. Specific cleaners are available for most decorative metals.

As previously mentioned, stone slabs are delivered to a retailer polished on one side. Honed, finished stone is achieved with 200- or 400-grit stones, which will produce an even, finely textured, nonreflective surface. Flame, thermal, and hammer finishes are technically distinct, but they look similar on a rough, coarse surface. Stone finished in a flame, thermal, or hammer finish nearly always appears significantly lighter than it would in a polished state.

Glass is made either plate or tempered. The differences affect its strength and physical properties but not its appearance. Distressed glass has noticeable folds and a smooth but faceted surface. Glass can be chemically etched or blasted with sand. It can be sanded, drilled, beveled, seamed, and polished.

Delivery and Installation

Delivery and installation is an important phase of the work. It requires care in securing and transporting the work and systematic installation at the site. The expense and time required for this phase can be substantial, so the delivery and installation needs to be carefully planned and incorporated in the cost of fabricating the furniture (Figure 8.33).

Figure 8.33 Installing furniture.

Repairing, Restoring, and Resurfacing

A clean dent can be repaired in wood furniture. Lightly sand in the direction of the grain to remove the finish in and around the dent. Apply a few drops of water to the dent. If necessary, place a moist cloth over the dent and apply a hot iron. In most cases, the moisture will draw the grain back flush to the original surface and minimize the need for filling. This process can be repeated as necessary, but generally the process is effective only up to three attempts.

All wood furniture acquires a patina and will become scratched over time. There are many ways to address scratches. Use a good grade of wax without silicones or hydrocarbons and steel wool as needed. Mix paste wax into a fine steel wool and rub firmly in the direction of the grain. After the wax dries, buff and polish the wax with a soft cloth. Dents can also be filled with a heated lacquer stick and a palette knife but furniture refinishing at this level is a specialty unto itself.

A CHRONOLOGICAL OVERVIEW OF TOOLS

Hand Tools

The evolution of hand tools from the Egyptian to the Greek civilization and into the Roman Republic is characterized by a general increase in the tools' strength but reveals little typological change. Copper was the standard metal used by the Egyptians for the bow drill, chisel, **awls,** and a range of adzes, axes, and toothed saws. Abrasives consisted of various stones and vegetable oils.

Greek carpenter's tools consisted of a rasp, plane, measuring instrument, a box of pigmented colors, a hammer, bow drill, heavy axe auger, gimlet, adze, and a punch. Improvements were also made in the handles of hand tools and in the materials of cutting surfaces.

Roman tools for making furniture were made of iron. Copper rasps with irregularly punched surfaces, saw blades with teeth set for traction cutting, a brace bit, a spoon bit, and a series of chisels were all improved due to the discovery of iron. An important tool for fabricating round chair legs was the turning lathe. The development of turning wood on a lathe generated an emphasis upon straight legs as load-bearing elements.

During the Middle Ages, the primitive lathe evolved into the leaf spring type: a frame with risers and a leaf spring operated by the feet of an artisan that allowed the worker to set it in motion and work in less awkward conditions. An important improvement in furniture making during this period involved the methods for joining materials together. Joints were made with pegs of harder wood or with hand-made nails; dovetail, mortise, and tenon joints were also used.

In the 16th century, the invention of the *perfect lathe* gave rise to a class of specialized craftsmen who collaborated with joiners. In 1568, woodblock-cutter Jost Amman records the existence of a carpentry workshop with 14 tools, the historian Joseph Moxon in 1703 mentions 30 tools in his *Mechanick Exercises: or the Doctrines of Handy Works,* and the Wynn Timmine catalog in 1892 lists 90.[2] By the Enlightenment, revolutionary changes had occurred in the tools and fabrication techniques of making furniture.

During the Enlightenment, fabricators developed better methods for representing shape and form using orthographic projection, which permitted greater control over work processes and the representational models employed in geometry, with ellipses, parabolas, and conical sections on rotatory bodies. Tools used during this period included 16 brace bits, screws, fretsaws, clamps, and workbenches equipped with iron vices. Pliers, chisels and gouges, squares, planes, and pincers were also common.

Machine Tools

In the early 19th century, under the pressure of the social, political, scientific, and technical revolutions of the age, a transformation occurred in woodworking shops that made it possible for furniture to be produced in limited quantities and in accordance with artisan traditions in keeping with local styles and tastes. Following the disappearance of the guilds and the rise of a liberal mercantile economy, production woodworking machines emerged for turning, planing, sawing, and milling. In addition, machines were able to produce standard pitched screws, nuts, and drill bits for the first time.

By the mid-1800s, the premier furniture in the made-by-machine category was the steam-bent beech wood *Model No. 14* chair produced by the Austrian company Gebrüder Thonet. Between 1859 and 1930, Thonet manufactured and sold 50 million of these chairs. By 1900, Thonet employed 5,000 people directly and 25,000 indirectly in other companies producing their products. At the height of production, Thonet was producing 15,000 pieces of furniture a day, 12,000 of which were chairs.

By the 1930s, the close working relationship between craft and machine production gave way to subdivisions of work in which the architect designed the prototypes and then submitted them to production industries for fabrication. Steel began to rise as a material in furniture production. Hollow steel tubes could be formed into many shapes and chromed. Bent plywood furniture designs by the Finnish architect Alvar Aalto exploited the elasticity of birch wood (a material also used to fabricate skis at the time).

In the 1950s, the industrial designer emerged as an independent professional skilled in designing with new technologies using resins, plastics, and upholstered works. The machinery necessary to fabricate plastic furniture was a significant up-front cost and required an enormous investment in large injection-molding machines, which could produce thousands of furnishings; mass production was necessary to recoup the initial investment in the machines. Mass production became the condition for economic recovery after World War II.

Hand Tools Used Today

Turning and carving is a specialized craft that requires a variety of chisels and gouges, which are usually beveled on both sides in order to work the wood at a variety of angles. Of all the fabrication processes used to work with lumber, carving has the closest link with craft (workmanship of risk) due to the human skill required. Like any cutting tools, chisels and gouges need to be kept sharp and maintained.

Sharp chisels are important tools in any workshop. Four types of chisels are needed for creating neat, accurate joints, removing waste, paring wood, and making mortises. A *firmer chisel* has a strong rectangular blade and comes in a range from ½- to 2-inch (1.27 cm to 5-cm) widths. In general, it is used for rough chiseling tasks. *Bevel-edged chisels* have two shallow bevels ground along the edges of the upper face suitable for cutting joints. *Paring chisels* have long blades for paring housings. *Mortise chisels* are strong and designed for cutting deep mortises. These chisels require a mallet to drive the tool firmly into the wood. For this reason, mortise chisels typically have a cap or metal ring to protect the handles from splitting.

Hand planes are used for a variety of purposes. A jointer plane is a long hand plane (24 inches [61 cm]) or more. It is used to remove warps and irregularities in lumber. *Jack planes* are shorter but are used for the same purpose. *Block planes* are small, lightweight, general-purpose hand planes.

There are two types of handsaws: ripsaws and crosscut saws. Japanese saws include cut-off and straight-cut saws. Generally, American saws cut on the push and Japanese saws cut on the pull. Another difference between American and Japanese saws is the quality and thickness of their blades. Japanese saws are made of thin folded steel and are razor sharp.

Power Tools Used Today

Most woodshops utilize a variety of power tools, which include table saws, jointers, planers, power sanders, and power drills (Figures 8.34–8.35). With the advent of power drills and drill presses, the traditional brace and bit all but disappeared. Electric power drills are powerful and easy to use. One should also investigate the battery-operated hand tools that are available.

When drilling through wood, the outgoing bore tends to create an outward explosion in the surface of the wood. This occurs in both flat and rounded surfaces, including large dowels. A tight, uniform backing applied to the wood being drilled will prevent this from happening. Drilling through dowels requires a jig in which the dowel should fit firmly. Prior to drilling dowel holes, consider using **Forstner bits** because they will ensure a quality result. Forstner bits are high-quality drill **bits** with a special serrated ring around the main point. This ring helps the bit stay on course and creates a clean, precise hole.

Figure 8.34 Woodshop with power tools, Miami University, Oxford, Ohio.

Figure 8.35 Disk sander.

Figure 8.36 Power drill.

Power drill presses (*pillar drills*) have a chuck that holds the required bit (Figure 8.36). The shank (thickness of the bit) generally ranges in size from ⅓₂ to ½ inch (0.8 mm to 1.27 cm), and drill types range from wood and metal multiuse drill bits to *Forstner* bits.

High-speed steel bits are used to cut wood or metal. Large drill bits are often made with a reduced shank so that they can fit into standard power drill chucks. *Spade bits* have long points for positioning on the exact center of a marked hole. These bits are also known as *paddle bits* due to their profile. Most power drill presses have an adjustable table, a feed lever, and, most significantly, a depth gauge that can be set to determine accurately the depth of a hole.

The power planer and power jointer are important power tools in any woodshop. Planers mill wood to a specific thickness. Planing lumber is limited to the width of the planer. Power jointers are important in creating 90-degree corners in milling lumber. Generally, lumber is first jointed, then planed. Once a 90-degree edge is made between two adjoining surfaces on a jointer, the lumber can be milled to its desired finished thickness.

In cutting metal, be certain to use a slower cutting speed for harder metals and keep a small amount of oil on the cutting surface at all times. Metal band saws are typically speed adjustable, cutting faster for softer metals such as copper and slower for harder metals such as carbon steel. **Kerf** marks and **burrs** left in the metal should be removed immediately with a file after each cut. Be especially careful of the burrs created when drilling metal and when grinding and welding metal (Figure 8.37).

When cutting plastic, use a blade specifically for this material. Push slowly and deliberately throughout each cut. Leave the protective adhesive sheet on the stock until all cuts are complete to minimize the risk of scratching the plastic. Take extra care when drilling acrylic. Drill slowly to avoid cracking the plastic and distorting the hole.

Metal and plastic can be folded. Sheet metal up to 12-gauge can be folded back onto itself. Care must be taken to ensure that the line of the fold is accurate and continuously

Figure 8.37 Student grinding a metal weld.

aligned. Sheet plastic such as acrylic can be folded by first heating along the edge of the fold and then carefully making the fold and securing it in place until the plastic cools.

Computer Numerical Control Devices

With the advent of the computer and computer-aided design (CAD), computer programs fueled the development of computer-aided manufacturing (CAM) and the use of CNC devices. These devices were initially expensive machines used for mass-produced items such as cars and planes, but recently they have begun to emerge in smaller and mid-sized craft shops throughout the world. CAD/CAM technologies have become firmly established and will likely become the means to design and fabricate a greater percentage of furniture in the future.

During the 1980s, furniture companies began to invest in their ability to achieve complicated cutting operations in a rapid, precise, and repetitive manner. Today, many furniture designers and companies use CAD software to produce digital geometric models and CAM software to specify how the digital design model will be fabricated. CNC devices translate the digital instructions into machine cutting operations to produce the furniture.

As smaller and mid-sized shops began to acquire digital technology, traditional craft methods began to incorporate CNC devices in the design and production of new works. Blue Dot.com, Ply Architects, Hariri and Hariri, Steven Kieren, and James Timberlake are some of the many design and architecture firms that have begun to achieve a productivity and high quality of work provided by digital software and CNC devices.

TECHNOLOGY: THE ART AND SCIENCE OF FABRICATION

Technology is a discourse between *techno* (making) and *logos* (thinking about the making). The art and science of fabrication guides how something is made. Regardless of the scale or scope of the project, the thesis reflects upon the correlations between the process of making and the completed furniture design. Within the process of furniture fabrication there is a vast body of empirical and scientific knowledge that links art with science, craft with theory, and workmanship of risk (craft) with workmanship of certainty (machine production). Design is never independent of technology. Design is often shaped by technology rather than the other way around.

Architect Frank Gehry initially relied upon *CATIA*, a computer program used in the aircraft industry, to model and fabricate unusual architectural designs utilizing compound curves. Following his early work with corrugated cardboard, Gehry's team has explored and produced woven, laminated maple chairs and a series of roto-molded polymer outdoor furnishings. Their work inspired many firms and designers to adopt similar computer-modeling programs in design.

Technology is the causeway of design, and its influence upon design is critical. Ernest Joyce's book *The Encyclopedia of Furniture Making* is a useful resource that focuses upon wood and woodworking techniques. Form and aesthetics depend upon technology. Change the way something is made, and it will affect the way it looks and works. Change the tools that one uses to design, and design will change as well.

Fabrication and production processes of contemporary furniture designs reveal a broad spectrum of technologies in use for designers, fabricators, and clients. This spectrum ranges from craft-based technologies (i.e., art, human skill, hand-made arts and crafts) to industrial-based technologies (i.e., industrial production, CNC machinery, axis mill machines, applied science). Furniture design, though, is still directly associated with social, cultural, and economic conditions, as well as with individual and collaborative fabrication efforts.

Consider the economic downturns that once prominent furniture production epicenters such as Detroit and Grand Rapids, Michigan, Buffalo, New York, and Meda, Italy, have experienced. This is one result of growing technological innovations. While these industrial centers experienced a dramatic decline in the number of human laborers used to produce furniture, CNC devices produce more furniture with greater precision in less time, with less cost to the consumer, and have had enormous social and economic impacts upon traditional fabrication methods.

Fabrication can be classified into two types of workmanship. Objects made by handcraft technologies (workmanship of risk) involve processes that are considered an art (*ars,* empirical knowledge). These processes can be thought of as distinct from industrial means of production (workmanship of certainty), often employing high-end manufacturing technologies such as CNC devices and robotic assemblages. The many processes of fabrication reveal a broad range of technologies from relatively low (craft-based) to relatively high (machine-based). One is not better than the other. Each has its strengths and weaknesses.

The technologies employed in making furniture at the industrial level tend to rely heavily upon industrial production, synthetic materials, expensive tooling, complex machinery, and carefully organized assembly processes. Companies such as Acerbis, Fiam, and Lowenstein are renowned for the technology they employ in the production of furniture. Acerbis is almost completely organized by CNC and robotic machines producing beautiful wood furnishings, including Mario Bellini's *Onda Quandra* (1988). Fiam uses a CNC device and robotic production processes to cut, form, and bevel glass furnishings such as the *Ghost* chair. Lowenstein, based in Fort Lauderdale, Florida, experienced enormous growth in the 1990s due to their decision to invest in and integrate with the newest finish technologies, which allow them to apply a final finish coat to their products and have it cure in less than 20 seconds. Lowenstein was able to finish furniture faster and with less cost than any comparable furniture

Figure 8.38 Pier Luigi and *artigani* in bottega di Pierluigi Ghianda, Meda, Italy.

company offering a similar product at the time. The technology enabled the product to get to market faster, with less cost, which helped the company increase its share of the institutional furniture market.

Smaller companies, prototypers, and craft shops tend to rely more upon human skill in the production of furniture. Small craft shops like Pierluigi Ghianda's custom woodworking studio in Meda, Italy (Figure 8.38), and the Nakashima home studio in New Hope, Pennsylvania, are examples of small custom shops that rely upon a balance between human skill and power woodworking tools to make furniture. The vast majority of furniture fabrication shops are somewhere between the craft shop and the automated factory.

Craft (Workmanship of Risk)

> Craftsmanship is defined simply as workmanship using any kind of technique or apparatus, in which the quality of the result is not predetermined, but depends on the judgment, dexterity and care which the maker exercises as he works. The essential idea is that the quality of the result is continually at risk during the process of making; and so I shall call this kind of workmanship "the workmanship of risk": an uncouth phrase, but at least descriptive.[3]

Craft is a time-honored tradition. It takes patience to craft a piece of furniture. Craft is the human skill involved in making, but recognition should never be the motivation. Motivation should be inwardly focused, having to do with passion and the satisfaction generated by craftwork. Traditional approaches to the subject of craft often emphasize the finished piece. However, the essence of craft lies in the human skill applied to the workmanship, not in the finished product.

Craft is rooted in the nature of workmanship and refers to the human skill in making. David Pye writes about craft in his book, *The Nature and Art of Workmanship,* stating that human technique has value but that quality workmanship is not dependent upon human technique.

For a craftsperson or artist, furniture design is about the process of making and is considered an art. For many individuals, it is an applied craft, as evidenced in the work of Antonio Gaudi or the unique, one-of-a-kind pieces of Wendell Castle, or a matter of design, as in the work of the Danish furniture designer Poul Kjærholm. It is difficult to draw a line between handcrafted furniture, fine art, and design, but it is important to try and do so because the effort can help clarify distinctions of one's own work. If furniture is hand crafted, signed, and original, can it be considered fine art? On the other hand, if art functions as furniture, can art be considered design? Can art be conceived by one person and made by another? In actuality, the polemic between *art* and *design* is of minimal interest to many furniture designers, but the notions and positions of the two terms can fuel a body of work and help maintain clarity and focus on why one does what one does as a furniture designer. This, at least, is helpful in placing one's work in the context of the work of others.

An industrial designer can engage a broad range of workmanship. Joe Columbo, Bruce Hannah, and Bill Stumpf have had others mass-produce their furniture designs. This is not to say that they don't have the desire or skill to make furniture; rather, it is a reflection upon the nature of engineered works conceived and intended for mass production. For the industrial designer, craft focusing on an individual work of art may be less important than the realization of standardized mass production. For most industrial designers, the goal is to generate exact replications through repeatable processes. The furniture designs of Achille Castiglioni, Antonio Citterio, and Ettore Sottsass fall within the category of design rather than art. One is not better than the other, but the distinction is important to realize.

Furniture produced at the highest levels of craft and furniture produced as contemporary or social art are generally considered art pieces. Craft is conceived and executed as a process-driven activity dependent upon human skill, regardless of the quality of the workmanship in the final product.

Machine Production (Workmanship of Certainty)

Most engineering advances used to fabricate contemporary designs rely upon industrial processes and repeatable means of production. Examples of rigorously tested and technologically sophisticated furniture can be seen in the office seating designs that have entered the marketplace during the past 20 years. The *Aeron* chair, the *Freedom* chair, the *Leap* chair, and the *Equa* chair are contemporary office icons that depend upon the workmanship of certainty and technological production. These chairs are examples of significant advances blending ergonomics, sustainable design concepts, new materials, and complex systems engineering. A popular office chair such as the *Aeron* chair is produced in vast numbers, with each chair made exactly like the one before it. The ability to repeat the process without deviation in any regard is key to the economic success of mass-produced design. In this regard, workmanship of certainty is mandatory. Precision tools and CAD machines are used to minimize variances between individual pieces. The idea that machines can cut, punch, and assemble with speed and accuracy gives designers the opportunity to design specifically for these industrial and digital production processes.

The engineering systems behind mass-produced office furnishings also employ extensive testing. The *Business and Institutional Furniture Manufacturer's Association* (BIFMA) describes guidelines and procedures for testing contemporary furniture. Established in 1973, BIFMA International is a not-for-profit trade association of furniture manufacturers and suppliers addressing issues of common concern. Examples of BIFMA testing include lateral force, caster and glide testing, upholstery, and flame resistance testing.

Between furniture crafted by hand and furniture fabricated by machine, some qualities are lost and some are gained. Many aspects of design and fabrication become critical in terms of their societal and economic impact. Consider the cost of human labor relative to the value of a single piece of furniture. A custom furniture shop may charge $50 to $60 an hour for labor, which can easily result in hundreds or thousands of dollars of labor for a single piece. In this model, low production runs are the norm, yet the model employs a relatively large number of skilled craftspeople, and this, in turn, has a broad impact upon a nation's social and economic life. The craftspeople circulate the company's earnings back into the local economy. Automation and machine fabrication minimize the need for a large employee pool trained in craft techniques. This results in fewer employees in the furniture industry and a higher investment in technical equipment and facilities. This too impacts the local economy. In a different way, the emphasis becomes more about the economic development and competitiveness of the industries.

chapter

9 Professional Practice and Marketing

Great designers seldom make great advertising men, because they get overcome by the beauty of the picture—and forget that merchandise must be sold.[1]
James Randolph Adams, *The International Dictionary of Thoughts, 1969*

FURNITURE IS A RELATIVELY expensive product to bring to market, which contributes to a limited customer pool. Further, consumers want more than comfortable and affordable furniture. Many want social status, beauty, structural integrity, and environmentally green design. The market is complex, driven by individual and societal needs and desires (Figure 9.1).

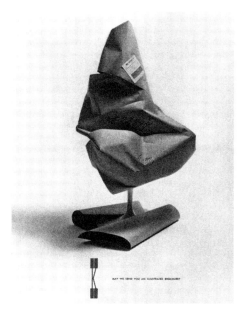

Figure 9.1 Poster of Saarinen's Tulip chair wrapped in Kraft paper, marketed by Knoll.

Figure 9.2 Wendell Castle's furniture exhibit at the Cincinnati Art Museum.

Throughout many developed countries, furniture is a mature product. Most markets have been saturated in the sense that almost everyone has furniture to satisfy basic needs. In these markets, it is the desire for new and better products that sparks demand. Furniture is conceived, fabricated, and marketed for specific niches, specific users, and specific functions.

Marketing efforts by furniture designers and furniture companies underscore a range of strategies due to the many different needs of consumers. Some designers and companies promote versatility of use, while others promote durability. Many promote *design,* which usually means well-composed, functional pieces. Others promote customer satisfaction and service. Some furniture is marketed as regionally or culturally branded, such as *Scandinavian design* or *Italian design.* Some furniture is marketed as fine art, as in the case of Wendell Castle's (Figure 9.2), George Nakashima's, or Sam Maloof's work. Galleries and museums collect pieces because of their craft, social meaning, cultural significance, or innovation in terms of material use or fabrication processes (Figure 9.3). A small amount of furniture is acquired by galleries

Figure 9.3 Trapholt Furniture Museum, Kolding, Denmark.

Figure 9.4 Ergo Kontormiljø—delivery van.

and museums and sold through auction and estate sales to collectors. Many office furnishings are branded as ergonomic products (Figure 9.4), including the *Aeron, Leap,* and *Freedom* chairs. Uniqueness is a desirable quality for some, while others prefer the value of regularity.

One priority that drives the vast majority of new works is the desire to make a similar product for less cost. This often results in reducing the quality of furniture's unseen aspects, relocating production to regions of the world where labor is less expensive, or increasing the technological efficiencies involved in the production of furniture.

Though it is correct to assume that designers and furniture companies respond to market demand, it is also correct to infer that they create market demand. Revolutionary designs take the market by surprise. Few people felt the need for inflated therapy or gym balls, beanbag chairs, or tubular metal chairs when these products first became available.

In some cases, designers anticipate a potential market and, by providing a solution, fill an emerging demand. The **bentwood** beech chairs of Gebrüder Thonet point to a match between these lightweight, inexpensive chairs and the restaurants, cafés, and residential spaces that emerged throughout Europe in the mid-19th century. The inspiration behind these chairs arose from an infusion of design, technology, cultural reflection, and sensitivity rooted in the idea of *zeitgeist*. The beech bentwood chairs produced in the late 1800s inspired generations of modern designers and contemporary fabricators (Figure 9.5).

Figure 9.5 Offspring designs: Thonet's bentwood (1880), Poul Kjærholm's PK 15 (1979), and PK 12 (1964).

Figure 9.6 Victoria and Louis Ghost chairs, designed by Philippe Starck. Glossy table designed by Antonio Citterio at the Kartell showroom in Helsinki, Finland.

Staff designers are full-time company employees who design and develop products in collaborative working environments for carefully researched markets. Furniture companies, such as Steelcase and Luxo Italiano, employ staff designers. They pursue specialized market niches by identifying their customer base and determine how best to reach it. Other furniture companies, such as Alias, Cassina, Herman Miller, Knoll, and B & B Italia, seek outside designers under contract and consulting arrangements. In some cases, designers must work only for the specific company, but in most cases, designers are free to consult with as many companies with which they can affiliate. Philippe Stark is an international design consultant who works with several prominent companies such as Alessi and Kartell (Figure 9.6).

INDUSTRY

Large furniture companies such as Fritz Hansen, Giogetti, Kartell, Knoll, Herman Miller, Vitra, and Zanotta have, to a degree, created and expanded new markets through the production of design goods (furniture marketed as design) (Figure 9.7). These companies differentiate themselves from other companies that produce period-replicated or conventional furniture. Large furniture companies employ distribution representatives, sales associates, and marketing directors, seeking ways to market furniture designs with contemporary building projects produced by architecture and interior design firms.

Figure 9.7 Coconut chairs, designed by George Nelson (1955), produced by Herman Miller (United States) and Vitra (Germany).

Competition generates a reluctance to share technical knowledge and resources with others, making it difficult to develop a shared pool of information among professionals. This results in proprietary knowledge and techniques that are kept secret, resulting in intellectual property with patents protecting finishes, designs, and so on.

Some furniture design companies market and distribute assembled products but outsource the fabrication of components and parts to others. Interflex uses Mario Terraneo's bottega in Meda, Italy, to fabricate a line of their beds. Alias outsources all production of their products to local and regional fabricators. Herman Miller assembles furniture in Zeeland, Michigan, but outsources the production of many components throughout the world.

Design consultants, like any consultant working for a large company, typically enjoy an independent and relatively risk-free working relationship with the industry. Payment for design services sometimes consists of an up-front one-time fee for design but very often results in a negotiated royalty. Royalties can vary, depending upon the designer's status and the anticipated volume of production. Typically, a designer will receive 3 to 5 percent of the *distributed cost* of mass-produced furniture.[2] The ramifications of this approach propel design into the realm of either expensive high-end works or affordable mass-produced furniture.

GREEN MARKETING

Green design was defined in Chapter 6 as being more complex and inclusive than *sustainable design.* Consequently, green marketing encompasses more than promoting the sustainability of a product. It is an opportunity to market how furniture is produced (socially and

Figure 9.8 Flat-pack Stool 60, Artek showroom, Helsinki, Finland.

technologically), how it is distributed, how it might be considered reusable or recyclable, and how it might eventually biodegrade. It is a chance to market the company behind the product for leadership in green design.

Fewer companies today are packaging their products with polystyrene, and more are using biodegradable cardboard and flat-pack distribution methods in response to concerns over chlorofluorocarbons (CFCs) that are produced in the production of polystyrene (Figure 9.8). How a product is distributed affects how green it is.

Size, weight, packaging, distance, and distribution costs are significant factors that affect the cost and resources needed to bring a product to market. Though Gebrüder Thonet first distributed chairs disassembled in the 1800s, flat-pack or knock-down furnishings became widely accepted by the public only in the 1960s. Gaetano Pesce's vacuum-packed *UP* series and *Il Sacco,* the original beanbag chair designed by Píero Gatti, Cesaré Paolini, and Franco Teadoro, greatly reduced the distribution cost of off-the-shelf furniture.

How a product is fabricated also determines how green it is. For example, the possible future ban of lead in soldering has pushed many firms to develop new techniques for joining metal. Various metal components are currently being powder-coated rather than spray-painted. Improved processes of finishing furniture can reduce environmental hazards; consequently, furniture production is continually evolving and, whenever appropriate, is being marketed as green design.

Targeting products that are green involves promoting furniture that:

- Produces low levels of VOCs
- Uses materials that are formaldehyde free, biodegradable, or renewable

Green products are often priced higher than conventional goods, but their life cycle may be longer and they are often cost efficient in the long run. The reality, however, seems to be that while people are willing to pay more for a green product, the degree of "how much more" is marginal.

RETAIL AND WHOLESALE

Retailers buy furniture directly from furniture companies at wholesale prices and sell furniture at retail prices in order to achieve a desired profit margin. Manufacturers generally do not provide floor items for display, nor do they provide furniture on loan or on consignment to retailers. Thus, retailers rely on the display and availability of in-house merchandise and special orders to generate and maintain sales (Figure 9.9).

Shopping by catalog has become popular. Rob Forbes' *Design Within Reach* (DWR) is a financially successful catalog and an on-line venue bringing design within reach to a growing market. *Smith Hawkin, Levenger, Sharper Image,* and *Frontgate* are further examples of well-organized sourcing and distribution companies for hard-to-find, easy-to-order products.

The North Carolina *Highpoint Furniture Market* occurs twice a year in October and April for one week. The principal focus is on wholesalers and retailers, sales representatives, and the press, with the primary emphasis placed upon generating sales and getting products to the market. On the last day of the Furniture Market, interior designers, architects, faculty, and students are allowed admission.

Figure 9.9 Kartell showroom, Helsinki, Finland.

Figure 9.10 ICFF—International Contemporary Furniture Fair, New York, 2005.

Figure 9.11 A pair of Ox chairs (designed by Hans J. Wegner, produced by Erik Jørgensen) at the International Furniture Fair (IFF), Copenhagen, Denmark 2006.

Similar to Highpoint, but more inclusive of designers, architects, and students worldwide, are the enormous international furniture fairs. The *Salone del Mobile* in Milan, Italy, organized by *COSMIT,* the Japanese furniture exhibition *TAGU,* the *Cologne Furniture Mart* in Germany, and *NEOCON* in Chicago's Mercantile Mart are examples of well-organized and well-attended furniture events where new products are unveiled and sold to wholesalers and industry professionals. The *International Contemporary Furniture Fair* (ICFF) in New York City and the *International Furniture Fair* in Copenhagen introduce contemporary furniture designs to the public (Figures 9.10, 9.11). A new annual venue for exhibiting and marketing furniture design is the *Las Vegas Furniture Fair.* These furniture exhibitions provide opportunities for designers and companies to exhibit and introduce new work.

Getting products to market is critically important. Furniture fairs help match sellers with buyers. Sales generated at an international furniture fair can lead to a significant annual percentage of gross income for a company. In these venues, new furniture designs are presented and aggressively marketed to the attendees and the press.

DESIGN FOR LESS

IKEA is a successful business that originated in Sweden and targets large metropolitan markets offering contemporary design solutions and inexpensive furniture and accessories. IKEA is in line with very successful *big box* retailers and has stores throughout the world (Figure 9.12a). In American cities such as Pittsburgh, the IKEA business model is to identify a critical mass of customers who can support the cost-effective operation in concert with a generally evolving product line. The IKEA customer is typically young, interested in design, and with a modest level of disposable income (Figure 9.12b). IKEA responds well to design trends and relies upon a high volume of sales and the introduction of new products each year to sustain growth. The process of purchasing furniture through IKEA is unique. Furniture is prepared flat-packed for customers to purchase from the distribution stores. Equally unique is the all-encompassing retail environment selling furnishings, accessories, lighting, rugs, food, and so on.

Figure 9.12a IKEA distribution outlet, Sweden.

Figure 9.12b IKEA at home and assembled.

ALTERNATIVE RETAIL

One traditional marketing approach used to generate sales is to host a warehouse sale. DWR has successfully organized and promoted weekend sales of overstocked and slightly damaged products at significant savings by utilizing warehouse storage close to regional and metropolitan airports in order to facilitate the distribution of furniture that otherwise would be difficult to sell.

Vintage design shops are everywhere. These are great places to find a Bertoia, Saarinen, or Eames chair or furniture designed by less well-known designers. Sometimes, remarkable designs (Figure 9.13) can be discovered in unexpected venues.

Guerrilla retail[3] is a term used to describe the sale of furniture in temporary places—off a truck, in a rental space, at an exhibit, at a kiosk on the sidewalk, or in a parking lot, plaza, and so on (Figure 9.14).

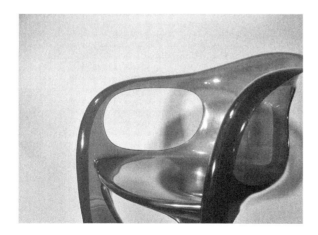

Figure 9.13 Remarkable compound curved plastic chair—considered vintage furnishing.

Figure 9.14 Used furniture priced to sell—vintage furnishing.

Figure 9.15 Paustian furniture showroom, Copenhagen, Denmark.

Figure 9.16 GUBI showroom, Copenhagen, Denmark, 2005.

Furniture showroom districts exist in major cities like New York, Chicago, Los Angeles, and Seattle. Bundling of showrooms is common, forming a concentrated *mall of design,* often in the same building or on the same street. Examples of concentrated districts are the *Pacific Design Center* in West Hollywood, California, the *International Trade Mart* in Dallas, Texas, and the *D & D Building* in New York City. In Europe there are areas in many cities that have become design districts in which showrooms are concentrated. *Paustian* and *GUBI* are two large furniture showrooms in Copenhagen that have contributed to the economic turn-around of an area that was previously an industrial and warehouse district (Figures 9.15, 9.16).

INDUSTRIAL ENTREPRENEURS: SILENT HEROES

Industrial entrepreneurs are the silent heroes behind the culture of design. They assume the economic risks and liabilities by leading their companies to invest in design. They establish markets through the production of goods as well as by responding to market demand. Individuals such as Aurileo Zanotta of Zanotta Spa, Alberto Alessi of Alessi, Busnelli of B & B Italia, Julio Castelli of Kartell, Louis Poulsen of Poulsen Lighting A/S, and Rolf Fehlbaum of Vitra all deserve their well-earned recognition. Industrial entrepreneurs create relationships with designers, fabricators, representatives, and retail store owners. They are informed about design and production, and are responsible for the welfare of their organization and its working relationships with designers. Their role is significant in shaping the industrial culture of furniture design and, on occasion, their vision has national and global impact.

Many larger furniture manufacturers have opened substantial showrooms, sometimes on site with their factories, to augment their printed catalog. This marketing trend began in the 20th century. Today, Cassina, Fritz Hansen, Flou, B & B Italia, Giogetti (Figure 9.17), GUBI, and

Figure 9.17 Giogetti showroom, Copenhagen, Denmark, 2006.

Vitra are some of the many furniture companies that have showrooms in close proximity to their factory and headquarters, blurring the line between gallery and retail store.

FURNITURE EPICENTERS

Epicenters of furniture design abound throughout the world. An epicenter is a place with a historical legacy regarding the design, production, research, distribution, or dissemination of furniture design. Epicenters are places where designers and industries have contributed to national and regional economies. In turn, these areas provide support and marketing venues to sustain greater economic success. The Italian Trade Commission established FORMA, whose purpose is to promote Italian furniture design throughout the world. The Danish Design Center was created in the 1960s to promote Danish companies' use of design and the success of Danish furniture designers worldwide. Often, regional economies help to support industrial epicenters, with nearby academic institutions that attract students and faculty into the profession.

Northern Italy

Milan, Italy, is home to thousands of designers engaged in architecture, interior design, and industrial design. Most are trained as architects. The Politecnico di Milano has nearly 15,000 students of architecture within its 7-year curriculum; and of the nearly 4,000 first-year students, 1,000 choose to pursue furniture, industrial design, and interior design as a focal track within the culture and curriculum of architecture. Many of these students will design furniture, and some will fabricate. Most will develop careers within a broad spectrum of related professional tracks while maintaining their affinity to, interest in, and passion for furniture design.

In addition to housing an enormous number of hopeful furniture designers, Milan is home to over 30 international journals that focus upon furniture design in both theme and content. *Ottagano, Domus, Arbitare,* and *Interni* are examples of notable international journals that regularly feature trends in furniture and showcase the designers. The magazines, journals, and books on Italian furniture design are the marketing engine behind the national and global success that Italy has enjoyed for the past 30 years. The concentration of significant furniture design magazines and journals marks Milan as a major design center that promotes Italian design worldwide.

Meda is a modest-sized city 1 hour north of Milan by train. It is located in the heart of Brianza, a region of northern Italy defined by Milan to the south, Como to the north, and Bergamo to the east. Meda is also an epicenter (but different from Milan), home to hundreds of furniture production and fabrication companies. For centuries, this region has maintained a tradition of furniture production that speaks to the workmanship of craft. Its history and the quality of its work make it an influential center of production. It is renowned for its cottage industries and the production of high-end furniture. *B & B Italia, Cassina, Giogetti, Flou, Zanotta,* and *Interfex* are some of the hundreds of furniture companies located in and around Meda. Over 33,000 custom fabrication shops (bottegas) and mid-sized companies produce furniture in Brianza. Nearly 20,000 shops employ fewer than ten *artigani* (craftspeople).[4]

Figure 9.18 Arne Jacobsen's Swan chairs at Fritz Hansen's press room.

East of Brianza is the region of Friuli in Udine—an area that has been linked with the yearly Italian exhibit *Promosedia.* In the region of Friuli, large quantities of moderately priced furniture are produced and distributed throughout the world. Technology employed in the production of these works is largely industrial. Friuli and Brianza are two distinct epicenters in Italy that have an international presence (albeit through noticeably different markets and marketing strategies) and generate a significant industrial base for Italy, Europe, and the world.

Scandinavia

Danish furniture was highly regarded in the 20th century for its craft in wood. Beech, birch, pine, and white oak were abundantly available and used to make furniture for years. In the 1960s, the quality of Danish furniture inspired industrial companies to sustain a high standard of design in their products. *Fritz Hansen, PP Møbler,* and *Rud. Rasmussen* of Copenhagen achieved high standards in production (Figures 9.18–9.20). Though Finland is technically not a Scandinavian country, it is culturally and socially con-

Figure 9.19 "The Chair," wooden frames in production at PP Møbler, Denmark.

Figure 9.20 Rud. Rasmussen's showroom and workshop, Copenhagen, Denmark.

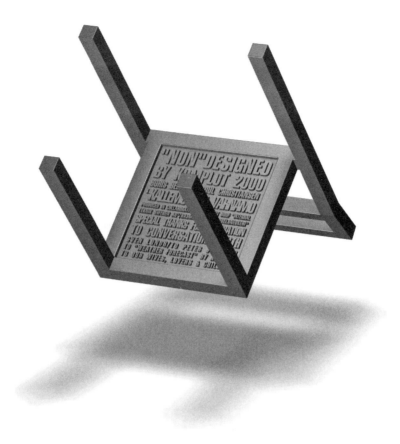

Figure 9.21 Branding and text applied to the underside of the Non Rubber chair, designed by Komplot Design (2000) for Källemo AB (Sweden).

sidered Scandinavian. The Finnish company *Artek,* located in Helsinki, helped to promote Scandinavian design throughout the world with the fabrication and distribution of the furnishings designed by Alvar Aalto.

Scandinavian furniture design, as it is known today, came about because a handful of world-class designers emerged from the same place and at the same time. During the 1950s, Arne Jacobsen, Verner Panton, Hans J. Wegner, Børge Morgensen, Finn Juhl, and Poul Kjærholm all sought the combination of function and refined beauty that presents itself in a natural way. Scandinavian furniture is notable for its restraint, workmanship, and direct correlation between form and function. Today, younger designers such as Niels Hvass and companies such as *Komplot Design, Hay, Hansen & Sørensen,* and *GUBI* are carrying the Danish tradition of furniture design and craft into the 21st century (Figure 9.21).

Other Epicenters

A short-list of other furniture epicenters throughout the world would include Paris, France; Barcelona, Spain; London, England; Amsterdam, Holland; Chicago, Illinois; Grand Rapids, Michigan; East Aurora, New York; and New York City. These epicenters often specialize in production, design, distribution, or marketing of furniture. Each of them maintains an industrial or design presence that has been developed and recognized as a center for a substantial period of time. Local regions and countries have invested in design centers and recognize how furniture design contributes to regional economies.

Branding

Industry giants such as *Bernhardt Company, Baker Furniture, the Bittner's Group, Thom Moser, Verbargs,* and *Arhaus* (Cleveland, Ohio) are examples of traditional and contemporary production companies that attempt to extend their market share by competing directly in the retail market and the public domain. They work to brand their merchandise, reaching customers directly through journals and magazine advertising and investing in retail-based showrooms. More often than not, they reach out to consumers interested in both current trends and traditional home furnishings. Their appeal is based upon the quality of workmanship, value, availability, and branded line of products.

Williams-Sonoma Home, Crate and Barrel, Armani, Casa, Pottery Barn, Target, West Elm, and many other retailers are joining the recent efforts of department stores such as *Macy's, Kohl,* and *JC Penney* to redefine domestic trend furniture. *Home goods* is a huge area and provides a great opportunity for furniture designers.

Artek, B & B Italia, Fritz Hansen, IKEA, Kartell, Knoll, Vitra, and *Zanotta* are furniture design and production companies. They have strong relationships within the culture of contemporary architecture and design in general. These companies market and advertise through a number of venues, including journals and magazines, art venues, furniture exhibitions, miniatures, and an extensive network of showrooms and retail stores (Figures 9.22–9.24). They maintain links with popular culture and the offices of leading architects and

Figure 9.22 *Alt for damerne*—March 1958, marketing the Egg chair, designed by Arne Jacobsen (1956), manufactured by Fritz Hansen.

Figure 9.23 "Easter Morning" for the *Saturday Evening Post,* May 16, 1959, by Norman Rockwell.

Figure 9.24 Miniature 1:6 models from the Vitra Miniature Collection at the Paustian furniture showroom, Copenhagen, Denmark, models produced by Vitra.

designers through marketing, aggressive pricing, production, and distribution strategies. Industrial production, economies of production, limits of distribution, and links with popular culture are extremely important in the conception and fabrication of contemporary works by these and many other companies.

On-line and web-based companies such as the California-based *Design Within Reach* (www.dwr.com), England's web-based outlet for contemporary works, *Habitat* (www.habitat.co.uk), *West Elm, Conrad's, Hold Everything, FrontGate, Sharper Image,* and Europe's *TopdeQ* (www.topdeq.com) have established a new and convenient way for people to search for and purchase furniture from their home and office using catalogs and the Internet.

BUSINESS

Many furniture designs never reach the marketplace. Putting a design idea into production requires investment, and investment requires economic viability. But equally important are the nature of the market at which the product is aimed and the degree to which furniture design can be protected from competition. The market value of the product must be greater than its cost to produce, market, and distribute in order to justify the investment required. The net profit should augment an acceptable return on the investment in plant and working capital.

Assessing the value and marketability of furniture design is difficult. The value of a design often depends upon the market niche at which the product is aimed: monogrammed beanbag chairs for children, vibrating massage loungers for the stressed, and lift chairs or wheelchairs for those in need. Furniture attracts niche market clientele and, more often than not, is marketed in such a manner.

Some market niches in the furniture industry are slow to adopt new technologies, whether or not these technologies enable a more durable, safer, or less expensive product. Those who desire traditional wood furnishings, stained and finished to appear handmade, most likely will continue to do so. These individuals will likely not seek out the latest polymer or recycled material incorporated in design. Likewise, those accustomed to sitting upright at the dining table will probably not adopt the Asian or Turkish model of sitting closer to the floor when sharing a meal. Markets are focused realities. This is as true today as it was centuries ago when Chippendale, Hepplewhite, and Sheraton worked to market their products.

What works well in one culture may not work in another. The cultural lifestyles and social norms of people need to be understood in conjunction with the furniture that is sought, desired, and needed by people finishing their home, office, or place of business in order to market effectively and attract consumers.

chapter

10 Historical Overview

History has remembered the kings and warriors, because they destroyed; art has remembered the people, because they created.[1]

William Morris

HOW SOCIETIES HAVE THOUGHT ABOUT DESIGNING, MAKING, AND USING FURNITURE

The history of furniture design emerges from the history of kings and queens, established and emerging societies, furniture makers, furniture designers, architects, interior designers, industrial designers, artists, historians, entrepreneurs, and consumers. Throughout history, furniture has helped people sit, rest, work, play, organize their possessions, and partition space. Furniture includes all the conceivable variations of objects and built-ins made to meet these functional needs as civilizations developed.

Furniture design reveals the thinking about and the making of objects and built-ins, encompassing evolving technologies, materials, and available resources that shape and, in turn, are shaped by cultural, political, and economic factors. And so, the history of furniture design is really a chronology of how societies have thought about designed, fabricated, and used an enormous anthology of furniture. If we seek to understand the challenges and conditions encountered in contemporary furniture design, we should look at the historical path that has shaped it thus far.

What was the first object used as furniture? Was it the ancient Egyptian coffin fabricated from wood and adorned with gesso, paint, jewels, glass, and gold to preserve the body for the afterlife? Or was it a stone ledge in a cave that Cro-Magnon man rested on? Was it a tree stump used to rest? Was it a transportable or stationary element used to or-

Figure 10.1 Skara Brae.

ganize possessions? Was it natural or worked by hand tools? When did furniture makers become furniture designers? What distinctions exist between hand-crafted pieces and mass-produced pieces? In what societies does furniture serve the middle class or the poor, not just the nobility or the affluent? Reflecting upon these questions generates an understanding about the nature of furniture design and the paradigms that shape its written history.

Consider the prehistoric stone houses at Skara Brae (circa 3500–2600 B.C.), located on the Orkney Islands north of Scotland. A prehistoric civilization built structures here entirely out of stone. What remains today are the built-in seats and platform sleeping spaces. In a harsh climate, these ancient buildings provoke some questions: Was furniture an inherent part of the structure of these dwellings? Did freestanding furnishings even exist? Though there is evidence of furniture in societies that predate the stone houses at Skara Brae, the image of a stone dwelling with interior stone platforms and no freestanding objects (Figure 10.1) raises further questions: Can architecture alone accommodate the functional and utilitarian needs of daily life relying solely upon platforms and built-in cabinetry? Do we need furniture? If furniture is inherently architectural, then what impact might mass production and industrialization have upon architecture and interior design?

The notion of furniture developing from an architectural lineage is widely accepted—especially among architects. Architectural practitioners and theorists from the past, including Marcus Vitruvius Pollio (1st century B.C.), Leon Battista Alberti (1404–72), and Alvar Aalto (1898–1976) have developed theoretical frameworks that address the subject of furniture design. Their writings, along with their built work, have influenced generations of designers. The Finnish architect Alvar Aalto explained:

"... A lamp and chair are always part of an environment. It has usually been like this: When working on the construction of a public building, I noticed that such furnishings and appliances were necessary to create the right unity, and then I designed them. The fact that later on they can also fit into another environment is another story."[2]

Aalto designed *Stool 60* in 1927 for the library he designed in Viipuri, Finland (see Chapter 4). Since then, over 1 million stools have been sold worldwide and are still in use today.

Furniture has deep architectural roots, reinforcing the concept of place and completing interior space, but it is also tethered to industrial production and craft. Driven by a combination of structural, utilitarian, and aesthetic concerns, furniture reveals a chronology of ideas beginning with the earliest societies that existed over 8,000 years ago.

THE EARLIEST CULTURES

Ancient Nomadic Societies

Before there were settled civilizations, there were nomadic societies. Before there were temples and houses, there were people living in tents, earth-mound structures, and caves. People traveled about freely as weather and terrain permitted.

Nomadic societies existed around the world and likely made for themselves a series of artifacts designed to make life better—physically, functionally, and spiritually. But what were their furnishings like? How did furniture help members of ancient nomadic societies in daily life?

Nomads can be categorized into three groups:

1. Hunting-and-gathering nomads (e.g., the African Pygmies, Cheyenne and Navajo Indians, Australian Aborigines, and indigenous people of Southeast Asia would have followed this way of life). These nomads moved from place to place to hunt animals and gather wild plants.
2. Pastoral nomads (e.g., the Bedouin of Arabia and northern Africa, the Fulani of Niger in western Africa, and the Hopi of the North American Southwest). These nomads traveled to find water and pasture lands for their herds.
3. Nomadic craft workers and merchants (e.g., the Lohar blacksmiths of India and the Gypsy traders of Eastern Europe). These nomads traveled seasonally to provide services.

Most nomads traveled in groups called *tribes, clans,* or *bands.* People ate, gathered socially, squatted to sit, and slept on the ground in tents, huts, and caves. Activities often occurred around a central fire.

Nomadic peoples had natural hide containers, which may have been one of the first indispensable articles of furniture for the storage of possessions. They also had wooden furnishings, textile rugs, and hammocks used for sleeping. Furniture had to be portable, easily dismantled, and light enough to carry long distances.

Prehistoric World Settlements

Under the conditions that existed in primitive civilizations, people needed a constant water supply and reasonable climatic conditions for settlements to root. It was not only in Mesopotamia and the Nile Valley that people were settling down to agriculture and the

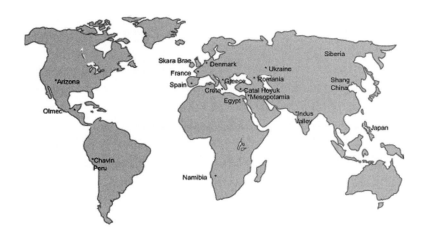

Figure 10.2 Map of the ancient world.

formation of settlements in the millennia between 6000 and 3000 B.C. (Figure 10.2). Along the upper Tigris River, the Assyrians were founding cities. In the valleys of Asia Minor and on the Mediterranean shores and islands, small communities developed into civilizations. Parallel developments were occurring simultaneously in regions of India, China, and the Americas.

As settled societies developed an infrastructure to produce functional possessions such as textiles, storage containers, and fundamental furniture pieces, inevitably a certain amount of trading developed.

PREHISTORY TO ANTIQUITY

Ancient Egypt

Early Dynastic Period (3100–2575 B.C.)

Egypt evolved from an unsettled society into a politically secure, economically strong, technologically advanced, and culturally unified civilization along the Nile River. Egypt was, and remains today, a land of few trees, but examples of wooden furniture have been preserved because they were buried in the tombs of kings and queens. Clearly, central trading among societies from different regions occurred in Egypt. Wood was imported and furniture was exported to neighboring countries. Craftsmen learned how to make and decorate a variety of freestanding furniture pieces (Figure 10.3). The furniture known to us from the Early Dynastic Period was well crafted, ornate, and fabricated using several materials. Craftsmen used a range of hand tools to manipulate wood, stone, metal, and glass. So important were the fabricators, along with the furnishings they made for the ruling society, that craftsmen were buried in royal tombs along with their tools.[3]

Significant knowledge about furniture making existed in the first Egyptian Dynasty (3200–2980 B.C.), based on evidence of the skill used to make mortise-and-tenon,

Figure 10.3 Egyptian craftsmen.

dovetail, and miter joints, copper and bronze fittings, and chests with bolted systems. Tools included mallets, copper and bronze saws, axes, chisels, adzes, and drills. Adzes were used to plane wood similarly to the way we use hand planes today. It is interesting to note that the hand tools and fabrication methods used in ancient Egypt remained constantly in use up to the early 19th century. The materials and tools used in ancient Egypt reveal a desire to fabricate beautiful, long-lasting pieces. The high quality of the workmanship indicates a culture thoughtful about developing fabrication processes and design principles.

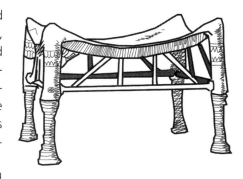

Figure 10.4 Drawing of an Egyptian stool.

Basketwork was made of coiled fibers, including palm, papyrus, reed, and alfalfa grass. Relatively small, low **X-chairs** were made resilient with interlaced cords and leather thongs (Figure 10.4). The use of grasses and plants in furniture illustrates that the Egyptians considered comfort in the chairs found in their tombs.

Danish professor Dan Svarth spent years researching, drawing, and modeling Egyptian furnishings at a 1:5 scale (Figure 10.5). He concludes that the ancient Egyptians used steambending technology to shape and form wood for their chariots and furniture. This is the first record of steam-bending technology used in the fabrication of furniture.

Ancient Egypt was a place of historical beginnings, many of which have influenced the history of furniture design in regard to typology, social status, form, and material. Significantly, 2600 B.C. is the date of the first known furniture designer. He was an Egyptian priest named Hesyre and was known to have designed furniture using 1:1 scale drawings of beds and other furnishings found at his tomb.[4]

Native Egyptian woods included acacia and African ebony, while cypress and cedar were imported from Syria and Lebanon.[5] Carved African ivory was commonly incorporated into

Figure 10.5 Models at 1:5 scale of Egyptian furnishings made by Dan Svarth.

Figure 10.6 Egyptian headrest.

Figure 10.7 Egyptian offering table, alabaster.

the legs of furniture. Ebony, due to its density and stability, enabled veneer techniques to develop. The use of these materials in furniture illustrates a desire for permanence and also points to active regional trade, experienced craftsmen, and the significance placed upon eating, sleeping, and the afterlife.

Old Kingdom (2575–2134 B.C.)

During the Old Kingdom, wooden coffins were fabricated with butt and miter joints secured with wooden dowels and shoulder miters. While dovetails, scarf joints, and halving joints were used, miter and shoulder miter joints exhibited sophisticated joining techniques, revealing how innovative the Egyptians were in using fabrication techniques. Whether or not the Egyptians invented these techniques or learned them from other societies, they increased the quality of workmanship and established a precedent for working with hand tools that lasted for millennia.

Beds and cosmetic boxes were used by both royalty and common people. Three- and four-legged stools were portable, practical, and easy to fabricate. Other furniture typologies from the Old Kingdom include bed platforms, chairs, game furnishings, storage chests, and tables. Storage chests were used as containers for clothing, cosmetics, household items, and jewelry. Most people slept on floor mats, but bed frames were used by the privileged. Bed platforms had elaborate footboard panels incorporated in their design, and rigid headrests were applied to support the head at the open and lower end of the platforms (Figure 10.6). Tables were generally rectangular and used for display, work, and dining. Smaller offering tables were fabricated with remarkable craft, often out of stone (Figure 10.7). Straight-backed and reclining chairs, with and without arms, were made of wood. Surviving chairs from various tombs illustrate beautifully carved open work, painted and decorated examples that incorporated **gilding, inlay,** and veneer work.

Archaic and Classical Greece

The city-states of ancient Greece fostered a personal spirit of inquiry and sought scientific and philosophical solutions to problems of daily life. Much of our understanding of ancient Greek furniture is based upon surviving pieces on display in museums, as well as the representation of furniture on painted vases and incorporated in sculptural relief. These artifacts

Figure 10.8 Decorated plate showing Greek reclining furniture.

provide knowledge regarding the fabrication and use of seven types of Greek furniture: chests, couches, footstools, klinai, klismos chairs, tables, and thronelike chairs. Greek furniture was used in a combination of practical and ceremonial functions tied to its developing democratic society, indicative of an egalitarian civilization. Most pieces were used for sitting, lounging, and eating (Figure 10.8).

Greece had an abundant supply of timber. Wood species such as oak, maple, beech, walnut, and willow made it unnecessary to use veneers. Marble and bronze were used in conjunction with or as a replacement for wood in special items, which denoted their importance for special functions. Wood joints were held together with tenons, hide glue, and nails. Carved, worked, and inlaid ivory, ebony, precious stones, and silver were common ornamentation for couches, chairs, and chests. In addition to the range of existing Egyptian tools, the Greeks improved upon the Egyptian hand plane. The introduction of the lathe around 700 B.C. enabled furniture legs to be turned round.

Figure 10.9 *Klismos* chair painted on a Greek vessel, circa 350 B.C.

The Greek **kline** was a couch with a headboard and footboard. It was used occasionally for eating with another person or reclining alone. *Klinai* were typically located in a room used for dining that later evolved into the Roman **triclinium.** For dining, a low table was used to hold food at the level of the recliner and could slide under the *kline* when not in use. The *kline* serves as a typological model for the contemporary recliner, as is evident in the origin of the word *recline.*

The **thronos** was a chair for the most important person present. It was used in both domestic environments and ceremonial environments. *Lekthoi* (loosely covered couches) were common but are not technically considered upholstery, which developed several hundred years later. The **klismos** (Figures 10.9, 10.10) was a wooden armless chair with outwardly curved legs. It was remarkably well proportioned and was associated with domestic Greek life between 700 and 400 B.C., as is evident in surviving Greek art and pottery decoration (see Chapter 4).

Figure 10.10 Interpretation of a Greek *klismos* chair fabricated by Kaj Gottlob (ca. 1921).

Etruria

Etruria was a prosperous settled society of linked city-states in northern Italy between 600–300 B.C. The Etruscans had established trade with Greece. Etruscan ideas about furniture design were adopted from Magna Grecia. The remains of magnificent murals from Etruscan tomb paintings, such as those from the towns of Cerveteri and Tarquinii, provide considerable insight into the comforts of the Etruscan way of life. The furnishings found in the carved and painted tombs reveal the importance placed upon the afterlife, though early tombs contained urns for ashes, not coffins for bodies.

A recurring theme in Etruscan tomb murals is the banquet—part of the religious ceremony at funerals. After the formal funeral ceremonies were complete, the relatives of the deceased would have been treated to a banquet, which the spirit of the departed was believed to attend. In Etruscan life, the banquet was a status event, indicating that the hosts had "arrived" in the estimation of the social elite. Lavish receptions were provided at which the guests reclined on couches, were waited on, and were entertained by musicians and dancers. Tables were covered with embroidered tablecloths on which dinner courses were served. The importance of the meal gave consequence to the furnishings used for dining.

Evidence of craftsmen working in wood, stone, bronze, textiles, and painting abounds. With the availability of bronze, a number of bronze chests, hardware, weapons, and domestic accessories, such as candlesticks, were fabricated as early as 700 B.C. The workmanship and design of small bronze tables were remarkable in their circular form, supported by paw-shaped feet and engraved with figures.

The Etruscans were active in the trading network surrounding the Mediterranean Sea. Their bronze artifacts have been identified as far west as Madeira, Spain, and as far north as Hassle, Sweden. This is an important point, demonstrating that furniture and furnishings have cultural and societal value as well as economic value. Through the exchange and trade of furniture, civilizations and societies adapted each other's cultural values.

The Romans

The Roman Republic (Figure 10.11) was marked by expansion based upon military strength and economic trade. Greece came under centralized Roman rule in 146 B.C. and began to influence Roman culture, including its architectural style and design vocabulary. Roman furniture was more elaborate than earlier Greek models. With the rise of the merchant class, the military class, and Roman citizenship, furniture began to function as a status marker, as described in Petronius' *Satyricon*.

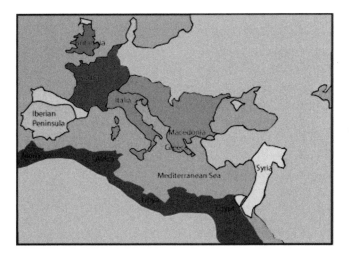

Figure 10.11 Map of the Roman Empire.

Figure 10.12 Roman study with furniture.

The Romans' settled mode of habitation resulted in new furnishings for the home (Figure 10.12). Rome was the place where the cupboard first developed because dishes and domestic accessories created the need and desire for increased display and storage. Small tables were fabricated of bronze, wood, and marble.

Our knowledge of Roman furniture also derives from the fresco paintings at Pompeii and Herculaneum, sarcophagi, and surviving examples made from marble, bronze, exotic woods, ivory, gold, and silver. In addition to the expanded realm of interior furnishings, outdoor furniture began to flourish in conjunction with the use and popularity of courtyards.

EARLY CHRISTIAN AND ISLAMIC CULTURES

Throughout medieval Europe and Asia, regional development thrived as clustered areas banded together politically and culturally. In 330 A.D., the Roman Emperor Constantine placed the new seat of the Eastern Roman Empire at Constantinople. With the new governing center, a developing Christian culture emerged throughout Eastern Europe and Asia Minor. Christian culture flourished, leading to the building of new churches and cathedrals and monastic interiors throughout Byzantium (Figure 10.13).

The stone that was used in the architecture around the area of Constantinople was superbly carved and revealed the desire to build permanent buildings. Ivory was commonly used in furniture, usually in the form of thick veneers. Carved ivory chairs from the 6th century were built like a box with the arms and back attached. Four-poster beds designed for drapery canopies were created at this time because of the need and desire for privacy and warmth. Generally, these furnishings were fabricated for the wealthy and the ruling class.

Figure 10.13 Byzantine writing table.

Emergence of Islamic Furniture (circa 610)

The roots of Islamic furniture can be traced to pre-Islamic and Persian societies, which had functional, simple furniture that later developed into more artistic and complex designs even before 610 A.D. In Islamic society, much of one's life was spent on the floor; therefore, the rug was considered one of the greatest possessions in a household and was used as furniture (Figure 10.14). People often slept on mattresses on the floor that were folded and stored in cupboards during the day.

The use of ornamentation was prevalent in pre-Islamic design and appeared in woven textiles as well as in carved and inlaid chests. The four basic types of ornament are calligraphy, vegetal patterns, geometric patterns, and abstract figural representation. This type of ornamentation was referred to in Europe as **arabesque** and was popular as a style until the early 17th century. (Although figural representation is prohibited by the Koran, abstract figural images do exist in woven rugs.) All four types of ornament assist in telling stories that helped to preserve Islamic history.

Geometric ornamentation reached a pinnacle in the Islamic world. Sources for the shapes and patterns existed in late antiquity among the Greeks, Romans, and Persians. The four basic shapes from which complicated patterns were constructed are circles, squares, the star pattern, and multisided polygons.

For centuries, Turks lived in Central Asia as a nomadic community in circular tents called yurts (Figure 10.15). Starting in the 11th century, they began migrating to Anatolia and began to settle. As a result of their settled life in Anatolia, the Turks developed the Turkish

Figure 10.14 Islamic prayer rug.

Figure 10.15 Turkish yurt.

house, which in turn generated an array of furniture shaped by their culture, traditions, and needs.

Anatolian Turkish houses were sparsely furnished before the 13th century. Furnishings were fixed and dependent upon the architecture in the form of shelves and built-in closets. However, the *besik* (cradle), *kavukluk* (shelf support for the headpiece of a religious cleric), *rahle* (support for the Koran), *sandik* (chest), and *sehpa* (stool) were used as portable furniture.

In a Turkish house, a child's first bed was the *besik* (cradle). Since it was designed to rock back and forth, the edges were shaped like an arc, above which was a holding bar with a covering raised or draped on the sides.

The *kavukluk* is a shelf composed of two or three elements and mounted on the wall in a home at the height of an average person. The traditional purpose of the kavukluk was to support the headpiece of a cleric, but it also is used as a shelf to support lighting equipment.

The *rahle* became a common type of furniture with the introduction of the printing press and the availability of the Koran to the masses (Figure 10.16). It is designed for a person to read the Koran and other books in a restful, sitting posture. The *rahle* is a small, often collapsible support, composed in an X shape that is formed by the

Figure 10.16 *Rahle,* Semsi Pasa Mosque; architect: Mimar Sinan, 1580.

insertion or folding of two wooden panels. Some *rahles* are stationary and incorporate horizontal desks and drawers. Originally, Korans were written on parchment paper using large characters, which resulted in volumes of great size and weight. The early *rahles* were therefore large, and some were designed with seats. They were adorned with valuable materials and hand-carved decoration.

The *sandik* was a chest used to store goods, clothes, various objects, food, and holy mantles. Most were made of wood that was carved, embroidered, inlaid, painted, or covered with fabric. Each chest had a unique lock system, and some had small compartments.

Mattresses used for sitting in nomadic Turkish tents were called *sedirs,* and these developed into divans after Turks settled in Anatolia. Divans were placed against interior walls in order to create space in the middle of the room. Surrounding the inside wall of a room, divans were upholstered with various textiles and carpets for comfort. Serving as models for thrones, they were produced with wooden splats and decorated with oriental motifs. Divans were called *ottomans* or *sofas* by Europeans and Americans.

Functioning as a device to carry the service tray, *sehpas* were proportional to the divan in size and were located next to, or in front of, the divan. They were either hexagonal or octagonal. Their tops were inlaid with tortoise shell, mother of pearl, ivory, gold, silver, or tile.

Woodworking techniques including openwork carving, mortise-and-tenon joinery, inlaying, overlaying, and painting were common decorative practices. Mother of pearl, ivory, tortoise shell, antler, and gold gilding were materials of decoration. Shellac, gum lacquer, wax, and special varnishes were also used. During the period of the Ottoman Empire, furniture-manufacturing centers were established in Bursa, Edirne, and Istanbul (capital cities). Each manufacturing center had its own style, and the furniture produced was named according to where it was manufactured, such as *Istanbul work, Adalar work, Edirne work,* or *Üsküdar work.*

MEDIEVAL SOCIETIES

The Romanesque period is marked by the spread of Christianity as a unifying culture throughout Europe, grafting pagan art from the north onto the more classical styles of the south. During this period, the Roman Catholic Church grew in power and influence despite the relocation of the papacy to Avignon, France, during the 1300s. Much that survives today from the Romanesque period is ecclesiastical, but there were relatively few differences between ecclesiastical and secular pieces other than the level of ornamentation. Many of the furnishings from this period were designed for the ruling class and the wealthy; most people still sat on rugs, platforms, simple stools, and the ground.

During the medieval period, regions utilized available natural resources and relied less upon trade. It was during the Romanesque period that walnut was harvested for furniture in Italy, Spain, and France. Walnut is an excellent wood for carving and **turning,** and it is not surprising that Italy, France, and Spain produced beautifully carved furniture. Oak was popular in Britain and the Netherlands. Oak is more difficult to carve than walnut, so furniture from Britain and the Netherlands was generally not elaborately carved. Pine and fir were common in Scandinavia and were carved easily. Scandinavians have enjoyed a long and rich heritage in the crafts going back to the beautiful, elaborate Nordic/Celtic carvings on their long boats and in their architecture.

At the time of the Norman invasion of Britain (1066), castles contained tapestries for warmth and aesthetics, yet they were sparsely furnished. The transient nature of political power and economic wealth, in conjunction with the ongoing reality of war and disease, offers some explanation for the sparsely furnished interiors during this time.

Gathering at the dining table was a social activity. Social dining usually occurred in the great hall of a castle. Social status was reinforced by where people sat. Often the king was seated under a tapestry, or his table was denoted in some manner. The spatial location of the table was also important, with the king's table placed at one end of the room. Trestle-type tables were fabricated from oak, making it easy to add or delete extensions, depending on the number of persons attending. These tables could be taken apart and stored when not in use.

While the medieval period saw the establishment of states and regional governments throughout Europe, furnishings remained transportable, by necessity, during these uncertain times. Words describing furniture during this time reinforced the concept of mobility. The Italian word *mobili,* the French word *meubles,* the German word *möbel,* and the Turkish word *mobilya* all refer directly to furniture.

One of the large stationary pieces of furniture in medieval Europe was the **armoire.** As the name implies, armoires were initially fabricated for holding armor and weapons. Over time, armoires evolved into domestic furniture for storing textiles and clothing. They were either built-in or freestanding, often painted inside and out in a provincial manner. They typically had one iron-hinged door. Due to their size and complex fabrication, several trades were employed in their fabrication. During the medieval period, armoires extended from northern Europe to the Alps. Particularly impressive Gothic armoires (**kas**) came from an area known today as Germany.

The stool was a standard piece of furniture during the Middle Ages. The X-shaped stool that was rooted in Greek tradition was referred to as a **cathedra,** implying authority for those who sat upon it. The term *cathedral* denoted the place where a bishop presided in church. In order to be a cathedral, a church had to contain the bishop's chair, or *cathedra.* The bishop's chair had an associated authority, and this concept has been passed down to current practice.

The *chair of estate,* reserved for the ruling lord, typically utilized a folding X-form. The importance of the chair, with arms as a symbol of authority, is a significant iconic reference that this piece of furniture has held up to the present. Chairs indicated rank and had embellishments incorporated in their designs to denote the hierarchy of family lines. During the Middle Ages, stools and benches were common forms of seating, and chairs were reserved for those with high social status. Today, an *endowed chair* gives special acknowledgment in academic research and in the culture of committees; the one presiding over the group is called the *chair* or *chairperson.* These examples are cultural successors of the Middle Ages.

Gothic chests, known as wooden **coffers,** grew in popularity throughout Europe and reached the height of their popularity by 1250. Metal hardware was added to wooden chests and wrapped the coffers. Their hardware, size, and decorative handwork distinguished the Gothic chests from earlier medieval chests.

Italian chests, known as **cassoni,** were uniquely personalized with carving, painting, or inlay work. Their form and decoration helped express personal identity, distinguishable among families.

The *box-seated chair,* popular in England, France, and the Netherlands, had a high back and enclosed arms. It typically incorporated a storage area under the seat. It was fabricated with panels beveled at the edges to enable a somewhat loose fit into **rails** and **stiles** of the frame. This joinery was common during the 15th and 16th centuries and represented a significant shift in fabrication technology, moving from dovetails and miter joinery to carpentry and building skills.

During the early Tudor period in England, a furniture type known as an *aumbry* was located in the bedchamber to store an overnight ration of food and refreshment. The Episcopal term *aumbry* describes a liturgical furnishing for storing the wine and bread of communion. The term *ambry* describes the container of the holy oils used for the distribution of the sacraments in a Catholic Church. All have the same etymological roots and emphasize the storage of food for common and ecclesiastical activities.

A significant typological division emerged in the 14th and 15th centuries involving two distinct types of **buffets.** One was a large buffet with stepped tiers for a grandiose display of household possessions. The other was smaller, with fewer tiers that were not stepped. Both types were used to display a growing collection of silver plates and glasses used for dining as well as formulating a visual class distinction by the display of treasures. Buffets and other household furnishings began to transform the home into something more than a place of shelter from the natural elements. As the home and social life in cities became secure, industry and population began to flourish.

The *Coronatia Chair* at Westminster Abbey (1420) is one of the few furniture pieces that were firmly attributed to a known master working under the order of King Edward I. Master Walter of Durham is the second individual credited with designing furniture in Western society. The recognition of design as a professional endeavor is significant and serves as a transitional link from the Middle Ages to the rebirth of 15th-century Europe.

Figure 10.17 Il Duomo, Florence Cathedral, Brunelleschi et al., 1420.

THE RISE OF EUROPE

The Renaissance

An emerging Renaissance had begun in Europe by the early 15th century. The rebirth is often cited to have originated in Florence, marking Filippo Brunelleschi's (1377–1446) completion of the dome for the cathedral in 1420 (Figure 10.17). Science, engineering, mathematics, human anatomy, perspective drawing, and new materials fueled a rebirth in the arts, furniture design, and architecture. The artist began to be admired as an inspired creator, which serves to mark the birth of the designer as we understand it today.

Craft **guilds** dominated the workshops during the Renaissance. Instead of igniting scientific and artistic revolutions, they restricted exploration and experimentation in design. A joiner was not allowed to inlay. Engravers were not allowed to do carpentry. Designers did not fabricate. Craftsmen had to satisfy their guild and not step beyond the prescribed division of labor. The segregation of skills generated excellence in workmanship within the trades but significantly limited creative exploration. The Renaissance marked the beginning of an important division between "hand" and "head," between art and science, and between craft and theory. It was a time in the history of furniture design when specialization and division of labor prevailed.

Figure 10.18 Canopy bed for
Christian IV, Kronen Slot, Denmark.

Leon Battista Alberti (1404–72) was a renowned architect and architectural writer who embodied the Renaissance in his built work and written treaties. He established principles that defined beauty as "the harmony and concord of all the parts achieved in such a manner that nothing could be added or taken away or altered except for the worse."[5] Ornament, according to Alberti, "gave brightness and improvement" to the works. He inspired many furniture makers to incorporate decorative motifs into furniture using proportional systems and a classical repertoire. Alberti had strong ideas about architecture, art, and design. Though he wrote proficiently, his ideas were not new. He adopted ideas from Vitruvius' and Aristotle's writings, and Alberti's success as an architect and his influence as a writer illustrate how significant the dissemination of historical knowledge can be.

Social distinctions were important during the Renaissance. Many furnishings were designed to express social status. Particular pieces included *the armoire, bed, buffet, cradle,* and *marriage chest.* For royal events and important social or political ceremonies, furniture was useful to denote class and rank. The *canopy bed* (Figure 10.18) recalled the canopy thrones used by kings. It extended beyond the need to create privacy and warmth for the sleeper. The canopy's material, size, and design expressed social status.

Traditional marriage chests were carved, gessoed, gilded, or painted to tell a story about the families of the couple being wed (Figure 10.19). They were typically produced in sets of

Figure 10.19 Italian cassone,
c. 1460.

Figure 10.20 Credence table.

two. One was fabricated for the bride and the other for the groom. They were the quintessential *mobile,* traveling with the bride and groom to establish their new home. These **dowry chests** became principal interior furnishings that contained the bride's dowry and the couple's personal possessions and were displayed prominently in the home. This tradition was carried into the 20th century as a *hope chest* to store household textiles and items, but it became more of a repository for symbolic or decorative memorabilia.

The **credenza** found its way to the home from a religious environment. The credenza is a sideboard, often draped in cloth to assist in dining, but it is related to the contemporary liturgical Catholic **credence table,** a small table located near the altar upon which the communion meal is placed before mass (Figure 10.20). Both terms share the Latin root *credere,* meaning "to believe."

During the 1400s, X-shaped folding chairs were popular for an informal and relaxed posture. In response to a growing desire for a more relaxed posture for the wealthy, two seating types emerged. The first was the *lit de repos,* a day bed with a raised back for daytime reclining. The second was a small, armless stool-like chair called the **sgabello.**

By 1500, the Italian Renaissance had produced a significant impact upon European art and design, especially among German artists. Albrecht Dürer visited Italy from Nuremberg and Augsburg. His prints and engravings helped to popularize Roman classicism in Central Europe. An emerging demand for classical furnishings generated an organization among craftspeople to legislate both the design and fabrication of classical pieces. The growing legislation resulted in a network of craft guilds throughout Europe. These guilds controlled the standards of quality in the fabrication of furniture (Figure 10.21).

Spanish, Portuguese, and Dutch seafaring expeditions resulted in the import of exotic materials. As a result of Dutch trade with the Far East and West Indies, ebony became available in limited supply to decorate plain oak furniture. Because ebony is an exceptionally

Figure 10.21 Emerging guilds.

strong wood, thinner members could be used, making it an excellent choice for inlay work and veneering.

Walnut was abundant in Southwestern Europe and a source of export for France and Spain. The increased availability of walnut provided carvers with greater opportunities to depict elaborate forms in furniture, built-ins, casework, and case goods.

During and following the Renaissance, published treatises and pattern books became popular throughout Europe due to the invention of the printing press in the mid-15th century and the prevalent use of woodcuts. Eight books by the Italian architect Sebastiano Serlio (1475–1554) were translated into English, French, and German. The illustrations in his architectural treatises about proportion and geometry had a significant influence on architects, designers, and fabricators throughout Europe. The French designer Androuet Ducerceau (1520–84) published furniture engravings that influenced the use of carving in major European centers. In 1550, Ducerceau presented objects with classical ideas of proportion that were overlaid with geometric patterns and representations of human and animal figures. Hughes Sambin (1520–1601), an architect, wood carver, and furniture maker, published a book on the diversity of the figures used in architecture. Sambin's book inspired figural representation, not only on many sculptural pieces of furniture, but also in the development of carving in low and high relief.

Craftsmen drew inspiration from Lorenz Stör's *Geometria et Perspectiva* (1567). This publication contained images of geometric forms intended to serve as perspective studies specifically for craftsmen working in wood, showing images of formal studies juxtaposed against a background of classical ruins.

Figure 10.22 Dutch 17th-century wardrobe closet.

With an increase in the number and type of articles of clothing that an affluent person wore, the **dresser** and **armoire** became significant furniture types in France and Italy around 1550. The armoire was larger than the dresser and was a precursor to the *wardrobe closet* (Figure 10.22). Related to both the dresser and armoire was the **cupboard,** a paneled box, either freestanding or wall-mounted, for storing equipment and food, used in dining. These large furnishings caused fabricators to rely upon more traditional carpentry skills, and this evolution generated further specialization and division of labor within the French, Italian, and German furniture centers. During this time, furniture companies began to emerge as a new industry. Through the resources available to a furniture company, guilds could work together in one organization to produce a variety of furniture.

The movable table with elaborate supports, connected by stretchers and typically covered with a carpet, became a popular furniture type in the 16th century. Movable and transformable tables and chairs (i.e., the gate-leg table and the chair/table) responded to the desire for flexibility in social and utilitarian function. This worked well in domestic settings, where houses were still quite small and rooms had multiple functions.

Antwerp, Belgium, was a center for the making of veneered and painted cabinets. These cabinets were worked in ebony or ebony veneer, with painters specializing in depicting mythological or classical scenes. Surrounding cities such as Amsterdam and Brussels followed Antwerp's lead in producing painted and veneered furniture.

Textiles were used to cover Dutch tables during this period and became one of the chief forms of social and class display. As a result, textiles were prominently used within residential and commercial interior spaces as tapestry wall hangings and as area rugs. Amsterdam was becoming a furniture-making center in tandem with its emerging political and growing economic base during the 15th century. This generated a prolonged focus on textiles incorporated in furniture design, which eventually led to the development of upholstered pieces in the 18th century.

By the end of the 15th century, Spain and Portugal had become wealthy countries. The Moors, who had conquered Spain in the 8th century (and lived there for over 700 years), were expelled in 1492. Although the Renaissance influenced Spain, the Moorish influence resulted in the distinctive Spanish style that used geometric systems, including ad quadratum (of the square), and strong contrasts in materials.

The gold and silver taken back to Spain and Portugal from Mexico and Peru were incorporated into furniture. With its superior fleet, Spain enjoyed trade with the Orient, which brought new lacquer finishes and frontal approaches to furniture design. A *frontal approach* is a formally arranged composition intended to be experienced straight on. Liberal use of decorative wrought iron characterized many pieces. Chair legs and arms were often turned and scrolled. The Spanish *scroll foot* was distinctive, as were the decorative nail heads shaped into roses and shells in various furnishings.

During the 16th century, the Spanish developed the idea that side tables and *cabinets-on-stands,* as well as chairs, should be used in specific positions within a room to define the architectural space. This spatial concept was central to the design and function of European Baroque furniture, which developed in France during the reign of Louis XIV (1643–1715).

The *fall-front cabinet* developed into a popular type of furniture known by the Spanish name **vargueño** (Figure 10.23). Upholstery and finely tooled leather were applied to many chairs and tables. Lisbon, Portugal, emerged as an active center for furniture makers.

In 1580, Phillip II unified Spain and Portugal. Because Spain ruled Mexico at the time, furniture makers in Mexico, like those practicing in Toledo or Lisbon, were required to be able to make a *vargueño,* an inlaid hip-joint chair, and a turned bed and table. Trade regulations forbade craftsmen to open a shop in the city without first being examined in their trade.

In England, joiners became recognized as the chief furniture makers during the reign of Queen Elizabeth I. But even within the joiners' guild, there were conflicts due in part to new fabrication techniques brought to England by the Flemish. *Board construction* began to replace *panel-set-in-frame* fabrication.

In the second half of the 16th century, many furniture makers developed framed-panel joinery, known as *rail and stile* construction, held together by pegs. The perfection of the

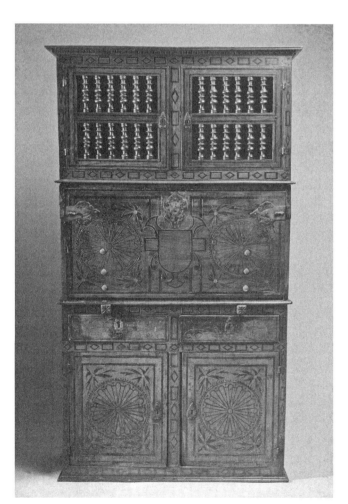

Figure 10.23 Spanish *vargueño,* walnut and oak, late 17th century.

miter joint greatly simplified the manufacturing of molded frames. Furnishings became lighter and more mobile.

In the 17th century, guilds began to evolve into training centers. They were active in governing the workmanship and behavior of members and in regulating the price and quality of manufactured goods. However, despite the power and strength attained in the early 16th century, guilds began to lose power due to their economic dependence on the Catholic Church. By the end of the 18th century, the Reformation and the dissolution of the monasteries resulted in political and societal shifts that limited the production of high-end furniture.

Nonetheless, craftsmen continued to function throughout Europe. As markets expanded, a new, rising middle class of English merchants and tradesmen reorganized themselves and received new charters, first from Queen Elizabeth I and later from King James I. Slowly, furniture companies began to emerge as early as 1570 with a dominance of joiners.

Baroque Period

The Baroque period began in the 17th century, originating in Southern Europe, and extended into the early 18th century. The Baroque style was influenced by the Bourbon dynasty (1589–1789) and by the prevailing fashions in Italy, France, Spain, and the Netherlands. Two cultural and economic forces shaped furniture of this period. First, there were large and complicated trade activities involving exotic and luxury goods in the Far East and with colonies throughout the world. Second, the Catholic Church began to consolidate power through the Counter Reformation during this period. Monasteries once again saw advances in furniture in both typology and quality due to their settled way of life. Demand for **lecterns,** cupboards, and stages for books, libraries, and desks flourished during the height of monastic life. Albrecht Dürer's etching of Saint Jerome in his study with a lion at his feet exemplifies an adorned, well-furnished monastic library.

In Southern Europe, Baroque furniture shared characteristics with Baroque art, emphasizing a strong contrast of light and material and a dramatic sense of theatricality (Figure 10.24). This was illustrated by the designs of the lavish show cabinets created during the Baroque era made from an array of exotic materials. In the Netherlands, a quieter northern style, referred to as the *Rembrandt style,* shared with architecture an interest in more naturalistic carving and realism.

As the Netherlands grew wealthier, Central Europe grew poorer. This resulted in a "folk quality" in many furnishings from Central Europe. In contrast, Sweden was the most economically powerful of the Baltic countries in the 17th century, and the quality of its furniture revealed its economic wealth.

The light-filled interiors depicted by the Flemish painter Jan van Eyck, as well as the interior spaces painted by Pieter de Hoogh and Jan Vermeer, portrayed a growing bourgeois way of life. During this time, distinctive theoretical texts on furniture and design permeated Europe. Grammars of ornament and patterns for *caryatids* were incorporated from surviving antique Greek and Roman pieces. Ten books on architecture, written by the Roman theorist Vitruvius, were republished in Strasbourg, Germany, in 1543. Printed copies of this classical history had a pronounced influence upon Northern European designers and makers of furniture.

The expanding divisions of labor created rivalries within trades, and the competition eventually developed both an insurgence and a resurgence of the guilds. A new joiners'

Figure 10.24 Baroque—carved plant ornament, marked by strong shadows and high contrasts.

guild developed in Northern Europe in 1519. With a range of furniture trades and the need for precise skills in fabrication, guild ordinances (i.e., regulations and standards of workmanship) became increasingly elaborate.

The French word for cabinetmaker, *ébéniste,* derived from *menuisier en ébène* (which literally means "someone who works with ebony wood"), was introduced to Spain, Portugal, France, and the Netherlands. Henry IV of France sent cabinetmakers to the Netherlands to study the work being done in ebony. French ebony cabinets on stands were entirely black.

Furniture fabricated in France at this time was considered quintessentially Baroque and influenced all of Europe. The most luxurious furniture designs were produced for two important French palaces—those of the Connétable de Montmorency (1568) and the Italian-born Queen of France, Catherine de Medici (1589).

The French nobility were given state apartments at Versailles. The interiors of these apartments involved great expenditure, but the rooms were essentially waiting rooms for people doing business with the king. The interiors contained lavish furnishings primarily to impress dignitaries. The rooms were called *sallés,* distinct from the word *chambres,* and were seldom used except as receiving rooms. However opulently the French nobility and the Medici family lived, bankers and successful merchants had, by comparison, basic furniture in their

Figure 10.25 French 18th-century bureau plat by André-Charles Boullé.

homes. This generated an inventory of well-crafted standard pieces, typical in well-to-do homes throughout Europe in the late 16th century.

Henry IV of France enacted the Edict of Nantes in 1558, which provided freedom of worship for Protestants working in France. In 1666, during the reign of Louis XIV, the government minister Jean-Baptiste Colbert founded the French Academy in Rome. The Academy sent French artists to study in Italy, thereby strengthening the tie between these two Catholic countries. In 1685, Louis XIV revoked the Edict of Nantes, resulting in the exodus of Protestant merchants and craftsmen to other countries that accepted Protestant workers, such as England, the Netherlands, and Switzerland. Many Protestants fled to the British colonies in the New World. This exodus had both a short-term and a long-term impact upon furniture design by generating an eclectic mixture of styles and fabrication techniques throughout the world.

André-Charles Boullé (1642–1732), the son of a Flemish cabinet maker, was born in Paris. In 1672, he accepted the position of *Ébéniste du Roi—Cabinet Maker of the King*. His work was admired and copied in Germany, resulting in **Boulle** furniture (Figure 10.25) utilizing a brass veneer over a wooden carcass, with tortoise shell, and mother of pearl inlaid in a brass sheet.

In 1682, Versailles was ready to receive the French court. Versailles, under the design team of Louis Le Vau, Charles Le Brun, and Andre Le Nôtre, was the ultimate attempt to create a center for political and cultural power in France. It was intended to overshadow the opulence of the recently completed Vaux le Vicômte, the residence of the former Minister of Finance. The interior designer and artist Charles Le Brun (1619–90) was appointed the first director of royal manufacturing at Gobelins. More significantly, Le Brun was the artistic coordinator of Vaux le Vicômte and Versailles and thus achieved a coordination of all aspects of the architecture and interior design. This was significant because the integration of architecture, interior design, and furniture design had never before been commissioned on such an enormous scale or with such opulence.

French Rococo Period

The **French Rococo** period (1715–74), was a time when important distinctions in an array of trades developed. The following terms identify some of the trades and craftsmen of the French Rococo:

1. **Ébéniste:** cabinet maker, working with ebony and a variety of other woods, who made veneered furniture
2. **Menuisier:** solid wood furniture maker
3. **Fondeur:** metal mounts maker
4. **Ciseleur:** bronze casting maker
5. **Vernisseur:** lacquerer
6. **Marqueteur:** maker of marquetry
7. **Doreur:** gilder

It remained a punishable offense for a furniture maker to cross trades. This made it difficult for those who possessed woodworking skills to work outside their primary trade and created a climate for specialists rather than generalists in furniture making. It is remarkable how coherent French furniture was, since so many guilds were involved in the fabrication of one piece. The *ébéniste's* job was to unite the efforts of the trades. Between 1743 and 1751, French cabinet makers were required to stamp their work with their names or initials followed by J.M.E.—*juré des menuisiers et ébénistes.*

Comfort and convenience became paramount in furniture design during the French Rococo period. Craftsmen at the court of Louis XV created furniture that was smaller in scale but elaborate in ornamentation (Figures 10.26, 10.27). Within the smaller furniture types of 18th-century

Figure 10.27 Hotel de Soubise, Paris, Salon Ovale de la Princess, 1737–40, by Germain Boffrand and Charles Natoire.

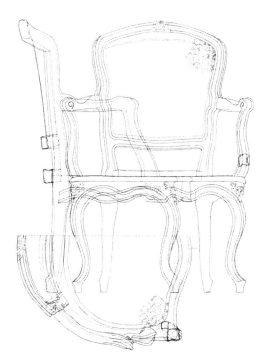

Figure 10.26 Study of a French Rococo chair.

Rococo, the development of comfort and social posture emerged, marking the beginning of *ergonomic design,* as well as the rise of gender-based aspects of furniture design. The wives and mistresses of male nobles decided which furniture to buy for their suites within the French courts, and this reality, in conjunction with the growing interest in comfort and social norms of posture and sitting, led to a proliferation of new forms and specialized pieces, and new methods of fabrication. The French Rococo was significant in this regard and laid the foundation for an emerging interest in extending the realm of furniture into the larger context of leisure, comfort, upholstery, ergonomics, and interior design.

England in the 17th and 18th Centuries

The greatest influence on furniture design in the 17th century resulted from the growth of trade within the British Empire. Finally, it had become economically possible to transport finished pieces of furniture as well as raw material by ship. A significant new source of furniture and raw material was India, and trade with India and its adjacent lands became known as the *Triangle Trade.* As a result of the Triangle Trade, an excellent tropical hardwood, West Indian mahogany, was obtained. The abundant supply of this hardwood, and its demand by the furniture trades, allowed solid wood furniture to replace traditional veneer pieces, which had previously been the norm.

Workers skilled in the techniques of **japanning** and *oriental lacquer* supplied Europe with new types of exotic finishes. Toward the end of the 17th century, imports from the Far East ignited a desire for painted and lacquered furniture (Figure 10.28). Solid wood furniture became popular because it withstood the voyage and climate better, while veneers buckled and split due to the climatic conditions during the sea voyages.

For a period of time in the 18th century, furniture was not signed; thus, relatively little is known about the fabricators. During this period, cabinet shops were small, often consisting of one master, one apprentice, and two journeymen. Outside of France, there were no strict guild systems. Furniture could be fabricated in a number of ways by many individual craftsmen. In addition, setting up a cabinet shop was not an expensive endeavor. The cost compared favorably to that of importing furniture from across the ocean.

William Kent (1684–1748) was a British architect and furniture designer whose work emulated Palladian classicism and was admired by Lord Burlington. He was renowned for the furniture he made for Lord Burlington and his friends, as well as for his interiors and his picturesque landscapes. By the mid-18th century, the Rococo style had reached its zenith. When the *Classical Revival* style became popular, critics began to speak out against extraneous curvilinear forms and demanded a return to less complex geometry. Attention returned to Roman classicism in particular (Figure 10.29).

Figure 10.28 English 18th-century japanned cabinet on stand—London, Charles II.

Figure 10.29 Neoclassical furniture, a return to Roman and Greek classicism.

Archeological publications flourished during this period. Robert Adam's *The Palace of the Emperor Diocletian at Spalato in Dalmatia* (1764) enabled wealthy patrons to derive inspiration for grandiose schemes. In 1753, William Hogarth stated in his *Analysis of Beauty,* "the S-shape suggests motion and the pleasure of wandering gives pleasure entitling the word beauty."[6] His view of beauty reinforced the spirit of the time and established a foundation for the emerging furniture designs of Thomas Chippendale and George Hepplewhite (a follower of the Neoclassical Adam style).

Thomas Chippendale (1718–79) was an English designer and cabinetmaker who incorporated a variety of patterns and styles in his work. Early **Chippendale** pieces had *cabriole* legs (Figure 10.30) with details including Chinese bamboo and open **fretwork.** In 1754, he

Figure 10.30 American Chippendale carved cabriole leg—with a "hairy paw" foot.

Figure 10.31 Pair of American side chairs, 1800.

wrote *The Gentleman and Cabinet-Maker's Director,* an up-to-date manual for urban colonial and English cabinetmakers. It was immensely successful and was reissued in 1762. Chippendale's drawings combined Chinese, medieval, and Rococo styles. His work, and particularly his chair designs, influenced a generation of cabinetmakers in North America (Figure 10.31). Chippendale's furniture emphasized carving rather than inlay. Carved details were applied rather than hewn from solid lumber. Therefore, Chippendale was able to maintain an inventory of applied designs, large and small, to satisfy every client. Mahogany was the favored wood because it was easy to work and carve, was stable, and had a beautiful, consistent grain. After Sir Robert Walpole repealed the import duty on mahogany in 1733, it became affordable and plentiful for making furniture.

The American Colonies and the Emerging United States

The plantation owners in the new American colonies turned to England for furnishings, but the vast majority of colonists were ordinary people from a variety of different cultures, who depended on what they could bring with them on their voyage or had to build their furniture from local woods. For these people, furniture was fabricated using primitive and regional woodworking technology.

The table became an important furnishing in the colonial home during the mid-17th century. It created a centered spatial zone in the home that was useful for work, social gatherings, tea, and shared conversations throughout the day. The American *gate-leg* table was used as an oval table in the center of the room and as a drop-leaf table placed against a wall (Figure 10.32).

Among the few personal possessions that traveled with families, chests were the primary furnishings brought from Europe. After a newly arrived family settled into a home, local lumber was used to craft additional furnishings. Wood turners could work with green

Figure 10.32 American 17th-century gateleg table.

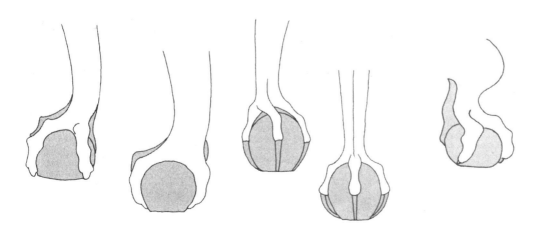

(unseasoned) wood such as white oak, ash, and red oak. In 1642, records from a joiner named Edward Johnson noted that towns were fast turning into urban communities.[7] The growing urban populations began to divide societies into trades and services.

William and Mary furniture (1689–1702) was named after Queen Mary, sister of King James II, and her Dutch husband, William of Orange. With their ascendancy to the English throne, several Dutch craftsmen emerged, whose collective work was influenced by Flemish design. The furniture under their reign was lighter and improved due to the strength of the wood used and the tools and methods employed in fabrication. What we now call **highboy** (Figure 10.33) and **lowboy** were characteristic of William and Mary styling and were central furniture pieces in the homes of the affluent.

Figure 10.33 Colonial highboy or chest on chest.

Queen Anne (1702–14) and the Age of Regionalism followed the reign of William and Mary. Although Queen Anne ruled England for only 12 years, this stylistic period lasted for nearly 40 years. In this era, the cabriole leg, the distinctive splat back, and the use of upholstery that emerged in the 17th century were renowned characteristics of the famous Queen Anne padfoot and **ball-and-claw-foot** chairs (Figure 10.34). Significant is the fact

Figure 10.34 American Chippendale—ball and claw variations from left to right: Philadelphia foot with prominent knuckles; squared-off New York foot; Newport foot with undercut talons; Newport foot, front view; Boston foot with rear-curving talon.

that these chairs were fabricated by individual components and made to order. This generated great variety in both design and production. Major urban centers throughout colonial settlements began to take on an ethnic or culturally unique characteristic of place enhanced by locally available material and local skill in furniture making. As a result, Boston, New York, and Philadelphia developed as distinct design centers reflecting popular local tastes. By the time of the Revolutionary War in 1776, 150 cabinetmakers were listed as working in Boston.

Newport, Rhode Island, was home to the Quaker family of cabinet makers Goddard and Townsend. They were known for **block front** *and shell carved* dressing tables and secretary bookcases. Their furniture pieces were fabricated from Honduran mahogany and were typically carved rather than inlaid. For over 30 years, Newport was a furniture-producing center where beautiful mahogany pieces for Newport's mercantile elite were fabricated.

The official treaty signed between the French, the British, and the American colonists on September 3, 1782, ended the struggle for independence and marked the return to peace and a fresh beginning for those living in the new United States. With a new sense of liberty, the *Federal style* (1780–1830) emerged, reflecting the aspirations of the republic. It was a classical style inspired by a renewed spirit of nationalism in conjunction with an interest in architecture and metaphor. The eagle, an ancient Roman Republican symbol, was adopted as an American symbol shortly after 1776. The American eagle served as an emblematic element in wood veneer and carved pieces found in buildings, in interiors, and on furniture (Figure 10.35). In addition, brass handles, knobs, and escutcheons were added for decoration. Cabinet maker Duncan Phyfe (1790–1830) and carver Samuel McIntire (1757–1811) were craftsmen who produced beautiful Federal-style work during this period.

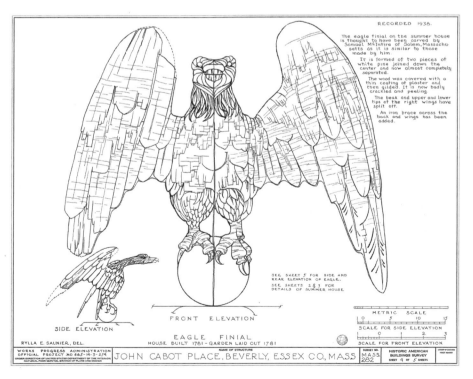

Figure 10.35 Eagle finial designed for John Cabot Place, Essex Co., Massachusetts.

The English cabinetmaker George Hepplewhite (d. 1786) was influenced by Adams Neoclassicism. His designs were lighter than those of Chippendale and were preferred by many for this reason (Figure 10.36). His *Cabinet-Makers and Upholsterer's Guide* and Thomas Sheraton's *Cabinet-Maker's and Upholsterer's Drawing Book* provided inspiration for many English and American furniture makers (Figure 10.37).

The Classical Style

The British brothers Robert and James Adam were both educated as architects. They developed a pronounced style after their return from Italy. Their work grew in popularity throughout England between 1760 and 1792 and had a profound effect on furniture styles in England and abroad, especially on the work of Hepplewhite and Sheraton. Their furniture was characterized by simplicity and delicacy. They designed sideboards, upholstered sofas, and daybeds. In response to the growing interest in classicism, many of their furniture designs incorporated animal heads, human figures, floral swags, and pendants.

Figure 10.36 American (Hepplewhite) card table (1800), mahogany.

Many people were attracted to the ideals of classical ornament, giving the work of the Adam brothers a strong following. The main source of inspiration for the young United States came from Greece and ancient Rome. The Greek ideal was a preferred standard on which to cultivate a new society. Ancient Greece, as well as English and French neoclassical furniture, influenced furniture design in America during the earlier 19th century.

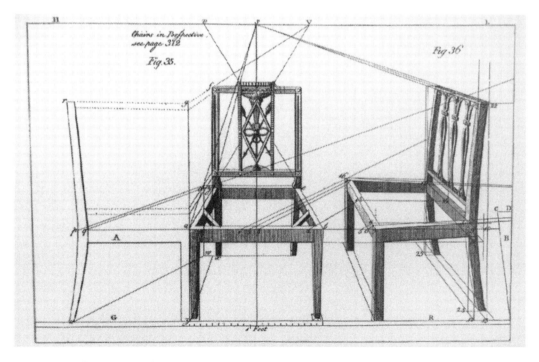

Figure 10.37 Thomas Sheraton's *Cabinet-Maker's and Upholsterer's Drawing Book.*

THE INDUSTRIAL REVOLUTION

All across Europe during the 19th century, cities began to host large expositions to show-case innovative cultural ideas, designs, and inventions. Munich, Germany, held its first an-nual exhibition in 1818, and subsequently Metz and Vienna, Austria, and Oporto, Italy, held exhibitions as well. These exhibitions showcased international culture including influences from Turkey, China, and Japan, and had great social and economic impact upon the culture of design. The *Great Exhibition*, the first recognized international exhibition, was held in 1851 at Hyde Park, London, in Joseph Paxton's recently completed *Crystal Palace*. This build-ing was a monumental undertaking of modular building utilizing prefabricated glass and iron components. The technology employed in its construction was similar to that used in the prefabricated furniture produced during the Industrial Revolution.

From an exhibition, a style that was promoted and admired would be rapidly dissemi-nated to all parts of the world by the press. With the world watching and encouraging new furniture designs, a complex eclecticism emerged, due in part to the improvements in indus-trial production, transportation, and communication.

In this new industrial era, museums began to be established. The new development in society helped to catalog ideas and styles from antiquity. The South Kensington Museum in London was famous for both the study and design of the decorative arts, serving as both a museum and a home for several international exhibitions. Today it is the Victoria and Albert Museum.

In 1851, Gebrüder Thonet of Boppard-am-Rhine, Germany, exhibited *bentwood furni-ture* in London at the Great Exhibition. By 1900, the Thonet company employed 5,000 work-ers producing 4,000 pieces a day, with another 25,000 people employed throughout Austria producing bentwood furniture. These pieces were of great inspiration to industrial produc-tion methods and influenced the rise of the Modern Movement (Figure 10.38).

Gebrüder Thonet exported modular, prefabricated, and unassembled bentwood furni-ture in kit form all over the world. This was the first documented case of a company pro-ducing knock-down pieces that provided a cost-effective means to distribute furniture to a

Figure 10.38 Le Corbusier chair, manufactured by Gebüder Thonet, 1925.

global clientele. Originally conceived and fabricated as laminated wood furnishings, bentwood technology came about because the laminated furniture tended to delaminate during the long ocean journeys to distribution ports throughout the world.

By the later 19th century, machines were assisting in the carving and cutting of wood. Machines were limited in their dexterity and other abilities, and machine carving had to be finished by hand. Therefore, furniture was relatively expensive to manufacture, but now multiple pieces could be inventoried. At the turn of the 20th century, furniture was made with both machines and hand tools—calling into question traditional paradigms of fabrication and the dependency upon craftsmanship.

During the 19th century, machine technology varied greatly by country and region. German cabinet makers were fine technicians and were considered to be the best at their craft, some of whom moved to Paris, the economic and cultural center for furniture design at the time. This assembly of talent in one large European center resulted in a melting pot of styles and growing eclecticism. This, in turn, helped to break down the sense of regionalism in design and fabrication and set the stage for the *International Style* that would emerge in Germany in the 20th century.

As the 19th century progressed, attention to handwork declined. Moreover, as labor costs continued to rise, the quality of workmanship decreased, especially after the First World War. In addition, the quality of timber declined, due in part, to kiln drying technology. The rapid reduction of the water content in freshly harvested lumber stressed the lumber, causing warping and bowing to occur more frequently. With a poorer stock of raw material and the expanding use of new technology, craftsmanship became less important. This negatively impacted traditionally designed and fabricated works, indirectly affecting the guilds and divisions between the trades.

With the ability to refine hardware and details using a greater variety of metals, the use of brass hardware became widespread in the third quarter of the 19th century. Inventive hardware and mechanically operated connections resulted in a new generation of mechanically transformative pieces. Mechanical furniture resulted from various patented inventions. Furniture such as the *In-a-Dor Murphy bed* or fold-down bed became popular space savers, finding their way into small apartments and sleeping cars in trains.

Throughout the second half of the 19th century, international exhibitions became forums for introducing innovation. The exhibitions were important cultural and economic events, exhibiting the "newest and the best" to a growing audience. However, in reality, the wealthy and the ruling class financed most of the exhibits. Significantly, their rise occurred in tandem with the Industrial Revolution, bringing new industrial materials, production methods, and mechanical types to the public. The Paris *Exposition Universelle,* first occurring in 1855, was organized to occur at 11-year intervals. *The Paris Exhibition* of 1900 marked design innovations leading into a new age. Following exhibits reinforced the age of mechanization, as seen in the Saint Louis exhibition in 1904, the Paris Art Deco exhibition in 1925, the 1933 Chicago World's Fair, and the 1939 World's Fair in New York City.

Technology enabled the production of nearly every kind of furniture. Eclectic works emerged, and with them a growing disconnect between the way something was fabricated and what it looked like, pushing design and production further apart.

The Industrial Revolution had a far-reaching impact on all aspects of society. Railroads allowed raw timber and completed furniture pieces to be transported long distances. This was the time when large numbers of books and periodicals were published. Books such as Henry Shaw's *Specimens of Ancient Furniture* (1836) presented drawings of early furniture pieces. Richard Bridgen's *Furniture with Candelabra and Interior Decoration* (1838) was also influential. Books that illustrated older styles helped rekindle a return to earlier forms and a revival of previous styles.

ECLECTICISM

In 1815, after the fall of Napoleon, Louis XVIII became King of France. Though he continued the revival of the classical styles that had been so popular in the court of his brother, Louis XVI, the Empire style soon evolved into the Bourbon "Restoration." This classical revival did not depend upon the precise rendition of former styles. Rather, updated versions of past styles came into being, mixing new technologies with older styles. This trend coincided with the enormous development of industrialization and the ability to mass-produce work. But as the French political structure came to an end with the revolution of July 1830 and with the end of the Bourbon line in 1848, new design ideas as well as fresh political incentives emerged.

In the mid-1800s, there was a growing and increasingly prosperous middle class whose new wealth and social aspirations provided opportunities for enterprising and inventive furniture manufacturers. Improved communication along with rail and ship transportation made new ideas and fabrication methods accessible to larger numbers of people. An example of this can be seen in the ebonized sideboard (Figure 10.39) with silver-plated fittings fabricated by E. W. Godwin (1833–86), an architect, interior decorator, and furniture designer, whose career began in Bristol, England. Godwin specialized in ecclesiastical and Gothic revival works, but his work was influenced by the asymmetry and simplicity of Japanese design. It was characterized by a careful balance of vertical and horizontal members, an ebonized finish, and contrasting hardware elements.

Figure 10.39 English 19th-century case good, designed by E. W. Godwin, cabinet maker Watt, ebonized wood/metal.

REVIVALS

By the end of the 19th century, Paris was indisputably the center of European furniture production. Furniture fabricated in Paris was typically well finished, with high-quality workmanship. Chair frames were often made of walnut due to the wood's stability and workability. By the 1880s, there were approximately 17,000 furniture workers in Paris, 2,000 of them fabricating the best and most expensive pieces (*meubles de luxe*), 14,000 making cheaper furnishings (*meubles courants*), and another 500 (*trôleurs*), whose job was to deliver their finished pieces around to the retail outlets. The huge Parisian furniture industry serviced almost 1,200 retailers, of which 50 were selling *meubles de luxe.* Despite the enormous number of furniture pieces being produced and fabricators making furniture, most designers looked backward, reviving older styles from eras long gone.

Italy remained a group of small states up to the mid-1800s but began to move toward nationhood with the *Exposizione dei Protti Dell'Industria Francesca* at Perugia. The Italians continued to emulate Renaissance carvings and styles almost to perfection. It was not until the highly personalized work of the Milanese furniture designer Carlo Bugatti (1856–1940) and the unification of Italy in 1879 that a new Italian style emerged. Though Bugatti's work featured unusual materials and non-Western motifs combined in a personal style, he designed and fabricated an enormous volume of furniture for wealthy Milanese for nearly 30 years before moving to Paris and focusing the remainder of his career on painting. His close association with art was typical of the northern Italians. Italy's global influence on furniture design would emerge later in the 20th century, when *artigiani* (craftspeople) and machine production technologies worked successfully together.

In the 1880s and 1890s, a Moorish influence arose. Due to the associations with harems and coffee shops, the impact of Moorish furniture upon Europe (save for Spain) was confined to semipublic spaces such as smoking and billiard rooms.

In the United States, lavish, deeply buttoned upholstered furniture in eclectic styles became popular in the form of three-seat sofas (Figure 10.40) and **love seats.** This furniture

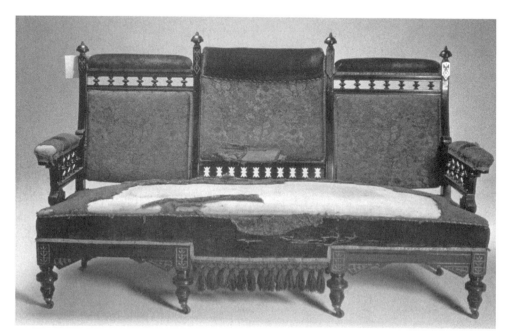

Figure 10.40 American sofa, upholstered, Mitchell & Rammelsberg Furniture Co. (established 1847, closed 1881). It is an eclectic mixture of Turkish and Japanese influences.

type developed during the Victorian era. It became an important piece for families, especially with young girls and a chaperone entertaining prospective suitors.

New markets, new products, and expanded trade were factors that created the unprecedented availability of furniture styles at the end of the 19th century. Furniture designs oriented to the emerging middle class looked similar to those fabricated a century before by hand for the ruling class. Taste had begun to pass from the palace to the parlor. Designers and consumers began to explore new ideas, seeking some of the lost qualities in craft from the previous century. As the revival period came to a close, the lack of quality in furniture was noticeable when viewed as a whole. As a consequence, there arose a demand for better workmanship, which in turn opened the door for a revival in craft and design.

CRAFT AND DESIGN

The 19th century witnessed the rise of architects as furniture designers. Architects had knowledge of both design and furniture fabrication and, in some respects, assumed the previous positions of *ébéniste* and *menuiser*. During this period, there was a growing culture of architecture and craft supported by an unprecedented outpouring of publications and treatises on beauty, furniture patterns, and craft. It was during this time that the *Arts and Crafts* movement began, marking a reaction to the Industrial Revolution and industrial production.

Alarmed by the poor quality, poorly designed products, minimal use of hand craftsmanship, and the environmental degradation of the Industrial Revolution, the architect Augustus Welby Pugin (1812–52) wrote his first book, *Gothic Furniture in the Style of the Fifteenth Century* (1835), which helped shape the Arts and Crafts movement. Much of his furniture was decorated with carving, but the carving did not hide the structure clearly stated in his designs. Pugin was specific about the distinction between structural necessity and applied decoration. He designed furniture in the medieval style, which was notable for its fabrication as well as its decoration.

The writings of Pugin and the teaching of John Ruskin (1819–1900), author of *The Seven Lamps of Architecture* (1849) and *The Stones of Venice* (1851–53), stressed the importance of structural frankness and fundamental truth in materials. These treatises were reminders to the burgeoning industrial revolutionists that mechanization would not capture the freedom and creative spirit of the craftsperson. Ruskin is considered to have been the founding father of the English Arts and Crafts movement. He believed in the total rejection of machine-produced products, saying that they were dishonest. He believed that machine-produced goods were inferior to works of skilled craftsmanship and called for a return to the practices of the medieval craft guilds.

Englishman William Morris (1834–96) was responsible for many improvements to common household objects such as the

Figure 10.41 English 19th-century Sussex (Morris) chair.

Figure 10.42 American bedstead, 1882–83, mahogany, designed and fabricated by Benn Pitman, Adelaide Nourse Pitman, and Elizabeth Nourse of Cincinnati, Ohio.

rush-bottomed *Sussex chair* (Figure 10.41). He and his company (Morris and Co.) hand fabricated traditional country furniture in response to the decline in the quality of contemporary furniture. Though Morris designed and fabricated work ranging from simple to elaborate furniture, his *Lesser Arts of Life* (1882) pointed out the difference between the necessary work-a-day furniture and the more elaborate "state furniture."

Benn Pitman (1822–1910) taught woodcarving at the Art Academy in Cincinnati, Ohio, and produced an extensive amount of unique wood-carved furniture during his long career (Figure 10.42). The success of his work and teaching in the Midwest paralleled the broad appeal of crafted and carved furniture throughout the United States at that time. Hand-worked furnishings became extremely valued during the mid-1800s and the demand fueled an emerging market for crafted works, which, in turn, evolved into the hybridization of craft and design during the late 1800s.

Arts and Crafts in Europe

According to Herman Muthesius, "arts and crafts were called upon to restore our awareness of the honesty, integrity, and simplicity in contemporary society. If this can be achieved, the whole of our cultural life will be profoundly affected. . . . If the new trends are genuine, then an original, lasting style will emerge."[8] Trend-setting furniture became popular at the

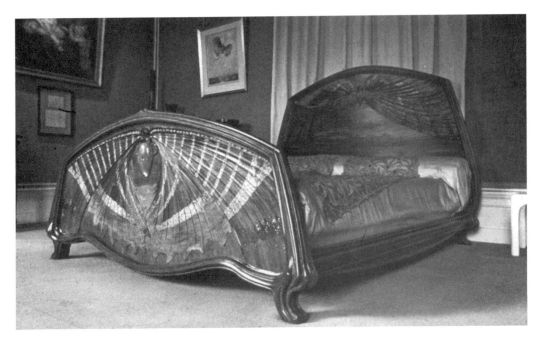

Figure 10.43 Émile Gallé, Dawn and Dusk bed, Ecole de Nancy.

end of the 19th century, inspired by designers, fine artists, architects, writers, and other professionals. It was this collection of tastemakers that spawned new movements of design that came to be known as *Arts and Crafts,* including the Gothic Revival, the Glasgow School, Art Nouveau, and the Vienna Secession. The authentic craftsmanship of furniture designed by the Scottish architect Charles Macintosh, by English architect C.F.A. Voysey, and other prominent designers became popular at the beginning of the 20th century.

Émile Gallé (1846–1904) worked with stained glass and designed furniture in Nancy, France. His works, along with those of the École de Nancy, founded in 1890, are traditionally cited as the origin of the French Arts and Crafts movement (Figure 10.43). The École de Nancy was a cooperative group organized for the production of the decorative arts. The cooperative idea was an attempt to make a complete design statement and create a unified look for everything from furniture to clothes, graphics, and architecture. It was here that elegant lines referencing flora and fauna found their way into tables, chairs, desks, windows, and doors. The French Arts and Crafts movement continued to evolve into the French Art Nouveau, while the work of Charles Robert Ashbee (1863–1942) of England had a simpler and somewhat machined aesthetic.

Designer and architect Charles Rennie Mackintosh (1868–1928) of Glasgow, Scotland, opened the door to a new spirit of modernism. Mackintosh created furniture and interior spaces whose designs were rooted in the tradition of Pugin and Morris. Many of his most famous furniture designs were fabricated for his architectural commissions, including the *Glasgow School of Art* (1897), the *Glasgow Tea Rooms* for Miss Cranston (1897), and *Hill House* (1902–04) located in Helensburgh, Scotland (Figure 10.44).

Figure 10.44 Charles Rennie Mackintosh, high-backed chairs, 1902.

Arts and Crafts in the United States

> The Arts and Crafts movement was inspired by a crisis of conscience. Its motivations were social and moral, and its aesthetic values derived from the conviction that society produces the art and architecture it deserves.[9]

The American segment of the Arts and Crafts period (1895–1915) was marked by a structural expression of simple form and handmade appearance (Figure 10.45). The primary tenet in design was *function*. This premise, along with a restrained use of ornamentation and a respect for the nature of the materials used, carried **Mission** furniture forward for a quarter of a century.

Gustav Stickley (1858–1942), was influenced by the ideas of John Ruskin and William Morris. Seeking to attain the values of handcrafted work, honesty of materials, beauty, and functional utility, Stickley produced Mission furniture at the turn of the 20th century in East Aurora, New York. In 1901, Stickley began to publish an influential magazine called *The Craftsman,* but soon after, Stickley's ideas about craft began to evolve toward the notion of industrialization, attempting to form a union between skilled craftsmen and machine production in furniture that could be marketed to the middle class.

The work of Gustav Stickley and the Roycrofters (1895–1938) featured copper fittings and prominent mortise-and-tenon joints, mostly fabricated from ammonia-fumed white

Figure 10.45 Sideboard, Shop of the Crafters, circa 1910.

oak. Their work encouraged handwork, and with it came a revived enthusiasm for craft and the skills necessary to make furniture by hand. Mission furniture was rectilinear, had subtle curved lines, and, when designed by Harvey Ellis (1852–1904), was usually inlaid with stylized floral motifs in colored wood.

Brothers Charles S. and Henry M. Greene (1870–1954) collaborated on many beautifully crafted residences that the two designed and built in Pasadena, California, at the turn of the century. Most renowned was their design for the Gamble House. They crafted wood-joined furnishings for their houses unique to the style of their architecture and sold custom furniture to clients.

Art Nouveau

Art Nouveau (1880–1910) emerged as a style from the opening of *Maison Art Nouveau*, a furnishing and novelty shop in Paris established by the dealer Siegfried Bing in 1895. The shop displayed furniture and designs for interiors such as glassware by Tiffany and Émile Gallé and exotic imported goods. The **Art Nouveau** movement was the first of its kind to occur throughout Europe at the same time. It transcended national boundaries and adopted regional and cultural references.

Hector Guimard (1867–1942) and Henry van de Velde (1863–1957) of Belgium settled in Paris and fabricated an array of furnishings emphasizing totally harmonious form (Figure 10.46).

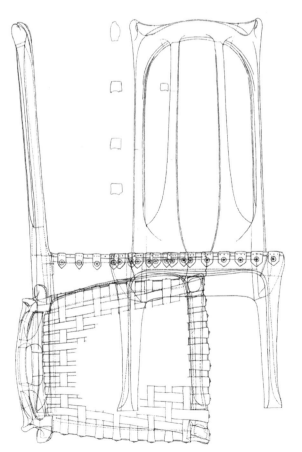

Figure 10.46 Chair by Hector Guimard (1900).

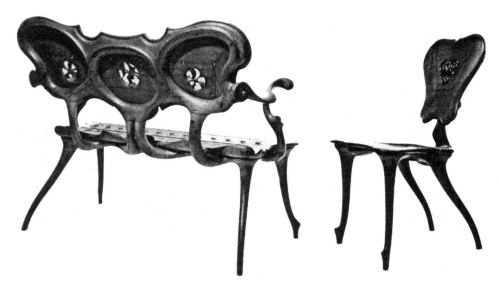

Figure 10.47 Chair and settee by Antonio Gaudi.

Otto Wagner (1841–1918) and members of the Vienna Secession, including Joseph Hoffmann (1870–1956), Koloman Moser (1868–1918), Adolf Loos (1870–1933), and Joseph Maria Olbrich (1867–1908), produced an exceptional body of work that inspired designers throughout the world. Though Hoffmann started his career as a practitioner of Art Nouveau, he soon turned away from its floral abstractions to develop a style that was severe and geometric. The furniture he designed was largely for his own buildings, though it is interesting to note that he did work with Michael Thonet and designed several chairs for him, including the famous *café* chair.

In 1903, Hoffmann and others started a cooperative venture called *der Wiener Werkstätte.* It lasted until 1932 and was noted for the integration of crafted and machine-produced works. In addition to producing furniture, it periodically exhibited the work of contemporary European designers such as Charles Mackintosh and Henry van de Velde. Until the First World War, the workshops produced furniture, leather goods, metal, glass works, and textiles and had a significant influence on modern architecture and furniture design.

Henry van de Velde (1863–1957) received his first significant acclaim for the interiors he exhibited at Dresden, Germany, in 1897. He played a leading role in the development of *Jugendstil,* the German and Austrian equivalent of Art Nouveau that literally means "youth style." His designs for furniture and tableware are of especially high quality. With ideas derived in part from John Ruskin and William Morris, he taught at his own school, the *Weimar School of Arts.*

Antonio Gaudi (1862–1926), an engineer, architect, and furniture designer, led the Art Nouveau movement from Barcelona, Spain, and completed a large body of work. Though Gaudi is renowned for his architecture, he designed many beautiful chairs and tables throughout his long career (Figure 10.47).

MODERNISM AND THE MACHINE AGE

In 1901, Frank Lloyd Wright (1869–1959) gave a talk at a meeting of the Chicago Society of Arts and Crafts entitled "The Art and Craft of the Machine." He declared that the furniture

Figure 10.48 Dining chair for the Susan Dana home, designed by Frank Lloyd Wright.

he designed was suitable for machine production and that machines should be abhorred only when they were set to replicate nonmechanical tasks such as carving. He wanted furniture to be machine made and affordable by a large number of people (Figure 10.48). Frank Lloyd Wright became an eminent American architect who created unique furniture pieces for most of his buildings. So important is his work that efforts have been made to preserve much of it, including the furniture and decorative elements within his buildings.

Between 1895 and 1915, Grand Rapids, Michigan, was commonly referred to as the "furniture capital of the world." There, American furniture companies such as the Limbert Furniture Company, Stickley Bros. Company, The Guild, the Michigan Chair Company, and the Grand Rapids Chair Company developed. Several years later, Steelcase, Herman Miller, and Hayworth emerged as enormously successful furniture companies. Originally producing furniture for the residential market, Herman Miller became the second largest office furniture producer in the United States. The company promoted its association with emerging designers Charles and Ray Eames and George Nelson. Steelcase developed a reputation for producing well-engineered office equipment and furniture, becoming the largest furniture company producing office systems and chairs for distribution throughout the world.

There was a steady advance throughout the *Machine Age* (1910–1945) in the design of machines, trains, boats, planes, and cars. However, the most profound development during this period was the advancement of science, citing the work and influence of individuals such as Albert Einstein and Max Planck. Science, engineering, and machines dominated all aspects of society, fueled in part by the Second World War and military advances from the war effort. New material technologies came into being with the use of tubular steel, bent plywood, and an array of new plastics. No longer was the world carved into unreachable quadrants. When new art movements emerged, they quickly spread throughout the world. Fine art trends exploded. The major art trends that rose after impressionism were cubism, surrealism, futurism, and fauvism.

With the rise of the Machine Age came *Art Deco,* which takes its name from the 1925 *L'Exposition Internationale des Arts Decoratifs et Industriels Modernes.* Arguably the most significant project during the Machine Age was the design and fabrication of the French ocean liner *Normandie.* Work on the Normandie began in 1935, and no expense was spared, calling into service many cabinet makers, metalworkers, silversmiths, glass workers, and ceramic craftsmen in France. From this time on, design in general took on a new direction—one that embraced the machine and new technology with open arms.

The furnishings of Le Corbusier (1887–1965) and his collaborators, Pierre Jeanneret (1896–1961) and Charlotte Perriand (1903–1999), exemplified a new spirit in furniture design that drew inspiration from the machine and industrialization. Designed for the *Salon d'Automne* in Paris in 1929 and the *Pavilion de l'Esprit Nouveau,* the *Chaise Longue* (1928), the *Grand Confort* chair (1928), and the *Siege de Repos* all embraced a machine aesthetic of tubular steel and black leather, drawing on ideals of modernism and theories outlined in Le Corbusier's book, *Towards a New Architecture* (Figure 10.49).

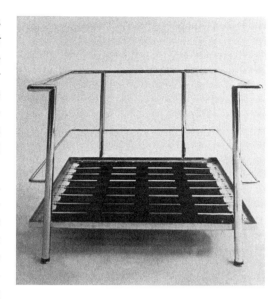

Figure 10.49 Tubular steel frame for Grand Confort, designed by Le Corbusier and Charlotte Perriand.

Gerrit Rietveld (1888–1964) was born in Utrecht, the Netherlands, and was trained as a cabinet maker and an architect. He designed and fabricated his *Red and Blue* chair in 1917 (see Chapter 4). In 1924, he designed the *Schröder House* in Utrecht. Rietveld designed and produced a great deal of furniture, nearly all of which embodied *De Stijl* principles, an approach in art and design based upon the abstraction of form and color. Throughout his career, he experimented with plywood, fiberboard, aluminum, upholstery, and bent metal (Figure 10.50). Theo van Doesburg (1883–1931), considered the father of *De Stijl,* was concerned with concepts of pure abstraction and developed a number of architectural projects and cubist furniture designs.

Figure 10.50 Upholstered lounge chairs, designed by Gerrit Rietveld.

The Bauhaus

Walter Gropius (1883–1969) founded the **Bauhaus** school in Dessau, Germany, in 1919. It precipitated a revolution in art, design, and architectural education whose influence is still felt today. In the words of Wolf von Eckardt, the Bauhaus "created the patterns and set the standards of present-day industrial design; it helped to invent modern architecture; it altered the look of everything from the chair you are sitting on to the page you are reading now."[10] Under Gropius' leadership, design and furniture created a modernist revolution demonstrating how materials and fabrication processes could inspire the design process. An example of this philosophical approach can be seen in Mart Stam's design of the first cantilevered tubular steel chair.

Ludwig Mies van der Rohe (1886–1969) was one of the defining figures of 20th-century design. He designed the *Barcelona Pavilion* and the famous *Barcelona* chair in 1928 (Figure 10.51). The chair became a classic, though it was not conducive to mass production because of the hand welding that was required for the side supports. It is also a remarkably heavy chair, making distribution expensive. Mies produced his *Brno* chair (1929–30) for the *Tugendhat* house in Brno, Czech Republic. Both the chair and the residence used similar fabrication techniques, which derived from similar design processes. Between 1930 and 1933, Mies was the Director of Architecture at the Bauhaus before moving to Chicago to teach at the Illinois Institute of Technology in 1938. The Knoll Group still produces his complete line of furniture.

Marcel Breuer (1902–81) was one of the most influential 20th-century furniture designers. Breuer studied art in Vienna before enrolling at the Bauhaus in 1920. There he studied furniture under Walter Gropius. Before setting up his own practice in Berlin in 1926, he designed the famous *Wassily* chair, the *B32,* popularly referred to as the *Cesca* chair, as well as a series of nesting tables (Figure 10.52). Before World War II, Breuer followed Gropius to the United States and taught at the Harvard Graduate School of Design. He also set up an architectural practice in Cambridge, Massachusetts, and worked on many architectural commissions for the next 20 years. In 1960, the Italian company Gavina revived production of a

Figure 10.51 Barcelona chair, designed by Mies van der Rohe (1928) for the German Pavilion in Barcelona, Spain.

Figure 10.52 Nesting tables, designed by Marcel Breuer.

number of his furniture pieces from the 1920s, and recently Knoll Studio produces several of his designs, reviving his contribution to modern furniture design almost half a century later.

Eileen Gray (1878–1976), an Irish-born designer and architect, was one of a handful of women who influenced the course of modern design. Her early work in Paris revealed Art Deco styling, but after 1922 her designs emulated the influence of De Stijl, cubism, and eventually modernist theories. Three of her more modernist works are the *Blocs Screen* (see Chapter 4), a lacquered screen with pivoting panels (1922), the *Transat* chair (a lacquered wood frame, metal hardware, leather-upholstered chair) designed in 1927 (Figure 10.53), and several versions of a cantilevered and adjustable tubular steel frame table with a glass top (1925–28).

Figure 10.53 Transat chair (1927), designed by Eileen Gray.

RISING HEROES OF EVOLVING MODERNISM

How did modernism affect society? Modernism was not broadly accepted until after World War II, when society began to look to the culture of design for leadership in social change. Exceptionally talented designers worked closely with artisans and craft shops throughout the United States and Europe during this time to bring the modern ideal into popular culture and to create furniture for everyday use. Many designers became prominent within this climate. Their work, working prototypes, and writings inspired a generation of furniture designers and helped develop the spirit of modernism.

Jean Prouvé (1901–84) was a French designer whose work has been recognized by his ingeniously simple method of fabrication that is typical of his furniture. His furniture design and architecture utilized industrial components and craft-based technologies (see Chapter 4). He was a prolific furniture designer who adopted modern ideas of form and function and was original and exploratory in his use of materials.

Carlo Mollino (1905–73) was an architect based in Turin, Italy. He had a prolific career designing and producing many beautifully crafted and ingeniously structured and curved furnishings. His love of airplanes, car racing, and experimenting with ideas of form and structure is evident in his curvilinear tables. Mollino worked from natural and animal shapes to establish a streamlined series of furniture designs. These pieces evolved from an appreciation of the shapes of Art Nouveau and the work of architect Antonio Gaudi. Mollino's work was more expressive, and often more sculptural, than that produced in Milan at the time. The changes in his style over the years responded to the evolving technology of bending and working with wood.

Alvar Aalto (1898–1976) was an architect from Helsinki, Finland. One of the most renowned modern furniture designers, Aalto combined his interest in furniture with his passion for architectural projects. His 1933 stacking stool, known as *Stool 60* (with a back—*Stool 65*), was designed for his library in Viipuri (see Chapter 4). Aalto's molded plywood lounge chair, *Paimio* (Figure 10.54), was designed and produced specifically for use

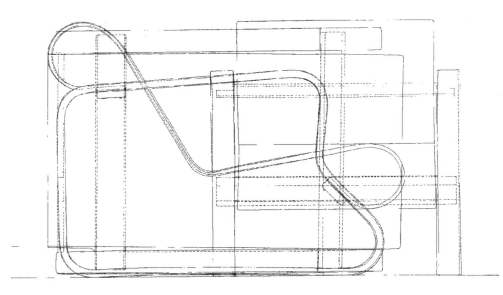

Figure 10.54 Paimio chair, designed by Alvar Aalto.

Figure 10.55 Florence Knoll and Eero Saarinen discussing the base of the Tulip chair.

by tuberculosis patients at his Paimio Sanatorium in 1930. The arms and base of the chair are laminated birch wood bent into a closed curve, and resilience is achieved in the scroll-shaped 3-mm plywood seat.

Later, Alvar and his wife, Aino Marsio, formed the Artek Company to fabricate his furniture using a combination of hand finishing and industrial production technologies. His revolutionary use of laminated plywood and Baltic birch captured world interest when his work was exhibited in London, Paris, and New York after World War II.

Eero Saarinen (1910–61) was a Finnish architect who worked for both Herman Miller and Knoll. He collaborated with his friend Charles Eames on many projects and experimented with plastics, metal, resin-reinforced glass fibers, and upholstery. Saarinen's work was sculptural, functional, comfortable, and ingeniously fabricated (Figure 10.55). Many of his chair designs, including the *Womb* chair with ottoman (1946–48), are still manufactured by Knoll.

Isamu Noguchi (1904–88) was a New York City–based freelance designer. His furniture and lighting were characterized by biomorphic form. He designed a beautiful glass-top coffee table with a biomorphic pivoting walnut base, several upholstered sofas, and an array of luminaires.

Arne Jacobsen (1902–71) was a Danish architect and designer whose work built upon Denmark's modern heritage. In 1950, Jacobsen decided to design furniture as a primary creative activity and began working with the Danish furniture manufacturer Fritz Hansen. The collaboration resulted in the production of the *Ant* chair (ca. 1951), the *Swan* chair

Figure 10.56 Egg and Swan chairs, designed by Arne Jacobsen, manufactured by Fritz Hansen.

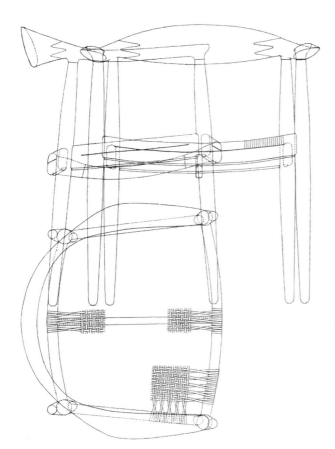

Figure 10.57 The Chair, designed by Hans J. Wegner (1949).

(1958), and the *Egg* chair (Figure 10.56). The *Ant* chair was one of the first of a series of chairs consisting of a molded plywood shell mounted on three chromed tubular steel legs. Its profile was the characteristic that led to its name. Jacobsen's lasting vision was of a building, its interior, and the furniture coming together as a complete, harmonious environment.

Hans J. Wegner (1914–2007) was a Danish architect whose chair designs (over 500) are remarkable for their craft, structural integrity, form, and comfort. His work fueled and paralleled a growing interest worldwide in Danish design and helped to foster a unique quality of Scandinavian design, which came to stand for craftsmanship, traditional values, and modern living—all working in harmony. Wegner worked for Arne Jacobsen for 5 years (1938–43) and in 1943 opened his own office in Gentofte, Denmark. In 1949 he designed *The Chair*, which is considered to be one of the classic chairs of the 20th century (Figure 10.57). The back and arm rests were combined in the design using a single subtle transformative curve. This feature, along with its woven cane seat, encapsulated the spirit of organic Danish modernism.

Charles (1907–78) and Ray Eames (1912–88) were a husband-and-wife design partnership. They met at the Cranbrook Academy of Art in Bloomfield Hills, Michigan, in the late 1930s. Charles collaborated on several molded plywood designs with Eero Saarinen that won first prize in a competition at the Museum of Modern Art in New York City in 1940. By

Figure 10.58 Ray and Charles Eames working together on the aluminum group desk chair, 1958.

1946, Ray and Charles Eames, as well as Saarinen, were exploring compound curves in sheets of laminated wood and introducing not only a new look but also a new degree of comfort in their revolutionary designs. After World War II, the Eameses designed a number of chairs and storage units that incorporated a wider range of materials including fiberglass, wire, and aluminum, many of which are still fabricated today by Herman Miller (Figure 10.58).

George Nelson (1908–86) was an architect who focused upon furniture, accessory design, and writing (Figure 10.59). His writing about modernist ideas of design and his long-term association with Herman Miller helped to consolidate the movement in American architecture and design, emphasizing how design could be practically applied in both home and office environments from the 1930s to the 1950s.

Harry Bertoia (1915–78) was born in Udine, Italy, and immigrated to the United States in 1930. He studied at the Cranbrook Academy of Art before setting up its metalworking department. After teaching at Cranbrook and working in California with the Eameses,

Figure 10.59 Marshmallow chair (love seat), designed by George Nelson and Irving Harper (1956) for Herman Miller.

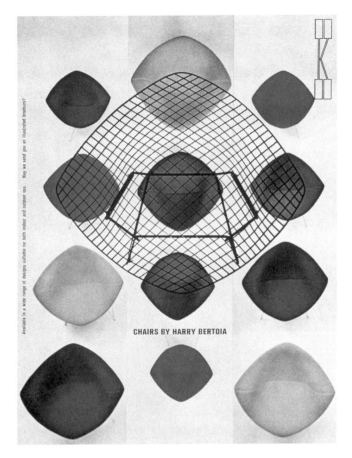

Figure 10.60 Wire Diamond chairs (1951), designed by Harry Bertoia for Knoll International.

Bertoia set up his own studio with the help of Knoll and produced the *Diamond* chair and a series of remarkable wire side chairs (Figure 10.60).

David Pye (1914–93) was a British master craftsman, a highly educated industrial designer, and Professor of Furniture Design at the Royal College of Art in London. His writings and teachings have long been major influences in the fields of woodworking and furniture design. He examined the relationship between design and workmanship. Pye wrote about the workmanship of risk, in which "the quality of the result is not predetermined, but depends on the judgment, dexterity, and care which the maker exercises as he works."[11] Pye contrasts this with the workmanship of certainty, in which "the quality of the result is exactly predetermined . . . always to be found in quantity production, and found in its pure state in full automation."[12] One of Pye's most important ideas is that hand craftsmanship is not always good, and manufacturing is not always bad.

Craft versus Design

Furniture craftsmen emerged in the United States soon after World War II, seeking to create works of beauty using handcraft technologies. They were somewhat resistant to the industrialization and mechanization in which the country was immersed and were often associated with studio furniture, which was crafted using machine and hand tools. George Nakashima, Wendell Castle, and Sam Maloof were renowned for their studio-based practices, producing some of the most refined and well-crafted furniture pieces from the post–World War II period to the 1980s, though the tradition continues today.

New Craftsmanship

New craftsmanship is marked by the hybridization of craft and industry. In this context, architects and designers work closely with industry to produce furniture that either depends upon industrial production processes or industrial materials. The results have a high degree of workmanship and pronounced qualities of form.

Frank Gehry (b. 1929) studied design and ceramics at the University of Southern California. After doing graduate work at Harvard, Gehry set up his practice in Los Angeles in 1962. His furniture is distinguished by a sense of form marked by a disciplined use of material. His corrugated cardboard chairs of the early 1970s (Figure 10.61) led to more technically challenging laminated maple veneer chairs in the 1990s (see Chapter 4), and recently, Gehry has produced a line of roto-molded plastic outdoor furnishings. Gehry's furniture designs weave together material, form, and an economy of fabrication.

Ron Arad (b. 1951) is a furniture designer whose work runs the gamut from individually crafted pieces to mass-produced furniture. He was born in Israel and has worked in his London-based studio (*One-Off*) designing and producing remarkable furniture throughout his professional career. The *Soft Big Easy* chair (1988–91) utilizes a steel and wood frame that supports a single block of variable-density expanded polyurethane, cut to shape by a CNC

Figure 10.61 Easy Edges, series of corrugated cardboard furnishings, designed by Frank Gehry for Knoll International.

Figure 10.62 Soft Big Easy, designed by Ron Arad for Moroso, 1988–91.

device and then covered with leather or fabric (Figure 10.62). His background and knowledge of materials and his practice of making full-sized prototypes using industrial materials and the skilled workmanship of a craftsman have resulted in a series of furniture pieces that embody the spirit of *new craftsmanship.*

THE 21ST CENTURY: THE DIGITAL AGE

In many interior and building projects, furniture design and selection have significant value in the generation and development of architectural and interior work. Academic and professional environments reinforce the notion that furniture design is a significant component of interior spaces. However, furniture design encompasses disciplines extending beyond architecture and interior design. In the context of expanded disciplines, the depth, breadth, and evolving body of knowledge of industrial design have inspired new work and new ideas about materials and production processes. Philippe Starck, Karim Rashid, and Marc Newson are contemporary designers who have been inspired by new materials and production processes, and their work, in turn, has inspired other designers.

Interesting parallels can be drawn between the historical context of the emerging field of *interior design* during the 20th century and that of *furniture design* in the 21st century. Furniture design is concerned primarily with objects in space designed and fabricated for a range of uses. Interior design is concerned primarily with space, interior construction technology, and the composition of elements in which a wide range of functions occur. Both fields engage material, detail, and joinery. Both address social use and function within a given cultural and societal context. Nevertheless, each field places an emphasis upon either the *frame* (space) or the *imprint* (object) in design.

Furniture design is a practice specialty but it emerges from one of several disciplines, depending upon how and where the designer is educated. From an academic perspective, furniture design is an interdependent activity. It is one part of what an industrial designer does, but it is also an important aspect of interior design, architecture, and fine art. Furniture designers venture into all of these fields. Primary relationships and parallels between industrial design and furniture design are timely in comparison. Industrial design developed from industrial engineering and the rise of the industrial arts movement of the 19th century. Industrial design infused the applied arts and the applied sciences using design to solve problems using a combination of engineering and aesthetic means. Many innovations of the 21st century come from industrial design, and furniture design is a perfect vehicle to adopt such innovation.

The field of furniture design continues to cultivate knowledge in the areas of ergonomics and human factors, fabrication technology, and material research. These areas are shaping and reforming academic and professional fields including (but not limited to) architecture, engineering, interior design, industrial design, fine art, applied arts programs, and vocational craft-based programs, as well as scientific research and advances in the fields of medical science, sociology, and cultural anthropology. The history of furniture design, by default, embraces these areas of study and contributes to evolving knowledge in the fields of human factors, digital, and material technologies.

In the 21st century, computer science, digital technology, and nanotechnologies have begun to influence society in general ways and furniture design in specific ways. Why has this occurred? Furniture design encompasses many far-reaching and specifically focused disciplines, technologies, and professions. It seems likely that society and furniture designers will continue to embrace these new technologies.

Despite the growing interest in digital technology, craftspeople ought to have a central role in design and fabrication, as they have for the past 5,000 years. Craftspeople will continue to help shape contemporary works, but they will need to share the field with a broader range of professionals due to the emergence of new materials and technological advances.

New Tools, New Materials, New Opportunities

Digital milling machines, high-end computer technologies, intuitive three-dimensional CAD modeling programs, new synthetics, and *smart materials* are helping designers and fabricators realize new furniture products. In addition to the assimilation of digital technologies, *green design* has become a significant, almost an inherent, aspect of design. We have seen and will continue to see new designs respond to the growing need to respect our physical and social environments.

Contemporary furniture designers seek to reveal new functional and utilitarian uses through the exploration and investigation of form, technology, and materials. The essence of invention depends upon *design thinking,* as well as understanding how to interweave material and fabrication technologies with social use and formal aspiration. Today, more than at any other time in history, designers have the capacity to extend the parameters of furniture design into new societal and formal realms. This thought brings the reader back to the premise and opening remarks presented in the first chapter of this book:

> Furniture design is deeply rooted in the human condition. It is a social science that belongs to the humanities, an applied art that draws upon many design fields, and a tangible reality that relies upon a working knowledge of materials and fabrication techniques. It is a holistic and all-embracing field of study.

Appendix

ENDNOTES

IMPORTANT DISTINCTIONS WERE MADE between the architect and the artisan (head and hand) in the 1400s during the rise of the Renaissance. Leon Battista Alberti's writing gets right to the point in articulating distinctions between thinking and making in architectural theory. Four hundred years later, the Industrial Revolution furthered the polemic between head and hand. Furniture entrepreneurs such as Michael Thonet began to pave the way for furniture design to emerge within the culture of mechanization and industry. Simultaneous with the rise of industry, writers and craftspersons such as John Ruskin, William Morris, and Gustav Stickley worked to rekindle the notion of craft and workmanship in furniture design. In the 20th century, the woodworker and educator David Pye clarified distinctions between craft (workmanship of risk) and machine production (workmanship of certainty) in his book, *The Nature and Art of Workmanship*. Sociologist Edward T. Hall and industrial designers Raymond Loewy and Norman Bel Geddes also contributed to the collective context of furniture design, though their perspectives were not always aligned. From ancient Rome to modern times, theorists have written treatises guiding the evolving culture of furniture design, which in turn have influenced generations of designers, fabricators, and educators. Their writings and works serve as references for all to access, understand, and debate.

Throughout the history of architecture and design, writers and theorists have found different ways of deconstructing wholes into parts with the goal of addressing all aspects of a subject in due course. A standard procedure is to construct a mental map or model of a given field and then to travel systematically through the field with map or model in hand as a guide—enabling relationships to emerge, which can result in a broader understanding of the subject. One of the first authors to conceive of a conceptual construct for the subject of architecture was Marcus Vitruvius Pollio.

Vitruvius was a Roman architect and theorist who wrote about architecture in the 1st century A.D. His architectural treatise, *The Ten Books on Architecture*, inspired Henry Wotton's phrase "firmness, commodity, and delight" in an attempt to present a comprehensive view of architecture. The deconstructive approach of subdividing a whole into parts is useful in breaking architecture into its components to clarify the subject without overwhelming the reader. Furniture design theory is no less complicated in this regard and, up to a point, has guided the organization of this book.

In the 20th century, many books and publications on furniture impacted academic, professional, and popular culture. John F. Pile, author of *Interior Design* and Professor of Design at Pratt Institute in New York City, structured several critiques on design into classifications that embrace purpose, structure, and visual expression. His books *Modern Furniture* and *Design Purpose, Form, and Meaning* do this well. Louis Sullivan, a Chicago architect who partnered with Dankmar Adler and once employed Frank Lloyd Wright, spoke and wrote about form and function in the most general and collective of meanings. The phrase "form follows function" is commonly attributed to Sullivan but was actually coined by Horatio Greenough.

Edward Lucie-Smith, author of *Furniture—A Concise History,* introduced an effective notion of taxonomy and typology in regard to furniture design by formulating four essential classifications: use, form, personal expression, and social status. David Pye, professor of Furniture Design at the Royal College of Art in London, England, provided insight into the areas of technology and production in his book, *The Nature and Art of Workmanship,* where he elaborated upon workmanship of risk (craft) and workmanship of certainty (machine production). Ernest Joyce contributed to the work of a generation of furniture designers and fabricators through his technical understanding and straightforward approach in writing about fabrication processes in his seminal book, *The Encyclopedia of Furniture Making.* Galen Cranz, professor of architecture at the University of California at Berkeley, contributed to the cultural and physiological notion of seating, ergonomics, and posture in her book, *The Chair,* an important discussion of seating within a sociological and cultural context. All of these excellent works contribute to the body of knowledge in furniture design.

Authors, designers, gallery and museum curators, faculty, students, and consumers organize design into various components, elaborating upon the components in some depth. In a gestalt psychology approach to design, where part-to-whole relationships are paramount but the parts are never as great as the whole, efforts to organize information and ideas into disparate categories are conceived and developed as a place to begin the journey but never to reside for long.

Scores of journals abound, from design-based publications such as *Domus, ID, Ottogano, Frame, Details,* and *Metropolis* to vocational journals such as *Woodshop* and *Fine Woodworking.* Books on the subject include a broad range of approaches with a focus on fabrication and production techniques. Other approaches include cataloging and documenting individual works and designers, as in Carol Soucek King's book, *Furniture—Architect's and Designer's Originals,* or Charlotte and Peter Fiell's *Modern Furniture Classics Since 1945.*

Though most books focus in depth on one topic and are written for selective markets, journals and publications often fall short in helping to reinforce or to cultivate a collective body of knowledge of furniture design that serves several markets. But with the growing interest and broad-based activity in furniture design, the time seems ideal to formulate a dialogue that transcends professional boundaries. More books are needed to introduce a broader range of ideas and individuals, and to contribute to the emerging discipline of furniture design.

REFERENCES

Industry

Industry arose during the 19th century. Selective furniture companies have since promoted the culture of design by publishing books, sponsoring gallery exhibitions, and coordinating international conferences. As industry has grown in political and economic strength, it has assumed a greater academic and cultural responsibility. A short list of contemporary furniture companies renowned for developing the culture of design includes Alessi, B & B Italia, Cassina, Fritz Hansen, Giogetti, Herman Miller, Kartell, Louis Poulsen, Olivetti, Thonet, Vitra, and Zanotta.

Museums, Galleries, and Exhibitions

Gallery exhibits on furniture design at the local, regional, national, and international levels have become common, educating the public and evolving paradigms about design. The *International Arts and Crafts* exhibit in London, Indianapolis, and San Francisco in 1996; the London exhibit *Icons,* focusing upon Italian furniture design in 1992; the *Design by Delight* exhibit in Indianapolis in 1990; and the retrospective exhibit of the work of the late Poul Kjærholm at the Louisiana Museum of Modern Art in 2006 are examples of furniture exhibits that have helped to promote the work of furniture fabricators and designers and, in doing so, have also shaped the culture of furniture design. The Cincinnati Art Museum exhibited Andrea Zittel's A–Z collection entitled "New Art 6" (1996) and has several pieces designed and produced by Wendell Castle in its permanent collection, a museum trend nationwide. The Museum of Modern Art in New York City has an extensive permanent collection of well-designed contemporary furniture—more than any museum or gallery in the world. The Kunst Industri Museet (Danish Museum of Art & Design) in Copenhagen is a remarkable resource for studying 19th- and 20th-century furniture. A brief list of galleries, museums, and special exhibitions is as follows:

COUNTRY	CITY	EXHIBIT, MUSEUM, or GALLERY
Australia	Sydney	Powerhouse Museum
England	London	Design Museum Victoria and Albert Museum
Czech Republic	Prague	Musée National des Techniques
Denmark	Copenhagen	Danish Museum of Decorative Art Danish Design Center
	Kolding	Trapholt Furniture Museum
France	Paris	Musée Nationale des Techniques Musée des Arts Décoratifs Musée National d'Art Modern Musée d'Orsay Fondation National d'Art Contemporain
Germany	Munich Weil am Rhein	Das Deutsche Museum Vitra Design Museum
The Netherlands	Amsterdam Rotterdam	Stedljk Museum Booymans van Beumijen Museeum
Italy	Milan	Salone del Mobile
Sweden	Malmo	Form Design Center
Switzerland	Zurich	Design Collection, Museum für Gestaltung
United States	Boston	Museum of Fine Arts, Boston
	Washington, DC	Cooper-Hewitt National Design Museum
	New York, NY	Museum of Modern Art National Academy of Design Cooper-Hewitt Museum Metropolitan Museum of Art International Contemporary Furniture Fair
	Highpoint, NC	High Point International Home Furnishings Market
	Chicago, IL	NEOCON World's Trade Fair (The National Exposition of Contract Furnishings)
	San Diego, CA	Mingei International Museum

Vitra's Chair Museum in Germany, located directly across the border from Basil, Switzerland, is home to Rolf Fehlbaum's permanent collection of over 1,500 chairs located and exhibited in an outstanding furniture museum designed by architect Frank Gehry. The Chicago Art Institute, with its permanent and traveling exhibits, and San Diego's Mingei International Museum in the heart of Balboa Park, exhibited *Heirlooms of the Future,* presenting several furniture pieces designed and produced by George Nakashima, Bob Stocksdale, Wendy Maruyama, Brett Hesser, Ron Kent, Gene Blickenstaff, and Sam Maloof.

Collectively, museum and gallery exhibits serve an important purpose in educating the public about furniture. Libraries such as the Furniture Library in Highpoint, North Carolina, and the Star Research Center in Grand Rapids, Michigan, are additional resources for historical and scholarly research in the field. International furniture fairs including the *Salone del Mobile* in Milan and those organized by COSMIT, as well as the *International Contemporary Furniture Fair* (ICFF) held annually in May in New York City, help shape and evolve the contemporary culture of furniture design.

Notes

Chapter 1 Introduction to Furniture Design

1. The terms *movable* and *equipment* are used to describe furniture in the following sources: *Webster's Illustrated Contemporary Dictionary,* (Encyclopedic edition, J. G. Ferguson Publishing Company, Chicago, 1988); *The American Heritage Dictionary of the English Language,* 4th edition (copyright © 2000 by Houghton Mifflin Company, published by Houghton Mifflin Company); *The Compact Oxford English Dictionary,* revised edition (Oxford: Oxford University Press, 2003); and www.dictionary.com.
2. Source: *The Compact Oxford English Dictionary,* revised edition (Oxford: Oxford University Press, 2003).
3. The organization of furniture using typological categories is a common approach. Edward Lucie-Smith, in *Furniture: A Concise History,* outlines four headings, "the first of which responds to the idea of function stating one can sit on a piece of furniture (stools, benches, and chairs); or else one puts things on it (tables and stands); sleeps or reclines on it (beds and couches); or uses it for storage (chests and wardrobes)" (p. 8).
4. Source: *The Compact Oxford English Dictionary,* revised edition, 2003.
5. *Structured play* is a phrase that faculty have used to describe the activity of design in the First Year Design Studio in the School of Architecture and Interior Design, College of DAAP at the University of Cincinnati.
6. Source: *The Compact Oxford English Dictionary,* revised edition, 2003.

Chapter 2 Function and Social Use

1. Gisela M.A. Richter. *Ancient Furniture A History of Greek, Etruscan and Roman Furniture* (Oxford: Printed at the Clarendon Press, 1926).
2. Ibid.
3. Sources that indicate heights for tables and counters include: Francis D. K. Ching, *Interior Design Illustrated* (New York: Van Nostrand Reinhold, 1987), pp. 64–69. Maryrose McGowan and Kelsey Kruse, *Interior Graphic Standards* (Hoboken, NJ: John Wiley & Sons, 2003), p. 173. Henry Dreyfuss Associates, *The Measure of Man and Woman,* revised edition (New York: John Wiley & Sons, 2002), pp. 25–28.
4. National Institute for Occupational Safety and Health Web site (Relevant Anthropometric Measures) and Wikipedia, the free online encyclopedia, *Design and Ergonomics:* en.wikipedia.org/wiki/Chair—Wikimedia Foundation Inc., February 2007.
5. Wikipedia, *Tatami:* en.wikipedia.org/wiki/Tatami.

6. Katie Weeks, "Slow and Steady," *Contract Source Guide,* 2006, p. 42, Contract Magazine, Nielsen Business Publications, USA.
7. *Action Office* brochure by Herman Miller.
8. Many office workstations are systems-based. *Herman Miller, Steelcase, Hayworth, Knoll, and Vitra* offer a variety of furniture systems designed as components that can be configured and arranged in a number of ways.
9. *Environment and Art in Catholic Worship* (EACW) is a provisional draft statement by the Bishops committee on Liturgy (BLL), Washington: published by the National Conference of Catholic Bishops (1978).
10. *Encyclopedia Britannica,* "Ambos," Vol. 1, p. 719 (1972).
11. Two sources: *The Oxford Dictionary of the Jewish Religion.* Ed. R.J. Zwi Werblowsky and Geoffrey Wigoden (Oxford: Oxford University Press, 1997). Ellen Frankel and Betsy P. Teutsch, *The Encyclopedia of Jewish Symbols* (Northvale, NJ: J. Aronson, 1992).
12. Martin Frishman and Hasan-Uddin Khan, *The Mosque: Islam and the Form of the Mosque,* pp. 35–37. New York: Thames and Hudson, 1994.

Chapter 3 Form, Spatial Organization, and Typological Orders

1. Edward T. Hall, *The Hidden Dimension* (Anchor Books, 1969). Hall coined the terms *sociofugal* and *sociopetal* in this book.
2. Ibid.
3. Kerry Capell, "How the Swedish retailer became a global cult brand," *Business Week,* November 14, 2005, p. 96.

Chapter 4 Furniture Case Studies

1. Edward Lucie-Smith, *Furniture: A Concise History* (London: Thames and Hudson, 1993), p. 25
2. Gisela M.A. Richter, *Ancient Furniture: A History of Greek, Etruscan and Roman Furniture* (Oxford: Printed at the Clarendon Press, 1926).
3. Klismosstol, drawn by Monica Hekk and Karin Hvidt, students at Danmarks Designskole (1989), Jens Overbye, Director of Spatial Design, DKDS, Copenhagen.
4. *The Compact Oxford English Dictionary,* revised edition 2003, and www.dictionary.com.
5. "The Chair: Handicraft and Industry," in *The Italian Chair,* Istituto Nazionale per il Commercio Estero, 1983. p. 29.
6. Thonet Barnestol, drawn by Hanne Meilsøe Dam, student at Danmarks Designskole (1989); drawing courtesy of Jens Overbye, Director of Spatial Design, DKDS, Copenhagen.
7. www.dwr.com/designers.

8. Sarah Booth Conroy, "Modern View of Marcel Breuer," *The Washington Post,* Oct. 11, 1981, Living section, p. L1.
9. www.designmuseum.org/design/marcel-breuer.
10. Ibid.
11. www.hermanmiller.com (*Action Office* brochure).
12. "Elegant Techniques, Italian Furniture Design 1980–1992," Electra, Milano, p. 43. Istituto Italiano per il Commercio Estero, Assaredo.
13. www.zittel.org.
14. Ibid.
15. www.hermanmiller.com.
16. www.steelcase.com/na.
17. Project description by Erik Skoven; interview and text given to the author, June 2006.
18. Ibid.

Chapter 5 Furniture Design Theory

1. *The American Heritage Dictionary of the English Language,* 4th edition (copyright © 2000 by Houghton Mifflin Company, published by Houghton Mifflin Company).
2. Ibid.
3. www.brainyquote.com/quotes/l/ludwigmies.
4. www.wikipedia.org and *Encyclopædia Britannica,* 11th edition (1972).
5. *The American Heritage Dictionary of the English Language,* 4th edition.
6. *Webster Illustrated Contemporary Dictionary,* Encyclopedic Edition (Chicago: J.G. Ferguson Publishing Co., 1987).
7. W. Jastrzebowski, "*An Outline of Ergonomics, or the Science of Work Based upon the Truths Drawn from the Science of Nature,*" originally published in *Nature and Industry* (1857), reprinted by the Central Institute for Labor Protection, (1997), Warsaw, Poland.
8. Each year the Bureau of Labor Statistics (BLS) gathers data on the number, rate, and characteristics of occupational injuries and illnesses occurring in the private sector by the U.S. Department of Labor, published by OSHA—Occupational Safety and Health Administration.
9. Ibid.
10. Clara A. Ridder, Basic Design Measurements for Sitting. Agricultural Experiment Station. University of Arkansas, Fayetteville, 1959. Hockenberry, Jack, Seating Design, NATO Symposium, 1980. Hockenberry's research was based on the work of Clara Ridder, introduced to the author by UC Industrial Design Professor Bradley Hammond. Using a seating machine to study and measure up-right seating profiles in different individuals, Clara Ridder's work resulted in an up-right seating profile known as the Ridder Curve.
11. *The American Heritage Stedman's Medical Dictionary,* 2nd edition (copyright © 2004 by Houghton Mifflin Company, published by Houghton Mifflin Company. All rights reserved).
12. J. J. Swearingen, C. D. Wheelwright, and J. D. Garner. *An Analysis of Sitting Areas and Pressure of Man* (Report 62-1) (Oklahoma City, OK: Civil Aero Medical Research Institute, 1962).
13. Paul Cornell, *The Biometrics of Sitting,* 2nd edition. This paper is an excerpt from a book by Marvin J. Dainoff, *People and Productivity: A Manager's Guide to Ergonomics* (Toronto: Holt, Rinehart, and Winston, 1986). ANSI/BIFMA Standard X5.1-1985. Note: The *American National Standards Institute* (ANSI) and the *Business and Institutions Furniture Manufacturers Association* (BIFMA) set minimum performance standards for chairs and stools.
14. A.C. Mandal, "Balanced Seating," www.mandal.com.
15. Ibid.
16. A.C. Mandal, "Balanced Sitting Posture on Forward Sloping Seat," www.mandal.com.
17. Edward T. Hall, *The Hidden Dimension* (Garden City, N.Y.: Doubleday, 1966), p. 1.
18. Robert Sommer, *Tight Spaces: Hard Architecture and How to Humanize It* (Englewood Cliffs, NJ: Prentice Hall, 1974), pp. 16–19.
19. Hall, *The Hidden Dimension.*
20. D.E. Berlyne, *Conflict, Arousal, and Curiosity* (New York: McGraw-Hill, 1960); S. Scott, "Visual Attributes Related to Preferences in Interior Environments," *Journal of Interior Design Education and Research,* Vol. 2, 1992.
21. www.wisdomquotes.com/cat_beauty.html—quotation on beauty compiled by Buckminster Fuller; copyright © 1995–2006 by Jone Johnson Lewis.
22. Leon Battista Alberti, *On the Art of Building in Ten Books,* ed. Joseph Rykwert (London: MIT Press 1991.).
23. "Aesthetics," *Encyclopædia Britannica,* 2006. www.britannica.com/eb/article.
24. Gyorgy Doczi, *The Power of Limits* (Boston: Shambhala Publications, 1981, p. 128.
25. John F. Pile, *Design Purpose, Form and Meaning* (New York: W.W. Norton, 1979), p. 58.
26. John F. Pile, *Modern Furniture* (New York: John Wiley & Sons, 1979).
27. John A. Kouwenhoven, *Made in America,* revised edition (Garden City, NY: Doubleday Anchor, 1962).

Chapter 6 Design

1. Carol Soucek King, *Furniture—Architects and Designers Originals* (New York: PBC International, 1994), p. 136.
2. Joy Malnar and Frank Vodverka, *The Interior Dimension* (New York: Van Nostrand Reinhold, 1992), pp. 29, 30–31.
3. Source: *The American Heritage Dictionary of the English Language,* 4th edition (copyright © 2000 by Houghton Mifflin Company, published by Houghton Mifflin Company).
4. Cynthia Leibrock, *Beautiful Barrier-Free A Visual Guide to Accessibility* (New York: Van Nostrand Reinhold, 1993), p. 82.
5. Interview with Jeff Arnold, May, 2006, manager of Paxton Wood Crafters, Cincinnati, Ohio, about international forest certification programs.
6. Ibid.
7. Text description given to the author by Emiliano Godoy, June 2006.
8. Martin Charter and Tischner, Ursula Tischner, *Sustainable Solutions Developing Products and Services for the Future* (Sheffield, UK: Greenleaf Publishing, 1991), Ch. 24.
9. Ron Mace, "Universal Design: Housing for the Lifespan of All People." (Washington, D.C.: U.S. Department of Housing and Urban Development, 1988).
10. Product Design is defined, "*the activity in which ideas and needs are given physical form, initially as solution concepts and then as a specific configuration or arrangement of elements, materials and components.*" Walsh, V., Roy R., and Bruce M. Winning, *By Design: Technology, Product Design*

and *International Competitiveness* (Basel: Blackwell, Oxford, 1992), p. 18.

11. www.malvino.com/intuitiv.htm; quote by Albert Einstein.

12. AIA Document D200 1995, "Project Checklist." This document contains a description of architectural design phases, which is also contained in Article 2.4 of AIA Document B141, 1997, "Standard Form of Agreement Between Owner and Architect with Standard Form of Architect's Services."

13. Ibid.

14. Ibid.

15. www.brainyquote.com/quotes/quotes/l/ludwigmies101419 .html. Van der Rohe is famous for his poetic aphorism, "God is in the details."

16. Ibid. (design phases).

17. Ibid. (design phases).

18. Stephen Bayley (British design critic), *Commerce and Culture,* From Pre-Industrial Art in Post Industrial Value. (A design museum book) London: Fourth Estate Publishers, 1989, Chapter 3.

Chapter 7 Materials

1. Materials Research Society (MRS), Materials Science and Engineering Web site: (The Intute Consortium), 2006. (The Materials Science & Engineering Career Resource Center) which is a service of TMS—The Minerals, Metals, & Materials Society. (about.com was founded in 1996.) (The Third Millenium OnLine).

2. Conversation about heat transfer with University of Cincinnati Professor Tom Bible, School of Architecture and Interior Design, May 2006.

3. Jerryll Habegger and Joseph H. Osman, *Sourcebook of Modern Furniture,* 2nd edition (New York: W.W. Norton, 1997), p. 279.

4. Ernest Joyce, *The Encyclopedia of Furniture Making* (New York: Sterling, 1987), p. 74.

5. Ibid. p. 1.

6. *Concepts in precompressed wood*—Erik Krogh, Professor DKDS. Course handout material, prepared by Professor Erik Krogh, Danmarks Designskole.

Chapter 8 Fabrication

1. www.brainyquote.com/quotes/quotes/a/alberteins103652 .html.

2. Istituto Nazionale per il Commercio Estero, *The Italian Chair* (Rome: n.d.), p. 30.

3. David Pye, *The Nature and Art of Workmanship* (New York: Cambridge University Press, 1968), p. 4.

Chapter 9 Professional Practice and Marketing

1. www.brainyquote.com/quotes/authors/j/james_randolph _adams.htm.

2. Interview with Boris Berlin of Komplot Design, June 2006.

3. Nigel Collett, "The New Look in Retail Design—Popping Up in a Street Near You," *Brand Republic,* June 14, 2005, p. 132.

4. Data gathered on Italian furniture production in 1989 during a 3-month study in Milan.

Chapter 10 Historical Overview

1. www.thinkexist.com. Quotation by William Morris (1834–96), British craftsman, early socialist, designer and poet, whose designs generated the Arts and Crafts movement in England.

2. Alvar Aalto, *The Complete Works,* Volume III (Zurich: Les Editions d'Architecture Artemis, Girsberger, 1963), p. 220.

3. Peter Philip, "Early Furniture," *Sotherby's Concise Encyclopedia of Furniture* (New York: Harper & Row, 1989), chapter 1, p. 14; Eternal Egypt Web site: The Eternal Egypt, 2005. "Building Tools," www.eternalegypt.org.

4. Interview with Professor Dan Swarth, Copenhagen, Denmark, June 13, 2006.

5. Leon Battista Alberti, Book 6, "On Ornament," Part 2, *On the Art of Building in Ten Books,* translated by Joseph Rykwert, Neil Leach, and Robert Tavernor (Cambridge, MA: MIT Press, 1991).

6. William Hogarth, *The Analysis of Beauty* (London: Printed by J Reeves for the author, 1753); Bernd Krysmanski, "Upsetting the Balance: William Hogarth and Roger de Piles," *The Site for Research on William Hogarth,* updated February 2005: www.fortunecity.de/lindenpark/hundertwasser/517/ balance.html.

7. Megan Aldrich, Victor Chinnery, Leslie Keno, Noël Riley, and William Stahl, "The Baroque," in *Sotherby's Concise Encyclopedia of Furniture,* chapter 3, p. 56.

8. Hermann Muthesius (*Das Englische Haus:* Entwicklung, Bedingungen, Anlage, Aufbau, Einrichtung und innenraum. Bd. pp. I-3. Berlin 1904–1905).

9. Gillian Naylor, *The Arts and Crafts Movement* (London: Trefoil, 1990 [first published 1971]), p. 7.

10. Wolf von Eckardt, "The Bauhaus," *Horizon,* IV, 2 (November 1961), p. 58.

11. David Pye, *The Nature and Art of Workmanship* (New York: Cambridge University Press, 1968), pp. 13–14.

12. Ibid.

Glossary

acrylic Synthetic polymer made from natural materials, such as coal, water, petroleum, and limestone. Produced as fibers, acrylics make soft, bulky fabrics and carpets. Produced in 4- by 8-foot (122 by 244-cm) sheets, they are colored and available in various thicknesses.

ad quadratum (By the square) A geometric system of proportion based on the ratio of the side of any square to its diagonal ($1:\sqrt{2}$).

ad triangulatum (By the triangle)

aesthetic From the Greek *aisthetikos,* pertaining to sensory perception. Generally, associated with the term *beauty.* Aesthetic is both a qualitative description and a reaction.

air drying A method of seasoning lumber by stacking it (usually outdoors) after being freshly cut. The circulation of dry air slowly dries the wood to 12–15 percent.

alloy A metallic substrate formed by blending two or more elements, one of which must be a metal.

altar A place of worship or sacrifice. A table in a Catholic or Episcopalian Church around which the Holy Eucharist is shared.

ambo In a Catholic or Episcopal Church, a liturgical furnishing from which the Bible is read. In the Greek Orthodox Church, an elevated platform in the nave from which the Gospel or Epistle is read aloud.

ambry An English wardrobe or cabinet, also spelled *aumbry,* the equivalent of the French armoire that preceded the cupboard. An ambry is the container for the Holy Oils in the Catholic Church.

animal glue Adhesive made from the skin and bones of animals.

anodizing A process of electroplating aluminum. Typically, the process deposits an oxide film on aluminum.

anthropometrics The physiology and measurement of the human body.

antiquing Process of making wood or fabric look old and used. Can be done by application, artificial weathering, distressing, etc.

apron Wood skirting placed at right angles to the underside of a tabletop, shelf, or seat of a chair, extending to the tops of the legs or bracket feet. It is also known as a skirt.

arabesque A style of ornament that originated in the Middle East and was popular in Europe until the early 17th century. It employs flowers, fruit, vegetal matter, text, and human figures to produce an intricate, continuous pattern of interlaced lines.

ark The built-in or freestanding furniture in a synagogue that contains the torah scrolls.

armoire A large, movable cupboard or wardrobe with doors and shelves for storing clothes. In the medieval period, armoires were used to store arms and suits of armor.

Art Nouveau A style of architecture and design that derived its name from Maison de l'Art Nouveau, a design shop in Paris. Dynamic and flowing lines characterized much of Art Nouveau.

Arts and Crafts Late 19th-century social, philosophical, and political craft revival movement led by John Ruskin and William Morris.

asymmetrical A condition in design that may have balance but not visual symmetry.

awl A small pointed tool, used for making holes or pilot holes for nails.

ball and claw Carved foot of an animal or bird claw clutching a ball used to terminate a cabriole leg that was popular in English furniture of the early 18th century.

barrel chair A chair originally made from half of a wine barrel. Typically fabricated from white oak with an incorporated loose seat cushion.

Bauhaus (1919–1931) German school of art and design founded by Walter Gropius and others with strong belief in the unity of the arts.

bed Furniture used to rest or sleep.

belt sander An electric power sander in which a continuous belt of sandpaper is rotated around rollers to sand wood.

bench A place to rest, with or without a back.

bentwood Wood that is bent rather than cut into shape, using steam to help shape it. The technique was perfected by Michael Thonet's company, Gebrüder Thonet, in the mid-19th century.

bergère A French fully upholstered, deep-seated armchair with closed-in sides.

Biedermeier Derived from the French Empire, an early 19th-century style developed by German craftsmen; named after an imaginary cartoon character that typified the middle-class German. Typically, it has painted rather than carved motifs on flat surfaces, often in black and gold.

BIFMA Business and Institutional Furniture Manufacturer's Association. This organization establishes guidelines for testing commercial-grade chairs.

bilateral symmetry Symmetrical balance in which a central axis cutting through the design produces two identical mirror images.

biomorphic Free-form organic shape, also called amoeboid, typical of the 1950s. Typically used to describe three-dimensional design.

bird's eye Mottled figure in sugar maple grain suggesting a bird's eye.

bit The end of a tool for cutting or boring. Used in hand and power drills. Bits are removable and interchangeable.

blind door Solid door on a case piece that conceals the contents.

blister An area of veneer that has separated from its mounting surface because the glue has failed.

block front A façade treatment on 18th-century case furniture in which the central vertical structure is recessed or composed of a concave center between its two sides.

blow molding Placing a hollow tube of molten thermoplastic in a mold and expanding it with air pressure.

board foot A piece of wood that is $1 \times 12 \times 12$ inches ($2.54 \times 30.5 \times 30.5$ cm), or a 144-cubic-inch equivalent.

bombé A French term describing the bulging, convex front and/or sides of case furniture. Bombé-type cabinets and chests are characteristic of Louis XV, late-18th-century Italian, Baroque, and Rococo works. Typically, bombé applies to commodes, bureaus, and armoires.

bookmatch Method of veneer matching pairs of adjacent slices of veneer as they are cut from the log and opened up similarly to the pages of a book. This produces a mirror image along the seam of the two flitches.

Boulle work A type of marquetry named after the cabinetmaker André Charles Boullé, who introduced it, using tortoise shell, silver, or brass inlay.

brass An alloy of copper and zinc. Brass is a base metal used for plating.

breakfront Case furniture having recessed and projecting sections on its façade where the center section projects forward beyond the two end sections.

bronze An alloy of copper, tin, and various other metals.

buffet French term referring to a sideboard used to store china, silver, and linens. The top surface is used as a counter for serving food. It usually has drawers as well as doors.

built-in Furniture that is permanently built into a structure. Casework includes built-in panels and cabinets.

bunk bed One bed stacked on top of another.

bureau Originally a red cloth covering a writing desk. Later, it referred to the desk itself. In the United States, the word designates a dresser.

burl Decorative wood from a growth on a tree with an extraordinary figure. Burl wood can occur in many different species. Elm is perhaps the best-known burl wood.

burr A thin, rough metal edge left after sharpening or cutting.

butterfly table A small folding table with splayed legs. The top has wing brackets underneath to support drop-leaf wings on either side.

cabinet A glass-fronted case good intended for the display of objets d'art.

cabinet scraper A thin piece of steel, either convex or rectangular, used for a final smoothing of wood before applying finish. Cabinet scrapers must be sharpened with an oilstone.

cabriole leg A furniture leg formed to resemble the stylized front leg of a capering animal that swells outward at the knee and inward at the ankle. It was popular in the early 18th century.

canapé A French sofa or upholstered settee for two or more people that came into use during the reign of Louis XIV.

canopy bed A bed with a frame around it to hold a fabric ceiling. During the Renaissance, the canopy bed was used in homes of the wealthy. During the Rococo and Victorian eras canopy beds were more common—made of wood (often carved) with a canopy top that could be closed for privacy and warmth.

canted A line or plane sloping at an inclined angle.

cantor stand A portable stand from which to sing or recite.

case goods Box-like furniture used for storage including bookcases, bureaus, chests, cabinets, and armoires.

casework Cabinets, cases, storage units, panels, and other fixtures that are built in or attached to the building.

cash-wrap In a retail store, the cash-wrap is a check-out counter, check stand, or check-out place to purchase items and often serves a dual function as the place to wrap purchases.

cassone Italian Renaissance term for a low chest with a lift-lid, hinged top. These chests were often made of walnut, elaborately carved, and used as a bridal or dowry chest.

caster A type of wheel mounted hardware applied to the bottom of furniture to help in moving about space. They are made from wood, rubber, metal, or plastic, and can lock or swivel.

cast glass The process by which glass is shaped by pouring it into a mold and allowing it to harden, or cure.

cathedra A variety of Roman seat furniture that was adopted as the "cathedral"—the chair of the bishop.

C-clamp An open clamp with one fixed and one screw-adjustable head, used for holding work pieces in position while gluing, etc.

cellaret A case on legs or a stand for wine bottles.

chair A piece of furniture for sitting, consisting of a seat, a back, and sometimes arm rests, commonly for use by one person. Chairs also often have legs to support the seat raised above the floor. Without back and arm rests, it is called a *stool*. A chair for more than one person is called a *couch, sofa, settee, loveseat* (two-seater without arm rest in between), or *bench*. A separate footrest for a chair is known as an *ottoman, hassock,* or *poof.* A chair mounted in a vehicle or theater is called a *seat.* Chairs as furniture are typically not attached to the floor and can be moved.

chair-table Armchair with a large round or rectangular back attached so that it can be converted to a table. Used in the Middle Ages.

chaise lounge Literally translated from the French as "long chair"; used for lounging. It is often used in bedrooms.

chamfer An angled surface planed on the edge of a piece of wood, usually at 45 degrees, either to soften a sharp edge or for aesthetic reasons.

checking The formation of small checks, splits, or flaws on the surface of lumber due to uneven seasoning.

chest A box with a lid and often a lock, used for storage.

chest-on-chest A highboy made by placing a small chest of drawers on a larger one.

Chippendale A style of furniture named after the furniture designer and maker Thomas Chippendale.

chrome A shiny, silver-colored metallic element that became commercially available in 1925, proving to be ideal as a plate on other metals, such as tubular steel, for decorative reasons and to prevent corrosion.

ciseleur Bronze casting maker.

coffee table A low table used in front of a sofa or couch.

coffer A low trunk for storing items that was a common furniture type from ancient times to the 18th century.

cofferer A craftsperson who fabricated coffers and chests in 17th-century Europe.

columbarium Case good or casework used to store the ashes of the deceased.

commode A French term for a chest with deep drawers on legs.

contact adhesive An adhesive that, when applied to two surfaces and brought together, creates an instant bond without the need for clamping.

contract furniture Furniture designed and fabricated for public places and the workplace. Usually marketed directly to the trade.

coping saw A small curve-cutting saw with a disposable blade held in tension using a sprung metal frame.

copper A ductile, malleable, corrosion-resistant metalic element. It is the only metal that occurs in large masses and has excellent electrical conductivity.

corner cupboard A triangular cupboard made to fit into a corner. It is usually a dining room china cabinet but may also be a curio cabinet in any room.

couch A 17th- and 18th-century term for a backless, upholstered lounge chair used for sitting and reclining. In common usage, it is often confused with a sofa or settee.

countersink A tapered hole that enables the head of a flat-topped bolt or screw to lie flush with or below the surface of a work piece.

craft Human skill (workmanship of risk).

credence table In a Catholic Church, a small table used to hold the bread and wine prior to the celebration of the Eucharist. An early Italian cabinet used for carving meats or displaying plates. It was the forerunner of the sideboard.

credenza Small buffet or sideboard with drawers or doors used during meals for serving, storing, or displaying.

creep The movement or deformation of materials over time when subjected to a constant load.

croft A small filing cabinet of the late 18th century with small drawers and a writing surface.

cross-banding Veneer banding inlaid at a 90-degree angle to the wood grain.

cupboard A paneled box, either freestanding or wall-mounted, for storing equipment and food, used in dining.

curly grain Grain with an irregular, wavy pattern. It is beautiful but difficult to work.

dado A flat groove, cut into the grain of one piece of wood, which holds the end of another piece within it.

daybed A twin-sized or single mattress on a frame used for sitting or sleeping. Also referred to as a *chaise longue*.

deacon's chair Chair for the deacon in a Catholic Church. Usually placed on the sacramental platform near the presider's chair.

design An active, creative process—implying conceiving, planning, or intending for a purpose. Used as a verb, a noun, and an adjective.

de Stijl An artistic movement concerned with the integration of painting, sculpture, and architecture that flourished in the Netherlands from 1917 to 1928. Its leaders included Gerrit Rietveld, Piet Mondrian, and Theo van Doesberg.

disk sander Usually used as a bench-clamped support sander that has a faceplate with an abrasive disk.

doreur French gilder of the 18th century.

dovetail joint An interlocking joint in which wedge-shaped pins and tails are cut to fit two pieces of wood together at right angles, producing a strong joint.

dowel A headless cylindrical pin, usually made of wood and often with small grooves or flutes along the length for air and glue to escape, used to attach pieces of wood together.

dowel pin A small brass or metal pin with a sharp point used to mark dowel positions. Similar to the pointed awl.

dowry chest A chest fabricated to store the trousseau of a prospective bride. Also known as a *hope chest*.

draw table Table with a flat leaf or leaves that extend from beneath the tabletop to increase the size of the table.

dresser A sideboard used to prepare or dress food. As used today, it indicates a chest for the storage of clothing.

drop front A hinged front of a desk that lowers to form a level writing surface. Also referred to as a *fall front*.

drop seat A shaped, upholstered seat designed to rest securely within the frame of the seat rail. Also referred to as a *slip seat*.

dust bottom Thin layer of wood that separates drawers to prevent dust from settling on the contents in the lower drawer.

easy chair Upholstered winged armchair with a high back.

ébéniste Maker of veneered furniture. A French term for a cabinetmaker who worked with ebony.

edge grain The quality of grain of wood produced by quarter sawing.

edge profile The detail or outline profile of the edge of a table or shelf. Typical edge profiles include ogee, chamfer, and bull-nose profiles.

empirical knowledge Knowledge that is self taught (learning by doing or synthesized from prior experience) such as carving, painting, and finishing.

enamel A colored, opaque composition derived from glass (silica), sometimes used as an inlay in furniture.

end grain The exposed wood fibers at the end of a piece of wood that has been cut across its grain.

ergonomics The science and art of fitting the task to the limits of the human body.

esquisse A sketch expressing the basic idea or concept. This drawing type stems from a methodology taught at L'Ecole des Beaux Arts in Paris at the turn of the 19th century.

étagère A small working table consisting of shelves or trays set one above the other to display items.

exposition of scriptures A furniture type in a Catholic Church on which the Bible is placed before and after each service.

fabrication A general term that describes the act of making furniture.

faux finish Paint-texturizing techniques that make a surface look old or imitate the patina found in antiques or other materials.

Federal style An architectural style that had a significant parallel in furniture design in the United States between 1780 and 1830. The source of inspiration came from the early republic in Greece. For the young emerging democracy, the Greek ideal was a preferred standard from which to cultivate a new society.

fiberboards Man-made boards manufactured from reconstituted wood fibers, particularly hardwoods, such as medium-density fiberboard and Medite II.

fiberglass A strong, lightweight structural material made of glass in fibrous form. It was developed in the United States in the 1930s and used by many designers in the 1950s, including Joe Colombo, Charles and Ray Eames, and Arne Jacobsen.

fiddle-back A chair splat or figured veneer shaped like a violin.

figure The natural grain pattern in a piece of cut wood.

finial An upright decorative object formed in a variety of turned shapes.

fire screen Made to screen the heat from an open fire. There are pole screen types with a screen on a tripod base and screens held upright by two vertical side supports.

flat grain The quality of the grain of wood produced by plain sawing. It is also called cathedral grain.

flitch An individual slice of veneer or an individual segment in a larger composite assembly of veneers. *Flitch* also refers to an assembled bundle of veneers typically arranged and numbered in sequence.

floating Solid wood construction fabricated so that it can expand and contract without damage by placing screws that hold the sides and top together in slotted screw holes.

fondeur A French craftsperson who made casts for metal mounts in the 18th century.

font A container for water. In a church, it contains holy water for baptism.

form The physical shape and structure of an object. The essence of a work, including its material, meaning, or purpose.

Forstner bit A drill bit used for cutting flat-bottomed holes or for drilling clean holes through wood.

French cleat Interlocking hardware devices used to secure a panel or case good to a partition.

French polish A traditional wood finish introduced in the 18th century made from a solution of shellac in alcohol, producing a mirror-like finish, but easily scratched or damaged by heat or water.

French Rococo Virtually synonymous with the Louis XV style given to a singular form of asymmetrical ornament that evolved from the Baroque style in France. It was widely used by French craftsmen from around 1720 to 1760.

fretwork Carved decoration consisting of a number of intersecting elements with open spaces between them.

furniture Stationary or movable articles that are used to make a space or building habitable. Examples include a broad range of tables, chairs, storage systems, and screens.

futon A traditional Japanese mattress stuffed with a natural fiber. The term now refers to a sofa bed with a frame and a removable mattress.

gallery Small fencelike border around a tabletop or case piece.

galvanic action A chemical corrosive reaction that occurs when two dissimilar metals are in contact with one another. The corrosive reaction is accelerated in the presence of humidity or moisture.

galvanized steel Steel coated with a thin layer of zinc to provide a more corrosion resistant surface.

gestalt The principle that the human eye sees objects in their entirety before perceiving their individual parts. From the German word for "form," it is based on a psychological theory developed by Max Wertheimer (1880–1943), Kurt Koffka (1886–1941), and Wolfgang Köhler (1887–1967) in 1930.

gift table In a Catholic Church, it is the table used to place baskets for collecting money.

gilding The process of applying powdered gold or silver leaf to a substrate to give the appearance of solid gold or silver.

gilt furniture Furniture that has gold leaf applied to its surface.

golden section A ratio that results when a line is divided so that the short segment has the same relationship to the long segment that the long segment has to the sum of the two parts. It works out to be a unique proportional relationship: 1:1.6182, as well as 0.6182:1.

grain The arrangement, direction, and size of the wood fibers in a length of wood.

green design More comprehensive than sustainable design. Green design is a general and inclusive term that considers distribution and packaging, biodegradability, the life-cycle of materials and products, off-gassing, the toxicity in fabrication or use, and a number of other important factors including environmental, human rights, labor standards, and more.

guild Trade association based on apprenticeship and mutually agreed-upon control of standards to protect the craft and its members. An early form of trade union.

haptic sensation The tactile and physical experience that results from touching and interacting with furniture.

hardwood The wood from a tree that has the seeds contained in a close ovary as opposed to being coniferous. Lumber that comes from deciduous or broadleaf trees, including such species as maple, cherry, and walnut. Most hardwoods are actually hard but some like bass or balsa wood, are soft.

heartwood The hard, dense, usable lumber of the tree between the pith (the center) and the sapwood.

hermetic Closed, self-contained.

hide glue Hide glue results from boiling animal bones and hooves down to a gelatinous mass, which is great for repairing antiques and has good workability, but its bonding strength is not as strong as PVA glues.

highboy A chest-on-chest that was made in the early 18th century in the American colonies.

hone A low sheen or dull finish applied to stone by grinding.

hope chest Colloquial American term for a dowry chest.

human factors A broad umbrella term that relies upon scientific research regarding the interface between the human body and built-form. Human factors data are objective and scientifically determined.

hutch An enclosed structure, often raised on uprights, of more than one shelf or tier.

iconostasis screen In Eastern Christianity, a wall of icons and religious paintings that separates the nave from the sanctuary in a church.

inlay The process of embedding a variety of materials into a wood or a stone surface to create a decorative effect.

intarsia The Italian term for inlay that was first used in the 14th century. A decorative use of wood, in which scrolls, arabesques, architectural scenes, fruit, etc., are reproduced by inlaying small pieces of colored woods in a background of wood.

interstitial space In-between space or resultant space such as a vestibule. Space that is generated by two or more intersecting spaces.

ischial tuberosities The two bones at the bottom of the pelvis that support 60 percent of a person's sitting weight.

iterative sketches A process in design used to investigate variations of selected aspects, while other aspects remain constant. Iterative sketches generally include a series of overlays used to investigate a detail of furniture, while the overall composition remains constant.

japanning A paint and varnish process that dates from the 17th century. It imitates oriental lacquer work.

joinery The process of attaching (joining) one piece of wood to another.

kas An early American wardrobe, of Dutch 17th-century origin, made of painted or paneled wood, usually elaborately carved and decorated.

kerf The groove or cut made by saw teeth in wood.

kickback The violent reaction of a work piece on a table saw when thrown by the machine blade.

kiln drying An artificial method of seasoning wood in a kiln to reduce the moisture content in air-dried lumber down to approximately 7 percent.

kline A Greek couch with a headboard and footboard used for reclining. It was used for relaxing, alone or with another person, or for eating a meal.

klismos An ancient Greek armless chair with concave (inwardly curved) saber legs and a concave back.

kneehole desk A desk with open space in the front center to accommodate the sitter's knees.

knock down Furnishings shipped unassembled or partially assembled.

kyphosis The inward compression of the vertebrae along the spine.

lacquer A resinous substance secreted by a scaled insect. A finish that originated in the Far East, in which resin, made from the sap of the lac (*Rhus*) tree, is applied to furniture in several layers to produce a smooth, hard-wearing surface.

lacquered A lacquered piece of furniture is generally finished using a nitrocellulose lacquer. There are catalyzed and precatalyzed lacquer finishes.

ladder-back chair A chair with horizontal back slats resembling the horizontal rungs of a ladder.

laminated Composed of layers of firmly united material (paper, wood, plastic, etc.), with resin or glue and compressed, sometimes under high heat and pressure.

lateral force Horizontal force applied to an object from the side.

lathe A machine consisting of a headstock containing a motor, tailstock, lathe, bed, and tool set used for the process of turning.

lazy susan A revolving tray or stand of wood or metal.

leather A generic name given to animal hides prepared by a currier.

lectern A podium used for speaking.

lexicon A stock of words belonging to a branch of knowledge.

love seat A small sofa designed to accommodate two persons.

lowboy A dressing table with drawers, typically with short legs.

lumbar lordosis The natural curvature of the spine when standing.

luster The visual quality of light caused by the reflection and refraction of light off a finished surface such as wood.

marborough legs A heavy, straight leg used on later Chippendale chairs and others.

marqueteur A maker of marquetry during the French Rococo period.

marquetry A decorative treatment in which small colored woods and wide varieties of other materials are applied to a piece of wood veneer that is then applied to the surface of furniture.

medium-density fiberboard (MDF) A close-textured, heavy, man-made board manufactured by gluing fine wood particles together with resin. It is used as a substrate for solid wood.

Melamine A plastic often used for laminate coatings, particularly on wooden kitchen surfaces and to make tableware. It resists melting or burning under heat.

mensa A small Roman table. The upper top portion of an altar table.

menuisier A French term for a solid-wood furniture maker denoting a wood carver or chair maker.

mihrab A niche in a mosque that indicates the shortest direction to Mecca.

millwork Finished woodwork and cabinetry that includes trim, molding, paneling, balustrades, etc. Elements conventionally made of wood that are applied and integrated into an interior space.

minbar A pulpit in a mosque that is next to the mihrab. The minbar traditionally has symbols of a gate, open door, and ascending steps incorporated in its design.

Mission style Product of the American Arts and Crafts period (1895–1915)—characterized by simple lines and craft details. Usually made of golden oak.

miter joint A corner joint at right angles where the pieces of wood that meet are cut to the same angle, typically 45 degrees.

mock-up A full or partial representation of the actual piece of furniture made from any material and used to study the measurements and aspects of design.

modernism An ideological or philosophical way of thinking about architecture and design. It is encapsulated by the phrase, *Form follows function.* The modernist idea is that function and utility can and should generate form.

Morris chair A large easy chair with arms. The seat back generally extends beyond the back to various angles. It was named after its inventor, William Morris.

mortise-and-tenon A type of joint consisting of a peg-and-hole configuration. The tenon is the projecting member and the hole is the mortised member.

Neoclassicism A mid-18th-century movement in art and architecture aimed at recreating the art and architecture of ancient Greece and Rome. It was a reaction to the excesses of Baroque and Rococo and part of a classical revival that prevailed into the 19th century.

nested tables Several tables sized from small to large, each one fitting under the next one.

nominal dimension The commercial size by which an item or material is known, but not the actual size. The nominal size of a stud is 2 by 4 inches (5.1 by 10.2 cm) and the actual size is 1½ by 3½ inches (3.8 by 8.9 cm).

occasional table A term applied loosely to any small table that can be used for different purposes and easily moved from one location to another.

off-gassing The dissipation of toxic fumes that are unpleasant and potentially harmful.

one-off One-of-a-kind piece.

ossuary A portable furnishing in a Catholic Church used to hold the ashes of a deceased person.

ottoman A low, upholstered seat or stool used as a footstool in front of an upholstered chair.

paradigm A culturally based perception of how things and actions are done.

parasthesia The result of pressure points applied to the body that can constrict the flow of blood and can result in a sensation of pins and needles, which eventually leads to numbness.

parquetry The decorative art of cutting out and laying geometric pieces of veneer to make patterns. It was used often on Louis XV furniture.

parti A parti communicates the basic physical and spatial components of a design. It can assume the form of a 3-D study or take the form of a sketch.

patina A surface condition produced by age, wear, or rubbing.

pedestal table A square or round table on a round center support. It was popular in England in the 18th century.

pembroke table A long, square-sided table with oval or square ends, usually on legs with casters. The leaves at the side drop nearly to the floor.

Perspex The trade name for a tough, light, translucent plastic that became popular in the 1930s. It has great flexibility, strong resistance to weathering, and is often used instead of glass.

pewter An alloy of tin with varying amounts of lead, copper, and antimony. In early America, used as a substitute for silver in household furnishings because of its lower cost.

pilot hole A small hole drilled into wood that allows the threads of a larger screw to bite into the wood without splitting it.

pin hinge Concealed hinge made of a metal peg, set into the end of a door, and fitting into the top and bottom of the frame.

pith The small, soft core of the tree trunk. It is completely unusable.

plain sawn The most economical way of cutting a log into lumber. Parallel longitudinal cuts create a cathedral grain to the lumber's face.

planer A machine used to plane smooth the face side and face edge of wood.

plastic Capable of being formed or molded, like clay. Any synthetic polymer substance that can be molded or formed, such as acrylic or polyester.

popliteal dimension The dimension from the underside of the knee to the bottom of the foot (or to the floor).

prayer rug A textile used by Muslims during their five daily prayers. The prayer rug helps to keep the worshipper clean and comfortable during prayer.

precompressed wood Wood that has been steamed and then placed in a compressor with significant compression force applied against the longitudinal direction, which severs the integrity of the wood's cellular structure. The wood is then fully pliable and remains so as long as the moisture remains in the wood. It is a remarkably flexible material and is easily shaped. Precompressed wood can be wrapped in plastic sheets and is usable for up to two months.

presider's chair In a Catholic Church, the chair for the presider of the Eucharist.

prie-dieu kneeler A high-backed kneeler with a narrow shelf, rail, or pad upon which the user may rest the arms while kneeling in the seat. Literally means "pray [to] God" and typically is used as a kneeler to pray.

processional cross A liturgical element, with or without a corpus and with or without an armature, used to mark the beginning of a service.

project The product of the design process.

proportion The mathematical or measurable relationships of a part, or parts, of a design, relative to other parts within a given field or frame of reference.

prototype An original fabrication to test and evaluate a design before producing the piece.

proxemics The study of how people communicate in and across space. The term was invented by anthropologist Edward T. Hall.

push-stick A stick with a notch cut in it, used to push wood into a machine cutter or blade.

quarter sawn A method of cutting a log into lumber by first cutting it lengthwise into quarters. Each quarter is then sawn at right angles to the annual rings. Quarter-sawn lumber was preferred by Stickley and Craftsman furniture.

quirk joint A narrow 90-degree channel cut into a material.

rabbet joint A rectangular recess or groove cut into the edge of a board when turning a corner between two boards.

rail The horizontal member in framing or paneling that connects to vertical posts.

reclining chair An upholstered chair or rocker that reclines.

relief Anything that projects from the background, such as relief sculpture.

rift sawn A method of cutting a log that results in the growth rings intersecting the face of the board at an angle between 30 and 60 degrees.

roll-top desk A writing desk enclosed by a curved, slatted panel.

roundabout chair A corner chair with a triangular front and usually a curved back. Also a term for the corner chair.

runner A horizontal connecting member used between the legs of a chair or case piece to strengthen its fabrication.

sapwood The newly formed outer wood located just inside the cambium layer of a tree trunk. Sapwood is generally lighter in color than heartwood.

scale A perceptual phenomenon that depends upon the size of something relative to another.

scoop seat A chair with a seat that has been hollowed to conform to the body.

seat pan The part of the chair on which one sits.

seat rail Horizontal rail that supports the seat of a chair.

seat rake The angle of the seat back to the seat pan in a chair.

secretary A drop-front writing desk, often with book shelves above and drawers below. *Secrétaire* is the French term.

sedia The Italian Renaissance box-form upholstered armchair.

settee A long, ornately carved and upholstered 17th-century seat or bench with a high back and typically high arms. Used by two or more people.

sgabello An Italian Renaissance stool-like wood chair designed with two trestle supports, an octagonal seat pan, and an inverted triangular back.

Shaker furniture Furniture made by 19th-century Shakers, pure in line and proportion.

silencer A thick, flannel-like, heavily napped fabric used under a tablecloth.

sofa Introduced in Italy in the late 17th century. Resembled a row of chairs joined together.

softwood The wood of a coniferous tree such as fir or pine, regardless of whether or not the wood is actually soft.

splayed Legs or trestle supports designed with an outward cant or slant.

stile The vertical member in framing or paneling that connects to the horizontal members.

stretcher A horizontal connecting member used between the legs of a chair or case piece to underbrace its construction in a H or X form.

substrate The material directly behind the veneer or laminate. Plywood and medium-density fiberboard are typically used as substrates for laminating high-pressure plastic laminate or adhering stone or tile to a counter.

symmetry A state of balance where a component (or several components) is mirrored along an axis.

tabernacle Liturgical furniture in a Catholic Church to contain the ciborium.

table A horizontal surface supported off the ground. Examples include conference table, dining table, kitchen table, side table, and work table.

tactile Capable of being experienced through the sense of touch.

tallboy An 18th-century English case piece with one chest of drawers on top of another. In America it is called a *highboy*.

tambour Half-round wood dowels glued to a backing material that allow a vertical sliding cover for a writing desk. Refers to a desk with a secretary top and slatted, sliding panels replacing the grille. Also refers to a piece designed to store and access writing, drawing, or paper supplies.

tanning The conversion of rawhide into leather.

tapering leg A leg that diminishes in thickness as it approaches the foot.

taxonomy The classification of information and ideas about a subject.

tempered glass Float glass that is heated, then rapidly cooled, causing it to harden and contract, which strengthens the glass to six times the strength of annealed glass.

thronos A throne-type chair for the most important person present.

torah table Liturgical furniture in a synagogue on which one reads the Torah.

torchere A floor lamp designed to cast light upward.

trestle A lateral, braced-frame support used on chairs and tables.

trestle table A table top supported by a braced frame (divided foot, horse), often consisting of two posts with feet, joined by a connecting member.

triclinium A couch surrounding three sides of a table in ancient Rome used to recline on and eat from. Also referred to as the *dining room* in ancient Rome.

trundle bed A low bed used in the American colonial period that could roll under a larger bed during the day.

tufting Upholstery held tightly with buttoning in a regular pattern.

turning Shaping legs or arms using a lathe.

twisted paper Thin rope made of braided paper, commonly used as a material for seat pans in many Scandinavian chair designs. It is literally twisted paper, which is biodegradable, readily available, local, inexpensive, and comfortable.

typology The organization of a subject based upon shared characteristics and attributes.

universal design Design attempts to meet the needs of people of all ages, abilities, and cognitive skills. Set forth as a concept by Ron Mace of the Center for Universal Design at North Carolina State University in 1990, universal design focuses on the "range of abilities" rather than the "limit of disabilities."

V-groove A shallow cut into the face of a material's surface. It usually has an angled or chamfered profile.

vargueño A Spanish drop-front writing cabinet on a chest or stand, popular in the 16th and 17th centuries.

varnish A transparent finish made from resinous material that dries to a hard shine.

veneer A thin layer of wood typically $\frac{1}{32}$–$\frac{1}{64}$ of an inch (0.8 mm to 0.4 mm) that is placed over or in another piece of wood to give the furniture the appearance of the outer wood material.

vernacular Furniture made locally or regionally, not necessarily by furniture professionals.

vernisseur French term for lacquerer.

volatile organic compounds Commonly referred to as VOCs. These compounds are organic chemical compounds that have high enough vapor pressures under normal conditions to significantly vaporize and enter the atmosphere. Sources include thinners and solvents.

voyeuse A chair designed with a narrow back supporting a padded and upholstered, curved crest panel used for conversation. The user sat with his or her back to the front of the chair in a straddle position and rested the elbows on the armrest.

webbing Latticed leather, jute, burlap, rubber, or metal used to support upholstery, whether coiled springs or loose cushions are used.

wheelchair A chair mounted on wheels for a person in need of mobility.

wickerwork Made by weaving rods of cane, rattan, or willow together to form a durable surface. Typically used to make seats for chairs.

Windsor chair A chair with a saddle-shaped wooden or rush seat, pegged legs, and back made of multiple turned spindles.

X-chair An ancient folding-type chair dating back to ancient Egypt and Rome and the Middle Ages.

zeitgeist A German expression that means "the spirit (Geist) of the time (Zeit)." It denotes the intellectual and cultural climate of an era.

Bibliography

BOOKS

Aalto, Alvar. *Verlag für Architektur,* Vols. 1–3. Zurich: Les Editions d'Architecture Artemis, Girsberger, 1963.

Adler, Mortimer J. *Aristotle for Everybody: Difficult Thought Made Easy.* New York: Bantam Books, 1980.

Alberti, Leon B. *On Painting,* Translated by John R. Spencer, 1956, revised edition. New Haven, CT: Yale University Press, 1966.

Alberti, Leon B. On the Art of Building in Ten Books, ed. Rykwert, Joseph. New York: MIT Press, 1991.

Alexander, Christopher. *Notes on the Synthesis of Form.* Cambridge, MA: Harvard University Press, 1964.

American Institute of Architects. *Architectural Graphic Standards,* 10th edition. New York: John Wiley & Sons, 2000.

Architectural Woodwork Institute. *Architectural Woodwork Quality Standards Illustrated.* AWI, Reston, VA 2003.

Ashby, Mike, and Kara Johnson. *Materials and Design: The Art and Science of Material Selection in Product Design.* Oxford: Butterworth-Heinemann, 2002.

Berlyne, D.E. *Conflict, Arousal and Curiosity.* New York: McGraw-Hill, 1960.

Berlyne, D.E. *Studies in the New Experimental Aesthetics: Steps Toward an Objective Psychology of Aesthetic Appreciation.* New York: Halsted Press, 1974.

Bevlin, Marjorie E. *Design through Discovery: An Introduction to Art and Design.* New York: Holt, Rinehart and Winston, 1989.

Blackburn, Graham J. *Illustrated Furniture Making.* New York: Simon and Schuster, 1977.

Blakemore, Robbie G. *History of Interior Design and Furniture: From Ancient Egypt to Nineteenth-Century Europe,* 2nd edition. Hoboken, N.J.: John Wiley & Sons, 2006.

Boger, Louis Ade. *The Complete Guide to Furniture Styles.* New York: Charles Scribner's Sons, 1969.

Bowman, John S. *American Furniture.* New York: Brompton Books Corporation, 1995.

Burchell, Sam. *A History of Furniture: Celebrating Baker Furniture—100 Years of Fine Reproductions.* New York: Harry N. Abrams, 1991.

Buttrey, D.N., ed. *Plastics in Furniture.* London: Applied Science Publishers, 1970.

Cabra, Raul and Dung Ngo, eds. *Contemporary American Furniture.* New York: Universe Publishing, 2000.

Caplan, Ralph. *By Design,* 2nd ed. New York: Fairchild Publications, Inc., 2005.

Casciani, Stefano. *Mobili Come Architectture, Il Disegno Della Produzione Zanotta.* Milan: Arcadia Edizioni, 1987.

Charter, Martin, and Ursula Tischner. *Sustainable Solutions: Developing Products and Services for the Future.* Sheffield, UK: Greenleaf Publishing, 2001.

Ching, Francis D.K. *Architecture: Form, Space, and Order,* 2nd edition. New York: Van Nostrand Reinhold, 1996.

Ching, Francis D.K. *Interior Design Illustrated.* New York: John Wiley & Sons, 1987.

Chippendale, Thomas. *The Gentleman and Cabinet-Maker's Directory.* New York: Dover Publications, 1966.

Colombo, Sarah. *The Chair.* The Ivy Press Limited, 1997.

Cooke, Edward, Jr. *New American Furniture: The Second Generation of Studio Furnituremakers.* Boston: Museum of Fine Arts, 1989.

Cranz, Galen. *The Chair: Rethinking Culture, Body, and Design.* New York and London: W.W. Norton, 1998.

Crochet, Treena. *Designer's Guide to Furniture Styles.* Upper Saddle River, NJ: Prentice Hall, Inc., 1999.

Curtis, William, J.R. *Modern Architecture Since 1900,* 3rd edition. London: Phaidon Press, 1997.

Diffrient, N., A.R. Tilley, and J. C. Bardagjy. *Humanscale 1/2/3.* Cambridge, MA: MIT Press, 1974.

Diffrient, N., A.R. Tilley, and J. C. Bardagjy. *Humanscale 4/5/6.* Cambridge, MA: MIT Press, 1974.

Diffrient, N., A.R. Tilley, and J. C. Bardagjy. *Humanscale 7/8/9.* Cambridge, MA: MIT Press, 1974.

Doczy, Gyorgy. *The Power of Limits.* Boston: Shambhala Publications, 1981.

Dormer, Peter. *Furniture Today—Its Design and Craft.* Penshurst Press, 1995.

Dormer, Peter, and Bill Dowell. "Anthropometry and Its Relationship to Chair Size Performance," proceedings of the 2nd Annual Conference for Managing Ergonomics in the 1990s, 1995.

Dryfuss, Henry, and Alvin Tilley. *The Measure of Man and Woman,* revised edition. New York: John Wiley & Sons, 2002.

Edwards, Clive. *Encyclopedia of Furniture: Materials, Trades and Techniques.* London: Ashgate Publishing, 2000.

Fabbro, Mario Dal. *Modern Furniture: Its Design and Construction.* New York: Reinhold, 1949.

Favata, Ignazia. *Joe Columbo.* Cambridge, MA: MIT Press, 1988.

Fiell, Charlotte, and Peter Fiell. *Modern Furniture Classics Since 1945.* Washington, DC: American Institute of Architects Press, 1991.

Fiell, Charlotte, and Peter Fiell. *1000 Chairs.* Cologne: Benedikt Taschen Verlag GmbH, 2000.

Fiell, Charlotte, and Peter Fiell. *Scandinavian Design.* Cologne: Taschen GmbH, 2005.

Fitzgerald, Oscar P. *Three Centuries of American Furniture.* New York: Gramercy, 1982.

Fleming, Fergus, and Alan Lothian. *Myth and Mankind: The Way to Eternity: Egyptian Myth.* London: Duncan Baird, 1997.

Foa, Linda. *Furniture for the Workplace.* Glen Cove, NY: PBC International, 1992.

Frishman, Martin, and Hasan-Uddin Khan. *The Mosque: History, Architectural Development and Regional Diversity.* London: Thames and Hudson, 1994.

Fuad-Luke, Alastair. *The Eco-Design Handbook.* London: Thames and Hudson, 2002.

Geest, Jan van. *Jean Prouvé's Furniture.* Koln: Taschen, 1991.

Gibson, Scott. *The Workshop—Celebrating the Place Where Craftsmanship Begins.* Newtown, CT: Taunton Press, 2003.

Gideon, Siegfried. *Mechanization Takes Command: A Contribution to Anonymous History.* (1948) New York: W.W. Norton, 1969 (by arrangement with Oxford University Press).

Grandjean, E. *Ergonomics in Computerized Offices.* Philadelphia: Taylor & Francis, 1987.

Greenberg, Cara. *Op to Pop Furniture of the 1960s.* A Bulfinch Press Book, Boston: Little, Brown and Company, 1999.

Habegger, Jerryll, and Joseph H. Osman. *Sourcebook of Modern Furniture,* 2nd edition. New York: W.W. Norton, 1997.

Hall, Edward T. *The Hidden Dimension.* Garden City, NY: Doubleday, 1966.

Heath, Thomas L. *The Thirteen Books of Euclid's Elements, Books 1 and 2.* New York: Dover Publications, 1956.

Heinz, Thomas A. *Frank Lloyd Wright Furniture Portfolio.* Salt Lake City: Gibbs-Smith, 1993.

Hennessey, James, and Victor Papanek. *Nomadic Furniture 1.* New York: Pantheon Books, 1973.

Hennessey, James, and Victor Papanek. *Nomadic Furniture 2.* New York: Pantheon Books, 1974.

Hepplewhite, George. *The Cabinet Maker and Upholsterer's Guide.* London: 1786 (New York: Dover, 1969).

Heskett, John. *Industrial Design.* New York and Toronto: Oxford University Press, 1980.

Hoadley, Bruce R. *Understanding Wood.* Newton, CT: Taunton Press, 1980.

Howe, Jennifer L. *Cincinnati Art—Carved Furniture and Interiors.* Athens: Ohio University Press, 2003.

Istituto Nazionale per il Commercio Estero. *The Italian Chair.* Rome, no date.

Jastrzebowski, Wojciech. "An Outline of Ergonomics or the Science of Work Based Upon the Truths Drawn from the Science of Nature." *Nature and Industry* (1857), reprint by the Centro Institute of Labor Protection, 1997, Warsaw.

Johnston, David. *The Craft of Furniture Making.* New York: Charles Scribner's Sons, 1979.

Joyce, Ernest. *The Encyclopedia of Furniture Making.* New York: Sterling Publishing Co. Inc., 1987.

Kieran, Stephan, and James Timberlake. *Refabricating Architecture.* New York: McGraw-Hill, 2004.

King, Carol Soucek. *Furniture Architects' and Designers' Originals.* Glen Cove, NY: PBC International, 1994.

Koehler, Arthur. *Identification of Furniture Woods.* Washington, DC: U.S. Department of Agriculture, 1926.

Koomen Harmon, Sharon. *The Codes Guidebook for Interiors.* New York: John Wiley & Sons, Inc. 1994.

Kouwenhoven, John A. *Made in America.* New York: Doubleday, 1951. Reprinted as *The Arts: Modern American Civilization.* New York: W.W. Norton, 1967.

Krogh, Erik. *Poul Kjærholm,* 2nd edition. Arkitektens Forlag. Copenhagen: F. Hendriksens Eftf., 2001.

Kuhn, Thomas S. *The Structure of Scientific Revolutions,* 2nd edition, enlarged. Chicago: University of Chicago Press, 1970.

Larrabee, Eric, and Vignelli, Massimo. *Knoll Design.* New York: Harry N. Abrams, Inc., 1981.

Le Corbusier. *Towards a New Architecture.* Architectural Press, 1927. Reprinted New York: Praeger, 1959.

Lefteri, Chris. *Plastics: Materials for Inspirational Design.* East Sussex, U.K.: Rotovision, 2001.

Lincoln, William A. *World Woods in Color.* Fresno, CA: Linden, 1986.

Livingston, Karen, and Linda Parry, eds. *International Arts and Crafts.* London: V & A Publications, 2005.

Lost Civilizations: Egypt: Land of the Pharoahs. Alexandria, VA: Time-Life Books, 1992.

Lucie-Smith, Edward. *Furniture: A Concise History.* London: Thames and Hudson, 1993.

Malnar, Joy Monice and Frank Vodvarka. *The Interior Dimension: A Theoretical Approach to Enclosed Space.* New York: Van Nostrand Reinhold, 1992.

Mandel, A.C. "The Seated Man (*Homo Sedans*), the seated work position, theory and practice." *Applied Ergonomics,* 1981.

Mang, Karl. *History of Modern Furniture.* New York: Harry N. Abrams, 1979.

Manzini, Ezio. *The Material of Invention.* Milan: Arcadia Edizioni, 1986.

Marek, Don. *Arts and Crafts Furniture Design.* Grand Rapids, MI: Grand Rapids Art Museum, 1987.

Miller, Craig R., et al, *Design in America: The Cranbrook Vision, 1925–1950.* New York: Harry N. Abrams, 1983.

Miller, Judith. *Furniture World Styles from Classical to Contemporary.* New York: Dorling Kindersley Limited, 2005.

Moffett, Marian, Michael Fazio, and Lawrence Wodehouse. *Buildings across Time: An Introduction to World Architecture,* 2nd edition. New York: McGraw-Hill Higher Education, 2004.

Morello, Augusto and Anna Castelli Ferrieri. *Plastiche E Design.* Milan: Arcadia Edizioni Srl, 1984.

Morgan, Morris H. *Vitruvius: The Ten Books on Architecture.* Cambridge, MA: Harvard University Press, 1914; New York: Dover Publications, 1960.

Mori, Toshiko, ed. *Immaterial/Ultramaterial: Architecture, Design, and Materials.* Harvard Design School in association with George Braziller, Cambridge, MA, 2002.

Mumford, Lewis. *Technics and Civilization.* New York: Harcourt, Brace, 1934.

Naytor, Gillian. *The Arts and Crafts Movement.* London: Trefoil, 1990.

Nelson, Karla J., and David A. Taylor. *Interiors,* 4th edition. New York: McGraw-Hill, 2007.

Ostergard, Devek E. *Bentwood and Metal Furniture, 1850–1946.* Seattle: University of Washington Press; New York: American Federation of Arts, 1987.

Oxford American Dictionary. Oxford: Oxford University Press, 1980.

Payne, Christopher. *Sotherby's Concise Encyclopedia of Furniture.* New York: Harper & Row, 1989.

Pile, John F. *Furniture, Modern and Post Modern.* New York: John Wiley & Sons, 1950.

Pile, John F. *Design Purpose, Form, and Meaning.* New York: W.W. Norton, 1979.

Pile, John F. *Modern Furniture.* New York: John Wiley & Sons, 1979.

Pile, John F. *Interior Design,* 3rd edition. New York: Harry N. Abrams and Prentice Hall, 2003.

Pile, John F. *A History of Interior Design,* 2nd edition. New York: John Wiley & Sons, 2005.

Piña, Leslie A. *Furniture in History.* Upper Saddle River, NJ: Prentice Hall, 2003.

Pye, David. *The Nature and Art of Workmanship.* New York: Cambridge University Press, 1968.

Quinan, Jack. *Frank Lloyd Wright's Martin House: Architecture as Portraiture.* New York: Princeton Architectural Press, 2004.

Richter, Gisela M.A. *Ancient Furniture: A History of Greek, Etruscan and Roman Furniture.* Oxford: Printed at the Clarendon Press, 1926.

Scarzella, Patrizia. *Steel and Style.* Milan: Arcadia Edizioni, 1984.

Schodek, Daniel, Martin Bechthold, Kimo Griggs, Kenneth M. Kao, and Marco Steinberg. *Digital Design and Manufacturing: CAD/CAM Applications in Architecture and Design.* Hoboken, NJ: John Wiley & Sons, 2005.

Schütze, Rolf. *Making Modern Furniture.* New York: Reinhold, 1967.

Scruton, Roger. *The Aesthetics of Architecture.* London: Methuen, 1979.

Sheridan, Michael. *Poul Kjærholm: Furniture Designer.* Humlebaek, Denmark: Louisiana Museum of Modern Art, 2006.

Sherrill, Sam. *Harvesting Urban Timber: A Complete Guide.* Fresno, CA: Linden, 2003.

Simpson, Chris. *The Essential Guide to Woodwork.* San Diego: Thunder Bay Press, 2001.

Smithson, Peter, and Karl Unglaub. *Flying Furniture.* Cologne: Die Deutsche Bibliothek, 1999.

Sommer, Robert. *Personal Space: The Behavioral Basis of Design.* Englewood Cliffs, NJ: Prentice Hall, 1969.

Sparke, Penny. *Design in Italy.* New York: Abbeville Press Publishers, 1988.

Sparke, Penny. *Furniture: Twentieth-Century Design.* London: Bell & Hyman, 1986.

Sparke, Penny. *A Century of Design—Design Pioneers of the 20th Century.* Hauppauge, NY: Barroons Educational Series, 1998.

Stem, Seth. *Designing Furniture.* Newton, CT: Taunton Press, 1989.

Tierney, William F. *Modern Upholstering Methods.* Bloomington, IL: McKnight & McKnight, 1965.

Trussell, John. *Making Furniture.* London: Dryad Press, 1970.

Vitruvius, Marcus Pollio. *The Ten Books on Architecture.* New York: Dover, 1960.

Vogel, Craig. *Aluminum: A Competitive Material of Choice in the Design of New Products, 1950 to the Present.* Essay on aluminum in design. Carnegie Museum of Art. New York: Harry A. Abrams, 2000.

Wake, Warren K. *Design Paradigms.* New York: John Wiley & Sons, 2000.

Wanscher, Ole. *The Art of Furniture: 5000 Years of Furniture and Interiors.* Reinhold, 1966.

Weizsäcker, Von E., Lovius, A., and Lovius H. *Factor Four: Doubling Wealth, Halving Resource Use.* London: Earthscan, 1997.

Whitford, Frank. *Bauhaus.* London: Thames and Hudson, 1984.

Wilhide, Elizabeth. *Living with Modern Classics: The Chair.* New York: Watson-Guptill, 2000.

Wilk, Christopher. *Thonet: 150 Years of Furniture.* Barron's Educational Series, 1980.

Zelleke, Ghenete, Eva B. Ottillinger, and Nina Stritzler. *Against the Grain: Bentwood Furniture from the Collection of Fern and Manfred Steinfeld.* Chicago: Art Institute of Chicago, 1993.

JOURNALS

Abitare, Editrice Abitare Segesta, Milan

American Furniture, University Press New England

Architectural Record, McGraw-Hill Companies

Architecture, Vnu Business Publications

Artichoke, Architecture Media Pty Ltd.

CasaBella, Arnoldo Mondadori Editore

Contract, Vnu Business Publications

Domus Magazine, Editoriale Domus, Milan

Fine Woodworking, Taunton Direct (Press), USA

Frame, Amsterdam, the Netherlands, info@framemag.com

Furniture and Cabinet Making, Gmc Publications Ltd

Furniture Production, Nigel Gearing Ltd

Furniture Today, Reed Business Information

ID, F & W Publications

Interior Design, Reed Business Information, New York

Interni, Arnoldo Mondadori Editore

Metropolis, Metropolis Magazine, Bellerophon Publications

Ottogono, Editrice Compositori

Woodcraft, Woodcraft Supply, Llc

Woodwork Magazine, Ross Periodicals Inc.

Woodworkers Journal, Woodworkers Journal

WEBSITES

Many on-line sources and Websites were helpful in developing the content of this book. Following is a brief list of sites that were especially noteworthy.

Department of Asian Art. "Lacquerware of East Asia." In Timeline of Art History. New York. The Metropolitan Museum of Art, 2000. (October 2004).

Design Addict, addict.com

Design History Society

Furniture Research at HighPoint University

The Metropolitan Museum of Art's Timeline of Art History

Illustration Credits

Chapter 1

Figure 1.1   Photo by Erik Skoven.
Figure 1.2   Copyright © William A. Yokel, 2005.
Figure 1.3   Courtesy of Rud. Rasmussen, Denmark.
Figure 1.4   Photo: Brian F. Davies.
Figure 1.5   Photo by Jim Postell.
Figure 1.6   Photo: Courtesy of Michael Toombs.
Figure 1.7   Chart by Jim Postell.

Chapter 2

Figure 2.1   Courtesy of Gil Born.
Figure 2.2   Photo by Jim Postell.
Figure 2.3   Photo by Jim Postell.
Figure 2.4   Courtesy of John Stork.
Figure 2.5   Photo by Jim Postell.
Figure 2.6   Courtesy of Cincinnati Art Museum, John J. Emery Fund. Accession No. 1945.64.
Figure 2.7   Drawing courtesy of Jim Postell.
Figure 2.8   Photo: Courtesy of Knoll, Inc.
Figure 2.9   Photo by Jim Postell.
Figure 2.10   Image courtesy of Kyle Barker.
Figure 2.11   Photo by Jim Postell.
Figure 2.12   Photographer Nick Merrick. Courtesy of Herman Miller Inc.
Figure 2.13   Photo by Jim Postell.
Figure 2.14   Copyright © William A. Yokel, 2005. Permission by Alyssa Thunberg, who is in the photo.
Figure 2.15   Copyright © William A. Yokel, 2005. Permission by David Fedyk and Whitney Hamaker, who are in the photo.
Figure 2.16   Historic American Buildings Survey, Walter Smalling, photographer, 1978.
Figure 2.17   Courtesy of Formica Corporation.
Figure 2.18   Courtesy of Gil Born.
Figure 2.19   Courtesy of Formica Corporation.
Figure 2.20   Photo courtesy of Cincinnati Art Museum. Accession No. 1962.457.
Figure 2.21   Installation view of the exhibition *William Christenberry: Architecture/Archetype* (October 5–November 21, 2001) at the Dorothy W. and C. Lawson Reed, Jr., Gallery, University of Cincinnati. Photo by Jay Yocis and courtesy of DAAP Galleries, University of Cincinnati. Photo copyright © 2001 University of Cincinnati. All artwork copyright © 2001 William Christenberry. All rights reserved.
Figure 2.22   Historic American Buildings Survey, Elmer R. Pearson, photographer, 1970.
Figure 2.23   Photo: Courtesy of Steelcase Inc.
Figure 2.24   Copyright © William A. Yokel, 2005.
Figure 2.25   Courtesy of John Stork.
Figure 2.26   Photo: Courtesy of Professor Sooshin Choi, as Proxy for Ola Abou-Sabe, Independence Technology L.L.C.
Figure 2.27   Source of image and photographer unknown.
Figure 2.28   Copyright © William A. Yokel, 2005.
Figure 2.29   Copyright © William A. Yokel, 2005.
Figure 2.30   Photographer Phil Schaafsma. Courtesy of Herman Miller Inc.
Figure 2.31   Photo: Brian F. Davies.

Figure 2.32	Photo courtesy of Erik Skoven and Fritz Hansen, Denmark.
Figure 2.33	Photo by Jim Postell.
Figure 2.34	*Poul Kjærholm—Furniture Architect.* June 23–15 October 2006. Photo: Jim Postell. Credit: Louisiana Museum of Modern Art.
Figure 2.35	Photo: Brian F. Davies.
Figure 2.36	Image courtesy of Peter Chamberlain.
Figure 2.37	Photo by Jim Postell.
Figure 2.38	Photo by Jim Postell.
Figure 2.39	Photo by Jim Postell.
Figure 2.40	Photo: Courtesy of Steelcase Inc.
Figure 2.41	Photo: Courtesy of Steelcase Inc.
Figure 2.42	Photographer Jim Powell. Courtesy of Herman Miller Inc.
Figure 2.43	Photo by Jim Postell.
Figure 2.44	Photo by Jim Postell.
Figure 2.45	Photo by Jim Postell.
Figure 2.46	Photo by Jim Postell.
Figure 2.47	Photo by Jim Postell.
Figure 2.48	Photo: Courtesy of David Lee Smith.
Figure 2.49	Copyright © Scott Hisey, 2004.
Figure 2.50	Courtesy of Library of Congress, Prints & Photographs Division, Reproduction No. 03037u.
Figure 2.51	Photo: Courtesy of Inci Ilgin, Associate Professor.
Figure 2.52	Photo by Jim Postell.
Figure 2.53	Photo by Jim Postell.
Figure 2.54	Photo: Courtesy of Patrick Snadon, Associate Professor, SAID, University of Cincinnati.
Figure 2.55	Photo: Courtesy of Roset USA. Photographer: Bernard Langenstein.
Figure 2.56	Photo by Jim Postell.
Figure 2.57	Photo: Courtesy of Julia Bryan.
Figure 2.58	Copyright © Scott Hisey, 2004.
Figure 2.59	Courtesy of Library of Congress, Prints & Photographs Division, Reproduction No. 3b46012u.tiff.
Figure 2.60	Courtesy of Formica Corporation.
Figure 2.61	Photo by Jim Postell.
Figure 2.62	Photo by Jim Postell.
Figure 2.63	Copyright © William A. Yokel, 2005.

Chapter 3

Figure 3.1	Photo courtesy of Erik Skoven in proxy for PP Møbler.
Figure 3.2	Copyright © William A. Yokel, 2005.
Figure 3.3	Photo by Jim Postell.
Figure 3.4	Photo: Courtesy of Cincinnati Art Museum (Change of Pace Exhibit, October 4, 1975–January 4, 1976).
Figure 3.5	Photo by Jim Postell.
Figure 3.6	Photo by Jim Postell.
Figure 3.7a	Courtesy of Erik Krogh, DKDS, Copenhagen.
Figure 3.7b	Photo by Jim Postell.
Figure 3.8	Photographers Craig Duggan/Hedrich Blessing. Courtesy of Herman Miller Inc.
Figure 3.9	Photo by Jim Postell.
Figure 3.10	Photo credit: Nathan Sayers for MetroNaps.
Figure 3.11	Photo: Courtesy of Julia Bryan.
Figure 3.12	Courtesy of John Stork.
Figure 3.13	Copyright © William A. Yokel, 2005.
Figure 3.14	Photo by Jim Postell.
Figure 3.15	Photographer Phil Schaafsma. Courtesy of Herman Miller Inc.
Figure 3.16	Photo by Jim Postell.
Figure 3.17	Drawn by Mette McLean and Sigurdur Stefansson, DKDS students. Courtesy of Jens Overbye, Lecturer, DKDS, Copenhagen.
Figure 3.18	Copyright © William A. Yokel, 2005.
Figure 3.19	Computer modeling by Carly L. Snyder.
Figure 3.20	Photo: Courtesy of Benjamin Meyer.

Figure 3.21a Design by the author. Computer model by Eli Meiners.
Figure 3.21b Photo by Jim Postell.
Figure 3.22 Drawing by Jim Postell.
Figure 3.23 Photo: Courtesy of Benjamin Meyer.
Figure 3.24 Photo by Jim Postell. Computer model by Steve Wethington.
Figure 3.25 Photographer: Miles De Russey. Courtesy Herman Miller.
Figure 3.26 Andrea Zittel. Image courtesy of Andrea Rosen Gallery, New York, and the Cincinnati Art Museum. Accession No. 1995.13.1-5.
Figure 3.27 Source of image and photographer unknown.
Figure 3.28 Photo: Courtesy of Steelcase Inc.
Figure 3.29 Copyright © William A. Yokel, 2005.
Figure 3.30 Photo by Jim Postell.
Figure 3.31 Design by Gülen Çevik and Jim Postell. Computer model courtesy of Eli Meiners.
Figure 3.32 Designers: Semprini/Cananzi 1989. Photo Credit: Emilio Tremolada.
Figure 3.33 Photo by Jim Postell.
Figure 3.34 Copyright © William A. Yokel, 2005.
Figure 3.35 Photo by Jim Postell.
Figure 3.36 Designer and Architect: Troels Grum-Schwensen. Manufacturer: Globe Furniture A/S, Denmark. Photography: Globe Furniture A/S, Denmark.
Figure 3.37 Photo taken by Jim Postell at the exhibition *Poul Kjærholm—Furniture Architect,* curated by Michael Sheridan, with permission from Susanne Hartz, Head of Press, Louisiana Museum of Modern Art, Humlebæk, Denmark.
Figure 3.38 Photo by Jim Postell.
Figure 3.39 Courtesy of Cincinnati Art Museum. Centennial Gift of Mr. and Mrs. Carl Bimel, Jr., in memory of Mrs. Carl Bimel, Sr. Accession No. 1981.471.
Figure 3.40 Photo by Jim Postell.
Figure 3.41 Courtesy Malene la Cour Rasmussen and Jørgen Rud. Rasmussen. Rud. Rasmussen/Denmark.
Figure 3.42 Design by Toshiyuki Kita, manufactured by Cassina, drawn by SAID student, School of Architecture and Interior Design, University of Cincinnati, and author.
Figure 3.43 Copyright © William A. Yokel, 2005.
Figure 3.44a Photo: Courtesy of Gerald R. Larson.
Figure 3.44b Historic American Buildings Survey, Jack E. Boucher, photographer, 1969.

Chapter 4

Figure 4.1 National Museum, Athens, Greece.
Figure 4.2 Drawing by Monica Hekk and Karin Hvidt, DKDS students. Courtesy of Jens Overbye, Lecturer, DKDS, Copenhagen, Interior Architect, MDD.
Figure 4.3 Computer rendering by Matthew Althouse.
Figure 4.4 Computer rendering by Matthew Althouse.
Figure 4.5 Courtesy of Cincinnati Art Museum. Gift of Mrs. Herbert N. Straus. Accession No. 1958.256.a-h.
Figure 4.6 Photo by Jim Postell.
Figure 4.7 Photo by Jim Postell.
Figure 4.8 Photo by Jim Postell.
Figure 4.10 Drawing by Carsten Engtoft Holgaard, Torben Kragh Jørgensen, and Pia Nielsen, DKDS students. Courtesy of Jens Overbye, Lecturer, Interior Architect, MDD.
Figure 4.11 Computer model by Nora Leuhmann.
Figure 4.12 Computer model by Nora Leuhmann.
Figure 4.13 Courtesy of John Stork.
Figure 4.14 Courtesy of John Stork.
Figure 4.15 Courtesy of John Stork.
Figure 4.16 Drawn by Hanne Meilsøe Dam, DKDS, Copenhagen. Courtesy of Jens Overbye, Lecturer, Interior Architect, MDD.
Figure 4.17 Copyright © William A. Yokel, 2005.
Figure 4.18 Computer model by Nora Leuhmann.
Figure 4.19 Drawing by Jim Postell.
Figure 4.20 Computer model by Nora Leuhmann.
Figure 4.21 Computer model by Nicole Desender.

Figure 4.22	Computer model by Sylbester Yeo and Michael Wigle.
Figure 4.23	Drawing by SAID student and author, School of Architecture and Interior Design, University of Cincinnati.
Figure 4.24	Photo courtesy Knoll, Inc.
Figure 4.25	Photo by Jim Postell.
Figure 4.26	Computer model by Nora Leuhmann.
Figure 4.27	Computer model by Nora Leuhmann.
Figure 4.28	Photo by Jim Postell.
Figure 4.29	Photo by Jim Postell.
Figure 4.30	Photo by Jim Postell, taken at the Alvar Aalto Museum, Jyväskyla, Finland.
Figure 4.31	Photo by Jim Postell taken at the Alvar Aalto Museum, Jyväskyla, Finland.
Figure 4.32	Courtesy of Herman Miller.
Figure 4.33	Photo by Jim Postell.
Figure 4.34	Photo by Jim Postell.
Figure 4.35	Photo by Jim Postell.
Figure 4.36	Photographer Phil Schaasfma. Courtesy of Herman Miller.
Figure 4.37	Courtesy of Herman Miller.
Figure 4.38	Computer model by the author and Nora Luehmann.
Figure 4.39	Photo by Jim Postell.
Figure 4.40	Photo by Jim Postell.
Figure 4.41	Computer model by Sylbester Yeo.
Figure 4.42	Computer model by Sylbester Yeo.
Figure 4.43	Computer model by Sylbester Yeo.
Figure 4.44	Photo: Courtesy of Knoll Inc.
Figure 4.45	Photo: Courtesy of Knoll Inc.
Figure 4.46	Computer model by Nora Leuhmann.
Figure 4.47	Courtesy of Herman Miller.
Figure 4.48	Courtesy of Herman Miller.
Figure 4.49	Photographer: Earl Woods. Courtesy of Herman Miller, 1979.
Figure 4.50	Photographer Steve Hall/Hendich Blessing. Courtesy of Herman Miller.
Figure 4.51	Drawing by SAID student and the author, School of Architecture and Interior Design, University of Cincinnati.
Figure 4.52	Photo by Jim Postell.
Figure 4.53	Computer model by Nora Leuhmann.
Figure 4.54	Photo courtesy Knoll, Inc.
Figure 4.55	Photo: Courtesy of Knoll Inc.
Figure 4.56	Computer rendering by Nora Leuhmann.
Figure 4.57	Computer rendering by Nora Leuhmann.
Figure 4.58	Photo by Jim Postell.
Figure 4.59	Computer model by Nora Leuhmann.
Figure 4.60	Photo by Jim Postell.
Figure 4.61	Photo by Jim Postell.
Figure 4.62	Photo by Jim Postell.
Figure 4.63	© Andrea Zittel. Image courtesy of Andrea Rosen Gallery, New York, and the Cincinnati Art Museum. Accession No. 1995.13.1-5.
Figure 4.64	© Andrea Zittel. Image courtesy of Andrea Rosen Gallery, New York, and the Cincinnati Art Museum. Accession No. 1995.13.1-5.
Figure 4.65	Image courtesy of Andrea Rosen Gallery, New York, and the Cincinnati Art Museum. Accession No. 1995.13.1-5.
Figure 4.66	Image courtesy of Andrea Rosen Gallery, New York, and the Cincinnati Art Museum. Accession No. 1995.13.1-5.
Figure 4.67	Image courtesy of Andrea Rosen Gallery, New York, and the Cincinnati Art Museum. Accession No. 1995.13.1-5.
Figure 4.68	Courtesy of Herman Miller.
Figure 4.69	Courtesy of Herman Miller.
Figure 4.70	Photographer Mike Stuk. Courtesy Herman Miller.
Figure 4.71	Photographer Nick Merrick/Hedrich Blessing. Courtesy Herman Miller.
Figure 4.72	Photo: Courtesy of Steelcase Inc.
Figure 4.73	Photo: Courtesy of Steelcase Inc.
Figure 4.74	Photo: Courtesy of Steelcase Inc.
Figure 4.75	Photo: Courtesy of Steelcase Inc.

Figure 4.76   Drawing by Erik Skoven.
Figure 4.77   Photo: Erik Skoven.
Figure 4.78   Photo: Erik Skoven.
Figure 4.79   Photo: Erik Skoven.
Figure 4.80   Computer model by Jim Postell.
Figure 4.81   Computer model by Jim Postell.
Figure 4.82   Photo by Scott Hisey.
Figure 4.83   Photo by Scott Hisey.
Figure 4.84   Photo by Gary Kessler, copyright 2005.

Chapter 5

Figure 5.1   Photo: Erling Christoffersen. Courtesy of Erik Skoven, DIS, and Danmarks Designskole, De-
               partment of Furniture and Spatial Design.
Figure 5.2   Drawing by DIS student. Courtesy of Erik Skoven.
Figure 5.3   Rooks Photography. Courtesy of Herman Miller.
Figure 5.4   Designed by Komplot Design. Photo: Komplot Design.
Figure 5.5a   Designed by Erling Christoffersen, Architect MAA, Designer MDD. Photographer: Ole
               Akhøj.
Figure 5.5b   Designed by Erling Christoffersen, Architect MAA, Designer MDD. Photographer: Ole Akhøj.
Figure 5.6a   Courtesy, Jonathan Bruns.
Figure 5.6b   Photo by Jim Postell.
Figure 5.7   Drawing by Randi Sigrid Andersen and Elsebeth Balsløw, DKDS students. Courtesy of Jens
               Overbye, Lecturer, Interior Architect, MDD.
Figure 5.8   Courtesy of Humanscale.
Figure 5.9   Courtesy of Gil Born.
Figure 5.10   Copyright © William A. Yokel, 2005.
Figure 5.11   Photo by Jim Postell.
Figure 5.12   Image courtesy of Peter Chamberlain.
Figure 5.13   Drawing: Courtesy of H. Bradley Hammond.
Figure 5.14   Image courtesy of Peter Chamberlain in proxy for Dr. Jirou Ohara. Image source: *Collection
               of Technical Body and Motion Measurements for the Designer,* Jirou Ohara. Shoukoku Pub-
               lishing, 1985.
Figure 5.15   Image courtesy of Peter Chamberlain in proxy for Dr. Jirou Ohara. Image source: see 5.14.
Figure 5.16   Courtesy Humanscale.
Figure 5.17   Photo: Courtesy of Benjamin Meyer.
Figure 5.18   Photo by Jim Postell.
Figure 5.19   Image courtesy of Peter Chamberlain.
Figure 5.20   Image courtesy of Peter Chamberlain in proxy for Dr. Enshu Moritani. Image source: *Furni-
               ture Design and Drawing.* Enshu Moritani. Umiyama Publishing, 1996.
Figure 5.21   Copyright © William A. Yokel, 2005.
Figure 5.22a   Photo by Bjørli Lundin.
Figure 5.22b   Photo by Bjørli Lundin.
Figure 5.23a   Photo by Bjørli Lundin.
Figure 5.23b   Photo by Bjørli Lundin.
Figure 5.24   Image courtesy of Peter Chamberlain.
Figure 5.25   Photo by Jim Postell.
Figure 5.26   Photo by Jim Postell.
Figure 5.27   Copyright © William A. Yokel, 2005.
Figure 5.28   Photographer Earl Jones. Courtesy of Herman Miller.
Figure 5.29   Photo by Jim Postell.
Figure 5.30a   Drawing by Jim Postell.
Figure 5.30b   Photo by Jim Postell.
Figure 5.31   Photo courtesy of Erik Skoven.
Figure 5.32   Body studies: SAID students, School of Architecture and Interior Design, University of
               Cincinnati.
Figure 5.33   Design and photography by Elizabeth Rajala.
Figure 5.34   Photo: Courtesy of Benjamin Meyer.
Figure 5.35   Photo: Courtesy of Benjamin Meyer.
Figure 5.36   Photo by Jim Postell.
Figure 5.37   Photo by Jim Postell.

Chapter 6

Figure 6.1a   *Poul Kjærholm—Furniture Architect.* June 23–15 October 2006. Photo: Jim Postell. Credit: Louisiana Museum of Modern Art.

Figure 6.1b   *Poul Kjærholm—Furniture Architect.* June 23–October 15, 2006. Photo: Jim Postell. Credit: Louisiana Museum of Modern Art.

Figure 6.1c   *Poul Kjærholm—Furniture Architect.* June 23–15 October 2006. Photo: Jim Postell. Credit: Louisiana Museum of Modern Art.

Figure 6.2a   Photographer George Heinrich. Courtesy of Herman Miller.

Figure 6.2b   Photographer Nick Merrick/Hedrich Blessing. Courtesy of Herman Miller.

Figure 6.3   Photo: Courtesy of Knoll Inc.

Figure 6.4   Courtesy of John Stork.

Figure 6.5   Photo by Jim Postell.

Figure 6.6   Copyright © William A. Yokel, 2005.

Figure 6.7   Photo by Jim Postell.

Figure 6.8   Drawing by SAID student and Jim Postell, School of Architecture and Interior Design, University of Cincinnati.

Figure 6.9a   Photo: Courtesy of Knoll Inc.

Figure 6.9b   Photo by Jim Postell.

Figure 6.10   Photo: Courtesy of Michael Toombs.

Figure 6.11   Drawing by Jim Postell.

Figure 6.12a   Sketch by Jim Postell.

Figure 6.12b   Permission by Florine Postell.

Figure 6.13   Photo by Janet Flory.

Figure 6.14   Courtesy of Gil Born.

Figure 6.15   Drawing by Jim Postell.

Figure 6.16   Photo courtesy of Erik Skoven.

Figure 6.17   *Poul Kjærholm—Furniture Architect.* June 23–15 October 2006. Photo: Jim Postell. Credit: Louisiana Museum of Modern Art.

Figure 6.18a   Photo: Courtesy of Professor Anton Harfmann, Associate Dean, DAAP.

Figure 6.18b   Photo: Courtesy of Professor Anton Harfmann, Associate Dean, DAAP.

Figure 6.18c   Photo: Courtesy of Professor Anton Harfmann, Associate Dean, DAAP. Permission by SAID student Joseph McGovern, who is in the photo.

Figure 6.19a   Photo: Courtesy of Professor Anton Harfmann, Associate Dean, DAAP. Permission by SAID student Vincent M. Calabro, who is in the photo.

Figure 6.19b   Photo: Lisa Ventre—University of Cincinnati.

Figure 6.19c   Photo: Lisa Ventre—University of Cincinnati.

Figure 6.20   Courtesy of Eames and Herman Miller.

Figure 6.21   Photo by Jim Postell.

Figure 6.22   Photo by Jim Postell.

Figure 6.23   Design by Komplot Design for Källemo AB (Sweden). Photo: Curt Ekblom.

Figure 6.24   Courtesy of Herman Miller.

Figure 6.25   Photo: Courtesy of Benjamin Meyer.

Figure 6.26a   Fabrication, Juan Zouain; design by Emiliano Godoy, 2005. Photo: Godoylab, 2005.

Figure 6.26b   Photo: Godoylab, 2005.

Figure 6.26c   Photo: Godoylab, 2005.

Figure 6.27   Photo by Jim Postell.

Figure 6.28   Designed by Komplot Design, manufactured by GUBI A/S, 2006. Photo Thomas Ibsen.

Figure 6.29   Photo by Jim Postell.

Figure 6.30   Courtesy of Humanscale.

Figure 6.31   Courtesy of Gil Born.

Figure 6.32   Computer modeling by Steve Wethington and Jim Postell. Image by Jim Postell.

Figure 6.33   Photo courtesy of Erik Skoven.

Figure 6.34   Sketch by Jim Postell.

Figure 6.35   Sketch by Jim Postell.

Figure 6.36   Drawing by DIS student. Image courtesy of Erik Skoven.

Figure 6.37   Photo courtesy of Erik Skoven.

Figure 6.38a   Courtesy of Gil Born.

Figure 6.38b   Courtesy of Gil Born.

Figure 6.39   Drawing by Jim Postell.

Figure 6.40a   *Poul Kjærholm—Furniture Architect.* June 23–15 October 2006. Photo: Jim Postell. Credit: Louisiana Museum of Modern Art.

Figure 6.40b *Poul Kjærholm—Furniture Architect.* June 23–15 October 2006. Photo: Jim Postell. Credit: Louisiana Museum of Modern Art.
Figure 6.41 Copyright © Scott Hisey, 2004.
Figure 6.42 Photo courtesy of Formica Corporation.
Figure 6.43 Photo by Jim Postell.
Figure 6.44 Courtesy of Gil Born.
Figure 6.45 Courtesy of Gil Born.
Figure 6.46 Photo: Drawing by Jim Postell.
Figure 6.47 Photo by Jim Postell. Permission by Michael Toombs.
Figure 6.48a Courtesy of Emiliano Godoy. Credit: Erika Hanson, 2005.
Figure 6.48b Courtesy of Emiliano Godoy. Credit: Erika Hanson, 2005.
Figure 6.48c Courtesy of Emiliano Godoy. Credit: Erika Hanson, 2005.
Figure 6.49 Photograph: John Curry, 2005.
Figure 6.50 Photo by Jim Postell. Permission by Michael Toombs.
Figure 6.51 Photo by Jim Postell.
Figure 6.52 Historic American Buildings Survey, Jack E. Boucher, photographer, 1985.
Figure 6.53 Photo by Jim Postell.
Figure 6.54 Photo by Scott Hisey.

Chapter 7

Figure 7.1 Photo by Jim Postell.
Figure 7.2 Photo by Jim Postell.
Figure 7.3 Photo by Jim Postell.
Figure 7.4 Photo by Jim Postell.
Figure 7.5 Photo by Jim Postell.
Figure 7.6 Photo by Jim Postell.
Figure 7.7 Photo: Brian F. Davies.
Figure 7.8 Designed by Pol Quadens. Courtesy of Pol Quadens.
Figure 7.9 Photo by Jim Postell.
Figure 7.10 Photo by Jim Postell.
Figure 7.11 Photo by Jim Postell.
Figure 7.12 *Poul Kjærholm—Furniture Architect.* June 23–15 October 2006. Photo: Jim Postell. Credit: Louisiana Museum of Modern Art.
Figure 7.13 Photo by Jim Postell.
Figure 7.14 Photo courtesy Knoll, Inc.
Figure 7.15 Photo by Jim Postell.
Figure 7.16 Photo by Jim Postell.
Figure 7.17 Copyright © William A. Yokel, 2005.
Figure 7.18 Drawing by SAID student, School of Architecture and Interior Design, University of Cincinnati.
Figure 7.19 Photo by Jim Postell.
Figure 7.20 Photo by Jim Postell.
Figure 7.21 Photographer unknown.
Figure 7.22 Photo by Jim Postell.
Figure 7.23 Photo by Jim Postell.
Figure 7.24 Photo by Jim Postell.
Figure 7.25 Photo by University of Cincinnati: Photographic Services. School of Design, University of Cincinnati.
Figure 7.26a Photo courtesy of Knoll International.
Figure 7.26b Photo courtesy Jim Postell.
Figure 7.27 Photo: Courtesy of Corky Binggeli, *Interior Design: A Survey* (John Wiley & Sons, 2007).
Figure 7.28 Photo by Jim Postell.
Figure 7.29 Courtesy and proxy for photographer: Erik Skoven.
Figure 7.30 Photo by Jim Postell.
Figure 7.31 Photography by Hedrich-Blessing, Chicago. Courtesy of Formica Corporation.
Figure 7.32 Photo by Jim Postell.
Figure 7.33 Copyright © William A. Yokel, 2005.
Figure 7.34 Copyright © William A. Yokel, 2005.
Figure 7.35 Photo by Jim Postell.
Figure 7.36 Designer unknown.
Figure 7.37a Photographer Nick Merrick/Hedrich Blessing. Courtesy of Herman Miller.

Figure 7.37b Designed by Komplot Design (2006) for GUBI A/S (Denmark). Photo: Thomas Ibsen.
Figure 7.38   Photo by Jim Postell.
Figure 7.39   Photo by Jim Postell.
Figure 7.40   Photo by Jim Postell.
Figure 7.41   Photo by Jim Postell.
Figure 7.42   Photo by Jim Postell.
Figure 7.43   Photo by Jim Postell.
Figure 7.44   Photo by Jim Postell.

Chapter 8

Figure 8.1   Photo by Jim Postell.
Figure 8.2   Courtesy of Erik Skoven.
Figure 8.3   Photo by Jim Postell.
Figure 8.4   Photo by Jim Postell.
Figure 8.5   Photo by Jim Postell.
Figure 8.6   Photo by Jim Postell.
Figure 8.7   Courtesy of Erik Skoven.
Figure 8.8   Photographer Charles Eames, Courtesy Eames. Courtesy of Herman Miller.
Figure 8.9   Courtesy of Cincinnati Art Museum, Gift of Melrose Pitman. Accession No. 1970.81.
Figure 8.10   Photo by Jim Postell.
Figure 8.11   Photo by Jim Postell.
Figure 8.12   Photo by Jim Postell.
Figure 8.13   Photo by Jim Postell.
Figure 8.14   Photo by Jim Postell.
Figure 8.15   Photo by Jim Postell.
Figure 8.16   Photo by Jim Postell.
Figure 8.17   Computer model by Ryan Newman.
Figure 8.18   Photo by Jim Postell.
Figure 8.19   Photo by Jim Postell.
Figure 8.20   Photo: Courtesy of Rud. Rasmussen.
Figure 8.21   Photo: Courtesy of Rud. Rasmussen.
Figure 8.22   Photo by Jim Postell.
Figure 8.23   Photo by Jim Postell.
Figure 8.24   Photo by Jim Postell.
Figure 8.25   Computer model by Ryan Newman.
Figure 8.26   Photo by Jim Postell.
Figure 8.27   Photo by Jim Postell.
Figure 8.28   Photo by Jim Postell.
Figure 8.29   Photo by Jim Postell.
Figure 8.30   Drawn and rendered by Jared Hoke, University of Cincinnati.
Figure 8.31   Photo by Jim Postell. Courtesy PP Møbler.
Figure 8.32   Photo by Jim Postell.
Figure 8.33   Photo by Jim Postell. Permission by Michael Toombs.
Figure 8.34   Photo: Courtesy of Gülen Çevik.
Figure 8.35   Photo by Jim Postell.
Figure 8.36   Photo by Jim Postell.
Figure 8.37   Photo by Jim Postell.
Figure 8.38   Photo by Jim Postell.

Chapter 9

Figure 9.1   Photo: Courtesy of Knoll Inc.
Figure 9.2   Photo: Courtesy of Cincinnati Art Museum (exhibit by Wendell Castle).
Figure 9.3   Copyright © William A. Yokel, 2005.
Figure 9.4   Photo by Jim Postell.
Figure 9.5   Photo courtesy of Erik Skoven.
Figure 9.6   Photo by Jim Postell.
Figure 9.7   Copyright © William A. Yokel, 2005.
Figure 9.8   Photo by Jim Postell.
Figure 9.9   Photo by Jim Postell.
Figure 9.10   Photo: Courtesy of Eli Meiners.

Figure 9.11   Photo by Jim Postell.
Figure 9.12a   Photo by Jim Postell.
Figure 9.12b   Copyright © William A. Yokel, 2005.
Figure 9.13   Image courtesy of Peter Chamberlain.
Figure 9.14   Image courtesy of Peter Chamberlain.
Figure 9.15   Photo by Jim Postell.
Figure 9.16   Photo courtesy of GUBI A/S Denmark.
Figure 9.17   Photo by Jim Postell.
Figure 9.18   Photo by Jim Postell.
Figure 9.19   Photo by Jim Postell.
Figure 9.20   Photo by Jim Postell.
Figure 9.21   Computer rendering by Komplot Design.
Figure 9.22   Courtesy of Erik Skoven and Fritz Hansen.
Figure 9.23   Printed by permission of the Norman Rockwell Family Agency. Copyright © 1959 the Norman Rockwell Family Entities.
Figure 9.24   Photo by Jim Postell.

Chapter 10

Figure 10.1   Photo: © Roger Butterfield.
Figure 10.2   Map courtesy of Corky Binggeli, *Interior Design: A Survey* (John Wiley & Sons, 2007).
Figure 10.3   Courtesy of John Stork.
Figure 10.4   Drawing courtesy of Corky Binggeli, *Interior Design: A Survey* (John Wiley & Sons, 2007).
Figure 10.5   Photo by Jim Postell.
Figure 10.6   Courtesy of Cincinnati Art Museum. Gift of the Cincinnati Museum of Natural History and Leland Banning. Accession No. 1990.1914.
Figure 10.7   Courtesy of Cincinnati Art Museum. Gift of L. Dow Covington. Accession No. 1909.92.
Figure 10.8   Photographer unknown; image modified by Jim Postell.
Figure 10.9   Courtesy of John Stork.
Figure 10.10   Photo by Jim Postell.
Figure 10.11   Courtesy of Corky Binggeli, *Interior Design: A Survey* (John Wiley & Sons, 2007).
Figure 10.12   Credit: *Thomas Hope's Greek and Roman Designs* (Dover Publications, 2005).
Figure 10.13   Courtesy of Corky Binggeli, *Interior Design: A Survey* (John Wiley & Sons, 2007).
Figure 10.14   Courtesy of Cincinnati Art Museum. Centennial Gift of Mr. and Mrs. Richard R. Markarian. Accession No. 1980.31.
Figure 10.15   Courtesy of Library of Congress, Prints & Photographs Division, Reproduction No. 20086u.tiff.
Figure 10.16   Architect: Mimar Sinan, 1580. Courtesy of Inci Ilgin, Associate Professor.
Figure 10.17   Photo: Courtesy of Patrick Snadon.
Figure 10.18   Photo by Jim Postell.
Figure 10.19   Courtesy of Cincinnati Art Museum. Gift of Mrs. Daniel H. Holmes in memory of Daniel H. Holmes. Accession No. 1933.9.
Figure 10.20   Photo by Jim Postell.
Figure 10.21   Courtesy of Erik Skoven.
Figure 10.22   Courtesy of Cincinnati Art Museum. Gift of Mr. And Mrs. Lucien Wulsin. Accession No. 1951.295.
Figure 10.23   Courtesy of Cincinnati Art Museum. Gift of Margaret Minster in memory of Leonard Minster. Accession No. 1986.769.a-c.
Figure 10.24   Jacques Stella, Baroque Ornaments, 2003 Dover Publications.
Figure 10.25   Cincinnati Art Museum Purchase. Gift of Mrs. E.L. Flagg, Reuben R. Springer, Mr. and Mrs. Rufus King, Mr. and Mrs. Alfred Traber Goshorn, Miss Mary Dexter, Miss Annie M. Howard, Reverend Alfred D. Pell, Benjamin Miller, and others, by exchange. Accession No. 1977.183.
Figure 10.26   Drawing by Dorthe Lautrup-Nissen, Lisbeth B. Lauritsen, and Tove Primdal, DKDS students. Courtesy of Jens Overbye, Lecturer DKDS, Copenhagen, Interior Architect MDD.
Figure 10.27   Photography: Courtesy of Patrick Snadon, Ph.D.
Figure 10.28   Courtesy of Cincinnati Art Museum. Gift of the Duke and Duchess of Tallyrand-Perigord. Accession No. 1954.525.a-b.
Figure 10.29   Photo by Jim Postell.
Figure 10.30   Photo by Jim Postell.
Figure 10.31   Courtesy of the Cincinnati Art Museum. Centennial Gift of Gloria Giannestras. In memory of Dr. Nicholas James Giannestras. Accession Number 1981.1.

Figure 10.32 Cincinnati Art Museum. Gift of Mr. Edmund Kerper (conversion of 1932 loan to accession. Accession No. 1977.138.

Figure 10.33 Courtesy of Cincinnati Art Museum. Bequest of Mary Moore Thomson in memory of her husband, Alexander Thomson. Accession No. 1981.519.

Figure 10.34 Photo by Jim Postell.

Figure 10.35 Library of Congress 00004a. Courtesy of Corky Binggeli, Interior Design: A Survey (John Wiley & Sons, 2007).

Figure 10.36 Courtesy of Cincinnati Art Museum. Gift of Mrs. William H. Chatfield. Accession No. 1956.358.

Figure 10.37 Photo by Jim Postell.

Figure 10.38 Manufactured by Gebüder Thonet, 1925. Courtesy of Cincinnati Art Museum (Change of Pace Exhibit, October 4, 1975–January 4, 1976).

Figure 10.39 Photo Courtesy Cincinnati Art Museum (Change of Pace Exhibit, October 4, 1975–January 4, 1976).

Figure 10.40 Courtesy of Cincinnati Art Museum, Henry Meis Endowment. Accession No. 1987.63.1.

Figure 10.41 Courtesy of Cincinnati Art Museum (Change of Pace Exhibit, October 4, 1975–January 4, 1976).

Figure 10.42 Courtesy of Cincinnati Art Museum. Gift of Mary Jane Hamilton in memory of her mother, Mary Luella Hamilton, made possible through Rita S. Hudepohl, guardian. Accession No. 1994.61.

Figure 10.43 Photographer unknown.

Figure 10.44 Courtesy Cincinnati Art Museum (Change of Pace Exhibit, October 4, 1975–January 4, 1976).

Figure 10.45 Courtesy of Cincinnati Art Museum. Gloria W. Thomson Fund for Decorative Arts. Accession No. 1989.107.

Figure 10.46 Drawn by Mogens Dorph-Petersen, Winnie Gludsted, and Kim Lundberg, DKDS students. Courtesy of Jens Overbye, Lecturer, Interior Architect, MDD.

Figure 10.47 Photo by Jim Postell.

Figure 10.48 Computer model by Sylbester Yeo and Jim Postell.

Figure 10.49 Courtesy Cincinnati Art Museum (Change of Pace Exhibit, October 4, 1975–January 4, 1976).

Figure 10.50 Photo by Jim Postell.

Figure 10.51 Photo: Courtesy of Knoll Inc.

Figure 10.52 Photo: Courtesy of Knoll Inc.

Figure 10.53 Computer model by Nora Leuhmann.

Figure 10.54 Courtesy of Erik Skoven.

Figure 10.55 Photo: Courtesy of Knoll Inc.

Figure 10.56 Photo: Courtesy of Erik Skoven in proxy for Fritz Hansen.

Figure 10.57 Drawing by Birgit Hougaard and Lene Jørgensen, DKDS students. Courtesy Jens Overbye, Lecturer, DKDS, Interior Architect, MDD.

Figure 10.58 Photo: Photographer Marvin Rand. Courtesy of Eames and Herman Miller.

Figure 10.59 Courtesy of Herman Miller.

Figure 10.60 Photo: Courtesy of Knoll Inc.

Figure 10.61 Photo by Jim Postell.

Figure 10.62 Photo by Jim Postell.

Index